Studies in Development Economics and Policy

General Editor: **Anthony Shorrocks**
UNU WORLD INSTITUTE FOR DEVELOPMENT ECONOMICS RESEARCH (UNU-WIDER) was established by the United Nations University as its first research and training centre and started work in Helsinki, Finland, in 1985. The purpose of the Institute is to undertake applied research and policy analysis on structural changes affecting the developing and transitional economies, to provide a forum for the advocacy of policies leading to robust, equitable and environmentally sustainable growth, and to promote capacity strengthening and training in the field of economic and social policy-making. Its work is carried out by staff researchers and visiting scholars in Helsinki and through networks of collaborating scholars and institutions around the world.

UNU World Institute for Development Economics Research (UNU-WIDER)
Katajanokanlaituri 6B, FIN-00160 Helsinki, Finland

Titles include:

Ricardo Ffrench-Davis and Stephany Griffith-Jones (*editors*)
FROM CAPITAL SURGES TO DROUGHT
Seeking Stability for Emerging Economies

Basudeb Guha-Khasnobis (*editor*)
THE WTO, DEVELOPING COUNTRIES AND THE DOHA DEVELOPMENT AGENDA
Prospects and Challenges for Trade-Led Growth

Aiguo Lu and Manuel F. Montes (*editors*)
POVERTY, INCOME DISTRIBUTION AND WELL-BEING IN ASIA DURING THE TRANSITION

Robert J. McIntyre and Bruno Dallago (*editors*)
SMALL AND MEDIUM ENTERPRISES IN TRANSITIONAL ECONOMIES

Vladimir Mikhalev (*editor*)
INEQUALITY AND SOCIAL STRUCTURE DURING THE TRANSITION

E. Wayne Nafziger and Raimo Väyrynen (*editors*)
THE PREVENTION OF HUMANITARIAN EMERGENCIES

Matthew Odedokun (*editor*)
EXTERNAL FINANCE FOR PRIVATE SECTOR DEVELOPMENT
Appraisals and Issues

Laixiang Sun (*editor*)
OWNERSHIP AND GOVERNANCE OF ENTERPRISES
Recent Innovative Developments

Studies in Development Economics and Policy
Series Standing Order ISBN 0–333–96424–1
(*outside North America only*)

You can receive future titles in this series as they are published by placing a standing order. Please contact your bookseller or, in case of difficulty, write to us at the address below with your name and address, the title of the series and the ISBN quoted above.

Customer Services Department, Macmillan Distribution Ltd, Houndmills, Basingstoke, Hampshire RG21 6XS, England

The WTO, Developing Countries and the Doha Development Agenda

Prospects and Challenges for Trade-Led Growth

Edited by

Basudeb Guha-Khasnobis

in association with the United Nations University – World Institute for Development Economics Research

First published 2004 by
PALGRAVE MACMILLAN
Houndmills, Basingstoke, Hampshire RG21 6XS and
175 Fifth Avenue, New York, N.Y. 10010
Companies and representatives throughout the world

PALGRAVE MACMILLAN is the global academic imprint of the Palgrave Macmillan division of St. Martin's Press, LLC and of Palgrave Macmillan Ltd. Macmillan® is a registered trademark in the United States, United Kingdom and other countries. Palgrave is a registered trademark in the European Union and other countries.

ISBN 1–4039–3483–5

This book is printed on paper suitable for recycling and made from fully managed and sustained forest sources.

A catalogue record for this book is available from the British Library.

Library of Congress Cataloging-in-Publication Data
The WTO, developing countries and the Doha development agenda : prospects and challenges for trade-led growth / edited by Basudeb Guha-Khasnobis.
    p.   cm. — (Studies in development economics and policy)
Includes bibliographical references and index.
ISBN 1–4039–3483–5 (cloth)
    1. World Trade Organization—Developing countries.   2. Free trade—Developing countries.   3. International trade—Developing countries.   4. Developing countries—Commercial policy.   5. Developing countries—Economic policy.   I. Title: World Trade Organization, developing countries and the Doha development agenda.
    II. Guha-Khasnobis, Basudeb.   III. Series.
    HF1385.W7833 2004
    382'.92'091724—dc22   2003070729

10   9   8   7   6   5   4   3   2   1
13   12   11   10   09   08   07   06   05   04

Printed and bound in Great Britain by
Antony Rowe Ltd, Chippenham and Eastbourne

Contents

List of Tables   vii

List of Figures and Box   xi

Foreword   xii

Acknowledgements   xiii

List of Abbreviations   xiv

Notes on the Contributors   xvii

Part I Overview

1 The WTO, Trade and Development: An Introduction   3
Basudeb Guha-Khasnobis

2 Developing Countries and the WTO Doha Round:
Market Access, Rules and Differential Treatment   10
Bernard Hoekman

Part II Agriculture

3 Trade Liberalization, Agriculture and Poverty in
Low-Income Countries   37
Kym Anderson

4 OECD Domestic Support and Developing Countries   63
Betina Dimaranan, Thomas Hertel and Roman Keeney

5 Impact of Trade Liberalization on Returns from Land:
A Regional Study of Indian Agriculture   92
Nilabja Ghosh

6 The Value of Agricultural Tariff Rate Quotas to
Developing Countries   130
Cathie Laroche Dupraz and Alan Matthews

Part III Manufacturing

7 Industrial Tariffs, LDCs and the Doha Development Agenda   161
Marc Bacchetta and Bijit Bora

8 Developed-Country Trade Barriers and the
LDCs: The Economic Results of Freeing Trade   190
Jon D. Haveman and Howard J. Shatz

9 The EU Everything But Arms Initiative and the LDCs   219
*Lucian Cernat, Sam Laird, Luca Monge-Roffarello and
Alessandro Turrini*

10 Export Subsidies: Theory, Evidence and the
WTO Agreement on Subsidies   261
Rajeev Ahuja

Index   287

List of Tables

2.1 Illustration of possible national priorities in different types of countries   13

2.2 Average unweighted tariff rates, by region, 1978–99   14

2.3 Frequency of core NTBs in developing countries, 1989–98   14

2.4 Trade shares of products affected by agricultural subsidies, 1995–98   17

2.5 Anti-dumping initiations per US dollar of imports, 1995–99   20

3.1 Average tariff equivalents of import market-access barriers to goods trade, by source and destination region, 1995   39

3.2 Sectoral and regional contributions to economic welfare gains from completely removing trade barriers globally, post-Uruguay Round, 2005   41

3.3 Percentage difference in sectoral output when all merchandise trade distortions remaining post-Uruguay Round are removed, 2005   43

3.4 Changes in sectoral trade balances when all merchandise trade distortions remaining post-Uruguay Round are removed, 2005   44

4.1 Producer support estimates and components, 1987 and 2000   65

4.2 Regional and sectoral aggregation   66

4.3 Trade specialization indices: $(X-M)/(X+M)$ 68

4.4 Share of developing-country trade with OECD, 1997   71

4.5 Experimental design   76

4.6 Implications of 50 per cent reduction in market price support for EU15 wheat, with re-instrumentation   78

4.7 Developing region welfare: EU15 wheat market price support reform   79

4.8 Change in average world prices due to comprehensive OECD domestic support reform   82

4.9 Developing region welfare changes: domestic support reform   83

4.10	World price effects of comprehensive 50 per cent market price support reductions for OECD agriculture, coupled with re-instrumentation	85
4.11	Developing region welfare changes: OECD re-instrumentation of agricultural support	86
5.1	Policy transition in rice market, 1991–2002	95
5.2	Estimates of net protection coefficients of rice in India, 1980–81 to 1992–98	96
5.3	Nutrient content, share in nutrient supply in country and policy scenario for fertilizers	100
5.4	Fertilizer import statistics, by ports, 1998–99	101
5.5	Rice (non-basmati) export statistics, by ports, 1998–99	102
5.6	Export of (non-basmati) rice from selected ports in India, 1991–2001	103
5.7	Calculation of fertilizer import price (all-India) and an estimate of protection	110
5.8	Calculation of farmgate export price and an estimate of protection of rice	113
5.9	Returns from paddy cultivation valued at prevailing and external prices	114
5A.1	Cost of cultivation of rice per hectare	123
5A.2	Fertilizer nutrient consumption and prices, by states	124
5A.3	Parameters underlying calculation of returns	125
5A.4	Estimated regression equation for fertilizer use, for yield adjustment	126
5A.5	Gains in returns at external prices from paddy cultivation estimated with alternative cost concepts	126
5A.6	Gains in returns at external prices from paddy cultivation: districts of Andhra Pradesh	127
6.1	Welfare gains for exporters due to the implementation of the TRQ	139
6.2	Relative importance of TRQ products and TRQ imports, by main commodity, average 1997–99	142
6.3	Usage of EU TRQs, by country grouping, average 1997–99	143
6.4	Preference margin on EU TRQ trade, average 1997–99	144
6.5	Rent created in EU TRQs, average 1997–99	146
6.6	Division of rents, by TRQ import arrangement	147
6.7	Value of rent estimated to accrue to developing countries on EU TRQ trade, average 1997–99	148
6.8	Average export prices, average 1997–99	150

7.1   Bound tariffs on industrial products: scope of bindings,
      simple averages, standard deviations and tariff peaks   165
7.2   Bound tariffs on industrial products: simple averages,
      by country and MTN category   168
7.3   Bound tariffs on industrial products: tariff peaks (share
      of tariff lines above 15%, by country and MTN category)   169
7.4   Bound tariffs on industrial products: scope of bindings,
      by country and MTN category   171
7.5   Distribution of binding coverage in Africa, Asia and
      Latin America   172
7.6   Applied tariffs on industrial products: simple averages,
      by country and MTN category   173
7.7   Applied tariffs on industrial products: tarrif peaks
      (share of tarrif lines above 15%, by country
      and MTN category)   174
7.8   Applied average tariffs on live, fresh, chilled or frozen
      crustaceans and prepared or preserved crustaceans   176
7.9   Tariffs on leather, leather clothing accessories
      and leather footwear   177
7.10 Tariff escalation on textile products: applied tariffs on
      textiles and clothing products   179
7.11 Duty-free imports into developed countries from
      developing countries and LDCs, 1996–2001   181
7.12 Pattern of MFN and preferential tariffs facing LDC
      exports of fish and fish products in selected markets   183
8.1   US and EU preference programmes   191
8.2   Eligible countries for US preferences programmes   196
8.3   Trade performance under the Caribbean programmes   201
8.4   Trade performance under the Andean Trade
      Preferences Act, 1991 and 2001   203
8.5   Trade performance under the African Growth and
      Opportunity Act, 2000 and 2001   204
8.6   Summary of tariff effects on Triad trade   208
8.7   Triad LDC imports and preferences programmes
      in force, 2000   209
8.8   Changes in Triad imports from LDCs as a result of
      eliminating all tariffs on LDC exports, 2000   212
9.1   European Union: major imports from LDCs, 2000   221
9.2   Selected LDC exports facing tariffs in the European Union,
      by major product category, 2000   223
9.3   EBA: the distribution of liberalized products, by sectors   224

9.4   Protection rates applied in the European Union on
        merchandise trade   229
9.5   Welfare changes   231
9.6   Exports, percentage changes   233
9.7   Sugar quotas allocation under the EC–ACP and
        EC–India preferential sugar regimes   246
9.8   European Union: top sugar exporters and their
        market share, 2000   250
9.9   Scenario (1): cane sugar – export changes   254
9.10 Scenario (2): cane sugar – export changes   254
10.1 CVD measures in force (as at 31 December 2002),
        against Brazilian exports   272
10.2 CVD measures in force (as at 31 December 2002),
        against Indian exports   274
10.3 CVD measures in force (as at 31 December 2002),
        against Korean exports   278

List of Figures and Box

Figures

5.1	Dual-channel market for rice	98
5.2	Exporters of urea, DAP and MOP fertilizers to India	102
5.3	Gains from free trade in output	115
5.4	Gains from free trade in output and input with yield adjustment	115
6.1	Welfare effects of a global TRQ with underfill	134
6.2	Welfare effects of a bilateral TRQ awarded to a more-competitive supplier with underfill	135
6.3	Welfare effects of a bilateral TRQ awarded to a less-competitive supplier with underfill	137
6.4	Assessed rent versus preference margin by commodity sector, annual average, 1997–99	146
8.1	US preference imports relative to total US imports	200
8.2	Growth rate of US total imports and US preference imports	201
9.1	EBA Scenario (1): trade-creation and trade-diversion effects	239
9.2	Scenario (1): bananas – total trade effects	240
9.3	Scenario (2): trade-creation and trade-diversion effects	242
9.4	Scenario (2): bananas – total trade effects	244

Box

5.1	Some policy steps taken with the launch of reforms	100

Foreword

The past decade of multilateral trade negotiations has witnessed an increasing divide between the developed and the developing countries on a range of issues, including market access, domestic support, competition policy, labour standards and the movement of 'natural persons'. The severity of the differences is apparent from the complete failures of at least two proposed rounds of talks – Seattle and Cancún. Although tariff barriers on average have declined under both the GATT and the WTO, there is considerable scepticism in the developing countries about whether the rule-based, reciprocity-driven organization is capable of fulfilling the special needs of developing countries. We all await an answer: can the WTO still reassert its development credibility?

On the positive side, the 'Doha Development Agenda' recognizes the concerns of developing countries explicitly and promises to seek an outcome that will resonate with their ongoing effort to reduce poverty, foster human development and ensure economic growth. This volume identifies the challenges faced as well as the opportunities to be taken and, based on selected case studies, provides important policy implications which can ensure that the new round of talks reasserts the developmental credibility of the current trade regime.

TONY SHORROCKS
Director, UNU-WIDER

Acknowledgements

UNU-WIDER gratefully acknowledges the financial contributions to the 2002–03 research programme by the governments of Denmark (Royal Ministry of Foreign Affairs), Finland (Ministry for Foreign Affairs), Norway (Royal Ministry of Foreign Affairs), Sweden (Swedish International Development Cooperation Agency – Sida) and the United Kingdom (Department for International Development).

I would like to thank Tony Shorrocks, Director of UNU-WIDER, for his support throughout the duration of this project. I am grateful to Janis Vehmaan-Kreula, secretary for this project, for her outstanding job on the editorial details, and Adam Swallow, Publications Editor, who worked hard to ensure an overall smooth transition of this project from its inception to completion.

BASUDEB GUHA-KHASNOBIS

List of Abbreviations

ACP	Africa, Caribbean and the Pacific
AGOA	African Growth and Opportunity Act
AMS	Aggregate measure of support
ANZ	Australia/New Zealand
AoA	Agreement on Agriculture
APEC	Asia-Pacific Economic Cooperation
APEDA	Agricultural and Processed Food Export Development Authority
ASEAN	Association of Southeast Asian Nations
ATC	Agreement on Textiles and Clothing
ATPA	Andean Trade Preferences Act
BFS	Bulletin on Food Statistics
CAP	Common Agricultural Policy
CBERA	Caribbean Basin Economic Recovery Act
CBTPA	Caribbean Basin Trade Partnership Act
CBI	Caribbean Basin Initiative
CEE	Central and Eastern European
CET	Common external tariff
CIF	Cost, insurance, freight
CMOS	Common market organization of sugar
COC	Comprehensive Scheme for Studying the Cost of Cultivation of Principal Crops (India)
COMESA	Common Market for Eastern and Southern Africa
CVD	Countervailing duty
DAP	Diammonium phosphate
DEPB	Duty Entitlement Pass Book
DES	Department of Economics and Statistics
DGCIS	Directorate General of Commercial Intelligence and Statistics
DSB	Dispute Settlement Body
EBA	Everything But Arms
EC	European Communities
ECA	Essential Commodities Acts
EEC	European Economic Community
EFTA	European Free Trade Area
EPAs	Economic Partnership Agreements
ERC	Expenditure Reforms Commission

EU	European Union
FAI	Fertilizer Association of India
FCI	Food Corporation of India
FDI	Foreign direct investment
FIPA	Foreign Investment Promotion Act
FOB	Free on board
FOD	French Overseas Department
FTA	Free-trade agreement
GATS	General Agreement on Trade in Services
GATT	General Agreement on Tariffs and Trade
GDP	Gross domestic product
GOI	Government of India
GTAP	Global Trade Analysis Project
HCI	Heavy Manufacturing and Chemical Industries
HS	Harmonized System
ICMS	Imposto Sobre Circulação de Mercadorias e Serviços (Brazilian excise tax)
IFI	International financial institutions
IPI	Industrial production tax
ITA	Information Technology Products Agreement
JIT	Just-in-time
LDCs	Least-developed countries
LFR	Less than full reciprocity
MDG	Millennium Development Goal
MENA	Middle East/North Africa
MFA	Multifibre Agreement
MFN	Most-favoured-nation
MOA	Ministry of Agriculture
MOP	Muriate of potash
MPS	Market price support
MSN	Maximum supply needs
MTN	Multilateral trade negotiations
NAFTA	North American Free Trade Agreement
NAMA	National Agri-Marketing Association
NTB	Non-tariff barrier
OECD	Organisation for Economic Co-operation and Development
PPP	Purchasing power parity
PRSP	Poverty reduction strategy paper
PSE	Producer Support Estimates
PTA	Preferential Trading Agreement
QR	Quantitative restrictions

RPS	Retention Price and Subsidy Scheme
RTA	Regional trade agreement
SACU	South African Customs Union
SAIL	Steel Authority of India Limited
SCM	Subsidies and Countervailing Measures Agreement
SDT	Special and differential treatment
SIC	Standard Industrial Classification
Sida	Swedish International Development Cooperation Agency
SIDS	Small Island Developing States
SME	Small and medium enterprises
SP	Special products
SPS	Sanitary and phytosanitary measures
SPS	Special preferential sugar
SSA	sub-Saharan Africa
STABEX	Commodity export earnings stabilization scheme
STTCL	Special Tax Treatment Control Law
SYSMIN	System for ACP mineral and mining exports
TERCL	Tax Exemption and Reduction Control Laws
TRIPS	Trade-related intellectual property rights
TRQs	Tariff Rate Quotas
TVE	Township and village enterprises
URAA	Uruguay Round Agreement on Agriculture
WTO	World Trade Organization

Notes on the Contributors

Rajeev Ahuja is a Senior Fellow at the Indian Council for Research on International Economic Relations (ICRIER), India.

Kym Anderson is Professor at the School of Economics and Executive Director at the Centre for International Economic Studies at the University of Adelaide, Australia.

Marc Bacchetta is a Counsellor at the Economic Research and Analysis Division of the World Trade Organization (WTO), Switzerland.

Bijit Bora is a Counsellor at the Economic Research and Analysis Division of the World Trade Organization (WTO), Switzerland.

Lucian Cernat is Associate Economic Officer at United Nations Conference on Trade and Development (UNCTAD), Switzerland.

Betina Dimaranan is a Research Economist at the Center for Global Trade Analysis, at Purdue University, USA.

Nilabja Ghosh is a Reader at the Institute for Economic Growth, New Delhi, India.

Basudeb Guha-Khasnobis is a Research Fellow and Project Director at UNU-WIDER, Finland.

Jon D. Haveman is a Research Fellow at the Public Policy Institute of California, USA.

Thomas Hertel is Distinguished Professor and Director at the Center for Global Trade Analysis at Purdue University, USA.

Bernard Hoekman is Policy and Research Manager at the World Bank, USA.

Roman Keeney is a Graduate Research Assistant at the Center for Global Trade Analysis at Purdue University, USA.

Sam Laird is Officer-in-Charge, at United Nations Conference on Trade and Development (UNCTAD), Switzerland and Special Professor of International Economics at the University of Nottingham, UK.

Cathie Laroche Dupraz is Coordinatrice DAA économie-gestion, Pôle d'enseignement supérieur agronomique de Rennes, Département Economie Rurale et Gestion, France.

Alan Matthews is Jean Monnet Professor of European Agricultural Policy, Department of Economic at Trinity College, Ireland.

Luca Monge-Roffarello is Economic Affairs Officer at United Nations Conference on Trade and Development (UNCTAD), Switzerland.

Howard J. Shatz is a Research Fellow at the Public Policy Institute of California, USA.

Alessandro Turrini is Associate Economic Officer at United Nations Conference on Trade and Development (UNCTAD), Switzerland.

Part I
Overview

1

The WTO, Trade and Development: An Introduction

Basudeb Guha-Khasnobis

There are sound theoretical reasons how free trade in an ideal world can augment world output by guiding resources to their best possible usages at any given point of time. Free trade is also endowed with considerable dynamic energy, which can sustain this efficient usage of resources over a period of time for a given country or group of countries, resulting in higher growth rates. Such beneficial effects of free trade are unambiguously true at an aggregate level, in the sense of making *every* country better off, although to different extents. However, theory does not say that free trade makes every individual better off. In fact, quite to the contrary, any reasonable theory of trade predicts that free trade has differential impacts on various population groups within a country. Thus, quite clearly, there are two potential sources of conflict which will affect any movement towards freer trade. The first source of conflict is the sharing of free trade benefits between countries. In this respect, the world trading community is divided into two broad groups, developing and developed countries, and their quarrels reflect essentially how to split the spoils of free trade. The second source of conflict is inherent within countries. Certain groups of people gain relatively more than others. Some groups may even lose from freer trade, at least in the absence of any redistribution of income by the government.

There are subtle differences in the ways the two sources of conflict manifest themselves. Developing countries as a group are *not* against freer trade, although they are often misunderstood as being so! Developing countries are basically unhappy about what they have received as benefits of a freer world trading regime relative to what they are being seemingly forced to offer. On the other hand, certain groups of population within both developing as well as developed countries *are* against freer trade because they stand to lose from it at least in the short run, in the absence of any guarantees for compensation.

These conflicts have been part and parcel of the successive rounds of the GATT and, since 1995, the WTO regime, during which the world community has been trying to move towards freer trade. The WTO regime, especially, has been increasingly turbulent, with the developing countries voicing their concerns about the development credibility of the new regime. The November 2001 'Doha Development Agenda' recognizes the concerns of developing countries explicitly and promises to seek an outcome that will resonate with their ongoing effort to reduce poverty, foster human development and ensure economic growth. Can the WTO reassert its development credibility by ensuring that Doha becomes truly the Development Round? What should be the negotiating strategy of the developing countries?

While examining the key features of the political economy of the trading system in Part I of the volume, we note in Chapter 2 that a necessary condition for success will be to recognize the political economy of reform, both at home and in partner countries. Little progress will be made on key issues unless there are major stakeholders within countries that perceive the overall package to be beneficial. Such 'domestic ownership' of WTO agreements is a prerequisite for multilateral negotiations to succeed. The primary onus for doing the groundwork necessary for an open domestic trade regime, a supportive investment climate and good human development policies relating to education and health lies with the respective governments. At the same time, development assistance must play an important role in helping to expand and improve the trade capacity that is needed for countries to benefit from better access to markets. Several commitments were made by both developed and developing countries in Monterrey in 2002. The priority is now to identify the policy measures seen by developing-country governments as urgent areas for action and to address the associated resource needs. It will be judicious to approach the problem of resource needs in a two-pronged manner. The first will be to try and enhance as well as stabilize export earnings for developing countries. The second is to create new and innovative sources of financing. The latter is the responsibility of the international community as a whole, especially the various aid agencies.

Ensuring that multilateral negotiations under its auspices shape world trade flows in ways that enable the developing countries to generate enough resources to meet growth and development objectives, is what the WTO needs to achieve if the scepticism regarding its development relevance is to be dispelled. The subsequent chapters in this volume have tried to assess the state of the world trading situation as it pertains to developing countries, in both agriculture as well as manufacturing. Will the political constituencies in the OECD allow it to reform its domestic support policy in a way that benefits the developing countries? How big are the regional disparities in the effects of agricultural trade reform in the developing countries? Are the Preferential Trading Agreements (PTAs) doing enough for the least developed countries? How much more can the United States, the European Union and Japan do to increase LDC exports? These are some of the questions the subsequent chapters try to answer.

Part II of the volume examines the liberalization of trade in agriculture, which remains one of the most contentious issues in WTO negotiations. According to estimates noted in Chapter 3, farm product markets remain the most costly of all goods market distortions in world trade. In fact, of all the economic gains to be had in 2005 from removing the barriers to trade in goods that will still be in place after all Uruguay Round commitments have been implemented, almost half (48 per cent) will come from agricultural and processed food policy reform in OECD countries. Another one-sixth of the welfare gains will come from reform of farm and food policies of developing countries. Thus it is essential that negotiations for agricultural trade liberalization continue without a pause. Evidence based on GTAP modelling also suggests that the gains from global trade liberalization in agriculture will be even more for some of the developing countries, if they carry out complementary reforms of their respective domestic policies as well.

Having said that, it is important to note that the welfare impacts on developing countries depend on whether they are net exporters or net importers of protected products as well as on the bilateral trade patterns. In Chapter 4, trade specialization indexes calculated since the 1970s for programme crops,[1] bounded between +1 and −1, describe the export (positive sign) and import (negative sign) orientation of each region. With few exceptions, these show substantial declines over this period. For example, Indonesia falls from −0.57 to −0.88 and ASEAN4 falls from +0.58 to +0.20. Several regions show shifts from net exporter to net importer status. For example sub-Saharan Africa's index falls from +0.39 in the 1965–75 period to −0.17 in the 1986–98 period, while the trade specialization index for Latin America outside of Brazil, Argentina and Mexico falls from 0.36 to −0.08. As these developing countries rely on imports of grains and oilseeds from the subsidized OECD economies, they are exposed to agricultural reforms that raise the prices of these specific products. The estimates from a GTAP model shows that an across-the-board, 50 per cent cut in all domestic support for OECD agriculture leads to welfare losses for most of the developing regions, as well as for the combined total group of developing countries. The 50 per cent cut in domestic support also results in large declines in farm incomes in Europe as well as North America. This makes such a reform package an unlikely political event. Chapter 4 suggests an alternative approach to reforming agricultural policies in the OECD, which would be to focus on broad-based reductions in market price support. In the European Union for instance, domestic support has increasingly replaced border measures. According to the chapter's modelling results, a shift from market price support to land-based payments could generate a 'win–win' outcome whereby farm incomes are maintained and world price distortions are reduced. This is indeed the direction charted by the OECD in its 'Positive Agenda for Reform' for agriculture (6 November 2002).

Just as with the case of reforming domestic support policy in the OECD countries, the political feasibility of any agricultural liberalization in the developing countries depends on exactly how it affects the farmers. The impact of trade liberalization on Indian rice exporters is taken up as a case study in Chapter 5. In the case of India, free trade in rice will certainly reduce its price and, similarly, free imports of fertilizer will raise its price. The exact geographic location of the farmers within India is particularly important. In the case of an exportable crop, the farmer's reference export price would be the FOB price at the port, less handling and transport charge from the production centre concerned. This means that farmers in an interior state or a remote centre would find themselves at a disadvantage compared to those in a location near a port. The farmer would gain from the export only if the external price exceeded the prevailing domestic price fetched. For traded input the farmer's price would analogously be the CIF import price at the port plus the handling and transport charges. Thus, in the context of large developing countries, there can be substantive differences in the impact of agricultural trade liberalization on the welfare of farmers, depending on where they are located. Any aggregate or average estimate of such welfare effects can be misleading, at least as far as the political feasibility of such liberalization, as well as the implication for poverty alleviation, are concerned.

On their part, developing countries may be well advised to focus their efforts on improved agricultural market access to the OECD economies. To this end, the use of tariff rate quotas (TRQs) was legitimized as a market access instrument in the Uruguay Round Agreement on Agriculture (AoA). The motivation behind this instrument was to guarantee minimum levels of market access and to safeguard current levels of access in the face of the high MFN tariffs resulting from tariffication. Whether and in what ways TRQ access should be extended is a subject of some interest in the Doha negotiations on further agricultural trade liberalization. A number of countries made proposals to improve the administration and size of TRQs in the Special Session on Agriculture at the start of the Doha negotiations. Chapter 6 focuses on the value of TRQ access to developing countries, whether under global or bilateral quotas, and finds that around 10 per cent of the EU's agricultural imports by value enter under TRQ arrangements, and developing countries account for over 60 per cent of these imports. TRQs, when they are binding, also create rents, and in many cases it is the rent element which becomes the most significant benefit of TRQ access. The majority of this rent (57 per cent) was appropriated by import agents as a result of the way TRQs are administered in the European Union. A reduction in in-quota tariffs, where they are currently positive, would be an effective means of providing some temporary compensation for the erosion of quota rents through MFN tariff reductions. Also relevant in some cases might be the introduction of specific changes in the licensing rules to ensure a greater transfer of the quota rents to developing country exporters – for example, by requiring export certificates be supplied by the exporting country.

Part III of this volume is devoted to market access issues in manufacturing. Chapter 7 examines where the WTO members stand with regard to their objective of achieving a substantial reduction of tariffs and eliminating discriminatory treatment in the area of non-agricultural tariffs. Two indicators are examined: the first is the percentage of MFN bound duty-free tariff lines for a sample of members, and the second indicator is the share of imports under MFN bound duty-free tariff items for a sample of members. Approximately 6 per cent of the total number of non-agricultural items in the sample of WTO members' tariff schedules is bound duty-free. This small number of duty-free items, even though they account for one-third of the value of world trade in industrial products, confirms that there is still a considerable amount to be achieved in multilateral tariff negotiations. The universal adoption of the MFN principle remains the ultimate goal of the ongoing process of such trade negotiations, but its all-inclusive character makes it a time-consuming, long-term possibility at best. PTAs are crucial as quick and stop-gap solutions. It is through PTAs that the rich and poor countries interact in more substantive ways. PTAs have proliferated in recent years, a phenomenon which is often cited as an indication that the WTO is a failing process. Without trying to under-estimate the gravity of some obvious problems with the WTO, one may differ with that interpretation and assert instead that the WTO has been an important catalyst in triggering PTAs and enhancing trade flows between countries.

The European Union, Japan and the United States offer a number of PTAs to developing countries. These include the well-known Generalized System of Preferences (GSP) and more recent ones such as the African Growth and Opportunity Act (AGOA, United States), the Everything But Arms Initiative (EBA, European Union) and the 99 Per Cent Initiative (Japan). The need to grant substantial trade preferences to the LDCs was emphasized in the Doha Ministerial Declaration. For the Caribbean beneficiaries, total trade under the programmes has expanded consider-ably since 1989. While total US imports from the 24 countries in this region rose more than 200 per cent between 1989 and 2001, total pre-ference trade rose more than 500 per cent. Similarly, in 2001, AGOA imports totalled almost US$8.2 billion, making almost 50 per cent of all imports from these countries duty-free. In Chapter 8, an econometric framework that makes the distinction between the *trade-reduction* and the *trade-diversion* effects was used to estimate the potential effects of removing *all* remaining tariffs in the Triad countries. Both the trade reduction and the trade diversion effects are bigger for the United States compared to other Triad economies. EU trade is the least sensitive. For the United States, on average, a 1 per cent increase in the average tariff reduces imports by 8.3 per cent. Further, a 1 per cent tariff preference leads to a 19.4 per cent increase in trade for the exporter in question. These numbers are reasonably large, suggesting significant benefits for LDCs from the unilateral preference programmes. Much more can be done, especially with respect to the US programmes.

The aggregate worldwide distribution of gains and losses of the EBA initiative was assessed using a computable general equilibrium (CGE) simulation model (GTAP). Partial equilibrium simulations were used to examine the effects of a complete removal of both tariff and non-tariff barriers (NTBs) faced by LDCs in the EU market. The results, reported in Chapter 9 showed moderate, but useful, welfare and trade gains from the EBA initiative, with the largest gains being recorded for sub-Saharan Africa. In particular, the EU sugar market appeared as the single most important source of change. The increased market access for LDCs comes mostly at the expense of other preference-receiving countries (ACP countries, in particular), although the changes are not large. There are some small negative effects on other countries that currently enjoy duty-free access to the EU market or enjoy MFN market access (for example, Polish and Romanian exports of live animals or US and Argentine exports of cereals). The estimates showed that only a handful of LDCs would see total trade increase by more than US$100,000, from a combination of trade-creation and trade-diversion effects. Malawi, the biggest winner, stands to increase its cane sugar exports by more than US$25 million. Other African LDCs (Madagascar, Tanzania and Zambia) are likely to see their cane sugar exports increase by between US$5–10 million. The only Asian LDC that shows incremental exports of more than US$100,000 is Myanmar. The estimates also suggest that Sudan is likely to see significant increases in its exports of molasses and cereals. The largest losers from negative trade diversion, in absolute values, are the current major ACP sugar exporters (Mauritius, Aruba, Fiji and Guyana).

The developing countries themselves are often pro-active in promoting their own exports. Chapter 10 discusses such export promotion measures – subsidies, to be specific – in three countries, South Korea, Brazil and India. A key message that emerges from the discussion is that export promoting subsidies were deemed as necessary in India and Brazil essentially to correct for the anti-export bias that existed in these countries due to their erstwhile import-substituting development strategies. Once overall reforms are implemented, such anti-export bias will be eliminated and reduce the need for subsidies on that count. However, even in countries that are outward-oriented to begin with, subsidies can be important instruments in wresting larger export market shares in the presence of imperfect competition. While the current agreements allow for export subsidies in selected developing countries for at least some time in the future, the fine print is rather cumbersome. Developing countries are seeking clarification of some of the existing clauses and would like to hope that these are interpreted in a manner which makes them truly useful.

Note

1. Programme crops are the grains and oilseeds which receive a large share of the domestic support in OECD countries.

2
Developing Countries and the WTO Doha Round: Market Access, Rules and Differential Treatment*

Bernard Hoekman

Introduction

The November 2001 'Doha Development Agenda' places development concerns at the core of WTO deliberations. The challenge is to achieve an outcome that supports poverty reduction and economic growth. The implementation problems associated with a number of WTO agreements, the addition of disciplines on intellectual property protection (TRIPS), and the persistence of tariff peaks and production and export subsidies for agricultural commodities in the OECD has led to a 'development credibility' deficit for the WTO. A precondition for the Doha Round to generate a good outcome from a development perspective is that the system becomes more balanced and has greater support of domestic stakeholders in developing countries.

Developing countries have historically played only a minor role in the multilateral trading system. Until the Uruguay Round (1986–93), their participation was *à la carte*, with many not making commitments. This changed with the entry into force of the WTO in 1995. Because of the so-called Single Undertaking, developing countries became subject to most of the disciplines of the many agreements contained in the WTO (*albeit* after transition periods had expired). At the same time, a number of the agreements increasingly came to be seen as having little benefit – indeed, in the case of some agreements (TRIPS) the perception rapidly emerged that benefits were highly skewed towards rich countries (Finger, 2002). The resulting 'Uruguay Round hangover' led to a great deal of scepticism regarding the benefits of WTO membership. Many governments and civil society of developing countries view the prospect of additional agreements and disciplines in the WTO with great suspicion. The Uruguay Round hangover has made them very aware of the downside of signing on to agreements that are ill understood and that have little if any backing by domestic stakeholders. Indeed, many developing countries are now actively seeking to improve their 'terms of trade' in the WTO.

However, industrialized countries appear to be less enthused about active multilateral engagement. Industry in OECD countries already operates in an environment where much of what they trade is duty-free (due to duty drawback and similar schemes, regional trade agreements (RTAs) and past negotiations that reduced MFN tariffs on their products substantially). And other interest groups have come to the fore that would like to introduce binding disciplines on non-trade policies such as labour standards and environmental regulation into the WTO and, more generally, seek to move the WTO 'behind the border'.

Developing country governments confront a three-fold challenge: inducing major trading partners to improve market access; ensuring that any multilateral trade rules support economic development; and convincing domestic stakeholders that there are significant net positive payoffs from further domestic trade reforms that are locked in via the WTO. Much of the burden of rebalancing the trading system to support economic development more effectively lies with developing countries. They are the major *demandeurs* and have the greatest stake in using the system to help them to adopt better domestic policies.

Success will require both reciprocity and increased attention to subjecting rule-making to economic cost-benefit analysis. The WTO process involves giving export interests that want better market access an incentive to put pressure on import-competing sectors to concede opening of the home market. With the spread of regional integration agreements and duty-free treatment provisions for imports used in export production, many multinationals now have less incentive to invest resources in support of traditional merchandise trade liberalization. As a result, reciprocity must be sought increasingly in other areas such as services and domestic regulatory policy commitments. The latter are more complex to negotiate. Negotiations to lower tariffs require little oversight from civil society as the outcome is generally welfare-improving. When it comes to domestic regulation it is not easy – and perhaps impossible – to trade 'concessions'. The practice to date has been to focus instead on the identification of specific rules that should be adopted by all – usually 'good practices' that have emerged over time in OECD countries. While these may be beneficial, adoption of such rules predominately impose implementation costs on developing countries (Finger and Schuler, 2000). The challenge here is to ensure that multilateral rules support development and to recognize that one size does not necessarily fit all.

The trade agenda at the national level

Success in integrating into the world economy is far from universal. In part, this reflects continued anti-export biases created by border trade policies and the absence of an enabling environment for supply-side responses to changed incentives to emerge. 'Behind the border' barriers to trade integration – for example, lack of access to finance, high-cost and low-quality distribution and transport services – are often important. To benefit from liberalization, measures to lower trade-related transactions costs and regulatory reforms may be called for to ensure that economic responses to liberalization are efficient, equitable and enduring. Priorities will differ depending on country circumstances. In some low-income economies priority areas for action are to strengthen institutions such as customs, reduce transport costs and ensure that export marketing and product standards are satisfied. In others, reducing tariffs and other trade barriers remain a priority. Table 2.1 provides a summary illustrative matrix mapping 'types' of countries against possible priority areas.

Border barriers

Despite significant liberalization by many developing countries, traditional trade policies continue to imply significant anti-export biases in a number of regions, most notably South Asia. Average (unweighted) tariffs in the Middle East and sub-Saharan Africa are in the 20 per cent range (Table 2.2). However, the 'border agenda' in many low-income countries is more institutional than trade policy-related. Although NTBs have come down substantially in most developing countries (Table 2.3), inefficiencies in public administration are often an impediment to trade. Customs clearance and logistics-related transactions costs can be a major disincentive for investment in tradable sectors, especially in activities that are time-sensitive or where it is important to be integrated into global production networks that operate on the basis of just-in-time (JIT) supply chain management. Exporters must have access to imported intermediate inputs at world market prices in order to be competitive. In countries where tariffs continue to be needed for revenue mobilization this requires well-functioning customs regimes that refund taxes paid on imported inputs – or, preferably, allow exporters to import inputs duty-free (so-called 'temporary admission' or 'green

Table 2.1 Illustration of possible national priorities in different types of countries

Country type	Traditional trade policies		Behind-the-border trade policies	
	Policy	Institutions	Policy	Institutions
Low-income: weak institutions, high fiscal dependence on tariffs	Reduce tariff dispersion; develop domestic tax bases	Strengthen customs; consider free trade zones as catalyst for exports	Enhance efficiency of transport and transit regimes; maintain competitive real exchange rate	Strengthen national capacity to design trade and regulatory policies; upgrade product standards bodies
Low-income: strong role of the state, high protection; high transactions costs	Reduce border barriers significantly; reduce tariff dispersion	Reduce red tape; adopt drawback or temporary admission customs schemes	Promote competition in service industries, including through FDI and privatization	Strengthen standards setting and certification bodies; efficient regulation to achieve social objectives
Transition economy	Maintain relatively low and uniform tariffs	Develop customs and related infrastructure	Develop legal and regulatory regimes for services	Develop national capacity to design/enforce regulatory policies
Middle-income: small, low average protection	Lower tariff peaks	Adopt *ex post* controls to facilitate trade	Enhance technology and E-commerce-related policies	Strengthen enforcement of prudential regulation
Middle-income: large, high protection	Reduce average and dispersion of protection	Reduce red tape; implement trade facilitation measures	Services liberalization; end monopolies; develop competition policy	Pro-competitive and prudential regulation; establish competition authorities

Source: Hoekman (2002).

Table 2.2   Average unweighted tariff rates, by region, 1978–99

Region	1978–80	1981–85	1986–90	1991–95	1996–99
Africa	38.2	29.3	26.9	22.3	17.8
East Asia	23.5	26.9	20.7	14.6	10.4
Latin America	28.1	26.4	24.1	13.9	11.1
MENA (ex-OPEC)	29.6	24.6	24.1	22.9	19.3
South Asia	NA	71.9	69.8	38.9	30.7
Europe/Central Asia	12.0	21.6	14.9	8.1	10.1
Industrial economies	11.9	8.9	8.2	6.8	6.1

Table 2.3   Frequency of core NTBs in developing countries, 1989–98, per cent

Country	1989–94	1995–98
East Asia and the Pacific (7)	30.1	16.3
Latin America and the Caribbean (13)	18.3	8.0
MENA (4)	43.8	16.6
South Asia (4)	57.0	58.3
SSA (12)	26.0	10.4

Note:
Parentheses indicate the number of countries per region for which data are available.
Source: World Bank.

channel' treatment). Many countries do not have well-functioning drawback regimes, creating anti-export bias.

The 'behind-the-border' trade agenda

A supporting legal and regulatory environment is vital for sustained growth. While this goes far beyond trade-related policy, elements of the associated 'behind the border' *trade* agenda include policies and institutions that support the ability of national firms to compete internationally. Meeting international standards for quality, health and safety is increasingly a precondition for contesting international markets. Many low-income countries are not adequately equipped to deal with rapidly tightening product standards and labelling requirements and confront major investment requirements in order to do so (Henson, Prebisch and Masakure, 2001; Wilson, 2001). The same is true of services. Reducing the cost of services that affect trade can easily have economywide welfare benefits that are a multiple of those associated with merchandise liberalization and, indeed, may be a precondition for benefiting from such liberalization.

Initiatives to strengthen private and public service institutions that support trade – access to credit, modernization of product standards conformity assessment systems – and to reduce the cost of key inputs (transport, telecoms, insurance, finance and so on) should be pursued in the context of an overall national strategic framework that identifies where the payoff to reform and public investment is largest. Careful policy analysis is needed to identify both priorities and options for reform. In many cases pro-competitive reforms will be needed, as greater competition (contestability of markets) will reduce prices and increase the variety of goods and services. Whatever the priorities are, in all countries there is a need for complementary macroeconomic, education, health and social policies. Separating the trade agenda from the development agenda more broadly defined is difficult, if not impossible. The key need is to integrate trade into the national development strategy. This is also necessary to be able to make an informed assessment of if, and how, issues should be addressed in the WTO.

The premise in what follows is that priority should be given to a 'traditional' market access agenda that focuses on the reciprocal reduction of barriers to trade in all products – goods *and* services – that is, including agriculture and labour-intensive manufactures such as apparel. There is still great scope to use traditional reciprocity dynamics to reduce barriers to trade and that is where the positive impact on development is likely to be the greatest.

Improving market access

A great deal of research has documented that there is still a large market access-related agenda (Anderson *et al.*, 2001; World Bank, 2001). The extent to which developing and industrialized country trade barriers are lowered, tariff peaks and escalation removed, export subsidies eliminated and production subsidies replaced with less trade-distorting measures will define to an important extent the development relevance of WTO talks.

MFN tariff rates of developed countries are less than 5 per cent on average. Indeed, much trade is now duty-free as a result of zero ratings, preferences and free trade agreements (FTAs). However, tariffs for some commodities are over 100 per cent (Hoekman, Ng and Olarreaga, 2002). Such tariff peaks – rates above 15 per cent – are often concentrated in products that are of interest to developing countries. In 1999, in the United States alone, imports originating in LDCs generated tariff revenue of US$487 million, equal to 11.6 per cent of the value of their exports to the United States, and 15.7 per cent of dutiable imports (US Department of Commerce, 1999).[1] Protection in OECD countries currently imposes costs on developing countries that exceed official development assistance flows (some US$45 billion per year). Benefits to developing countries from abolishing their own protection are over US$60 billion. Global protection of trade in merchandise costs the world economy some US$250 billion (Hertel and Martin, 2000). If current policies restricting trade in services are considered, the figure can easily double or triple (Stern, 2002). Add in the trade-chilling effect of instruments of contingent protection (anti-dumping, safeguards) – see below – and the real income gains from elimination of redundant red tape at borders and it is clear that the benefits of reducing market access barriers are enormous.

Because average tariff barriers in developing countries are higher than in industrialized nations, much of the potential welfare gains from reducing trade barriers will arise from own liberalization. The large potential payoff from reciprocal tariff liberalization provides a strong rationale for developing countries to engage in traditional GATT-type tariff negotiations – greater efficiency in home markets and cheaper access to imports will be complemented by better access to export markets. This argument applies to LDCs as well. As noted by Winters (1999), a useful mnemonic in this connection is WYDIWYG: what you do is what you get. When it comes to trade policy, the payoffs to negotiations and liberalization are primarily a function of domestic action – the extent to which own protection is reduced.[2] Three sectors matter greatly for developing countries: agriculture, textiles and clothing and services.

Agriculture

Despite the fact that the inclusion of agricultural policy disciplines in the Uruguay Round has justifiably been hailed as a major achievement, it must be recognized that the primary effect of the Uruguay Round was simply to bring agriculture back into the trading system. The commitments that were made – the ban on quantitative restrictions, the resulting tariffication of border protection in this sector, the minimum market access commitments implemented through TRQs, the agreement to lower export subsidies and reduce the aggregate measure of support (AMS) – did not do much to lower agricultural protection. The effective level of protection has diminished little since the conclusion of the Uruguay Round in 1995.

Total net transfers from consumers and taxpayers to farmers in OECD countries equalled 76 per cent of the farm gross value added in 1986–88;

in 2000, after implementation of all Uruguay commitments, they still amounted to 62 per cent of gross value added. Although the producer nominal protection coefficient (the ratio of prices received by producers to the border price) fell from 58 to 35 per cent between 1986–88 and 1999–2001 in the OECD, the number of active farmers declined over this period as well. As a result, support per farmer has continued to rise in many OECD countries – by 31 per cent in the United States and 60 per cent in the European Union (Anderson, 2003; Messerlin, 2003).

Highly distorting agricultural support policies in many OECD countries has a major detrimental effect on developing countries, including LDCs. Indeed, 18 per cent of LDC exports on average comprise goods that are subsidized in at least one WTO member, compared to 3–4 per cent for other countries (Table 2.4). A similar observation holds for imports – 9 per cent of LDC imports involve products that are subsidized, compared to 3–4 per cent for other countries. Numerous analyses have documented the detrimental effects of OECD policies on developing countries. For example, sugar is one of the most policy-distorted of all commodities, with OECD protection rates frequently above 200 per cent (Mitchell, 2003). Producers in those countries receive more than double the world market price. OECD support to sugar producers of US$6.4 billion per year roughly equals developing country exports. US subsidies to cotton growers totalled US$3.9 billion in 2002, three times US foreign aid to Africa. These subsidies depress world cotton prices by around 10 per cent, cutting the income of poor farmers in West Africa, Central and South Asia, and poor countries around the world. In West Africa alone, where cotton is a critical cash crop for many small-scale and near-subsistence farmers,

Table 2.4 Trade shares of products affected by agricultural subsidies, 1995–98, average per cent

Country	Domestic support		Export subsidies	
	Exports 1995–98	*Imports 1995–98*	*Exports 1995–98*	*Imports 1995–98*
All countries (143)	3.6	3.7	4.4	4.4
Industrial countries (23)	3.1	3.3	4.0	3.9
Developing countries (90)	4.2	4.2	5.0	5.0
LDCs (30)	17.8	8.9	16.7	13.1

Note:
Parentheses indicate the number of countries per region for which data are available.
Source: Hoekman, Ng and Olarreaga (2003).

annual income losses for cotton growers are about US$250 million a year (Baffes, 2003).

The Doha call for elimination of agricultural export subsidies is clearly of great importance for developing countries that have a comparative advantage in the products affected, both directly and indirectly. While attaining this objective will undoubtedly be difficult, the benchmark is clear and is a good one. The primary need is to establish a deadline to achieve it. Matters are more difficult when it comes to other subsidies. In principle, decoupling domestic support payments from production makes sense. Given that there is a rationale for subsidies in many contexts and that the revealed preference of many governments to use subsidies, it would appear more effective to focus on reduction of border barriers and the abolition of explicit export subsidies. This would automatically impose serious constraints on the feasibility of production subsidies by greatly increasing their costs (Snape, 1987).

From a trade perspective, reducing border barriers is critical. Hoekman, Ng and Olarreaga (2003) find that a 50 per cent global tariff cut will have a much greater positive effect on exports and welfare of developing countries than a 50 per cent cut in subsidies, even if the analysis is limited to the set of commodities that is currently subsidized by at least one WTO member. The reason for this is that tariffs are often very high for subsidized products, frequently taking the form of non-transparent specific duties. While minimum market access commitments negotiated during the Uruguay Round – implemented through TRQs – ensure some access, in many cases the TRQs are small, and the effect of the tariffs is to support high domestic price levels.

This does not imply that negotiations can neglect domestic support policies. Most developing countries oppose further agricultural trade liberalization in an environment that is characterized by continued large-scale support for OECD farmers. Past experience has demonstrated that the gains from own liberalization are attenuated because of the market segmenting effect of OECD subsidy policies. Indeed, own liberalization in some instances – for example, India – has proven to be politically unsustainable as farmers are subjected to large world price swings and import surges of subsidized commodities (Gulati and Narayanan, 2002). Substantial reduction in OECD agricultural support policies is therefore not just important for developing countries in its own right – in that it generates direct benefits for the many economies that are (potential) net exporters – but is critical from a political economy perspective. It is necessary to create the conditions to allow developing country governments to pursue domestic reforms. That is, subsidy reforms in OECD countries are necessary, although not sufficient, for developing countries to maximize the gains from the current WTO negotiations on agriculture, as this will require own liberalization.

Also important are effective safeguard mechanisms. Safeguards are often the only available instrument to developing country governments to respond to OECD intervention that leads to import surges and periods of low-priced imports. In the absence of effective safeguard mechanisms that can be invoked when import surges harm domestic farmers, many countries will not want to substantially reduce tariff bindings for agricultural products (as high levels of bound tariffs allow governments to raise applied rates unilaterally if deemed necessary up to the level of the tariff binding). Large differences between the level of a tariff binding and the applied tariff rate creates uncertainty and reduces the relevance of GATT rules. While bringing bound rates down towards applied rates is beneficial and should be an objective, linking such a process to the removal of export subsidies; decoupling of domestic support and substantial reductions in OECD tariff peaks can help ensure that such reforms are implemented.

Textiles and clothing and contingent protection

Although the WTO Agreement on Textiles and Clothing requires the abolition of all textile quotas by 1 January 2005, tariff barriers to trade in this sector remain high. As important is the uncertainty of access generated by the threat of contingent protection (safeguards and especially anti-dumping). Anti-dumping has become a frequently used instrument in both industrialized and developing countries. Not only have developing countries become frequent users of anti-dumping, but on a per-dollar of import coverage basis they are the most intensive users of anti-dumping (Table 2.5).

The existence of anti-dumping induces rent-seeking behaviour on the part of import-competing firms, and creates substantial uncertainty regarding the conditions of market access facing exporters. Investigations have a chilling effect on imports (they are a signal to importers to diversify away from targeted suppliers) and are often facilitating devices for the conclusion of market sharing or price-fixing agreements with affected exporters (see Blonigen and Prusa, 2001 for a survey of the evidence). The best policy in this regard has been known for a long time – abolish the instrument. Safeguards are a better and more honest instrument to address the problem anti-dumping is used for – providing import-competing industries with time to adjust to increased foreign competition (Finger, 1996). Greater discipline on the use of the instrument could involve determining the impact on the economy of imposing duties through

Table 2.5 Anti-dumping initiations per US dollar of imports, 1995–99

Country/economy initiating	Against all economies	
	No. of anti-dumping initiations	*Initiations per US dollar of imports index (USA = 100)*
Argentina	89	2125
South Africa	89	2014
Peru	21	1634
India	83	1382
New Zealand	28	1292
Venezuela	22	1174
Australia	89	941
Colombia	15	659
Brazil	56	596
Israel	19	418
Chile	10	376
Indonesia	20	330
Mexico	46	290
Turkey	14	204
Korea	37	185
Canada	50	172
European Union	160	130
United States	136	100
Malaysia	11	97

Source: Finger, Ng and Wangchuk (2001).

so-called 'public interest clauses' – current legislation and WTO rules impose only weak procedural disciplines on import-competing industries and do not give users of imports a voice. The problem is a political economy one: a necessary condition for reform is greater mobilization of countervailing forces in the domestic political arena.

Services

There is a huge market access agenda in services trade, one that spans foreign direct investment (FDI) as well as cross-border trade, and where to date only limited progress has been made in the WTO (Mattoo, 2001).[3] Here again the greatest gains to developing countries would come from reforming their own policies. In contrast to tariffs, services trade and investment restrictions do not generate revenue for the government. Instead, they tend to raise costs for users, imposing a 'tax' on the whole economy.[4]

Market access and regulation are closely intertwined. Services are activities where there is often need for some type of regulation to address market failures or achieve social (non-economic) objectives. A good case can be made that many of the 'backbone' services that are critical to development – transport, energy, telecoms, finance – increasingly have become industries where network externalities are important. Regulation to ensure that markets are contestable needs to focus not only on 'traditional' types of entry barriers – outright bans, licensing, and the like – but on the ability to connect to the network at a reasonable price, apply the relevant technologies, and so on. Designing and enforcing policies to achieve this is not trivial. In many cases, regulatory thinking and economic analysis is still evolving rapidly when it comes to network industries, and technological developments may make specific types of interventions redundant or counterproductive. Careful assessments of the implications of alternative types of international cooperation – which may be regional rather than multilateral – are required to determine what options might be most appropriate for developing countries.

Market-access focal points and negotiating modalities

Many countries have proposed the use of tariff-cutting formulae to reduce tariffs on merchandise trade – both manufactures and agricultural. This is a good approach, especially if a non-linear formula is used that reduces high tariffs (peaks) much more than low tariffs. The request–offer approach used in the Uruguay Round can easily increase the variance in protection, gives greater negotiating leverage to large countries and allows peaks to remain in place. A Swiss-type formula, as proposed by the Chair of the WTO market access committee, is much preferable.[5] However, it is important that at the same time WTO members also agree on an end point or final objective. A Swiss type of formula can greatly reduce the average level of protection and the dispersion of tariff rates, but ideally needs to be complemented by a decision that the end point or ultimate objective should be the complete removal of tariffs on goods that are of export interest to developing countries. Given that average OECD rates for manufactures are already low, a possible focal point here would be the complete elimination of tariffs by these countries by 2015 – the target date for the achievement of the Millennium Development Goals.

Given that OECD countries have already bound virtually all their tariff lines at applied rates, any formula that gives weight to both *additional* bindings (increases in the ratio of the number of bound to unbound lines) and reductions in the absolute difference between bound and applied rates, will automatically give credit to developing countries in terms of attaining an agreed target level of liberalization. What this implies is that formulae need to focus on *bound* rates and not exclusively on applied tariff rates.

The efficiency of the service sector is a major determinant of competitiveness (most services are inputs into production). Services are therefore of great importance to developing countries and there are substantial opportunities both to expand exports and to liberalize further access to developing-country markets. While the latter will bring the greatest gains, opening by developed countries of temporary access to service markets for natural service providers – so-called mode 4 of the GATS – and a binding of the current liberal policy set that is applied to cross-border trade (modes 1 and 2 of the GATS) – would be both valuable and assist governments in pursuing domestic reforms. Opening of developed country labour markets to allow temporary entry by foreign workers equal to 3 per cent of the current workforce would generate welfare (real income) gains that exceed those that could be attained from full merchandise trade liberalization. In addition, many developing countries have begun to exploit the opportunities offered by the Internet and telecommunication networks to provide services through cross-border trade. Currently such trade is largely free of restrictions, and this desirable state of affairs should be locked in through the GATS.

Given that there are only limited sector-specific commitments on national treatment and market access in the GATS, the simplest benchmark would pertain to the sectoral coverage ratio and/or the number of sectors where no restrictions on national treatment and market access are maintained (Hoekman and Kostecki, 2001). For many developing countries the coverage of specific commitments is well below 25 per cent of all services and modes of supply. Binding the status quo would help reduce uncertainty, while pre-committing to future reform can help increase the relevance of the GATS. Given the importance of movement of natural services providers as a mode of contesting foreign service markets for developing countries, explicit quantitative targets for 'mode 4' visas could be considered – for example, a minimum share of total service sector employment (Walmsley and Winters, 2002). Even if not used as the focal point for negotiations, this can be a metric for judging the outcome of negotiations.

The terms of a potential deal could involve mode 3 concessions by developing countries – made on a case-by-case basis – against comprehensive mode 1 and mode 4 commitments on the part of developed countries that are made on the basis of a 'formula' (model schedule or template) (Mattoo, 2001). While national concessions on mode 3 should be sensitive to the type of service – in particular, the need for complementary regulation – developing countries have a lot to gain from both dimensions: making own mode 3 commitments will help improve economic performance and expand employment; the same dynamics are generated as a result of better access to services markets through modes 1 and 4.

Reciprocal MFN liberalization and unilateral trade preferences

Historically, the strategy of developing countries in the GATT–WTO has been to limit the reach of reciprocity by seeking 'differential and more favourable treatment'. Special and differential treatment (SDT) provisions in the WTO span three core areas: *market access*, through trade preferences granted to developing countries and acceptance that developing countries make fewer market access commitments than developed countries in trade negotiations; *exemptions* or deferrals from some WTO rules; and *technical assistance* to help implement WTO mandates. Only the second of these is legally enforceable – preferences and technical assistance are so-called 'best endeavours' commitments. There is general dissatisfaction with SDT provisions among both developed and developing countries as the current system has not worked especially well. SDT is a major agenda item for the Doha Round. What follows discusses preferences; the next section turns to the issue of the scope of WTO rules.

A major factor affecting negotiating modalities on market access is that developing countries have been granted preferential access to rich country markets. This raises the question whether market access preferences should be deepened and extended as opposed to an effort that centres on MFN liberalization on a reciprocal basis. It also raises the question of what to do about the erosion of preferences that is unavoidable given further MFN-based liberalization. For many products exported by low-income countries, tariffs in high-income countries may be zero as a result of trade preference schemes. The EU Everything But Arms (EBA) initiative and the US African Growth and Opportunity Act (AGOA), in particular, offer deep preferences to beneficiary countries that can satisfy eligibility constraints.

Trade preferences for many developing countries tend to be limited for tariff peak items as these are by definition 'sensitive' products that are often excluded or subject to some type of quantitative limitation. Much of the economic literature concludes that preferences do little good, and may even do harm (Hoekman, Michalopoulos and Winters, 2003; World Bank, 2003). Reasons for this include:

- *Countries benefiting from preferential access are subject to rules of origin.* These may be so strict (constraining) that countries are forced to pay the MFN tariff because they cannot satisfy the requirements. Research reveals that utilization rates are often much less than 100 per cent (Brenton, 2003; Inama, 2003).
- Often goods in which developing countries have a comparative advantage are the most 'sensitive' products that have the *highest tariffs.* Preferences for these products are frequently limited.
- Preferences are uncertain, subject to unilateral change or withdrawal, and to non-trade conditionality (satisfaction of labour rights, environmental requirements, etc.).
- Preferences can give rise to *serious trade diversion* as the set of goods that beneficiary developing countries produce and trade will tend to overlap with other developing countries that are not beneficiaries.
- Even in cases where preferences have value – that is, they apply to highly protected sectors in donor countries and thus generate rents – in practice, these rents will not accrue completely to the recipient country. Instead, a share of the rents, perhaps most of them, will be *captured by importers* (distributors, retailers).
- Fears of preference erosion may spur efforts to *maintain preference margins,* in the process impeding both multilateral liberalization efforts and own reforms by recipient countries.

There is an acute danger that substantial progress on market access through a formula approach will be impeded because of concerns by countries that this will erode the value of their current preferential access. The danger is that this may give scope to preference-granting countries to delay implementing tariff reductions for products that are important for other developing countries (and their own welfare). The same is true for agricultural subsidies. Some developing countries are indirectly benefiting from OECD domestic support because they have preferential access to the protected market – the European Commission sugar regime is an example. The preferences therefore potentially create incentives for an 'unholy alliance' with OECD farm interests, at the cost of less global liberalization.

One way forward would be to agree on a single preferential tariff rate – zero – for all products currently benefiting from GSP status in developed countries (as is the case presently in the United States), thereby removing all partial preferences. However, extending preferential duty-free access to large countries such as India and China will be very difficult politically. A major reason why duty-free access for much of Africa and the LDCs could be implemented is that these countries account for less than 0.5 per cent of world trade. Given the political reality that developed nations will not grant larger developing countries unconditional preferential market access, and that this is not first best in the first place – given the benefits of own reforms – this will have to occur through reciprocal, MFN liberalization.

In order to assist low-income developing countries to benefit from market access opportunities a significant increase is needed in technical and financial assistance to expand supply capacity and improve the investment climate in low-income countries. The need for this is acute in absolute terms, but is made even stronger as the trading system moves in the direction of lower MFN trade barriers and the consequent erosion of preferences for those countries that currently benefit from effective preferential access. One option that could be considered as an alternative to maintaining preference margins is for OECD countries to help current developing country beneficiaries adjust through direct income support-type instruments (targeted at affected farmers and firms and decoupled from past production levels). More generally, what is required is assistance to help affected countries deal with the associated adjustment costs by supporting diversification into other activities, retraining, and so forth.

WTO rules and special and differential treatment

A precondition for developing countries to benefit from WTO membership is 'getting the rules right' – ensuring that they support development. Most developing countries are latecomers to the multilateral trading system – a fact that explains why many present WTO rules predominantly reflect the interests of rich countries and the status quo disciplines that already have been put in place by them. Thus, the much greater latitude that exists in the WTO for the use of agricultural subsidization, for example, reflects the use of such support policies in many developed countries. The same is true for the permissive approach that has historically been taken towards the use of import quotas on textile products – in principle, prohibited by GATT rules. More recently, the inclusion of rules on the protection of intellectual property rights (TRIPS) has strengthened perceptions that the WTO contract is unbalanced.

The Single Undertaking approach in the Uruguay Round led to the inclusion into the WTO of rules in many areas of a regulatory nature. This was the culmination of a process started in the Tokyo Round (1973–79). It shows few signs of abating – witness the focus on competition law, FDI policy, transparency in government procurement, trade facilitation and environmental policy. Calls for deeper integration at the multilateral level range from coordinated application of national policies to the harmonization of regulatory regimes. A key question from a development perspective is to determine the rationale for proposals to pursue deeper integration and, if so, whether the WTO is the appropriate forum for this.

'Getting the rules right' requires evaluating and understanding the implications of alternative rules. This is not straightforward, especially when it comes to the regulatory, 'behind-the-border' policies that are increasingly the subject of multilateral discussions. Too often deliberations in the WTO are not informed by economic analysis or a good understanding of the costs and benefits of specific proposals or rules, or how these costs and benefits are distributed across or within countries.

One consequence of this is reflected in the substantial effort that has been expended over the years to provide 'special and differential treatment' (SDT) for developing countries in the WTO (Hudec, 1987; Finger, 1991). A good case can be made that efforts to enhance the development relevance of the WTO need to distinguish the issue of SDT – the principle that poorer countries should be granted 'better than MFN' treatment – from the broader issue of ensuring that WTO rules and disciplines support development. The second dimension is by far more important. This goes well beyond the specific language that is found in WTO agreements relating to developing country interests. Instead, it revolves around whether a particular WTO rule makes sense for developing countries to implement (Hoekman, Michalopoulos and Winters, 2003).

The Doha Ministerial Declaration reaffirmed the importance of SDT by stating that 'provisions for special and differential treatment are an integral part of the WTO agreements'. It called for a review of WTO SDT provisions with the objective of 'strengthening them and making them more precise, effective and operational' (para. 44). The Declaration also states that 'modalities for further commitments, including provisions for special and differential treatment, be established no later than 31 March 2003' (para. 14). However, in the event efforts in 2002 to come to agreement on ways to strengthen and operationalize SDT provisions have not been successful so far. Looking forward, the experience with Uruguay Round implementation and the Doha discussions on SDT in 2002–03 suggest that a new approach is needed.

Recognizing differential interests and capacities

As noted previously, the primary challenge from a development perspective is to get the rules 'right'. This requires engagement by developing country stakeholders and economic analysis of the implications of proposed rules at the national level. Given the resource and skill constraints that prevail in many countries, this is indeed a huge challenge. One way of recognizing these constraints is through SDT provisions that give countries the assurance that rules will apply only once a nation has put in place the preconditions needed to benefit from implementation. Even if countries consider a set of rules to be in their interest, other issues may constitute a more urgent priority for investment of scarce administrative and financial resources. These observations suggest the need for 'differentiation' among developing countries in determining the reach of WTO rules. The need for this is greatest for 'resource-intensive' disciplines – that is, those that require significant complementary legal, administrative and institutional investments or capacity; or that will potentially give rise to large net transfers out of developing countries (as could be the case under the TRIPS agreement, for example).

The basic rationale for differentiation is that certain agreements or rules simply may not be immediate development priorities and/or require that other preconditions be satisfied for implementation to be beneficial. These preconditions can be proxied by the attainment of a minimum level of *per capita* income, institutional capacity, or economic scale. Some WTO disciplines may not be appropriate for very small countries in that the regulatory institutions that are required may be unduly costly – that is, countries may lack the scale needed for benefits to exceed implementation costs.[6]

Several options could be considered to take into account and operationalize country differences in WTO agreements. Such 'rule-related SDT' could involve:[7]

- Adopting a 'rule of thumb' that makes a group of countries eligible to 'opt-out' of provisions that entail substantial implementation costs until such time as they have passed certain economic *development-related benchmarks or eligibility criteria*. This would imply revisiting the current set of country groups recognized in the WTO: the LDCs (a UN-defined group); other developing countries (a 'self-designated' group), and developed countries. It would also require consensus as to which agreements this SDT would apply to.
- An *agreement-specific approach* involving country-based criteria that are applied on an agreement-by-agreement basis to determine whether

(when) agreements should be implemented. This could be linked to the provision of technical assistance and development of a national action plan for ultimately assuming the WTO obligations concerned.

- A *country-based approach* that places trade reforms priorities in the context of national development plans such as the poverty reduction strategy papers (PRSP), and would employ multilateral surveillance and monitoring to establish a cooperative framework under which countries are assisted in gradually adopting WTO norms as part of a more general programme of trade-related reforms.

A common feature of these options is that they entail more narrowly defining eligibility for temporary exemptions from WTO rules and devoting much more attention to determining the economic costs and benefits of implementation of rules. None of the options will be easy to operationalize. Country classification inevitably creates tensions among different developing countries as to which countries would be counted in and which out. What constitutes 'resource-intensive', for example, and the extent to which specific agreements will give rise to large implementation costs are questions that will require analysis, both general and country-specific. Countries or analysts may disagree about the magnitude of assessed costs and benefits. Determining criteria that could be used in the implementation context will require input from stakeholders, government agencies and development institutions. While this could help to strengthen the coherence of policy at both the national and international levels, it would also make the WTO negotiation and enforcement process much more complex.

Widening the set of actors involved in implementation of a new approach towards SDT may reduce the risk of inducing countries to adopt and pursue a programme of trade and regulatory reform that may not in fact be suited to the country concerned. However, care would need to be taken to ensure that this did not lead to cross-conditionality. Many countries were concerned in the Uruguay Round about avoiding possible 'cross-conditionality' between the WTO and international financial institutions (IFIs); this led to a ministerial declaration on 'coherence' to call for 'avoiding the imposition on governments of cross-conditionality or additional conditions' resulting from cooperation between the WTO and the IFIs.[8]

Several options may therefore be feasible in recognizing country differences in the ability to benefit from implementation of resource-intensive rules. The choice of type of approach requires considerable thought and discussion. Arguably, what matters most at this point is that WTO members recognize that capacities and priorities differ hugely across the membership and consider alternative approaches along the lines sketched out above. Given the steady expansion of the WTO into regulatory areas, this would help make 'development relevance' more than a slogan. A new approach towards SDT that is anchored much more solidly on economic analysis and a national process of identification of development priorities could do much to enhance the 'ownership' of the institution in developing countries. Whatever is done, it is important that transparency and predictability is preserved, to avoid wasteful strategic behaviour and to target SDT to those countries that are most in need of it. In determining SDT eligibility, non-negotiability once a deal has been reached is critical.

A first step could be to establish a broad-based, high-level group operating under the auspices of the WTO General Council to explore different options, possible mechanisms and details of an alternative approach, including establishing criteria to determine which rules are resource-intensive in implementation, with recommendations to be made before the end of the Doha Round. The terms of reference of such a working group should be relatively broad and include both national economic policy-makers and representatives of the international development community.

Conclusion

The challenges confronting developing countries seeking to expand their international trade are primarily domestic. Necessary conditions are an open domestic trade regime, a supportive investment climate and a host of complementary policies relating to education, health, infrastructure, etc. The WTO negotiating agenda often will have little bearing on the priority issues and needs that must be addressed on the ground in developing countries. The primary beneficial role that the WTO can play is to foster the reduction of barriers to trade – in goods and services – on a reciprocal basis. As far as multilateral policy disciplines are concerned, a precondition for benefits to result is to get 'the rules right' – to ensure that they support development. Getting 'the rules right' requires analysis and participation by stakeholders. One size may not fit all, especially when it comes to the regulatory, 'behind-the-border' policies.

Historically, the strategy of developing countries has been to seek SDT: unilateral trade preferences from developed countries, rejection of reciprocity in the exchange of market access commitments; and exemptions or deferrals from some WTO rules. Preferences have not proven to be very effective as an instrument of development. They often come laden with restrictions, product exclusions and administrative rules that prevent beneficiaries from utilizing them fully. Even when effective, they divert trade away from equally poor but excluded developing countries. Irrespective of trade diversion costs, preferences do little to help most of the world's poor, as they live in countries such as India and China that are granted only limited preferences, if any, for products in which they have a comparative advantage.

Multilateral non-discriminatory liberalization of trade in the goods and services, in which many developing countries tend to have a comparative advantage, is a more effective and efficient approach to expand trade opportunities. This should include a binding commitment by developed countries to abolish export subsidies and decouple agricultural support policies. The pursuit of these objectives would be more supportive of development than one that continues to emphasize preferential access to markets and non-reciprocity. This is both because own liberalization is beneficial and because a non-discriminatory approach would result in reduction in barriers to trade maintained by middle-income as well as developed countries. The former are increasingly important potential markets, and have been among the most dynamic traders in recent years (World Bank, 2003).

As far as WTO rules are concerned, especially new rules on 'behind-the-border' policies, the priority is to ensure that any negotiated disciplines support development and are seen to do so in developing countries. This is a critical precondition for 'ownership' of WTO agreements. However, even good agreements may not be a priority for some countries, especially the poorest and smallest, nor are the benefits likely to be proportional in all countries. The experience after the Uruguay Round with implementation of agreements by developing countries has demonstrated that limiting recognition of differential capacities and levels of development to uniform transition periods and non-binding offers of technical assistance is inadequate. Adopting a new approach to SDT that is firmly grounded on economic analysis that reflects national circumstances would do much to enhance the development relevance of the WTO.

Development assistance must play an important role in helping to expand and improve the trade capacity that is needed for countries to benefit from better access to markets. Policy reforms and trade-related investment needs should be determined on a country-by-country basis as part of the national processes used by governments to identify priorities. Technical and financial assistance should be driven by national considerations, not by the WTO agenda. However, additional assistance will be needed to help low-income countries adapt to a gradual reduction in trade preferences following further non-discriminatory trade liberalization, and to assist poor net-importing countries to deal with the potential detrimental effects of a significant increase in world food prices should this materialize. Major commitments were made by both developed and developing countries in Monterrey in 2002 – the priority now is to identify the policy measures seen by developing-country governments as urgent areas for action and to address the associated resource needs.

Notes

* Thanks are due to Carsten Fink, Will Martin, Aaditya Mattoo and Marcelo Olarreaga for helpful comments and suggestions on an earlier draft and to Francis Ng for data. This chapter draws in part on joint work in progress with Costas Michalopoulos and L. Alan Winters. The views expressed are personal and should not be attributed to the World Bank.

1. This calculation excludes Angola, 95 per cent of whose exports are oil-related and not dutiable. The LDCs comprise 49 low-income countries, mostly in Africa.

2. Fiscal constraints may imply that low-income countries need to maintain tariffs above the average prevailing in more advanced economies for revenue collection purposes. In such cases, countries should consider greatly reducing the dispersion in duty rates by moving towards a uniform tariff (Tarr, 2002).

3. Walmsley and Winters (2002) estimate the global gains from allowing temporary entry of both skilled and unskilled labour services equivalent to 3 per cent of the current workforce in OECD countries would be some 1.5 times greater than the gains from merchandise liberalization.

4. Stern (2002) surveys the literature.

5. The formula approach that was suggested by the chair in May 2003 is an augmented 'Swiss' formula that makes the cut in tariffs a function of the initial average level of protection. It is defined as: $T_1 = B \times NAV \times T_0 / (B \times NAV + T_0)$, where T_1 is the final (bound) tariff; B is a parameter to be chosen; NAV is the initial national average tariff; and T_0 is the initial (bound) tariff. The proposal is that all countries bind at least 95 per cent of all tariff lines and value of imports. The factor $B \times NAV$ equals the maximum coefficient of the Swiss formula used in the Tokyo Round. The Chair also proposed that specific tariffs be converted into *ad valorem* equivalents, that tariffs in sectors of interest to developing countries be reduced to zero (on a reciprocal basis); that developing countries have a transition period that is three times longer than for developed countries; and that LDCs be exempted from tariff-cuts altogether. While in principle a good approach, LDCs should consider participating in the tariff-cutting and binding process – not participating removes an opportunity to further reduce anti-export bias and the dispersion in rates of protection.

6. For example, despite remarkable reductions in customs clearance times that have been achieved by some LDCs (sometimes from weeks to days or hours, as in

Senegal), the customs regimes in many participating countries are characterized by long clearance times, a plethora of informal fees and inadequate performance monitoring indicators. Many countries are struggling to implement the Agreement on Customs Valuation and to work with and reform other institutions whose actions impinge on customs efficiency such as security and enforcement.

7. These options are discussed further in Stevens (2002), Prowse (2002), Wang and Winters (2000), and Hoekman, Michalopoulos and Winters (2003).

8. Declaration on the Contribution of the World Trade Organization to Achieving Greater Coherence in Global Economic Policymaking, 15 December 1993.

References

Anderson, K. (2003) 'How Can Agricultural Trade Reform Reduce Poverty?'. Background paper prepared for the UN Millennium Project Task Force on Trade.

Anderson, K., B. Dimaranan, J. Francois, T. Hertel, B. Hoekman and W. Martin (2001) 'The Cost of Rich (and Poor) Country Protection to Developing Countries' *Journal of African Economies*, 10(3): 227–57.

Baffes, J. (2003) 'Cotton Market Policies: Issues and Facts', Washington, DC: World Bank, mimeo.

Blonigen, B. and T. Prusa (2001) 'Antidumping', NBER Working Paper 8398, Cambridge, MA: NBER.

Brenton, P. (2003) 'Integrating the Least Developed Countries into the World Trading System: The Current Impact of EU Preferences under Everything But Arms', Policy Research Working Paper 3018, Washington, DC: World Bank.

Finger, J. M. (1991) 'Development Economics and the GATT', in J. De Melo and A. Sapir (eds), *Trade Theory and Economic Reform*, Oxford: Basil Blackwell.

———— (1996) 'Legalized Backsliding: Safeguard Provisions in the GATT', in W. Martin and L. A. Winters (eds), *The Uruguay Round and the Developing Economies*. Cambridge: Cambridge University Press.

———— (2002) 'The Doha Agenda and Development: A View From the Uruguay Round', Manila: Asian Development Bank.

Finger, J. M. and P. Schuler (2000) 'Implementation of Uruguay Round Commitments: The Development Challenge', *The World Economy*, 23: 511–26.

Finger, J. M., F. Ng and S. Wangchuk (2001) 'Antidumping as Safeguard Policy', World Bank Working Paper 2730, Washington, DC: World Bank.

Gulati, A. and S. Narayanan (2002) 'Managing Import Competition When Developing Countries Liberalize Trade: The Indian Experience', IFPRI, mimeo.

Henson, S., K. Preibisch and O. Masakure (2001) 'Review of Developing Country Needs and Involvement in International Standards-Setting Bodies', www.dfid.gov.uk.

Hertel, T. and W. Martin (2000) 'Liberalizing Agriculture and Manufactures in a Millennium Round: Implications for Developing Countries', *The World Economy*, 23: 455–70.

Hoekman, B. (2002) 'Strengthening the Global Trade Architecture for Development: The Post-Doha Agenda', *World Trade Review*, 1: 23–46.

Hoekman, B. and M. Kostecki (2001) *The Political Economy of the World Trading System: The WTO and Beyond*, 2nd edn, Oxford: Oxford University Press.

Hoekman, B., C. Michalopoulos and L. A. Winters (2003) 'More Favorable and Differential Treatment of Developing Countries: Towards a New Approach in the WTO', Washington, DC: World Bank, mimeo.

Hoekman, B., F. Ng and M. Olarreaga (2002) 'Tariff Peaks in the Quad and Least Developed Country Exports', *World Bank Economic Review*, 16: 1–22.

——— (2003) 'Reducing Agricultural Tariffs versus Domestic Support: What's More Important for Developing Countries?', World Bank Development Research Group and Centre for Economic Policy Research, mimeo.

Hudec, R. E. (1987) 'Developing Countries in the GATT Legal System', London: Trade Policy Research Centre.

Inama, S. (2003) 'Trade Preferences and the WTO Negotiations on Market Access', Geneva: UNCTAD, mimeo.

Mattoo, A. (2001) 'Liberalizing Trade in Services', Washington, DC: World Bank, mimeo. www.worldbank.org/trade.

Messerlin, P. (2003) 'Agriculture in the Doha Agenda', Policy Research Working Paper 3009, Washington, DC: World Bank.

Mitchell, D. (2003) 'Sugar Policies: Opportunity for Change', Washington, DC: World Bank, mimeo.

Prowse, S. (2002) 'The Role of International and National Agencies in Trade-Related Capacity Building', *World Economy*, 25 (9): 1235–61.

Snape, R. (1987) 'The Importance of Frontier Barriers', in H. Kierzkowski (ed.), *Protection and Competition in International Trade*, London: Basil Blackwell.

Stern, R. (2002) 'Quantifying Barriers to Trade in Services', in B. Hoekman, P. English and A. Mattoo (eds), *Development, Trade and the WTO: A Handbook*, Washington, DC: World Bank.

Stevens, C. (2002) 'The Future of SDT for Developing Countries in the WTO', Institute for Development Studies, University of Sussex, mimeo, May.

Tarr, D. (2002) 'Arguments for and Against Uniform Tariffs', in B. Hoekman, P. English and A. Mattoo (eds), *Development, Trade and the WTO: A Handbook*, Washington, DC: World Bank.

US Department of Commerce (1999) *US Merchandise Trade: Selected Highlights*, Washington, DC: US Government Printing Office.

Walmsley, T. and L. A. Winters (2002). 'Relaxing Restrictions on Temporary Movement of Natural Persons: A Simulation Analysis', University of Sussex, mimeo.

Wang, Z. K. and L. A. Winters (2000) 'Putting "Humpty" Together Again: Including Developing Countries in a Consensus for the WTO', CEPR Policy Paper 4.

Wilson, J. S. (2001) 'Bridging the Standards Divide: Recommendations for Reform from a Development Perspective', Washington, DC: World Bank, mimeo, www.worldbank.org/trade.

Winters, L. A. (1999). 'Trade Policy as Development Policy', Paper presented at the UNCTAD X High-level Round Table on Trade and Development, www.unctad.org.

World Bank (2001) *Global Economic Prospects and the Developing Countries: Making Trade Work for the World's Poor.* Washington, DC: World Bank.

——— (2003). *Global Economic Prospects and the Developing Countries: Realizing the Development Promise of the Doha Agenda*, Washington, DC: World Bank.

Part II
Agriculture

3
Trade Liberalization, Agriculture and Poverty in Low-Income Countries

Kym Anderson

At the Fourth Ministerial Meeting of the World Trade Organization (WTO) in Doha in November 2001, members agreed to launch the next comprehensive round of multilateral trade negotiations (MTNs). The attempt to do so at the previous Ministerial Meeting in Seattle in late 1999 was aborted, not least because developing-country members believed they had not benefited sufficiently from the preceding Uruguay Round. That belief still persists, and the poorer developing countries of South Asia and sub-Saharan Africa (SSA) in particular remain sceptical that a new round of negotiations will benefit them – notwithstanding the substantial focus on their development concerns in the Doha Ministerial Declaration (WTO, 2001b).

If the poorer developing countries of South Asia, SSA and elsewhere are to become constructively engaged in this next attempt to liberalize trade multilaterally, they need to be convinced that they will receive sufficient gains from trade reform to warrant the inevitable costs of negotiation and adjustment. They and the donor community also need to be convinced that trade reform will alleviate rather than add to poverty and food insecurity in their countries. The net food-importing developing countries, and those currently receiving tariff preferences or food aid, are especially worried that they will be made worse off by agricultural trade reform.

This chapter offers an economic assessment of the opportunities and challenges provided by the Doha Development Agenda's MTN round for low-income countries seeking to trade their way out of poverty. After a brief discussion of the links between poverty, economic growth and trade, it reports modelling results showing that farm product markets remain the most costly of all goods market distortions in world trade. It then focuses on what such reform might mean for countries of South Asia and SSA in particular, both without and with their involvement in the MTN reform process. What becomes clear from that comparison of modelling results is that if those countries want to maximize their benefits from the Doha Development Agenda, they need also to free up their own domestic product and factor markets so their farmers are better able to take advantage of new market-opening opportunities abroad. The chapter then addresses other concerns of low-income countries about farm trade reform: whether there will be losses associated with tariff preference erosion, whether food-importing countries will suffer from higher food prices in international markets, whether China's WTO accession will provide an example of trade reform aggravating poverty via cuts to prices received by Chinese farmers, and the impact on food security and poverty alleviation. The chapter concludes with lessons of relevance for low-income countries for their own domestic and trade policies.

Links between poverty, economic growth and trade

Throughout most of the nineteenth and twentieth centuries, the number of people in the world in absolute poverty (defined as living on less than the equivalent of US$1 per day in 1985 PPP terms) had been increasing almost continually (Bourguignon and Morrisson, 2002). Since the late 1970s, however, the number has declined by more than 200 million, or from 15 to 7 per cent of the global population; and the number on less than US$2 per day has declined by 450 million, or from 40 to 19 per cent of the world's people, according to new estimates by Sala-i-Martin (2002).

Remarkable though that recent achievement has been in such a short period, Sala-i-Martin's data suggest there are still 350 million on less than US$1 and almost 1 billion on less than US$2 per day – most of whom are in Asia and SSA.[1] Since poverty alleviation for those remaining poor people is a high priority, efforts have been made to understand the reasons behind successful alleviation. The evidence presented by Sala-i-Martin suggests that economic growth differences have been largely responsible for the differences in poverty alleviation across regions, a finding supported by numerous other studies (for example, Dollar and Kraay, 2002). Initiatives that boost national economic growth rates are therefore likely to be helpful in the fight against poverty, *ceteris paribus*.

Trade liberalization is one such initiative that tends to boost economic growth.[2] But it also alters relative prices, so its net effect on poverty reduction depends also on the signs of those relative product and factor price changes. If the price changes are pro-poor, then they will reinforce any positive growth effects of trade reform on the poor.

Potential gains from the WTO's Doha Development Agenda

Tariffs facing poor-country exports to other markets are high. At the end of the Uruguay Round negotiations, the tariff equivalent of import market access barriers to goods trade were low for minerals and energy raw materials and for most manufactures entering developed country markets (the exceptions being textiles and clothing); but they were high for numerous manufactures entering developing-country markets and even higher for agricultural goods entering both rich and poor countries (Table 3.1). Since developing-countries' interests in market-access opportunities abroad are primarily in either farm products and/or light manufactures such as textiles and clothing – goods that are the most protected in world trade (see also WTO, 2001a) – they have a great deal to gain potentially from the Doha Round.

That fact is reflected in a recent set of empirical estimates using a model of the global economy known as the GTAP (Global Trade Analysis Project),

Table 3.1 Average tariff equivalents of import market-access barriers to goods trade, by source and destination region, 1995, per cent

Exporting region	Importing region		
	High-income	*Low-income*	*World*
Agriculture			
High-income	16	22	18
Low-income	15	18	16
World	16	20	17
Manufactures			
High-income	1	11	4
Low-income	3	13	7
World	2	12	5
Minerals/energy			
High-income	0.1	1.3	0.4
Low-income	0.4	5.2	2.4
World	0.2	3.0	1.1

Source: Hertel *et al.* (1999).

which is an applied general equilibrium model based in Purdue University (Hertel, 1997).[3] According to estimates in Anderson *et al.* (2001), of all the economic gains to be had in 2005 from removing the barriers to trade in goods that will still be in place after all Uruguay Round commitments have been implemented, almost half (48 per cent) will come from agricultural and processed food policy reform in OECD countries (Table 3.2) – even though such products in those countries contribute only 4 per cent of global GDP and less than one-tenth of world trade. Another one-sixth of the welfare gains will come from reform of farm and food policies of developing countries.

Textiles and clothing reforms will be the next biggest contributor, although they appear small by comparison with agricultural reform: their potential global welfare contribution is only one-ninth that of agriculture's (7 per cent compared with 65 per cent). This big difference reflects two facts: one is that projected distortions to prices for agriculture are more than twice those for textiles and clothing in 2005; the other is that textiles and clothing contribute only 1.5 per cent to the value of world production and 5 per cent to the value of world trade, half or less of the shares for farm products (Anderson *et al.*, 2001).

Two assumptions are crucial in generating the results reported in Table 3.2, however. One is that China and Taiwan, having joined the WTO at the end of 2001/start of 2002, enjoy the same accelerated access to OECD markets under the Uruguay Round Agreement on Textiles and Clothing (ATC) as other developing countries that were already WTO members. The other crucial assumption is that OECD countries fully implement the spirit of the ATC by the end of 2004 – that is, they remove remaining import quotas and do not replace them with similarly protective instruments such as safeguard measures. Dropping either of those assumptions reduces very substantially the estimated gains from Uruguay Round implementation (Anderson *et al.*, 1997), and therefore will raise the potential gains from textile and clothing reform in the next and subsequent WTO rounds above that reflected in Table 3.2.

The distribution of the gains across regions that would result from full trade liberalization is clear from Table 3.2. As always, most of the gains accrue to the liberalizing region. For example, all but one-tenth of the gains from high-income countries removing distortions to their trade in farm and food products accrues to those countries. Even so, that farm trade reform contributes more than one-quarter of the total welfare gains to developing countries from rich countries liberalizing their merchandise trade. That is more than the contribution of rich countries' barriers to textile and clothing trade, and over half the contribution of all other

Table 3.2 Sectoral and regional contributions to economic welfare gains[a] from completely removing trade barriers globally, post-Uruguay Round, 2005, per cent of total global gains

Liberalizing region[b]	Benefiting region[b]	Agriculture and food	Other primary	Textiles and clothing	Other manufactures	Total
High-income	High-income	43.4	0.0	-2.3	-3.2	38.0
	Low-income	4.6	0.1	3.5	8.8	16.9
	Total	48.0	0.0	1.3	5.6	54.9
Low-income	High-income	4.4	0.1	4.1	10.9	19.5
	Low-income	12.3	1.0	1.4	10.9	25.6
	Total	16.7	1.1	5.5	21.7	45.1
All countries	High-income	47.9	0.1	1.9	7.7	57.5
	Low-income	16.9	1.0	4.9	19.6	42.5
	Total	64.8	1.1	6.8	27.3	100.0

Notes:
[a] The estimated value of the global welfare gain is $254 billion in 1995 US dollars. No account is taken in these calculations of the welfare effects of environmental changes associated with trade liberalization, which could be positive or negative depending in part on how environmental policies are adjusted following trade reforms.
[b] High- and low-income here are shorthand for developed and developing countries.

Source: Anderson et al. (2001).

manufacturing trade barriers. As for developing countries liberalizing their own farm and food policies, three-quarters of the benefits therefrom stay with the developing countries themselves, and those policies contribute almost half of the gains from those countries' overall merchandise trade reform.

WTO members were right, therefore, to insist that agricultural reform must continue into the new century without a pause. In particular, developing countries as a group have a major stake in the process of farm policy reform continuing: according to the model results in Table 3.2, farm and food policies globally contribute 40 per cent of the cost to developing economies of global goods trade distortions. Textile and clothing policies also harm them greatly, but barely one-third as much as farm policies.[4] Table 3.2 shows that 60 per cent of the contribution to developing countries from trade liberalization – and 72 per cent of that from farm trade liberalization – will come from reforms by developing countries themselves.[5]

The above GTAP modelling study found that full liberalization of rich-country farm policies would boost the volume of global agricultural trade by more than 50 per cent, but would cause real international food prices to rise by only 5 per cent on average. For the subset of low-income countries that would remain net food-importing economies after such a reform and thereby suffer a deterioration in their terms of trade, the extent of the rise in their food import prices would be small.

However, developing countries will gain less if they abstain from reforming their own policies. To illustrate the point, the effects on low-income countries in SSA and South Asia are examined first without and then with those economies participating in reform (drawing on more recent results reported in Anderson and Yao, 2003). If all regions other than South Asia and SSA were to remove their trade distortions remaining after the end of 2004 (when all Uruguay Round commitments are to have been implemented), the world economy would structurally adjust to allow each region to exploit its comparative advantages even more; SSA and South Asia would have to undertake some structural changes within and between key sectors even if they chose not to join in such a trade reform (Table 3.3(a)). In particular, agriculture would expand at the expense of labour-intensive manufacturing in those low-income countries. However, SSA would expand its agricultural output more, and contract its manufacturing more, if it also undertakes reforms itself than if it stands aside from reform. The trade balance for the different product groups is affected by the above production effects plus changes in consumption, following relative price and income changes. By comparing Tables 3.4(a) and 3.4(b) it is evident that net food imports are less for SSA and

Table 3.3 Percentage difference in sectoral output when all merchandise trade distortions remaining post-Uruguay Round are removed, 2005

(a) Reform in all regions except SSA and South Asia

	South Africa	Other SSA	India	Other South Asia
Rice	6	1	12	9
Wheat	18	2	6	6
Other cereal grain	114	85	1	1
Vegetables, fruit, nuts	1	0	1	1
Oil seeds	2	3	−1	2
Other crops	43	−8	−2	1
Plant fibre	−12	11	−2	0
Livestocks	28	15	0	1
Other food products	28	2	−2	29
Meat and dairy products	38	14	1	3
Forestry fish	2	0	0	1
Energy mineral	−2	0	1	2
Vegetable oils, fats	0	0	−4	−5
Textiles and wearing apparel	−8	−2	−10	−16
Other manufactures	−7	0	3	11
Services	0	0	0	0

(b) Reform in all regions including SSA and South Asia

	South Africa	Other SSA	India	Other South Asia
Rice	4	−1	19	18
Wheat	−3	−6	15	7
Other cereal grain	171	90	1	2
Vegetables, fruit, nuts	1	9	0	−3
Oil seeds	−5	−1	0	7
Other crops	61	9	−2	−4
Plant fibre	−10	−1	−2	−1
Livestocks	−6	54	0	6
Other food products	22	3	1	38
Meat and dairy products	−6	0	2	8
Forestry fish	7	4	0	3
Energy mineral	29	7	6	3
Vegetable oils, fats	0	2	−15	−17
Textiles and wearing apparel	1	−13	5	29
Other manufactures	−8	−5	19	60
Services	1	0	2	4

Source: Anderson and Yao (2003).

Table 3.4 Changes in sectoral trade balances when all merchandise trade distortions remaining post-Uruguay Round are removed, 2005, 1995 US dollars billion

(a) Reform in all regions except SSA and South Asia

	South Africa	Other SSA	India	Other South Asia
Rice	−54	28	1,897	397
Wheat	−50	44	671	48
Other cereal grain	1,016	1,815	50	1
Vegetables, fruit, nuts	−114	−8	67	−17
Oil seeds	−79	48	119	39
Other crops	2,427	−2,068	28	−108
Plant fibre	−106	589	30	−70
Livestocks	21	365	6	4
Other food products	5,062	339	−494	3,232
Meat and dairy products	2,954	569	153	130
Forestry fish	−4	−54	0	−25
Energy mineral	−436	−198	185	−297
Vegetable oils, fats	−145	−22	−186	−70
Textiles and wearing apparel	−498	−143	−7,159	−6,315
Other manufactures	−8,066	−469	4,552	3,484
Services	−1,927	−836	80	−433

(b) Reform in all regions including SSA and South Asia

	South Africa	Other SSA	India	Other South Asia
Rice	−82	−54	2,565	689
Wheat	−152	−252	1,736	163
Other cereal grain	1,681	1,911	67	0
Vegetables, fruit, nuts	−66	881	−118	−590
Oil seeds	−62	68	224	−175
Other crops	3,609	1,704	−647	−2,001
Plant fibre	−73	158	−244	−782
Livestocks	73	1,146	−3	7
Other food products	4,976	230	195	3,530
Meat and dairy products	−480	−239	458	36
Forestry fish	29	270	−234	−148
Energy mineral	6,760	4,442	−410	−3,381
Vegetable oils, fats	−125	−46	−1,292	−585
Textiles and wearing apparel	−605	−1,490	629	3,706
Other manufactures	−14,086	−8,054	−5,068	1,698
Services	−1,398	−676	2,142	−2,168

Source: Anderson and Yao (2003).

South Asia following the removal of remaining trade barriers in 2005, but more so when those developing countries participate in the reform.

The results in Anderson and Yao (2003) suggest that SSA's economic welfare gain is twice as great from participating in than from standing aside from further trade liberalization. However, most of that greater gain goes to the South African Customs Union (SACU). The reason that 'Other SSA' as an aggregate does not gain more is that the very considerable gains from more efficient resource use will be offset by an adverse change in the region's terms of trade when all of those countries expand their primary product exports simultaneously.

That finding raises the question: would the economy of each SSA country be better off if its government did not participate in the next WTO round? The answer is: 'certainly not'. On the contrary, their economy's welfare would be even worse if their government did not participate, for several reasons. One is that it would forgo the economic efficiency gains from reforming its own policies while still suffering the terms of trade loss from others' reforms (since any one of those countries is too small for its own policy choice to alter the terms of trade significantly).[6] Second, it would forgo the opportunity to seek through the negotiations greater market access for its particular exports to other countries. And, third, there is the promise in this next round that any participating poor economies that lose from taking part in the multilateral liberalization could secure much more compensation than in previous rounds, in the form of technical assistance and funds for trade policy capacity-building (WTO, 2001b).

It is thus in the national economic interest of such countries to be pressured from abroad to commit to such reform, painful though that may be politically for its governments. The political pain tends to be less, and the prospect for a net economic gain greater, the more sectors the country involves in the reform. The economic gain is prospectively greater the more sectors it involves because a wider net reduces the possibility that reform is confined to a subset of sectors that are not the most distorted. (When so confined, resources might move from the reformed sector to even more inefficient uses, thereby reducing rather than improving the efficiency of national resource use.)

If these were not enough reasons for national governments in SSA to become active participants in the Doha Round, including embracing trade reform at home, there are at least three other reasons for doing so. One is that the more each country is prepared to provide trading partners with greater access to its own market, the more those partners are willing to reciprocate by providing greater access to their markets. That benefits exporters in all countries, offsetting the loss of domestic political support from import-competing producers. The second reason is that once a country binds its reform commitments, as required under WTO, its government is better able to resist the temptation to give in to political pressure to reverse that reform. And the third reason has to do with the spread of globalization, which is raising the net political benefits of opening up markets versus remaining protectionist and interventionist. The dramatic falls in the costs of doing business across national boundaries mean not only that the rewards from opening one's own economy to foreign trade and investment flows have risen, but also that the costs of *not* adopting and maintaining an open, stable and transparent set of economic policies are also rising. If, as a result of these globalization forces, the governments of developing economies choose to embrace more reform at home, it makes sense to capitalize on that decision by using the next WTO round to demand greater access to trading partners' markets in return.

Qualifications to the global modelling results

There are three other important sources of gains from trade reform that are not captured in the above results – namely, gains from reform to trade in services, gains from increasing competition and economies of scale and dynamic gains. They are discussed in turn below. The next section then addresses the question of whether it matters that global trade liberalization erodes poor countries' tariff preferences.

The nature of service sector policies makes estimating their effects much more difficult than is the case for barriers to goods trade. Nonetheless, preliminary empirical attempts suggest that restrictions on services trade and investment flows are very substantial, particularly by developing countries (Findlay and Warren, 2000). Moreover, the GATS negotiations during the Uruguay Round resulted in almost no commitments to lowering those impediments (Hoekman, 1996). During that round many developing countries considered the negotiations that led to the GATS as something they had to put up with in order to get agriculture and textiles 'concessions'. Yet the gains to developing countries from opening up their services markets, as for developed countries, would be enormous. Those gains would come not just directly to consumers but also to producers who purchase services as intermediate inputs into their goods production. Farmers in particular would benefit from services reform because they depend heavily on such things as transport services to get their produce to domestic and overseas markets (Anderson and Hoekman, 2000).

Other attempts at measuring distortions to services trade together with mark-ups by imperfectly competitive firms also are beginning to bear fruit. A study by Francois (2001) includes one set of estimates of the tariff equivalent of those distortions in a version of the GTAP model that also incorporates imperfect competition and scale economies. Specifically, that study assumes monopolistic competition exists in the non-primary sectors involving economies of scale that are internal to each firm. These modifications amplify the estimated gains from trade considerably. For example, that study finds that if applied tariff rates for both goods and services were to be cut in half, the global gains would be US$385 billion, of which 51 per cent would be due to services reform. The 49 per cent due to halving tariffs on goods trade (US$192 billion) in the Francois study compares with the above estimate (where no imperfect competition is assumed) of around US$250 billion from totally removing all tariffs on merchandise trade. The key point to draw from this comparison is that the gains from trade reported above should be interpreted as lower-bound estimates for at least two reasons: because they apply only to goods trade, leaving aside the important distortions prevalent in services markets; and because they are based on the assumption that there are no economies of scale and that perfect competition prevails in all sectors.

Both aspects of this point are especially important for SSA. With respect to policies at home they are important partly because that region has among the highest barriers to services trade (Francois, 2001, Table C.2), and partly because the region's national economies are small and hence those services trade barriers translate into a high degree of monopolistic activity and diseconomies of small scale.

None of the studies reported above draws on a truly dynamic economic model. They measure well the effects of producers reallocating their resources and consumers adjusting their purchases when relative product prices change with trade reform, but they do not measure the impact of such reform on investment behaviour. Yet we know from experience that when markets are freed up, investors divert their funds towards expanding the now more-profitable activities and away from the now less-profitable ones. They are also willing to invest more in aggregate, because of the reduced uncertainty associated with binding the reforms in WTO schedules. That boost to investment applies even more following the reductions in barriers to foreign investment and hence international technology transfers since the 1980s. Thus economic growth is boosted by that diversion and expansion of investment funds, over and above the boost in output from reallocating existing resource endowments.

This additional effect is omitted from most empirical modelling efforts, for two reasons: partly because it takes much longer for analysts to build and to run dynamic models than comparative static ones, and partly because the extent to which investors respond to changing incentives is less well understood and hence cannot be included with as much certainty as the other behavioural characteristics that are common to both comparative static and dynamic models. Keeping that in mind, it is nonetheless instructive to note the results of a recent study that examined the range of outcomes generated as the responsiveness of productivity to openness is varied.

The World Bank (2002, Chapter 6) conducted a study very similar to the one reported above, and obtained very similar results when its version of the GTAP model was in comparative static mode (a global welfare gain from complete liberalization of merchandise trade of US$355 billion per year by 2015, compared with the present study's estimate of US$254 billion as early as 2005 when the world economy would be somewhat smaller, and with agricultural policies still responsible for about two-thirds of that gain). When their same model was switched into dynamic mode, however, that global gain increased two- to three-fold over reasonable ranges of productivity responsiveness parameters. This adds further weight to the claim that the earlier welfare results should be considered as very much lower-bound estimates of the gains from trade liberalization.

In short, developing countries have much to gain economically from taking part in the next round of WTO negotiations to liberalize trade, and more so the more they are willing to embrace reform at home so as to enable their firms to take greatest advantage of the opportunities provided by the opening up of markets abroad. And this applies especially to agricultural trade reform.

Does it matter that global trade reform erodes tariff preferences?

In the past, many developing countries have put their negotiating efforts more into seeking extensions of preferential trading schemes than into cuts to remaining MFN barriers to trade in agricultural, textiles or other products. That first option is currently still before them in at least two forms: through some extensions to tariff preferences to developing countries; and through expanding subregional free trade areas.

There are several types of preferential access schemes that have been designed to mitigate the effects of high tariffs on exports from developing countries to advanced economies. They range from very broad ones with minor tariff concessions, such as the GSP, to market-specific ones such as the EU provision of duty-free access for certain volumes of certain products from certain developing countries (mostly former colonies of EU member states) in ACP (formerly the Lomé Convention, now the Cotonou Agreement), to the new EU proposal for duty- and quota-free access for most exports from the LDCs (as classified by the United Nations). To what extent are these arrangements stepping stones or stumbling blocks towards better market access abroad for poor African countries? In particular, how effective are these arrangements as compared with MFN liberalizations under the WTO in delivering benefits to the poorer economies (as distinct from just being easier politically for national governments to sign)?

ACP developing countries that have been granted preferential access to EU markets for some of their exports typically consider themselves privileged, believing that it enables them to compete better in those markets. Not only do they not have to pay the same import duty as other foreign suppliers, but also they receive the EU domestic price, which is higher than the international price to the extent of the protection afforded by the tariff on non-ACP imports.

Beneficial though this might sound, such an assessment ignores four important points. First, many other equally poor but non-ACP developing countries are harmed by the ACP preferences. This was made abundantly clear in the 1990s during the infamous dispute-settlement case that was brought to the WTO concerning the EU banana import regime. One background study showed that for every dollar of benefit that the banana policy brought to producers in ACP countries, the regime harmed non-ACP developing country producers by almost exactly 1 dollar – and in the process harmed EU consumers by more than 13 dollars (Borrell, 1999a). It is difficult to imagine a more inefficient way of transferring welfare to poor countries, since EU citizens through direct payments, could have been thirteen times as effective in helping ACP banana producers and not hurt non-ACP banana producers at all. Such wasteful trade diversion is avoided under non-discriminatory MFN liberalizations that result from multilateral trade negotiations under the WTO.

Second, the additional production that is encouraged in those ACP countries getting privileged access to the high-priced EU market is not internationally competitive at current prices (otherwise it would have been produced prior to getting that preferential treatment). Indeed the industry as a whole might not have existed in the ACP country had the preference scheme not been introduced.[7] In that case, its profits are likely to be lean despite the scheme, and would disappear if and when the scheme is dismantled. Efforts to learn the skills needed, and the sunk capital invested in that industry rather than in ones in which the country has a natural comparative advantage, would then earn no further rewards.

Third, the ACP preferential access scheme under the Lomé Convention has not been a reciprocal agreement – that is, the developing countries were not required to open their markets to EU products. While that makes life easy for ACP politicians, it contributes nothing to the removal of the wasteful trade-restrictive policies of the ACP countries. This contrasts with market-access negotiations under WTO, which are characterized by reciprocity: you receive greater access to my markets (on an MFN basis) on the condition that your trading partner receives a similar degree of improvement in access to your markets.

Fourth and perhaps most importantly, the ACP preference scheme reduces very substantially the capacity for developing countries as a group to press for more access to EU markets. It does this in two ways: by reducing the number of such countries arguing against protection, and by creating a subset of developing countries supporting the EU protectionist stance (in order to continue to receive the high domestic prices in the EU market). This point is crucial, and yet it is often not appreciated. Perhaps if these preferences had not been offered in the first place, developing countries would have negotiated much more vigorously in previous GATT rounds for lower tariffs on agricultural and other imports into the European Union. That in turn would have placed greater pressure on Japan and others to reduce their agricultural protectionism also. The end result would have been higher international prices for agricultural products that, for developing-country producers as a group, might have been more than sufficient to offset the lower prices received in the EU market for a subset of those producers.

A similar set of provisos can be made about the European Union proposal to extend preferences for UN-designated LDCs. That initiative would provide duty- and quota-free access to the European Union for exports of all merchandise except arms (Cernat, Laird and Turrini, 2002; see also Chapter 9 in this volume). It received in-principle, best-endeavours endorsement at the 4th WTO Ministerial in Doha in November 2001, but without any specific timetable.[8]

Liberal though that proposal sounds, we should note that it does not include trade in services (of which the most important for LDCs would be movement of natural persons, that is, freedom for LDC labourers to work in the European Union or other high-wage countries).[9] Also, a number of safeguard provisions is included in addition to the European Union's normal anti-dumping measures. Furthermore, access to three politically sensitive agricultural markets – bananas, rice and sugar – would be phased in by the European Union only gradually over the years to 2010 (and would be subject to stricter safeguards). Not surprisingly, it is these three products, but especially sugar, that offer the greatest potential for growth in trade from LDCs to the European Union (see Cernat, Laird and Turrini 2002, Figure 4.1).

Several empirical studies of the proposal have already appeared. A World Bank study by Ianchovichina, Mattoo and Olarreaga (2001) compares the EU proposal, from the viewpoint of SSA, with recent initiatives of the United States and Japan. Their GTAP modelling results suggest that even the most generous interpretation of the United States' Africa Growth and Opportunity Act (which they model as unrestricted access to the United States for all SSA exports) would benefit SSA very little because the US economy is already very open and, in the products where it is not (for example, textiles and clothing), SSA countries have little comparative advantage. Likewise they find that the Japanese proposal of free access to Japan's market for industrial products helps SSA hardly at all, since the region exports few industrial products. By contrast, the EU proposal, especially if it were to apply to all QuAD countries (the European Union, the United States, Canada and Japan), would have a sizeable effect on SSA trade and welfare – provided agriculture is included in the deal. Just from EU access alone, SSA exports would be raised by more than US$0.5 billion and SSA economic welfare would increase by US$0.3 billion per year (an 0.2 per cent boost). This is very similar to an estimate by UNCTAD/Commonwealth Secretariat (2001, Chapter 3).

The estimated benefits are not surprising given that agriculture and food products account for more than half SSA exports. These items are highly protected in the EU and other Quad countries, and little is provided for them in the way of preferential access under the GSP. The results overstate the benefits of the EU proposal, however, as this World Bank study assumes that all SSA countries (excluding relatively wealthy South Africa and Mauritius), not just the LDCs among them, would get duty- and quota-free access.

Another World Bank study, by Hoekman, Ng and Olarreaga (2002), uses a partial equilibrium approach and looks at the benefit of the EU initiative for LCDs not just in SSA but globally. It finds that trade of LDCs would increase by US$2.5 billion per year if all Quad countries provided them with duty- and quota-free access on all merchandise.[10] However, almost half of that increase would come as a result of trade diversion from other developing countries. The authors suggest this is trivial because it represents less than 0.1 per cent of other developing-countries' exports (about US$1.1 billion).[11] That misses a similar point to the one made above, however. It is that if the forty-eight LDCs are given such preferences, they will become advocates *for* rather than *against* the continuation of MFN tariff peaks for agriculture and textiles – diminishing considerably the number of WTO members negotiating for their reduction. It may be true that reductions in agricultural and textile tariffs would help LDCs much less than they would help other developing countries, as the study by Hoekman, Ng and Olarreaga (2002) finds; but the gains to consumers in the Quad would be more than sufficient to allow them to increase their aid to LDCs to compensate for the loss of income from preference erosion. To put the point in a blunter but more general way, trade can be worse than direct aid if the trade is preferential and thereby distortionary.

Would food-importing countries not lose from higher international food prices?

Among the net food-importing developing countries, some fear agricultural protection cuts by OECD countries will lead to higher international food prices for their imports. Yet even those developing countries need not lose out from farm support cuts abroad. If, for example, they are close to self-sufficiency in food without price supports (as are many net food-importing countries in Asia and SSA), and reform abroad raises the international price of food, they may switch to become sufficiently export-oriented that their net national economic welfare rises. A second possibility is that the developing country's own policies are sufficiently biased against food production that the country is a net importer, despite having a comparative advantage in food. In that case, it has been shown that the international price rise can improve national economic welfare, even if the price change is not sufficient to turn that distorted economy into a net food exporter (Anderson and Tyers, 1993). That comes about because the higher price of food attracts mobile resources away from more-distorted sectors, thereby improving the efficiency of national resource allocation. Because of these two possibilities, the number of poor countries for whom a rise in international food prices might cause some hardship is much smaller than the number that are currently not net exporters of agricultural products. What about those developing countries whose comparative advantage is gradually moving from primary products to (initially unskilled) labour-intensive manufactures, as in South Asia? While that industrialization lowers their direct interest in agricultural trade reform abroad, it heightens their keenness to see barriers to exports of textiles and clothing lowered. That interest in textile trade expansion should be shared by agricultural-exporting developing countries, for if South Asia could export more manufactures, it would tend to become a larger net importer of agricultural products. Conversely, lowered industrial-country barriers to agricultural trade would reduce the need for the more land-abundant developing countries to move into manufactures in competition with the newly industrializing ones. Scope clearly exists for the two groups to band together and negotiate as a single voice calling for barriers to both farm and textile trade to be lowered, so that each group can better exploit its comparative advantage to the direct benefit of the vast majority of poor people in both.

Is China not an example where trade reform will add to poverty via lower domestic prices for farm products?

Because China's accession to the WTO involves a decline in the domestic price of some farm products, and because farm households in China are among the country's poorest, that trade reform is often pointed to as an example of one that will exacerbate poverty. To explore that possibility, a set of empirical studies was commissioned by the World Bank. The GTAP model was used to generate the changes in product and factor prices expected from the commitments to reform that China made in its WTO accession negotiations. These were then mapped to the earning and spending patterns of various household types and regions in China as revealed in China's rural and urban household surveys. The results suggest that the conventional wisdom – that China's WTO accession will impoverish its rural people via greater import competition in its agricultural markets – need not prevail. One needs to keep in mind that, even if prices of some (land-intensive) farm products fall, those for other (labour-intensive) farm products could rise. Also, the removal of restrictions on China's exports of textiles and clothing will boost town and village enterprises (TVEs), so demand for non-farm workers in rural areas may grow even if demand for farm labour in aggregate falls.

New estimates of the likely changes in agricultural prices as a result of WTO accession are drawn on to examine the factor reward implication of China's WTO accession empirically using the GTAP model. Results reported in Anderson, Ianchovichina and Huang (2002) suggest farm–non-farm and Western–Eastern income inequality may well rise but rural–urban income inequality need not. That conclusion is supported by a more detailed study of households by Chen and Ravallion (2002). They find negligible impacts on inequality and a small reduction in poverty in aggregate, but some variance across households and regions. Farm households tend to lose, especially those highly dependent on feed grain production (in Northeastern China) and in hinterland regions with weak links to the booming non-farm sectors and eastern provinces. But the losses are at most very small, amounting to less than 5 per cent of household income. Facilitating the transfer of some labour from less-lucrative farm activities to now more-lucrative non-farm work could (with the usual remittances back to the farm household) be sufficient to ensure all gain from China's WTO accession.

The study by Anderson, Ianchovichina and Huang (2002) also examines how much difference it could make if the *hukou* system that restricts rural–urban migration were to be abolished. Their results suggest that the sign of the effects could be switched to favour the poorer farm households – albeit at the expense of the richer non-farm ones – if the remaining WTO accession-related reforms were to be accompanied by reform of the *hukou* system that allowed some members of those households to obtain higher-paying non-farm employment and repatriate earnings back to their farm family. And of course aggregate national economic welfare would be enhanced by that labour market reform as well. This illustrates the general point that gains from trade reform will be greater the more liberal are domestic product and factor markets.

Would poverty and food insecurity not increase in low-income countries because of higher international food prices?

The impact of trade liberalization on income distribution, and thereby on poverty, is not always clear: even though the effects of trade policies on capital owners and workers have been studied by trade theorists for centuries, applying that theory to the real world turns out to be a complex empirical task (McCulloch, Winters and Cirera, 2001; Hoekman, Ng and Olarreaga, 2002). This is because the economywide effects depend (a) on the shares of households' income from different productive factors such as labour and land, whose prices will have changed (depending on the size of the changes in relative producer prices, factor substitutability, factor intensities and factor mobility between sectors), (b) on their expenditure shares on different products (whose consumer prices also will have changed and not necessarily to the same extent as producer prices, not least because of marketing margins) and (c) on any changes in net transfers to them (for example, increased handouts, decreased taxation, more remittances from urban relatives). Those complexities make it difficult to generalize *a priori*, or even in the face of empirical modelling studies when they report effects of reform just on production, trade, prices and aggregate economic welfare. Even so, some observations are nonetheless worth making about the effects on poverty and food security of reducing agricultural protectionism globally.

Most low-income countries in SSA have not propped up the producer price of food. In so far as an international food price rise is transmitted domestically, the vast majority of the poor would benefit directly. This is because they are in farm households and are net sellers of food. Even poor landless farm labourers who are net buyers of food would benefit indirectly from agricultural trade liberalization via a rise in the demand for their unskilled labour, assuming that that raises their wage sufficiently to more than offset the rise in food prices. Since the more affluent people in cities would find it relatively easy to pay a little extra for food, the only other major vulnerable group is the underemployed urban poor. But even they may not be worse off because the trade reform would be likely to generate a more-than-offsetting increase in the demand for their (often informal sector) services.

What about the impact of reform on food price variability and other aspects of food security, especially as it affects the poorest households? Contrary to popular belief, trade liberalization is much more likely to reduce than raise food insecurity for the vast majority of the world's poor. 'Food security' means always having access to the minimum supply of basic food necessary for survival. The key to that, in addition to peace and greater efficiency in the functioning of staple food markets, is strengthened purchasing power of the poor. That is, enhancing food security is mainly about alleviating poverty. The rate of food self-sufficiency is at most only a supplementary indicator, and only while there remains a perception that food insecurity rises when the level of food self-sufficiency in basic foods falls much below 100 per cent.[12]

Eliminating all agricultural policy distortions in developed countries would raise international prices for agricultural products on average, and reduce their variance by 'thickening' the market, which would stimulate production in non-protected countries. According to one study (Diao, Somwaru and Roe, 2001), that would boost the value of agricultural exports of developing countries by 24 per cent while dampening their agricultural imports by just 2 per cent. That suggests that food self-sufficiency in many low-income countries would rise. Since a high proportion of the poorest households in developing countries are producers and net sellers of food, they would also benefit from such reform. In both respects, therefore, food security for the vast majority of households in low-income countries should be enhanced on average. Those same households would be helped even further if agricultural price-depressing policies were in place domestically and these were removed. The latter reform also boosts self-sufficiency in agricultural products and thereby boosts even further perceived food security in those economies.

The Diao, Somwaru and Roe (2001) study estimates that eliminating developing countries' own agricultural price distortions would boost their farm export value by a further 6 per cent. True, the households that are net buyers of food in such economies will face higher food prices; but whether they become less food-secure depends also on what happens to their earnings (and/or transfers). If they are landless rural poor, their earning prospects will have risen along with the growth in demand for farm labour. As for urban households, the vast majority of them are more affluent than those in rural households and so can well afford to pay higher market prices for food. This suggests that only a small proportion of households in low-income economies would be net food buyers at risk of becoming more food-insecure as a result of rising domestic food prices following trade liberalization.

What about in low-income economies, where agricultural trade liberalization means lower domestic prices for agricultural products because such countries that have kept domestic food prices above international levels via import restrictions? It is true that removing those distortions will reduce farm incomes in those countries (albeit by more for larger than smaller farms). Certainly urban households will benefit from lower food prices. However, food self-sufficiency will fall – and it is the fall in both farm earnings and food self-sufficiency that focuses the attention of those who argue that agricultural trade liberalization is bad for poor farm households.

Focusing on just the direct effects of agricultural trade policy reform can be misleading, however, not least because it does not take account of the fact that such reform is typically done in the context of multilateral, economywide liberalization. Being multilateral means that other countries' farm protection cuts raise international food prices and so less of a price fall occurs than when a country cuts its agricultural protection unilaterally. And being economywide means that the decline in demand for farm labour is more or less than offset by a growth in demand for labour in expanding non-farm industries.

In short, at least two points are worth stressing. First, eliminating agricultural policy distortions in developed countries would increase the mean and decrease the variance of international prices for agricultural products, which would stimulate production in other countries. That suggests food self-sufficiency would rise in those low-income countries that transmit international prices to their domestic market. Second, since a high proportion of the poorest households in low-income countries are producers and net sellers of food, they would be key beneficiaries of such reform. In both respects, therefore, food security for the vast majority of households in low-income countries should be enhanced on average. Those same households would be helped even further if they had been subject to price-depressing domestic policies and these were removed. The latter reform also boosts self-sufficiency in agricultural products and thereby boosts perceived food security even further in those economies. The households that are net buyers of food in such economies would face higher food prices, but whether they become less food-secure depends also on what happens to their earnings (and/or transfers). If they are landless rural poor, their earning prospects will have risen along with the growth in demand for farm labour. As for urban households, the vast majority of them are more affluent than those in rural households and so can well afford to pay higher market prices for food. This suggests that only a small proportion of households in low-income economies would be net food buyers at risk of becoming more food-insecure as a result of rising domestic food prices following trade liberalization.

Conclusions and policy implications

Low-income countries have much to gain from the WTO's Doha Round of trade negotiations. In particular, they have a strong vested interest in working together to push simultaneously for the freeing up of trade in both farm and textile products.[13] Achieving that end will require some opening up of developing economies themselves as a *quid pro quo*, but that will benefit rather than hurt the poor in their own economies – especially if it includes reducing the relatively high levels of protection currently afforded many capital-intensive manufacturing industries and the service sector. And it will be politically easier to do in agriculture the more developed countries reform their farm policies and thereby raise the mean and lower the variance of international food prices.

Nonetheless, in some African countries at least, preparedness to move further down the reform path would be greater if mechanisms were introduced that increased perceived food security. How a country attains its optimal level of food security is a moot point. If a society would feel too food-insecure under laissez faire, bearing in mind the above considerations, then what needs to be determined is a sense of (a) its willingness to pay for more security by various means and (b) the costs of those insurance measures. One such measure involves encouraging the holding of food stocks above those that would be commercially viable – a public good that is explicitly allowed for in Annex 2 of the WTO's AoA. The optimal level of encouragement is that which boosts stocks so that the marginal social benefit in terms of food security equals the marginal social cost of that intervention. Costs are non-trivial, however. Storage and interest costs and the costs of spoilage and quality deterioration can amount to more than 20 per cent a year. The cost part of the calculation also would need to include the risk of government failure if stocks were to be managed by an inefficient (or corrupt) public agency.

If greater domestic production capability was considered by society to be one of the desirable means of boosting food security (because of a perception that food import dependence is too unreliable), there are far less costly ways of achieving that than via protection from food imports. For example, boosting production alone, rather than also taxing consumption as with an import barrier, would be a lower-cost and less trade-distortive means of achieving that end. Even more effective could be improvements in land tenure and more investment in the stocks of primary factors used in food production: agricultural research, rural human capital and rural infrastructure. That would provide an especially high payoff in situations where, as in so many countries, there has been gross underinvestment in these activities in the past. Simultaneously, production could be boosted in many low-income countries simply by better clarifying and enforcing land rights, since they are a key source of collateral for securing loans for productive investments by farm households.

Where targeted programmes to boost the earning capacity of the poverty-stricken (for example, via basic education/training) are still not enough to boost their food security in the short term, targeted consumer subsidies to provide that core group with food staples are much less costly than general subsidies to all food consumers via price-depressing agricultural policies. Food aid that is targeted to just that group could be readily provided by the international community without depressing very much the prices received by farmers in recipient countries.[14] And greater technical and economic cooperation in the areas of agricultural research, rural education and health and rural infrastructure may be important co-requisites of trade policy reform if developing countries are to be convinced that they would gain unequivocally from the Doha Round.

Notes

1. World Bank estimates (for example, Collier and Dollar, 2002, Figure 3) also indicate a decline in the number of poor, but they suggest those numbers on less than US$1 per day are several times larger, possibly as many as 1.2 billion in 2000.
2. The link between openness and economic growth, while not completely unambiguous and universal, is strong, and there is no evidence that openness is harmful to growth (see the discussion in McCulloch, Winters and Cirera, 2001, Chapter 2). Trade's impact on growth can be much reduced in the absence of liberal domestic markets, macro stability and appropriate institutions and infrastructure, however, since those are all necessary to enable producers to respond to changes in international market signals. For a comprehensive survey of the links between trade, growth and poverty, see Berg and Krueger (2002). A survey of the empirical evidence is available in Winters, McCulloch and McKay (2002).
3. The GTAP model is a standard, multi-region model that is currently in use by several hundred researchers in scores of countries on five continents. The Version 4 data base builds on contributions from many of these individuals, as well as the national and international agencies in the GTAP Consortium.
4. It should be recognized that these results ignore the effect of tariff preference erosion. In so far as a developing country receives such preferences at present in OECD markets, the above results slightly overstate the potential gains from their reforms. This point is taken up below.
5. Martin (2001) points out that since the mid-1980s the share of developing countries' agricultural exports that is going to other developing countries has risen from less than 30 per cent to more than 40 per cent.
6. For empirical support for this proposition, see for example Anderson and Strutt (1999) with respect to Indonesia. The point is made strongly also in the volume on the Uruguay Round edited by Martin and Winters (1996).
7. Alternatively, the ACP scheme may have caused an existing industry to become less competitive. An extreme example of an industry that has ossified as a consequence of regulations introduced to share the expected benefits of EU preferences is sugar in Mauritius (Borrell, 1999b).
8. In Paragraph 42 of the Ministerial Declaration (WTO, 2001b) it simply says: 'We commit ourselves to the objective of duty-free, quota-free market access for products originating from LDCs.'
9. On the potential gains from freeing international trade in unskilled labour services globally, see Walmsley and Winters (2002).
10. This and other estimates of gains from preferential market access provisions need to be discounted to the extent that rules of origin, sanitary and phytosanitary (SPS) barriers, anti-dumping duties and the like limit the actual trade allowed. For a detailed analysis of these types of restrictions on

EU imports from Bangladesh in recent years, see UNCTAD/Commonwealth Secretariat (2001, Chapter 5).
11. The impact outside the LDC group would be far from trivial for Mauritius, however, since the vast bulk of its exports are quota-restricted sales of clothing and sugar to the European Union and United States. See the discussion in UNCTAD/Commonwealth Secretariat (2001, Chapter 6).
12. Diaz-Bonilla, Thomas and Robinson (2001), provide charts showing that both the LDCs and the net food-importing developing countries have enjoyed much faster growth since the 1970s in total exports than in food imports, with the former being three–five times the latter.
13. Within agriculture, developing countries' interests in Doha agenda items align closely with those of the Cairns Group of non-subsidizing agricultural-exporting countries (Bjornskov and Lind, 2003). See Cairns Group (2002) for its proposal on market access in the Doha Round.
14. If such subsidies are paid only in the towns and cities, however, this increases the risk of excessive, socially costly migration out of agriculture of the sort analysed by Harris and Todaro (1970).

References

Anderson, K., B. Dimaranan, J. Francois, T. Hertel, B. Hoekman and W. Martin (2001) 'The Cost of Rich (and Poor) Country Protection to Developing Countries', *Journal of African Economies*, 10(3): 227–57.

Anderson, K., B. Dimaranan, T. Hertel and W. Martin (1997) 'Economic Growth and Policy Reforms in the APEC Region: Trade and Welfare Implications by 2005', *Asia-Pacific Economic Review*, 3(1): 1–18.

Anderson, K. and B. Hoekman (2000) 'Developing Country Agriculture and the New Trade Agenda'. *Economic Development and Cultural Change*, 49(1): 171–80.

Anderson, K., E. Ianchovichina and J. Huang (2002) 'Impact of China's WTO Accession on Rural–Urban Income Inequality and Poverty', Paper for the World Bank project on WTO Accession, Policy Reform and Poverty Reduction in China, Washington, DC: World Bank (June).

Anderson, K. and A. Strutt (1999) 'Impact of East Asia's Growth Interruption and Policy Responses: The Case of Indonesia', *Asian Economic Journal*, 13(2): 205–18.

Anderson, K. and R. Tyers (1993) 'More on Welfare Gains to Developing Countries from Liberalising World Food Trade', *Journal of Agricultural Economics*, 44(2): 189–204.

Anderson, K. and S. Yao (2003) 'How Can South Asia and Sub-Saharan Africa Gain From the Next WTO Round?', *Journal of Economic Integration*, 18(3).

Berg, A. and A. O. Krueger (2002) 'Trade, Growth and Poverty', Paper presented at the Annual World Bank Conference on Development Economics. Washington, DC.

Bjornskov, C. and K. M. Lind (2003) 'Where do Developing Countries Go After Doha? An Analysis of WTO Positions and Potential Alliances', *Journal of World Trade*, February.

Borrell, B. (1999a) 'Bananas: Straightening Out Bent Ideas on Trade as Aid', Paper presented at the World Bank/WTO Conference on Agriculture and the New Trade Agenda from a Development Perspective, Geneva, 1–2 October.

———— (1999b) 'Sugar: The Taste Test of Trade Liberalization', Paper presented at the World Bank/WTO Conference on Agriculture and the New Trade Agenda from a Development Perspective, Geneva, 1–2 October.

Bourguignon. F. and C. Morrisson (2002) 'Inequality Among World Citizens: 1820–1992', *American Economic Review*, 92(4): 727–44.

Cairns Group (2002) 'Negotiating Proposal on Market Access', Submission to the Committee on Agriculture Special Session, JOB(02)/1126, Geneva: WTO, September.

Cernat, L., S. Laird and A. Turrini (2002) 'The EU's Everything But Arms Initiative and the Least-Developed Countries', Paper prepared for the UNU-WIDER research project conference on The Impact of the WTO Regime on Developing Countries, Helsinki, 4–5 October.

Chen, S. and M. Ravallion (2002) 'Household Welfare Impacts of China's Accession to the WTO', Paper prepared for the World Bank project on WTO Accession, Policy Reform and Poverty Reduction in China, Washington, DC: World Bank, October.

Collier, P. and D. Dollar (2002) *Globalization, Growth, and Poverty*, New York: Oxford University Press for the World Bank.

Diao, X., A. Somwaru and T. Roe (2001) 'A Global Analysis of Agricultural Reform in WTO Member Countries', Background Paper for a USDA Project on Agricultural Policy Reform in the WTO: The Road Ahead, ERS-E01–001, Washington, DC: US Department of Agriculture.

Diaz-Bonilla, E., M. Thomas and S. Robinson (2001) 'Trade Liberalization, WTO and Food Security', Washington, DC: International Food Policy Research Institute, October, *Mimeo*.

Dollar, D. and A. Kraay (2002) 'Growth is Good for the Poor', *Journal of Economic Growth*, 7(3): 195–225.

Findlay, C. C. and A. Warren (eds) (2000). *Impediments to Trade in Services*: *Measurement and Policy Implications*, London: Routledge.

Francois, J. (2001) *The Next WTO Round: North–South Stakes in New Market Access Negotiations*, Adelaide: Centre for International Economic Studies and Rotterdam: Tinbergen Institute.

Harris, J. R. and M. P. Todaro (1970) 'Migration, Unemployment and Development: A Two-Sector Analysis', *American Economic Review*, 60(1): 126–42.

Hertel, T. W. (ed.) (1997) *Global Trade Analysis: Modeling and Applications*, Cambridge and New York: Cambridge University Press.

Hertel, T., K. Anderson, J. Francois, B. Hoekman and W. Martin (1999) 'Agriculture and Non-Agricultural Liberalization in the Millennium Round', Paper for the World Bank/WTO Conference on Agriculture and the New Trade Agenda from a Development Perspective, Geneva, 1–2 October.

Hoekman, B. (1996) 'Assessing the General Agreement on Trade in Services', in W. Martin, and L. A. Winters (eds), *The Uruguay Round and the Developing Countries*, Cambridge and New York: Cambridge University Press.

Hoekman, B., F. Ng and M. Olarreaga (2002) 'Eliminating Excess Tariffs on Exports of Least Developed Countries', *World Bank Economic Review*, 16: 1–21.

Ianchovichina, E., A. Mattoo and M. Olarreaga (2001) 'Unrestricted Market Access for Sub-Saharan Africa: How Much is it Worth and Who Pays?', CEPR Discussion Paper 2820, London: Centre for Economic Policy Research, June.

Martin, W. (2001) 'Trade Policies, Developing Countries, and Globalization', Policy Research Report, Washington, DC: World Bank.

Martin, W. and L. A. Winters (eds) (1996) *The Uruguay Round and the Developing Countries*, Cambridge and New York: Cambridge University Press.

McCulloch, N., L. A. Winters and X. Cirera (2001) *Trade Liberalization and Poverty: A Handbook*, London: Centre for Economic Policy Research.

Sala-i-Martin, X. (2002) 'The World Distribution of Income (Estimated from Individual Country Distributions)', NBER Working Paper 8933, Cambridge, MA, May.

UNCTAD/Commonwealth Secretariat (2001) *Duty and Quota Free Market Access for LDCs: An Analysis of Quad Initiatives*, Geneva: UNCTAD and London: Commonwealth Secretariat.

Walmsley, T. and L. A. Winters (2002) 'Relaxing Restrictions on Temporary Movement of Natural Persons: A Simulation Analysis', University of Sussex, *Mimeo*.

Winters, L. A., N. McCulloch and A. McKay (2002) 'Trade Liberalization and Poverty: Empirical Evidence', University of Sussex, *Mimeo*, September.

World Bank (2002) *Global Economic Prospects and the Developing Countries: Making World Trade for the World's Poor*, Washington, DC: World Bank.

WTO (2001a) *Market Access: Unfinished Business: Post-Uruguay Round Inventory and Issues*, Special Study, No. 6, Geneva: World Trade Organization.

———— (2001b) *Doha WTO Ministerial 2001: Ministerial Declaration*, WT/MIN(01)/DEC/1, Geneva: World Trade Organization, 14 November.

4

OECD Domestic Support and Developing Countries

Betina Dimaranan, Thomas Hertel and Roman Keeney

Introduction

Most studies of global agricultural trade liberalization are primarily focused on market price support – that is, agricultural support provided indirectly through border measures, either import barriers or export subsidies, designed to boost domestic relative to world market prices. In the late 1980s, this form of support accounted for about 75 per cent of total producer support in agriculture in the member countries of the Organization for Economic Cooperation and Development (OECD) (OECD, 2002a). Prior to the Uruguay Round Agreement on Agriculture (URAA), this was also the only area of agricultural protection under negotiation in the international arena. A very important innovation in the URAA was to put domestic subsidies on the table. More specifically, support policies are placed in 'boxes' according to their impact on international trade. Those policies that have 'no, or at most minimal trade-distorting effects or effects on production' are placed in the 'green box' and are not subjected to reduction requirements under the URAA. Those policies that are deemed to be trade-distorting are placed in the 'amber box' and are subjected to reductions. However, if the payments are accompanied by programmes aimed at limiting production, they may be placed in yet a third box, the 'blue box'. As a consequence, they are exempt from the negotiated reductions in support. This third box has since come under scrutiny and there have been proposals to subject it to successive reductions as well – or potentially eliminate this box altogether.

As a result of the URAA, the share of producer support provided by market interventions has gradually fallen, so that it now accounts for only two-thirds of total support (OECD, 2002a). This trend may continue as proposed EU reforms involve further efforts to 'decouple' support from world prices (*The Economist*, 2002).[1] The goal of this chapter is to assess the likely impact of such decoupling on developing-country welfare. In the process of making this assessment, we also pay special attention to the impact of reforms on real farm income in the reforming OECD countries, as the farm lobby is a powerful political force and operates as an important constraint on reform efforts. Owing to these dual objectives of the chapter, there are necessarily two rather distinct parts to our analysis. First, we must assess the direct impact of domestic support in the OECD countries on OECD agriculture – specifically farm incomes, production and subsequently trade. Then we must assess the impact of these changes on the developing countries. Before embarking on this analysis, we first turn to an historical overview of domestic support and OECD trade with developing countries.

Background to domestic support and developing country trade

Overview of domestic support in the OECD

The OECD uses the concept of Producer Support Estimates (PSE) as the principal indicator in monitoring and evaluating agricultural policy developments. The PSE is 'an indicator of the monetary value of gross transfers from consumers and taxpayers to agricultural producers, measured at the farm-gate level, arising from policy measures that support agriculture, regardless of their natures, objectives or impacts on farm production or income'. It comprises market price support, payments based on output, payments based on area planted/animal numbers, payments based on historical entitlements, payments based on input used, payments based on input constraints, payments based on overall farming income and miscellaneous payments (OECD, 2001). The different measures vary in terms of their effects on farm income in the OECD countries, as well as their effects on trade and hence their impact on the welfare of developing countries.

Table 4.1 presents the changes in the overall PSE and its component parts for selected OECD countries in 1987 and 2000. The PSE are smallest for Australia and New Zealand. These are largely made up of market price support and variable input subsidies. In Australia, for both years, the majority of market price support has been applied to grains and milk, while most of the applications of subsidies on variable inputs are applied to meat and meat products. By 2000, most of the PSE had been

Table 4.1 Producer support estimates and components, 1987 and 2000

OECD region	Year	PSE %	Percentage share in PSE, by support type				
			Market price	Output	Variable input	Land-based	Historical entitlement
Australia	1987	7.87	42.23	0	36.57	0	0
	2000	5.56	24.48	2.76	49.66	2.06	5.04
Canada	1987	35.84	49.80	18.84	14.09	15.36	0
	2000	19.50	51.22	7.12	6.43	7.63	11.29
EU15	1987	45.02	85.92	5.51	5.49	2.74	0
	2000	38.34	58.75	5.22	6.64	25.42	0.64
Japan	1987	67.28	90.68	2.56	3.95	0	0
	2000	64.06	91.05	2.80	4.34	0	0
Korea	1987	69.47	98.76	0	0.78	0	0
	2000	72.56	95.86	0	2.45	0	0
New Zealand	1987	8.87	26.79	0	70.36	0	0
	2000	0.74	54.43	0	40.31	0	0
Switzerland	1987	72.96	81.53	1.31	8.56	6.06	0
	2000	71.38	59.09	3.96	5.64	11.27	15.86
United States	1987	27.01	50.82	5.69	14.21	26.60	0
	2000	21.94	32.01	18.85	13.61	7.18	21.51

Source: OECD PSE/CSE Data base 2001.

eliminated in New Zealand, with large reductions in variable input subsidies in meat and meat products. In the case of Japan and Korea, the PSE have remained relatively unchanged in both level and in composition. The PSE rates have been highest historically for Switzerland, but here a fair amount of decoupling has occurred, with the share of market price support in the total falling from 82 per cent in 1987 to 59 per cent in 2000.

It is in the United States, Canada and the European Union where sizeable cuts in the PSE show up over this period – although the May 2002 US Farm Act has reversed this trend for that country. In the European Union, there has been a decided shift in the composition of support, with the share provided by market price support falling in favour of increased land- and headage-based payments. In Canada, market price support as a PSE share is nearly the same but market price support (MPS) for grains has been greatly reduced while there has been a large increase in milk MPS. Most support in Canadian grains is now provided via input (including land) and output subsidies, as well as historical entitlements. In the United States, the PSE has been more moderately reduced, with a large portion of the reduction coming from the elimination of market price support. In 2000, historical entitlements had become a much more important component of the PSE in US grains.

This change in the mix of producer support in some of the OECD countries is potentially quite important. It is also expected to continue – and perhaps accelerate – under a new WTO round. For insights on the potential impact of changes in the level and mix of domestic support, we turn below to the existing literature on this topic. But, first, let us consider the potential impact that these reforms will have on developing countries. To understand this, we must first examine the trade links that will transmit price and quantity changes from OECD countries to developing countries.

Overview of developing-country trade patterns

Developing countries are an enormously diverse group. Some are net exporters, and some are net importers of the temperate products that OECD countries tend to protect. Some are closely tied into the OECD markets – by virtue of geography or perhaps historical trade preferences. Others are more reliant on other developing countries for their food supplies and export markets. The strength of the trade links of a developing country with the OECD countries will play an important role in the impact of OECD domestic support reform on the developing country. This section provides an overview of the trade patterns of developing countries *vis-à-vis* the OECD countries in agriculture and food products. Data are summarized for the regional and commodity aggregation used in the study in Table 4.2.

Table 4.2   Regional and sectoral aggregation

OECD countries	
ANZ	Australia and New Zealand
Japan	Japan
Korea	South Korea
USA	United States
Canada	Canada
Mexico	Mexico
EU15	European Union
EFTA	European Free Trade Area
CEU	Hungary and Poland
Turkey	Turkey
Developing countries	
China	China
Indonesia	Indonesia

Vietnam	Vietnam
ASEAN4	Malaysia, Philippines, Singapore, Thailand
India	India
RsoAsia	Rest of South Asia
Argentina	Argentina
Brazil	Brazil
RlatAm	Rest of Latin America
FSU	Former Soviet Union
MENA	Middle East and North Africa
Tanzania	Tanzania
Zambia	Zambia
R_SSA	Rest of sub-Saharan Africa
ROW	Rest of World
Programme commodities	
pdrice	paddy rice
wheat	wheat
crsgrns	coarse grains and cereals nec.
oilsds	oilseeds
rawsgr	sugar cane, sugar beet
pcrice	processed rice
refsgr	sugar
Livestock and meat products	
ruminants	cattle/sheep, wool
nonrumnts	animal products nec.
rawmilk	raw milk
rummeat	meat: cattle/sheep
nrummeat	meat products nec.
dairy	dairy products
Other agriculture and food	
othcrops	vegetables and fruits, plant-based fibres, other crops
vegoilfat	vegetable oils and fats
othprfood	other processed food
mnfc	manufactures
srvc	services

Note: nec. is not elsewhere classfied.

Table 4.3 reports the average trade specialization indices for three decades over the period 1966–98 for the aggregated regions in this study. Trade specialization indices are calculated as: $(X-M)/(X+M)$, where X are exports and M are imports. The value of the index ranges from -1 for a country which imports, and does not export, a particular commodity and $+1$ for a country which is specialized as an exporter of the commodity. Table 4.3 separately identifies the aggregated commodity groups – programme commodities,[2] livestock and meat products and other agriculture and food products. Among the developing countries, Argentina has maintained its export specialization in programme

Table 4.3 Trade specialization indices: $(X - M)/(X + M)$

Regions	Programme commodities			Livestock and meat products			Other agriculture and food		
	1965–75	1976–85	1986–98	1965–75	1976–85	1986–98	1965–75	1976–85	1986–98
ANZ	0.95	0.97	0.94	0.99	0.98	0.98	0.13	0.10	0.32
Japan	−0.94	−0.96	−1.00	−0.96	−0.96	−0.96	−0.60	−0.67	−0.82
Korea	−0.90	−0.82	−0.90	−0.14	−0.73	−0.85	−0.23	−0.23	−0.21
USA	0.59	0.78	0.81	−0.04	0.16	0.24	−0.08	−0.04	0.00
Canada	0.55	0.72	0.76	0.13	0.32	0.40	−0.18	−0.18	−0.09
Mexico	0.19	−0.87	−0.83	0.03	−0.41	−0.54	0.66	0.56	0.36
EU15	−0.74	−0.56	−0.27	−0.49	−0.05	0.13	−0.48	−0.37	−0.17
EFTA	−0.91	−0.89	−0.76	−0.08	−0.02	−0.04	−0.27	−0.27	−0.08
CEU	−0.51	−0.71	0.03	0.57	0.44	0.50	−0.20	−0.28	−0.15
Turkey	−0.54	0.25	−0.51	0.04	0.55	−0.32	0.86	0.79	0.43
China	−0.17	−0.55	−0.18	0.87	0.69	0.38	0.22	0.36	0.28
Indonesia	−0.57	−0.88	−0.88	0.13	−0.11	−0.30	0.74	0.71	0.52
Vietnam[a]	n.a.	−0.37	0.85	n.a.	−0.65	−0.01	n.a.	−0.10	0.48
ASEAN4	0.58	0.49	0.20	−0.74	−0.30	−0.34	0.48	0.55	0.38
India	−0.58	−0.15	0.43	−0.40	−0.24	−0.10	0.43	0.24	0.44
RsoAsia	−0.59	−0.16	−0.40	−0.43	−0.70	−0.67	0.45	0.13	−0.02
Argentina	0.97	0.99	0.96	0.99	0.92	0.75	0.64	0.71	0.78
Brazil	0.58	0.15	0.29	0.51	0.47	0.35	0.79	0.85	0.66
RlatAm	0.36	0.07	−0.08	−0.17	−0.23	−0.23	0.56	0.56	0.57
FSU[a]	n.a.	n.a.	−0.63	n.a.	n.a.	−0.59	n.a.	n.a.	−0.31

MENA	-0.91	-0.97	-0.94	-0.80	-0.94	-0.87	-0.01	-0.54	-0.45
Tanzania[a]	n.a.	n.a.	-0.40	n.a.	n.a.	0.18	n.a.	n.a.	0.69
Zambia	-0.35	-0.40	-0.40	-0.88	-0.78	-0.59	-0.38	-0.15	0.34
R_SSA	0.39	-0.13	-0.17	0.37	-0.05	-0.25	0.68	0.54	0.53
ROW	-0.10	-0.43	-0.66	-0.27	-0.50	-0.45	-0.16	-0.25	-0.43

Note:
[a] The time-series trade data for Vietnam start in 1976 while that for the former Soviet Union and Tanzania start in 1992.

Source: Authors' calculations from bilateral time series data in GTAP 5 data base.

crops over the period. Economic reforms in Vietnam and India have permitted these countries to shift from being moderate net importers to being net exporters of programme crops. The net export position of the ASEAN4 region has seen a decline over the period and Indonesia's net import position has worsened. China's net export position has improved. The Middle East/North Africa (MENA) region has been a consistently strong net importer of programme commodities. Among the OECD countries, Australia/New Zealand (ANZ) has been consistent in its net export position. The United States' and Canada's net export position has strengthened over the period. The EU15 and EFTA have substantially reduced their net imports as a share of total trade, while Japan and Korea remain consistent net importers of programme commodities over the entire period. Overall, we conclude that increased domestic support for programme crops appears to have contributed to improvements in the net trade position of the OECD countries in programme crops, at the expense of developing countries.

Turning next to livestock products, we see from Table 4.3 that China, Argentina and Brazil are net exporters. The specialization indices for these countries, however, have declined over the years. On the other hand, the net import positions of India and ASEAN4 in these products have diminished markedly. In the OECD countries, the ANZ region stands out as a strong net exporter of livestock and meat products. Japan is a strong net importer and Korea's net import position has increased over the period. On the other hand, the United States, Canada and the European Union have seen increases in their trade specialization indices over the period. Increased domestic support for livestock products in these countries appears to have contributed to their net export position.

Most of the developing countries are consistent net exporters of the aggregate group of other agriculture and processed food products. Among the OECD countries, Mexico, Turkey and ANZ are net exporters while the other OECD countries in our aggregation are net importers. Thus we have a rough division between temperate products (programme crops and livestock), where OECD domestic support plays an important role and where developing countries are largely net importers, and tropical products for which developing countries are largely net exporters.[3]

Focusing next on developing-country bilateral trade with the OECD, Table 4.4 reports separately the share of each developing country's total trade that is specifically with OECD countries. Tanzania, Zambia and Indonesia rely on the OECD market as a destination for more than

Table 4.4 Share of developing-country trade with the OECD, 1997

Developing countries	Programme commodities		Livestock and meat		Other agriculture and food	
	Exports[a]	Imports[b]	Exports[a]	Imports[b]	Exports[a]	Imports[b]
China	52	76	60	85	55	44
Indonesia	78	58	69	95	27	44
Vietnam	13	56	74	82	24	40
ASEAN4	40	48	54	71	47	44
India	27	75	52	85	31	24
RsoAsia	23	66	61	81	62	18
Argentina	23	58	38	35	57	36
Brazil	48	21	71	33	50	36
RlatAm	47	63	77	69	47	51
FSU	37	23	50	80	48	63
MENA	43	66	73	80	66	60
Tanzania	89	31	54	60	54	25
Zambia	86	7	69	93	65	43
R_SSA	63	49	77	82	69	62
ROW	62	73	59	66	62	61

Notes:
[a] Exports to OECD countries as share of each developing country's total exports of the commodity group.
[b] Imports from OECD countries as share of each developing country's total imports of the commodity group.
Source: Authors' calculations from GTAP 5 data base.

three-quarters of their exports of programme commodities. On the other end of the scale are Vietnam, Argentina and the rest of South Asia, each of which relies on the OECD market as destination for less than a quarter of their programme commodity exports. This indicates that a strong net exporter like Argentina competes with the OECD in third markets for programme commodities. On the import side, the OECD is the source of more than two-thirds of total programme commodity imports of countries like China, India and the rest of South Asia and the MENA region. For these countries, reductions in domestic support for OECD agriculture will mean higher-priced imports. Reforms in OECD market price support may significantly affect the trade patterns in these countries. On the other hand, those developing countries that rely heavily on the OECD as an export destination, or that compete with OECD products in third markets stand to gain from measures that decouple domestic support from production decisions.

Even greater dependence on the OECD countries as an import source is exhibited by countries like China, Indonesia, Vietnam, South Asia, FSU, MENA, Zambia and the rest of SSA in the case of livestock and meat products, with each importing more than 80 per cent of their total imports of these commodities from the OECD. Bilateral exports and imports of developing countries for other agriculture and food commodities are generally less concentrated on the OECD.

Literature review

The earliest work assessing the impact of different methods of agricultural support on prices, and factor returns in agriculture is that of Floyd (1965). He compared the impact of price supports with output restrictions and mandatory land retirement. He did not consider the possibility of producer payments based on land use. However, input-based payments have become increasingly common in recent years. Hertel (1989) developed a series of propositions relating to the impacts of a wider range of support measures on production, net exports, employment, land rents and farm income. He placed these on both an equal-cost and equal-PSE basis for a single-product, agricultural sector in the absence of pre-existing support. A few key points emerged from this paper. First of all, subsidies on variable inputs that substitute for fixed factors (for example, land) in agriculture have a greater impact on output, and hence trade, than do equal cost output subsidies. Such variable input subsidies also moderate the share of producer support that accrues to land and other fixed factors. On the other hand, subsidies to land, such as the per hectare payments currently made in the European Union, have a more modest effect on output, while leading to higher land rents than under an equal cost output subsidy. Finally, when compared to an output subsidy of equal cost, export subsidies have a larger impact on exports, agricultural production, employment and land rents, provided the elasticity of export demand exceeds the domestic demand elasticity.

Of special interest for the present chapter is the OECD (2001) report on *Market Effects of Crop Support Measures*. In this report, the authors compare the impacts of a wide range of producer support across OECD countries. They find that the movement from market price support and output subsidies to land-based payments is a 'win–win' scenario in most countries – with farm income rising and world price impacts of support falling.[4] From the point of view of this chapter, this suggests an interesting possibility, namely that re-instrumentation of producer support for agriculture in OECD countries could conceivably maintain OECD farm incomes, while contributing to enhanced welfare on the part of developing-country exporters. This hypothesis will be explored in greater detail below.

A separate study, also undertaken at the OECD (OECD, 2002b) analysed the impact of further agricultural trade reforms on developing countries using two modelling frameworks. The OECD AgLink model is used to examine the impacts of reductions in market price support, while the GTAP model is used to examine the impacts of cuts in both market price support and direct payments to producers. They look at relatively broad groups of developing countries, and they do not consider more elaborate reforms in which the mix of measures is changed in an attempt to maintain farm incomes.

In contrast, Frandsen, Jensen and Yu (2002) use a modified version of the GTAP model to examine the impact of further decoupling of domestic support in the European Union. Their emphasis is on the budgetary and macroeconomic effects of these policy reforms among OECD countries. They argue that further decoupling of EU agricultural policies would reduce budgetary exposure in the European Union as well as bring it into compliance with potentially stricter WTO disciplines on domestic support. They also find rather substantial changes in world prices – particularly for meat products – although they do not examine the issue of overall developing country welfare explicitly, and they restrict themselves to EU reforms.

Since the early 1990s, there has been a large number of global, general equilibrium, analyses of trade liberalization – some of which include domestic support (these include Hertel *et al.*, 1996; Elbehri *et al.*, 1999; Hertel and Martin, 1999; Anderson *et al.*, 2001; Rae and Strutt, 2002). Most of these studies are based on the GTAP data base and modelling framework. However, the GTAP data base has not been particularly well suited to the analysis of domestic support issues. Versions 1–4 of the GTAP data base treated all domestic support as an output subsidy. Version 5 introduced a first-cut disaggregation of support across inputs but it still suffers from some important limitations (Gehlhar and Nelson, 2001; Frandsen, Jensen and Yu, 2001). Furthermore, the standard GTAP model is not well suited to analysis of domestic support issues, due to its relatively simplistic treatment of factor markets. One contribution of the present chapter is to address these limitations.

Methodology

Model design

This chapter assesses the impact of changes in both the mix and the level of domestic support in OECD countries on the welfare of farm households in the OECD and on the national welfare of developing countries. Therefore, it is not enough to say that world prices will rise or they will fall. The welfare impacts on developing countries will depend on whether they are net exporters or net importers of protected products. It will also depend on the bilateral trade patterns discussed earlier. In short, we need a global trade model with bilateral trade flows explicitly treated. One such framework is offered by the GTAP data base and associated models, used by a number of the previous studies.

For purposes of this study, we constructed a special-purpose version of the GTAP data base and model designed to make it more appropriate for the analysis of domestic support. We adopt, as our starting point, the general framework proposed by the OECD (2001) in which factor demand and supply relations play a central role. The most valuable contribution of the report resides in the Annexes, where extensive literature reviews are available for the European Union and for North America. The authors provide central parameter values for the key elasticities of substitution, as well as for factor supply elasticities (see OECD, 2001, Tables A1.3 and A1.4). We have restructured the GTAP model in order to take advantage of this information and it is to these features that we now turn.

We begin by segmenting the factor markets for labour and capital between agriculture and non-agriculture. A key parameter in the OECD analysis is the elasticity of factor supply for farm-owned inputs. The values of these parameters proposed by the OECD are reported in Dimaranan, Hertel and Keeney (2003, Table 6). The values are less than one, which is a sharp contrast to the usual assumption of perfect factor mobility used in most computable general equilibrium (CGE) analyses. This means that commodity supply is also less responsive, and more of the benefits of farm subsidies (or losses from their elimination) will accrue to farm households.

The OECD report also attempts to come up with supply elasticities for purchased inputs. However, there is little econometric evidence to draw on here. One advantage of the general equilibrium framework is that these commodity supply responses are endogenously determined – as a function of the factor market assumptions as well as the cost structure of the industry. Therefore, we dispense with the OECD estimates of input supply for fertilizers and other purchased inputs. The supply prices for the 18 different intermediate inputs are endogenous in the model and determined by the interaction of supply and demand in each of these markets.

On the factor demand side, we employ a nested-CES production function which can be calibrated to the three key elasticities of substitution available from the OECD report. Specifically, we postulate that output is a CES composite of two input aggregates. The first of these is a purchased input aggregate, while the second is a value-added aggregate. The individual inputs in each of these groups are assumed to be separable from one another – with a common elasticity of substitution (CES). The purchased input and value-added aggregates are themselves each a CES function of individual farm inputs. This gives us a total of three CES substitution parameters. They are calibrated to the OECD central values for the Allen partial elasticities of substitution between: (i) land and other farm-owned inputs, (ii) land and purchased inputs and (iii) among purchased inputs. These parameters are not critical for our analysis of the non-OECD impacts since domestic policies in these countries are unchanged in our simulations. Accordingly, we simply set these parameter values equal to those from Mexico for all non-OECD countries in the model.

Given our interest in tracking real farm income and the overall measure of support for OECD agriculture, we also add some additional equations to the model to determine these variables. Real farm income is based on payments to endowments in the farm sector, adjusted for depreciation and the farm sector's share of national net taxes. To obtain real farm income, we deflate this by the regional household's price index which is computed in the standard GTAP model. In some simulations, real farm income is treated as exogenous, and a policy instrument is endogenized in order to maintain this target level of income.

The computation of PSEs in the GTAP model is complicated by the fact that traded commodities are differentiated by origin. So the model tracks bilateral trade and there is no unique world price. Therefore, the domestic–world price gap is measured as a trade-weighted combination of bilateral import and export prices. In the case of market price support, this price gap is applied to output in order to compute the change in PSE associated with a given policy change.

Finally, given the importance of the trade elasticities to our analysis, we have incorporated recent estimates, implemented at the disaggregated GTAP level, based on the methodology outlined in Hummels (1999). He used detailed trade, tariff and transport cost data for a variety of importing countries in North and South America to estimate a differentiated products model of import demand. The variation in bilateral transport costs permits him to get quite precise estimates of these parameters – in sharp contrast to much of the earlier work in this area.

The remainder of the model follows the standard GTAP framework, with sectors producing output under perfect competition and constant returns to scale. Consumer demands are modelled using the non-homothetic, CDE functional form, calibrated to estimates of price and income elasticities of demand. Bilateral trade flows are modelled using the Armington approach under which products are differentiated by origin. Bilateral transport costs between countries are explicitly modelled, and a global 'bank' serves to close the model with respect to global savings and investment.

Data and aggregation

The study uses an aggregation of a revised version of the GTAP 5 data base (Dimaranan and McDougall, 2002). In the GTAP 5 data base, all the different components of OECD PSE data except for market price support are distributed into four classifications of domestic support, namely: output subsidies, intermediate input subsidies, land-based payments and capital-based payments. In contrast to GTAP 5, the land-based payments were revised to handle payments on historical entitlements separately. Their effect is now neutral across programme commodities. The region and sector aggregation of the GTAP data base used in the study is as laid out in Table 4.2.

Experimental design

Three sets of simulations are used in this chapter to analyse the impacts of changes in OECD domestic support on developing regions. The experimental design is outlined in Table 4.5.

The first set of experiments involves a 50 per cent liberalization of border measures relating to wheat in the EU15 while allowing area payments to adjust to maintain the real farm income level in the EU15. This re-instrumentation simulation provides the first insight into

Table 4.5 Experimental design

Policy reform and re-instrumentation for EU wheat	EU wheat land subsidy is allowed to adjust to maintain a constant real farm income condition when market price support is reduced by 50 per cent
50 per cent cuts in OECD domestic support	Comprehensive reform of domestic support in OECD for all countries and all commodities: 50 per cent cuts in all domestic support instruments
50 per cent cuts in OECD market price support with re-instrumentation	Comprehensive reform of market price support, including 50 per cent cuts in tariffs and export subsidies, with a compensating increase in payments to land, designed to stabilize real farm income in each OECD country

changes in model variables that result from a politically feasible reform scenario. In addition, the focus on reform in a single region–commodity pair provides a good starting point for examining the mechanisms underlying the welfare impacts on developing regions occurring from OECD reforms.

The final two sets of experiments consider more comprehensive reforms in which first domestic support and then market price support are cut by 50 per cent in all OECD countries. In the second simulation, domestic support is endogenized to offset the adverse impacts of cuts in market price support for OECD farm incomes.

Results and discussion

Policy re-instrumentation

A primary obstacle to reducing support in OECD agriculture is the adverse impact on farm incomes. Given the differential impact of the various methods of support used in OECD countries,[5] there appears to be scope for re-instrumentation of support. This point is made quite clearly by Dewbre, Anton and Thompson (2001), who show that market price support is a relatively inefficient means of transferring income to farmers and furthermore, that it does so at the expense of relatively large distortions in world markets. They show that, in contrast, land-based payments are highly effective at transferring income to farmers, while reducing world market price impacts of OECD agricultural policies. We therefore turn next to a simulation in which market price support for EU wheat production is further reduced (by 50 per cent from 1997 levels), yet farm income is maintained at current levels by increased land-based subsidies.

As shown in Table 4.6, reducing MPS by 50 per cent and maintaining farm incomes via area payments results in an 8.6 percentage point increase in the power of the *ad valorem* land subsidy (treated as a negative tax in the model). Note that we have not increased the set-aside requirement in this case, since output falls due to the reduction in domestic prices. The increased subsidy to wheat land results in increased returns to land employed in the wheat sector, which in turn attracts more land to this activity. With overall production declining, this policy leads to a more extensive form of wheat production, with a decline in the use of labour, capital and purchased inputs per hectare of land.

The decline in wheat production and increase in consumption due to lower domestic prices causes wheat exports from the EU15 to fall. This is

Table 4.6   Implications of 50 per cent reduction in market price support for EU15 wheat, with re-instrumentation

EU15 variable	Percentage change
Change in area payments	−8.6
Land rents	0.3
Wheat acreage planted	0.0
Labour use	−3.4
Capital use	−3.3
Output price	−0.7
Output quantity	−3.3
Export price	0.6
Export quantity	−7.5
World price	0.4
Equivalent variation	US$ million
EU15	187.8
OECD–FSU aggregate	246.7
Developing region aggregate	−69.0

Source: Authors' simulations.

further reinforced by the reduction in export subsidies for wheat. Thus the export price of EU wheat rises. This re-instrumentation leads to an increase in efficiency in the EU economy and a subsequent welfare gain of US$188 million. With the exception of Argentina and Zambia, the developing countries lose from higher wheat prices. The aggregate welfare loss to developing countries totals US$65 million in this case.

Impacts on developing countries

The developing country impacts of the EU wheat reform summarized in Table 4.6 are decomposed by region and welfare contribution in Table 4.7. Here, we follow the approach of Huff and Hertel (1996), whereby regional welfare can be explained by allocative efficiency effects and the terms of trade effects. The allocative efficiency effects are due to second-best effects where a country benefits positively from increased activity in industries that are taxed and negatively from the expansion of subsidized industries. The terms of trade effects come from changes in a country's export prices relative to changes in its import prices. A country benefits positively from an increase in its export prices and is negatively impacted by a net increase in the prices of goods that it imports. As noted previously, since the developing-country impacts of OECD reform are transmitted through international

Table 4.7 Developing region welfare: EU15 wheat market price support reform, US$ million

Region[a]	Equivalent variation			Terms of trade components		
	Total	Alloc. efficiency	TOT	World price	Export price	Import price
LDC total (−0.67)	−65.5	−9.6	−55.2	−34.7	12.7	−33.2
China (−0.91)	−4.8	−2.8	−1.8	−2.1	2.5	−2.2
Indonesia (−1.00)	−3.1	−0.1	−3.0	−3.4	0.7	−0.3
Vietnam (−1.00)	−0.0	−0.0	−0.0	−0.1	0.1	−0.0
ASEAN4 (−0.97)	−3.9	−0.9	−3.0	−3.6	2.5	−1.9
India (−0.83)	−0.4	−0.2	−0.2	−1.8	1.3	0.3
RsoAsia (−1.00)	−6.3	−1.1	−5.0	−4.2	0.1	−1.0
Argentina (1.00)	7.0	0.8	5.9	5.8	0.3	−0.2
Brazil (−0.96)	−3.6	−1.0	−2.5	−3.7	0.8	0.4
RlatAmer (−0.86)	−10.1	−1.6	−8.3	−6.5	4.4	−6.2
MENA (−0.88)	−29.6	−2.0	−27.6	−11.7	0.8	−16.7
Tanzania (−1.00)	−0.1	−0.0	−0.1	−0.1	0.0	0.0
Zambia (0.76)	0.0	0.0	0.0	−0.0	−0.0	0.0
R_SSA (−0.94)	−10.4	−0.8	−9.6	−3.2	−0.8	−5.5

Note:
[a] Specialization indices in italics.
Source: Authors' simulations.

markets, it is hardly surprising that the resulting change in the terms of trade for these countries (TOT in Table 4.7) accounts for the bulk of the developing-country losses. Furthermore, with the exception of Argentina and Zambia, all of the developing countries are made worse off due to the EU15 wheat reform.

It is challenging to sort out the impact of changes in export and import prices of different commodities in order to explain why a given country experiences a terms of trade gain or loss. A helpful approach to decomposing the terms of trade effects is provided by McDougall (1993) who decomposes the percentage change in the terms of trade for a given region into three separate effects – the world price effect, the export price effect and the import price effect:

$$tot_r = \sum_i S_i^{Xr} p_{Xir} - \sum_i S_i^{Mr} p_{Mir} \qquad \text{terms of trade effect}$$

$$= \sum_i (S_i^{Xr} - S_i^{Mr})(p_{wi} - p_w) \qquad \text{world price effect}$$

$$+ \sum_i S_i^{Xr}(p_{Xir} - p_{wi}) \qquad \text{export price effect}$$

$$- \sum_i s_i^{Mr} \; (p_{Mir} - p_{wi}) \qquad \text{import price effect}$$

The world price effect equals the sum over all traded commodities of the product of a country's net trade share (the difference between export and import shares for commodity i), $(S_i^{Xr} - S_i^{Mr})$ and the change in the price of i (for example, wheat), P_{wi} relative to an index of average world prices for all products, P_w (lower case variables denote percentage change, so the difference in these two price changes represents the percentage change in the price ratio). The world price effect is positive in the case of a net exporter of a commodity for which EU reform means higher world prices. However, from Table 4.7 (see specialization indexes in parentheses for each country) we know that most of these developing countries are net importers of wheat. Therefore this component contributes negatively to their welfare.

The MENA region suffers the worst deterioration in terms of trade due to the world price effect, owing to MENA's heavy reliance on imports of wheat. Examining the entries in the world price effect column of Table 4.7, we see that Argentina, which is a substantial net exporter of wheat, is the one country which experiences a welfare gain from the higher world wheat prices.

The second component in the terms of trade decomposition is the export price effect which is the sum of export share-weighted relative price changes where the relative price change is the ratio of the exporter's price for commodity i, P_{Xir}, relative to the worldwide average price for commodity i, P_{wi}. Of course, if these commodities are perfect substitutes, then this effect disappears since the two prices will not differ in the case of a homogeneous commodity. The degree to which the two prices can diverge is influenced by the degree of product differentiation in the market for commodity i. There is product differentiation in all commodities in this model since the Armington trade structure ensures that wheat produced in one country is differentiated from wheat produced in another.

The export price effects in Table 4.7 are uniformly positive, with the exception of Zambia and the rest of SSA. These positive entries reflect the fact that increased EU imports of wheat result in higher EU exports of other products, and thereby lower EU export prices. Since the world average price for all goods is a weighted average of all export prices, most non-EU export prices rise, relative to the average.

The import price component of the terms of trade decomposition is the mirror image of the export price effect and refers to the import share-weighted change in the country-specific import price index, P_{Mir} relative to the average world price index, P_{wi}. Developing countries tend to receive subsidized imports from the European Union, and so it is hardly surprising that elimination of these subsidies results in higher average prices for composite wheat imports. This effect is particularly important for MENA, rest of Latin America and rest of SSA.

Impacts of comprehensive OECD agricultural reforms on developing countries

Having worked through the basic mechanisms by which domestic support and protection of OECD markets will affect the developing countries, we now 'scale up' this analysis of one specific commodity to the global level by examining the combined impact of cuts in support for all agricultural products in all OECD countries. We begin by examining the impact of a 50 per cent cut in domestic support, then turn to an experiment akin to the one discussed before whereby market price support is cut by 50 per cent, while domestic support in the form of area payments rises to stabilize OECD farm incomes.

Cutting domestic support in the OECD

The first column of Table 4.8 reports the average world price impacts of cutting domestic support for all agricultural commodities in the OECD by 50 per cent. It is immediately clear that domestic support policies have the strongest impact on programme crops and ruminant livestock (primarily beef). These are the commodities where the world price increases are greatest. Sugar and dairy, where the bulk of protection remains at the border, actually shows small price declines, as land and labour shifts out of programme crops into other activities. This causes other crop prices to fall as well.

The remaining columns of Table 4.8 decompose the total world price effect by type of domestic support policy instrument. Despite the import-ance of land-based payments for programme crops in the European Union and United States, it is the intermediate input subsidies that contribute most to the world price effects for these crops stemming from domestic support policies in the OECD. For example, 1.7 per cent of the 4.9 per cent increase in the world price of wheat following this cut in domestic support is attributed to the cut in intermediate input subsidies. This is due to the fact that they are both important in the overall mix of support (see Table 4.1) as well as highly distorting of world trade. In the case of the strong increase in the price of ruminant meat, this is largely due to the subsidies on animal numbers (capital subsidy).[6] The impact of this domestic support reduction scenario on developing country welfare is reported in the first column of Table 4.9. As can be seen from this table, developing countries as a group lose from this cut in OECD domestic support (Column (1)). The notable exceptions are Argentina, Brazil and India. Columns (2) and (3) of this table decompose these welfare effects into their allocative efficiency and terms of trade components. As with the previous wheat example, the bulk of the developing-country losses are due to the deterioration of their terms of trade. The only case where the allocative efficiency effect dominates is for China. This is largely driven by the interaction between reduced oilseed imports from the United States, interacting with a very high pre-WTO accession tariff on these imports. That tariff has since been dramatically reduced as part of China's WTO accession process (Ianchovichina and Martin, 2002) so this effect is no longer empirically relevant.

Table 4.8 Change in average world prices due to comprehensive OECD domestic support reform, 50 per cent reduction

Commodity	World price change	Contribution by tax/subsidy to world price change			
		Output	Intermediate input	Land	Capital
pdrice	0.26	0.12	0.34	0.05	−0.23
wheat	4.91	1.03	1.68	1.11	1.09
crsgrns	5.5	1.42	1.79	1.02	1.27
oilsds	3.53	0.92	1.21	0.79	0.6
rawsgr	−0.58	0.09	0.14	−0.33	−0.48
othcrops	−1.5	−0.01	−0.03	−0.69	−0.77
ruminants	4.3	0.48	0.95	−0.38	3.25
nonrumnts	0.54	0.26	0.45	−0.14	−0.02
rawmilk	0.21	0.14	0.81	−0.33	−0.4
pcrice	0.27	0.13	0.12	0.06	−0.03
vegoilfat	0.97	0.2	0.34	0.24	0.2
refsgr	−0.06	0.05	0.06	−0.03	−0.15
rummeat	2.21	0.31	0.56	−0.11	1.44
nrummeat	0.43	0.17	0.28	−0.06	0.04
dairy	−0.19	0.14	0.36	−0.27	−0.43
othprfood	0.22	0.06	0.11	0.07	−0.03
mnfc	0.12	0.01	0	0.1	0.01
srvc	0.11	0.01	0	0.1	−0.01

Source: Authors' simulations.

Table 4.9 Developing region welfare changes: domestic support reform, US$ million

Region	Equivalent variation			Terms of trade components		
	Total	Alloc. efficiency	TOT	World price	Export price	Import price
	(1)	(2)	(3)	(4)	(5)	(6)
China	−69.1	−69.6	18.5	−51.8	137.1	−66.8
Indonesia	−13.6	0.8	−12.4	−54.5	35.5	6.6
Vietnam	−8.2	−1.9	−6.6	−10.0	5.8	−2.4
ASEAN4	−15.2	4.9	−15.9	−47.4	113.4	−81.9
India	35.9	15.2	22.8	−22.9	38.6	7.1
RsoAsia	−44.2	−3.3	−39.7	−57.2	17.2	0.3
Argentina	157.3	26.2	120.5	183.1	−53.1	−9.5
Brazil	200.2	73.3	94.9	1.1	88.5	5.3
RlatAm	−214.3	−29.9	−183.4	−244.7	101.8	−40.5
MENA	−270.1	−50.6	−217.7	−315.9	83.1	15.1
Tanzania	−7.0	−1.2	−4.9	−7.1	1.8	0.4
Zambia	0.0	0.2	−0.3	−1.4	0.4	0.7
R_SSA	−126.1	−16.0	−108.0	−149.7	31.1	10.6
ROW	17.1	27.7	−9.4	−221.4	285.9	−73.9
LDC total	−357.3	−24.2	−341.6	−999.7	887.0	−228.9

Source: Authors' simulations.

As before, we can decompose the terms of trade effect into its component parts to obtain some further insight into the source of the developing country losses. This is done in the subsequent three columns of Table 4.9. Note that the world price effects are dominant, and negative, followed in magnitude by the export price effects which are positive for developing countries as a group. The import price effects are negative, and considerably smaller in absolute value.

The world price effects can be broken down further by commodity and region (see Dimaranan, Hertel and Keeney, 2003, Table 12). Recall that the world price effect is positive when the price rises and the country is a net exporter and negative when it is a net importer. For a world price decline, it is precisely the opposite.

Recall that the world price rises were most dramatic for the programme crops and for ruminant meats, while the biggest price decline is for other crops (Table 4.8). Furthermore, recall from Table 4.3 that developing countries tend to be net importers of programme crops and livestock products, and net exporters of other crops. Therefore, it is not surprising that the largest losses are for wheat, coarse grains, ruminant products (net importers with a world price rise) and for other crops (net exporters with a declining world price). From the point of view of an individual region/country, MENA and rest of Latin America are among the hardest hit by these effects.

Recall, however, that our analytical framework takes into account the differentiation of products by country of origin. So the export price effect can potentially offset or reinforce the world price effect, depending on whether developing-country export prices rise or fall, relative to the world average. The product differentiation aspect of the analysis further reinforces the adverse impacts on developing countries for wheat, coarse grains, oilseeds and ruminant products. However, in the case of other crops, which are quite highly differentiated, the rise in developing-country export prices, relative to the world average, generates an overall gain. Developing countries also benefit overall from developments in the global markets for manufactures and services.

In addition to the losses incurred by developing countries from the cuts to domestic support in the OECD countries, there are substantial declines in OECD farm incomes. The largest decline is in the EU15 (–16 per cent), followed by EFTA (–13 per cent), then the United States (–5 per cent) and Canada (–3.5 per cent). The losses in most other OECD countries are under 1 per cent, due to relatively more reliance on border measures (Japan and Korea, see Table 4.1) or lower levels of support (Australia and Canada). From a political economy point of view, this kind of reform looks like a difficult one to sell. Therefore we turn to an alternative type of comprehensive reform.

Re-instrumentation of agricultural support in the OECD

We simulate an alternative type of comprehensive, OECD reform focusing on reductions in market price support. Specifically, tariffs and export subsidy rates in the OECD countries are cut by 50 per cent. Domestic support is permitted to increase in order to compensate producers for the resulting loss in income. As with our EU wheat example, we use the land-based payments to compensate producers, since they are the most efficient and least trade-distorting of the instruments currently in use.

Table 4.10 reports the world price effects of the re-instrumentation experiment. Column (1) reports the total effect, while columns (2)–(7) break this total into the parts attributable to tariffs in the major OECD markets, as well as export subsidies. The first thing to note is that the world price effects on programme crops and ruminant products are far

Table 4.10 World price effects of comprehensive 50 per cent market price support reductions for OECD agriculture, coupled with re-instrumentation

Commodity	World price change	Contribution of import tariffs				Contribution of export subsidies	
		EU	USA	Japan	Other OECD	EU	Other OECD
	(1)	(2)	(3)	(4)	(5)	(6)	(7)
pdrice	0.711	0.145	−0.004	0.44	0.088	0.039	0.003
wheat	0.794	0.072	−0.028	0.28	0.106	0.344	0.02
crsgrns	0.954	0.005	−0.074	0.122	0.145	0.744	0.012
oilsds	0.408	0.077	−0.068	0.26	0.127	0.008	0.004
rawsgr	0.205	0.14	0.063	0.036	−0.047	−0.007	0.02
othcrops	0.171	−0.008	0.049	0.092	0.022	−0.002	0.018
ruminants	0.031	−0.102	0.015	0.079	−0.016	−0.014	0.069
nonrumnts	−0.119	−0.088	0	0.045	−0.065	−0.016	0.005
rawmilk	0.182	0.08	0.048	0.031	−0.074	−0.004	0.101
pcrice	−0.209	−0.306	0.019	0.071	0.001	0.004	0.002
vegoilfat	−0.095	0.018	−0.022	−0.008	−0.089	0.005	0.001
refsgr	0.071	0.005	0.044	0.023	0	−0.002	0.001
rummeat	−0.068	−0.103	−0.011	0.039	0.006	−0.004	0.005
nrummeat	−0.184	−0.125	−0.001	0.021	−0.065	−0.014	0
dairy	−0.167	−0.14	0.004	0.012	−0.023	−0.021	0.001
othprfood	−0.347	−0.099	−0.005	−0.016	−0.231	0.003	0.001
mnfc	−0.025	−0.01	−0.002	−0.009	−0.003	−0.001	0
srvc	−0.024	−0.008	−0.002	−0.008	−0.005	−0.001	0

Source: Authors' simulations.

more modest than those following the domestic support experiment. In general, the average world price of crops rises, while the average world price of livestock products falls. The largest contributor to the higher rice prices is the Japanese tariff cut. In the case of wheat prices, EU export subsidies, followed by Japanese tariffs, are the largest contributions to the increase. The situation is similar for coarse grains, where the majority of the world price impact is traced back to the elimination of EU export subsidies. The average world farmgate price of sugar rises due to cuts in the EU and US import tariffs. Meat and dairy prices worldwide are heavily influenced by the EU tariff cuts. With a large share of the world's output in the European Union, lower prices in that market contribute to a decline in the world average price. Finally, in the case of other food products, the 'other' OECD countries' tariffs appear to play the largest role.

Table 4.11 reports the welfare impacts of the re-instrumentation experiment. In sharp contrast to the domestic support experiment, most developing countries gain from the liberalization. Only China, ASEAN4 and rest of South Asia lose, and these losses are relatively small. As before, the overall effects, as well as most of the individual country effects, are dominated by the terms of trade changes. Two notable exceptions are China and MENA, where the allocative efficiency effect dominates the terms of trade effect and changes the regional welfare outcome. In the case of China, this is due to a reduction in other processed food output, which shows a much higher rate of taxation than other sectors in this aggregation of the Version 5 GTAP data base. This gives rise to an efficiency loss. For MENA, the source of the large efficiency gain is due to the increase in imports. MENA's imports of everything excepting programme crops tend to increase only modestly. However, this region has very high rates of protection on many of these products imported from the European Union and EFTA – indeed much higher than for most other products. Other processed food products is a

Table 4.11 Developing region welfare changes: OECD re-instrumentation of agricultural support, US$ million

Region	Equivalent variation			Terms of trade components		
	Total	Alloc. efficiency	TOT	World price	Export price	Import price
	(1)	(2)	(3)	(4)	(5)	(6)
China	−59.8	−78.3	24.8	−4.1	57.6	−28.8
Indonesia	−6.3	−4.2	−1.5	−14.2	18.3	−5.6
Vietnam	4.4	−1.5	6.8	−0.4	8.3	−1.1
ASEAN4	−34.3	−16.8	−16.2	−21.5	32.6	−27.3
India	0.6	−17.9	19.0	−2.8 r	26.0	−4.2
RsoAsia	−17.7	−5.4	−12.3	−11.3	6.8	−7.9
Argentina	71.2	6.2	61.8	20.1	49.4	−7.7
Brazil	102.2	47.8	40.6	2.7	47.2	−9.4
RlatAm	238.6	26.3	199.0	−3.8	243.1	−40.4
MENA	15.6	56.6	−40.7	−31.4	61.2	−70.6
Tanzania	3.3	0.6	2.1	0.7	1.6	−0.2
Zambia	0.2	−0.1	0.3	0.1	0.4	−0.1
R_SSA	90.5	17.2	72.7	11.8	76.2	−15.3
ROW	28.9	25.6	4.5	−0.4	15.7	−10.8
LDC total	437.3	56.0	360.8	−54.5	644.4	−229.4

Source: Authors' simulations.

case in point, with an average bilateral tariff of 165 per cent on imports from the EFTA region. Thus when other processed food products from EFTA increase, as a result of trade liberalization in that region, there is a substantial efficiency gain for the MENA region. However, in the aggregate, these efficiency gains are only a small portion of the total developing-country gains from the re-instrumentation experiment. The breakdown of the total regional terms of trade effects into their component parts in columns (4)–(6) of Table 4.11 reveals that, unlike the domestic support scenario, the across-the-board cut to market price support is most strongly influenced by the export price effect. With all OECD countries increasing their imports, and hence their exports, the average price of OECD exports falls for most products. This depresses the world average price of most products, leaving the developing countries with a favourable position for their export prices, relative to the world average. Both the world price effect and the import price effect are still negative, but these are dominated by the strong positive change in developing-country export prices.

Further exploration of the export price effect by commodity and region (reported in Dimaranan, Hertel and Keeney, 2003, Table 15) revealed that apart from the programme commodities, almost all the export price effects are positive, reflecting the general tendency of OECD export prices to fall, relative to those of the developing countries. The total export price effect by commodity, summed over all the developing countries, shows the largest positive effects for other crops and other processed food products. On a commodity basis, the only negative total terms of trade effect pertains to wheat and coarse grains. All other commodities show a total terms of trade effect that is positive for the developing countries.

Summary and conclusions

Long-term support for agricultural programme commodities in OECD countries, coupled with disprotection in many developing countries, has left many of the latter increasingly dependent on imports. As the developing countries have come to rely on imports of grains and oilseeds from the subsidized OECD economies, they have become much more exposed to agricultural reforms that raise the prices of these specific products. As a result, we find that an across-the-board, 50 per cent cut in all domestic support for OECD agriculture leads to welfare losses for most of the developing regions, as well as for the combined total group of developing countries. The 50 per cent cut in domestic support also results in large declines in farm incomes in Europe and, to a lesser degree, North America. This makes such a reform package an unlikely political event.

An alternative approach to reforming agricultural policies in the OECD would be to focus on broad-based reductions in market price support. This has been occurring in a number of OECD countries, most notably the European Union, where domestic support has increasingly replaced border measures. As demonstrated in this chapter, the basic economic principles of agricultural support policies suggest that a shift from market price support to land-based payments could generate a 'win–win' outcome whereby farm incomes are maintained and world price distortions are reduced. This is the direction charted by the OECD in its recent 'Positive Agenda for Reform' for agriculture (OECD, 2002a). We formally examine such an agricultural reform scenario, implementing a 50 per cent cut in market price support for OECD agriculture, with a compensating set of land payments designed to maintain farm income in each of the member economies. This comprehensive reform scenario results in increased welfare for most developing countries, with gains on other commodities offsetting the terms of trade losses from higher programme crop prices.

The preference for a continued focus on cuts in market price support, instead of shifting the emphasis to domestic support cuts is also reflected in two recent papers by other authors on this same general topic. Rae and Strutt (2002) conclude from their GTAP-based comparison between border measures and domestic support that improved market access generates far greater trade and welfare gains than domestic support cuts. This leads them to propose that trade negotiators' attention be focused squarely on cuts to border measures before turning any attention to domestic support.[7] Hoekman, Ng and Olarreaga (2002) focus on developing-country impacts of OECD agricultural policies using a very different approach, but they reach the same conclusion as this chapter.[8] They find that cuts to tariffs will generate much larger global welfare gains and positive gains to developing countries, whereas cuts to domestic support lead to smaller global welfare gains and losses for developing countries.

In summary, we conclude that most developing countries will be well advised to focus their efforts on improved market access to the OECD economies, while permitting these wealthy economies to continue – indeed, even increase – domestic support payments. Provided these increased domestic support payments are not linked to output or variable inputs, the trade-distorting effects are likely to be small, and they can be a rather effective way of offsetting the potential losses that would otherwise be sustained by OECD farmers. This type of policy re-instrumentation will increase the probability that such reforms will be deemed politically acceptable in the OECD member economies, while simultaneously increasing the likelihood that such reforms will also be beneficial to the developing economies.

Notes

1. More recently it appears that France and Germany will oppose such reforms (*The Economist*, 2003).
2. The programme commodities referred to in this chapter comprise paddy rice, wheat, coarse and cereal grains, oilseeds, raw sugar, processed rice and refined sugar. The first four are the crops for which the GTAP data base has OECD domestic support data. Processed rice and refined sugar are included since these are the traded form of rice and sugar, respectively.
3. In order to keep the tables manageable, the 'Other Agriculture' category also includes food products. If this latter were removed, we would see even more significant net exports from the developing countries.
4. One cautionary note – as anticipated in the results of Hertel (1989) – is that a shift towards variable input subsidies could have the opposite effect, with larger world price impacts and smaller farm-income benefits
5. This is expounded at length in a longer version of this chapter (Dimaranan, Hertel and Keeney, 2003) which reports on the results of stylized simulations. The results show that with an equal PSE increase, a subsidy on variable inputs produces the largest effect on wheat output, exports and prices. Compared to market price support, an output subsidy has a larger effect on output, producer prices and farm income. Subsidy payments to land used in production of wheat have the smallest effects on output, exports and price of wheat.
6. These results can be compared roughly to those of Rae and Strutt (2002), by noting that they omit the land- and capital-based payments from their domestic support scenario, arguing that these are largely 'blue box payments' and therefore exempt from cuts under the URAA.
7. Unlike this study, Rae and Strutt (2002) focus solely on cuts in domestic support provided through output and variable input subsidies (their proxy for 'amber box' measures).
8. Their analysis is based on a highly disaggregated, econometric model that assumes that products are perfect substitutes.

References

Anderson, K., B. Dimaranan, J. Francois, T. Hertel, B. Hoekman and W. Martin (2001) 'The Cost of Rich (and Poor) Country Protection to Developing Countries', *Journal of African Economies*, 10(3): 227–57.

Dewbre, J., J. Anton and W. Thompson (2001) 'The Transfer Efficiency and Trade Effects of Direct Payments', *American Journal of Agricultural Economics*, 83(5): 1204–14.

Dimaranan, B., T. Hertel and R. Keeney (2003) 'OECD Domestic Support and Developing Countries', WIDER Discussion Paper 2003/02, Helsinki: UNU-WIDER.

Dimaranan, B. V. and R. McDougall (eds) (2002) *Global Trade, Assistance, and Production: The GTAP 5 Data Base*, Center for Global Trade Analysis, Purdue University, West Lafayette, Indiana.

The Economist (2002) 'Europe's Farms: Will These Modest Proposals Provoke Mayhem Down on the Farm?', 13–19 July: 42–3.

————— (2003) 'The Case for the Defence', 9 January.

Elbehri, A., M. D. Ingco, T. Hertel and K. Pearson (1999) 'Agriculture and WTO 2000: Quantitative Assessment of Multilateral Liberalization of Agricultural Policies', Paper presented at the Conference on Agriculture and the New Trade Agenda in the WTO 2000 Negotiations, Geneva, 1–2 October.

Floyd, J. E. (1965) 'The Effects of Farm Price Supports on Returns to Land and Labor in Agriculture', *Journal of Political Economy*, 73(2): 148–58.

Frandsen, S., B. Gersfelt and H. G. Jensen (2002) 'Decoupling Support in Agriculture: Impacts of Redesigning European Agricultural Support', Paper presented at the Fifth Annual Conference on Global Economic Analysis, Taipei, Taiwan, 5–7 June.

Frandsen, S., H. G. Jensen and W. Yu (2001) 'Domestic Support in Agriculture–Version 5 of the GTAP Database: The Case of the European Union', Paper presented at the Fourth Conference on Global Economic Analysis, Purdue University, West Lafayette, Indiana, June.

Gehlhar, M. J. and F. J. Nelson (2001) 'Treatment of Domestic Agricultural–Support and Implications for Reductions: The Case for the United States', Paper presented at the Fourth Conference on Global Economic Analysis, Purdue University, West Lafayette, Indiana, June.

Hertel, T. (1989) 'Negotiating Reductions in Agricultural Support: Implications of Technology and Factor Mobility', *American Journal of Agricultural Economics*, August: 559–73.

Hertel, T. and W. Martin (1999) 'Would Developing Countries Gain from Inclusion of Manufactures in the WTO Negotiations?', Paper prepared for the World Bank's Conference on Developing Countries and the Millennium Round, WTO Secretariat, Centre William Rappard, Geneva, 19–20 September.

Hertel, T., W. Martin, B. Dimaranan and K. Yanagishima (1996) 'Manufactures Trade in a Changing World Economy', in W. Martin and L. A. Winters (eds), *The Uruguay Round and the Developing Countries*, New York: Cambridge University Press.

Hoekman, B., F. Ng and M. Olarreaga (2002) 'Reducing Agricultural Tariffs versus Domestic Support: What's More Important for Developing Countries?', Paper presented at the International Agricultural Trade Research Consortium Conference on 'The Developing Countries, Agricultural Trade and the WTO', Whistler, 16–17 June.

Huff, K. M. and T. Hertel (1996) 'Decomposition of Welfare Effects in the GTAP Model', GTAP Technical Paper 5, Center for Global Trade Analysis, Purdue University, West Lafayette, Indiana.

Hummels, D. (1999) 'Toward a Geography of Trade Costs', University of Chicago, Illinois, mimeo.

Ianchovichina, E. and W. Martin (2002) 'Economic Impacts of China's Accession to the WTO', Washington, DC: International Trade Department, World Bank, mimeo.

Martin, W. and L. A. Winters (eds) (1986) *The Uruguay Round and the Developing Economies*, New York: Cambridge University Press.

McDougall, R. A. (1993). 'Two Small Extensions to SALTER', SALTER Working Paper 12, Industry Commission, Canberra.

OECD (2001) *Market Effects of Crop Support Measures*, Paris: Organization for Economic Cooperation and Development.

———— (2002a) *Agricultural Policies in OECD Countries: A Positive Agenda for Reform*, Paris: Organization for Economic Cooperation and Development.

———— (2002b) *The Medium-Term Impacts of Trade Liberalisation in OECD Countries on the Food Security of Non-Member Economies*, Paris: Organization for Economic Cooperation and Development.

Rae, A. N. and A. Strutt (2002) 'The Current Round of Agricultural Trade Negotiations: Why Bother about Domestic Support?', Paper presented at the Fifth Annual Conference on Global Economic Analysis, Taipei, Taiwan, 5–7 June.

5
Impact of Trade Liberalization on Returns from Land: A Regional Study of Indian Agriculture

Nilabja Ghosh

Introduction

The international economic order envisaged in the WTO agreement is one of fair competition among nations bringing out efficient production patterns. The beneficial effect of this order on a large developing country like India, however, hinges on the ability of free trade to generate rapid growth in output along with rising income for large numbers (Becker, Mitra and Balseca, 2002) of people. The largest section of India's population still depends on agriculture for a livelihood and a most desirable possibility expected from the new regime would be the commercial success of this sector, drawing on the natural advantages of the immobile and internationally non-tradable factors devoted to it and also the ability to access certain tradable factors such as fertilizer that confer a qualitative change on the immobile factors. Agriculture in India, however, remains shrouded in a mesh of internal controls and distortions and this chapter attempts to unravel the underlying market reality by raising the query: would farmers in the country gain by exporting grains when free-market forces are allowed to operate? The question is addressed within a limited coverage only. First, the chapter considers only non-basmati rice,[1] which holds a special place in Indian agriculture. Second, the reference time point, 1998–99, pertains to the most recent year for which information could be collected and during which rice apparently enjoyed competitive advantage and exports proved successful. The external prices prevailing at the point are subject to the then current international trade realities.

Several studies have demonstrated India's comparative advantage in rice and the product emerged as a prominent export item responding to the economic reforms of the 1990s. Suited to the soil and climate of the country, it is cultivated extensively and by all classes of farmers. It is a labour-intensive crop but its dominance in crop patterns is positively associated with the level of poverty and weak infrastructure within the country (Ghosh, 2002). Under the existing conditions the prospect of rice export offers a potential to deal a frontal blow to rural poverty. The Government of India actively supported the prospect by procuring grains at minimum support prices and selling to exporters, among other measures. Consecutive years of good monsoons helped the supply side and the exports additionally served to alleviate the storage problems arising in the public domain.

In trying to measure the impact of trade liberalization on the returns from cultivation the chapter considers at length the marketing channels that are encountered by the farmers under a dual system where both the public and the private sectors operate. The effect of trade is deemed to come from both the output market and input market where the input is tradable. The gains from export are perceived to flow back to the farmer (Bhagwati, Panagariya and Srinivasan, 1998). The calculation of this flow is also difficult, for various reasons. First, in India there is no systematic and clear-cut method of marketing the product from farm to ship. Even if one ignores the public–private duality, the marketing methods of private traders are unique to the situation and also to their strategies and objectives and researchers have resorted to empirical approximations or firm-specific surveys. Second, the private trader in any case does not provide or publish any systematic record of operation and cost. Third, the dominance of the public sector in the market and the distortions induced would make such cost figures, even if available, unrepresentative of the free-trade situation. Fourth, there is no clear definition of the export or border price concept to assess the competitiveness or gain in a free-trade situation. Prices in overseas markets are usually considered, but they are found to be at variance with realized prices. Fifth, international demand and supply often depend on which part of the country they are viewed from. Sixth, prices in international markets are volatile and sensitive to the trading decisions of the home country. Finally, the prevailing situation is complex, in flux as policies undergo continual change. Not only is output market distorted by policy mixes, the input market is shrouded in an even more complex regime of protection shared non-transparently by farmers and manufacturers.

In the absence of definite patterns and recorded information from the private trader information provided by the public sector operator the

Food Corporation of India (FCI) is used in the present study although the FCI enjoys economies of scale and monopoly powers that private traders do not. Cost of transport has been based on the cheaper-mode railways and for export prices actual FOB prices at the ports of economic relevance are considered. If India enters freely into the export market for rice, its price will certainly go down and similarly if India steps up its imports of fertilizer its price will go up. This chapter makes a conservative estimate through a restrictive small-country assumption. The year under consideration seems favourable for India, modest in respect of global fertilizer price and buoyant in respect of exchange rate and export price of rice in comparison to the trend during the 1990s[2] and the gains from free trade have therefore been made subject to rather optimistic assumptions. While this confers a bias to the results, it can be anticipated that with a more realistic assumption, where global prices are sensitive to India's exports of rice and imports of fertilizer, the returns would be unchanged. The prevailing trade regime is pertinent to the computation of the returns and for an understanding of their limitations. The policy that is evolving is essentially double-edged, with both input and output markets impacting on farmer's gains in contradictory ways. Since data on input use at the crop level is yet unavailable for the reference time point, approximations have been made about the technology by looking at the survey data available for an adjacent period in the 1990s. Fertilizer is treated as the single major tradable input and also as a contraining input to production. The policy on both fronts and the role of ports in trading are discussed next as background to the method of price calculation laid down later. The theoretical frameworks of analysis and data issues are also described, along with the results.

The rice market in India at a cross-roads

The rice market comes under the purview of the Government of India's foodgrain policy, which originated in a time of shortage in the 1940s. The historic Bengal famine and the Second World War, events taking place against the background of a low-productivity agriculture and abysmal market integration in India, brought the state to intervene in the market without any long-term vision. In the 1960s, developments that strengthened the government's will for a long-term policy were (1) poor crop performance and resulting food shortages, (2) shortage of foreign exchange for imports, (3) two successive wars and the political unacceptability of food aid from the United States, (4) availability of new technology for agrarian development and (5) the new optimism that farmers in traditional agriculture were capable of responding to economic incentives (Krishna, 1963; Schultz, 1964). All this laid the foundation of the FCI in 1965, in keeping with the socialistic spirit of the time. A price policy promulgated soon after and followed in subsequent decades, designed to be executed by the FCI, integrated several conflicting objectives (Tyagi, 1990; Mellor and Ahmed, 1988). It aimed to provide incentives to the farmer, prevent distress selling and usher in self-sufficiency in grains. It also aimed to protect consumer interest through low food prices, stabilize prices, hold buffer stocks and serve the needs of the poor and the vulnerable.

The rice market remains a dual-channel market with a residual private trade inhibited by not only the dominance of FCI but also by a multitude of other controls. The private grain trader is discouraged by unexpected government policy changes, low-priced open sales by FCI, excessive inter-seasonal price stability that offers little margin from trading, coercive levies and low priority in allocation of credit and railway wagons. The state governments also impose various control orders on movement and storage under the 1955 Essential Commodities Act (ECA).

The shortage situation, however, changed as foodgrain production and foreign exchange reserves reached sustainable levels and markets became more integrated (Kumar, 1997; Sharma, Ghosh and Kumar, 2001). The food policy itself has now come under serious review with the general spirit now moving in favour of a free market, India's participation in the WTO and an urgent need to exploit the advantage of the AoA. However, the government's domestic interventionist role (Table 5.1) still hides the true competitive advantages in the country and gives distorted signals. Rice cultivation spans several states due to favourable soil and climate;

Table 5.1 Policy transition in the rice market, 1991–2002

Year	Import	Export	Domestic
1991	Canalized through FCI	Negative list Licensed	Dual-channel
1997	Canalized through FCI	Negative list Quantitative restriction (QR) Minimum export price	Dual-channel
1999	Free	Free	Dual-channel
2002	State trading Solely on commercial consideration Tariff Other safety measures	Free	Dual-channel

India is the world's largest rice producer after China. Rice is a water-intensive crop, both rainfed and irrigated, grown in multiple seasons or rotated with other crops. Intensive cropping is often associated with ecological stresses and the resource cost of growing rice is not easily quantifiable. Rice is also a labour-intensive product, with labour constituting about 30 per cent of the cost and constitutes the livelihood of a significant part of India's population.

Opening up rice trade to the world market is a contentious issue considering that food security and farmers' livelihood are vital issues in Indian polity (Rao, 2001; Vyas 2001). Studies by Gulati *et al.* (1994), Datta (1997) and Chand (1999) agreed on the comparative advantage of India in rice through measures of the nominal protection coefficient.[3] The results of these studies are summarized in Table 5.2. Since internal distances act as a protection for imports and disprotection for exports (Nouroz, 2001) handling and freight charges are of crucial importance. In the absence of a well-documented marketing record the Gulati and Chand studies approximated these as 5 per cent of reference price, where the reference price itself is different in the studies and Datta accessed information from industry sources.

Rice, both basmati and non-basmati, emerged as items of export during the 1990s taking India from an insignificant place in global export market to a share of 16 per cent (FAO, 1998). Within India's exports of agricultural goods, rice has grown from 2.3 per cent in the triennium 1991–92 to

Table 5.2   Estimates of net protection coefficients of rice in India, 1980–81 to 1992–98

Author	Gulati et al. (1994)	Chand (1999)	Datta (1997)
Ref. years	1980–81 to 1992–93	1988–89 to 1997–98	1994–95
Ref. port	Calcutta		Kandla
Ref. price domestic	Procurement price	Delhi market price transmission to producers	Price at Karnal, Haryana
Ref. price import	International price, Bangkok	FOB price	FOB price at Kandla
Ref. centre	AP, Punjab, India	India	India
Marketing charges	5% domestic ref. price	5% domestic ref. price	From industry sources
NPC	0.46–0.47	0.71–0.89	0.78–0.79
	Fair average quality	Non-parboiled	Different varieties

Sources: Gulati *et al.* (1994); Datta (1997); Chand (1999).

1993–94 to 9.5 per cent in 1994–95 to 1996–97 and further to about 10 per cent in 1997–98 to 1999–2000.

Market channels and institutions

While retaining a major portion of the output themselves, farmers market only about 30–40 per cent of paddy (World Bank, 1999) and of this about 50 per cent enters the centrally administered market operated by the FCI and other state agencies. The remaining grain goes by the private channels, which is the so-called 'open market', although regulated and impacted by various state rules and activities. The FCI freely procures from the market and also coerces levies from millers.

Rice export is now freely allowed and the exportable grains trace a course from the farmer to the exporter in two parallel channels, as shown in Figure 5.1. The whole process can be divided roughly into three major phases: (a) farm to mill, (b) mill to port gate and (c) port gate to ship. Phase (a) has two further sequences, one from farm to market, operated by the farmer and the other from market to mill, operated by the farmer, trader or public agent. Phase (b) is operated by the trader or the FCI and the final phase (c) is now in the hands of the exporter. The transaction at each point has an implication for the remuneration that percolates to the farmer. The marketing process is elaborated in Appendix 1.

The cost structures generated in the two channels are diverse, although some studies (Gulati, Sharma and Kahkonen, 1996; Sidhu, 1998) have suggested that the FCI faced a higher cost structure as compared to the private trader. The FCI's role as distributor in commercially unattractive sectors accounts largely for this weakness and makes comparison difficult.

Fertilizer pricing in India: a review

The RPS

The success of the high-yielding seed depended on the superior response of crops to chemical fertilizers and success came at a tremendous cost in terms of budgetary subsidies. With the urge for self-sufficiency and import substitution, the government not only pursued an active food policy but also sought to control the fertilizer sector to make fertilizers affordable to farmers and promote technology adoption. Since India was deficient in a production facility for essential fertilizers, imports were necessary, but following the oil shock of 1974 the government went a step beyond canalization of imports to protect and build up a strong domestic industry. The fertilizer industry has always claimed policy attentions on account

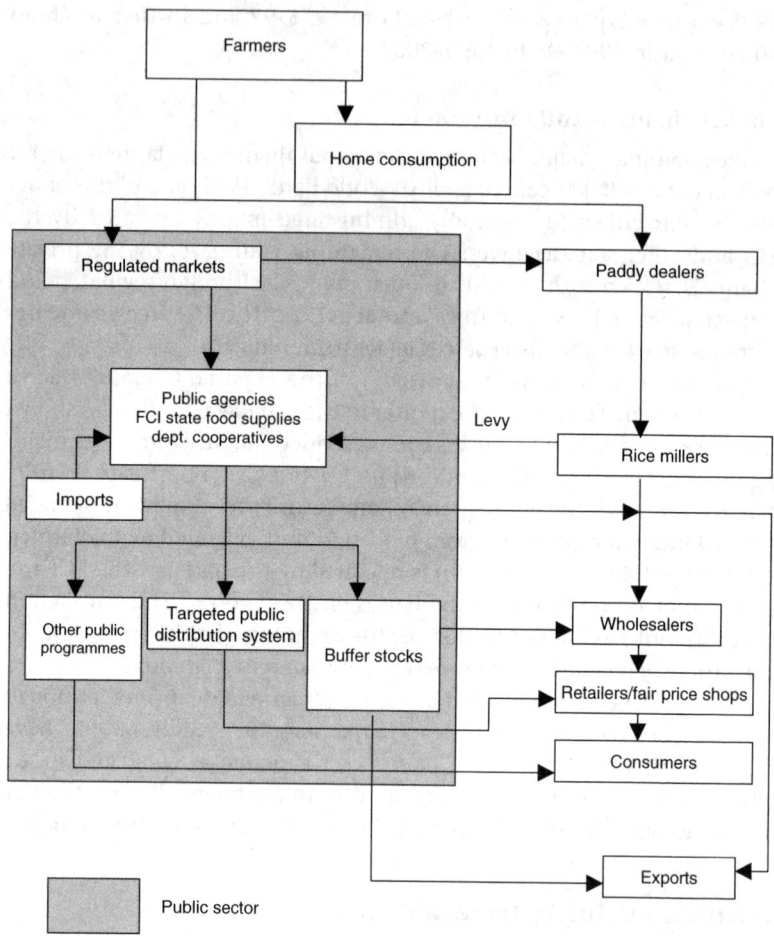

Figure 5.1 Dual-channel market for rice

of its dependence on oil or natural gas as the basic raw material or feed-stock and thereby its links with the international oil market. The industry also has a profound interaction with the national oil/gas sector which is highly regulated and caters to several other key sectors of the economy such as power and transport. On the supply side, the burgeoning fertilizer industry was offered concessional pricing of feedstock while the feedstock choice itself changed over time with availability of technology and resource and strategic considerations. On the sale side, a complex scheme (see Appendix 2) known as the Retention Price and Subsidy Scheme (RPS) was in place to protect farmers.

The RPS came under increasing attack because of the subsidy burden imposed on the budget, its complex and non-transparent nature and its inconsistency. The subsidy has increased over the years, mainly because the farmgate price of fertilizer has not adjusted to the feedstock prices. While the political weight of a strong farm lobby is associated with this, the small and marginal farmers who also benefit from the subsidy are of particular concern. On the other hand, it is contended that a large part of the subsidy (about 40 per cent, as of the 1980s) goes to protect the fertilizer industry and to feedstock-importing agencies, as these prices are also administered (Gulati, 1989; Gulati and Narayanan, 2000). Since the latter agencies are all state-owned, their surplus essentially represents intra-government transfers.

Reforms

The decontrol of phosphatic (P) and potassic (K) fertilizers is a landmark reform in the sector. Urea, the most important nitrogenous fertilizer, is still controlled and the fertilizer industry – spanning public, private and cooperative sectors – is protected by canalized imports and the RPS, or its modified versions. The partial reforms created nutrient imbalance in soil when prices of decontrolled fertilizer responded to market forces and the government reacted by introducing ad hoc concessions which are a form of continuing subsidies to P and K fertilizers. The steps taken to free the fertilizer market from state controls and integrate it with the global market were accompanied by vigorous political resistance and political indecision arising from user problems, as borne out by Box 5.1. The fertilizer industry is also compelled, but not without reservations, to face pathbreaking changes as feedstock pricing move towards import parity.[4]

India depends on imports in varying degrees for all three major fertilizers and with the progress of WTO implementation this dependence is likely to increase.[5] Urea under RPS faces a uniform maximum price fixed by the national polity. On the other hand, DAP and MOP fertilizers for nutrients P and K, although imported and distributed privately, also face a nationally uniform sale price rather than market-determined prices at regional levels, depending on distances and local conditions. The latter also enjoy concessions with a bias in favour of domestic producers (Table 5.3).

Box 5.1 Some policy steps taken with the launch of reforms

1. On 25 July 1991 some of the nitrogenous fertilizers, excluding urea (CAN, AS, AC),[1] were decontrolled and prices of other fertilizers were increased by 40%.
2. After three weeks, the price hike was revised to 30% and small and marginal farmers were exempted.
3. The dual pricing method was again abandoned as not more than 5% of farmers were said to have benefited.
4. On 25 August 1992 the government decontrolled P and K and abolished RPS for P. But the nitrogenous fertilizers were brought back under control.
5. The sale price of urea was again reduced by 10%, RPS was retained.
6. To moderate the price increase of decontrolled fertilizers, concessions were introduced. Other advantages relating to freight, exchange rate and customs duty were extended.
7. In 1994 the same N fertilizers were decontrolled and the urea price was raised by 20%. Further increases occurred in 1997, 1999 and 2000–01.

Note:
1. Calcium ammonium nitrate, ammonium sulphate and ammonium chloride, respectively.

Table 5.3 Nutrient content, share in nutrient supply in country and policy scenario for fertilizers

Fertilizer (nutrient)	Nutrient content %	Nutrient supply %	Policy
Urea (N)	46 (N)	63 (N)	RPS/Group-based concession State trading
DAP (N,P)[a]	(18,46)	53 (P)	Decontrolled Concessions
MOP (K)[b]	(60)	65 (K)	Decontrolled Concessions

Note:
[a] DAP = Diammonium phosphate.
[b] MOP = Muriate of potash.
Source: FAI.

Ports in India's external trade

The competitive advantages enjoyed by a country, and thereby the direction and nature of trade, will influence, and be influenced by, the size, location and efficient distribution of the ports. As a result, a competitive relation is also expected to grow up among a country's ports. The advantage of a port depends on the hinterland served (Weigend, 1958), the internal transport cost, the overseas regions/markets served and the associated shipping or freight rates. The port's own internal advantages in terms of access, handling equipment, labour availability and quality of service are no less important, and there is a significant overlapping of the catchment area among ports.

India has an extensive coastline supporting 11 major and 149 minor ports managed respectively by the Port Trusts under the central government and the state governments (GOI, 2002). Corporatization and privatization of ports are also under way. The major ports, Kandla and Mumbai in the west and Madras (Chennai), Vishakhapattanam, Calcutta–Haldia in the east, are the most dominant ports.[6] Indian ports are constrained by congestion (Datta, 1997) and there is an overwhelming concentration on the western port, Kandla. Although distances should be a major factor for trade, Tables 5.4 and 5.5 show that significant amounts of fertilizer imports are made from eastern ports like Madras and Vishakhapattanam even though fertilizer is procured dominantly from nations in the west (Figure 5.2) and non-basmati rice is exported

Table 5.4   Fertilizer import statistics, by ports, 1998–99

Port	Quantity (tonnes)	Value (Rs '00,000)	Unit value (Rs/kg)	Share % (quantity)
Kandla – free trade zone	297,204	19,406.3	6.53	5.97
Bhavnagar	275,360	20,692.91	7.51	5.53
Kandla – sea	522,359	43,012.84	8.23	10.49
Vishakhapattanam	1,564,925	119,372.43	7.63	31.42
Madras	655,922	36,271.34	5.53	13.17
Bombay	5,351	364.77	6.82	0.11
Calcutta	40,214	1,830.93	4.55	0.81
Total	4,980,981	341,379.69	6.85	67.50
Others	1,619,646	100,428.17	6.20	32.50

Source: DGCIS.

Table 5.5   Rice (non-basmati) export statistics, by ports, 1998–99

Port	Quantity (tonnes)	Value (Rs '00,000)	Unit value (Rs/kg)	Share % (quantity)
Bombay	237,231	26,500.77	11.17	6.02
Calcutta	18,845	1,865.61	9.90	0.42
Haldia	29,138	2,867.18	9.84	0.65
Kakinada	948,429	95,516.11	10.07	21.69
Kandla – sea	1,162,626	122,543.96	10.54	27.83
Nhava Shiva	5,201	559.51	10.76	0.13
Vishakhapattanam	31,947	3,246.88	10.16	0.74
Madras	21,081	2,657.08	12.60	0.60
Others	1,911,390	184,627.43	9.66	41.92
Total	4,365,888	440,384.53	10.09	100.00

Source: DGCIS.

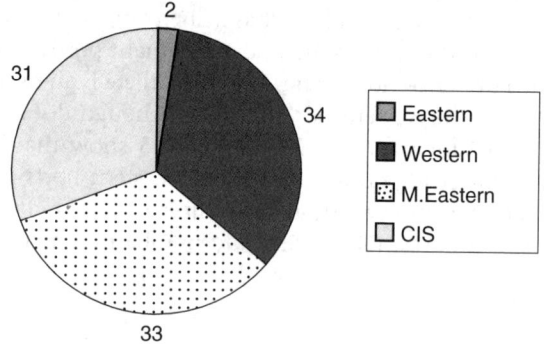

Figure 5.2   Exporters of urea, DAP and MOP fertilizers to India, per cent

both from eastern and western ports like Kakinada (22 per cent) and Kandla (28 per cent), respectively. Differential prices are fetched or paid across the ports.

The six ports Mumbai, Kandla, Calcutta–Haldia, Kakinada, Madras and Vishakhapattanam together accounted for 69 per cent of rice exports in the 1990s but with a high dispersion rate measured by the coefficient of variation (CV) of 116 per cent (going up to 206 per cent) in 1994–95. The year 1995–96, which witnessed the highest export of 4.5 million tonnes, also saw a more even distribution among the ports with a lower CV. Each port has been subject to volatility across time as seen from the CV computed in Table 5.6. However, Kandla, which handles the highest

Table 5.6 Export of (non-basmati) rice from selected ports in India, 1991–2001 (tonnes)

Port Year	Bombay (sea)	Kandla (free trade zone and sea)	Calcutta Haldia (sea)	Kakinada (sea)	Madras (sea)	Vishakhapattanam (sea)	Others ports	Total export all ports	CV (%) ports[a]
1991–92	15,451	356,474	103	28,250	1,862	–	9,795	411,935	194
1992–93	48,348	172,099	60	29,985	1,515	–	3,612	255,619	145
1993–94	7,924	499,268	581	34,441	574	–	22,399	565,187	202
1994–95	7,553	323,464	8,960	1,289	1,233	3,008	102,988	448,495	206
1995–96	528,237	1,503,521	31,503	700,738	101,525	285,437	1,389,738	4,540,699	94
1996–97	306,258	935,652	7,145	165,905	60,315	85,652	428,113	1,989,040	122
1997–98	172,935	827,604	9,386	209,370	48,982	83,445	370,076	1,721,798	123
1998–99	237,231	1,162,626	18,845	948,429	21,081	31,947	1,945,729	4,365,888	119
1999–00	115,199	426,841	2,405	239,246	27,496	16,404	430,202	1,257,793	116
2000–01	85,784	184,292	3,866	–	27,707	85	381,460	683,194	133
Decade 1991–2001									
Average	152,492	639,184	8,285	235,765	29,229	50,598	508,411	1,623,965	117
CV %	104	67	115	132	107	167	121	93	–
Share %	9.4	39.4	0.5	14.5	1.8	3.1	31.3	100.0	–

Note:
[a] Coefficients of variation (CV) across time and across the six sea ports or port groups.
Source: DGCIS, computed.

volume, also experiences least volatility. Calcutta–Haldia, followed by Madras, has the lowest record of export, which falls short of 0.1 million tonnes.

Data and theoretical framework

Trade liberalization is defined in a broad context of aligning domestic prices with international prices through both domestic and external sector reforms. The comparison is made between returns in the prevailing price situation under existing levels of controls and regulations on the one hand and the hypothetical situations where external market prices are realized for output and traded inputs on the other. The regional dimension emanates from the diversity in technology, yield rate, local factors and location in relation to relevant ports, all of which reflect on the domestic prices and the incidence of trade on prices.

Such a study has to be based on information on various aspects drawn from varied sources. While official publications from government or non-government departments such as the Department of Economics and Statistics (DES), Comprehensive Scheme for Studying the Cost of Cultivation of Principal Crops (COC) and Bulletin on Food Statistics (BFS) under the Ministry of Agriculture and the Fertilizer Association of India (FAI) and the Directorate General of Commercial Intelligence and Statistics (DGCIS) produce published data on crop, fertilizer and foreign trade statistics, there is no readily available published data on many other aspects, especially those related to internal trade. In the total absence of published and systematic records of private trade operations, this chapter relies to a large extent on information provided by the Government of India (GOI), which also operates in a dual-channel foodgrain market and a partially decontrolled fertilizer market. Discussions with officials of FAI, FCI and the Agricultural and Processed Food Export Development Authority (APEDA), and information supplied by these organizations, have proved crucial in this study.

The measure of returns depends on the definition of revenue and cost used in the calculation. The COC information is basically meant to calculate farm costs for all categories to arrive at a government minimum support price (Appendix 3) faced by the farmers on inputs supplied from own resources or purchased from market. To the extent that agriculture is viewed as a commercial enterprise comparable to other sectors such as industry, the returns per hectare could be measured as a profit, with farmers' own labour and resources included as cost at market prices. Essentially this corresponds with the use of a concept denoted 'C2' by

COC, in which all paid-out and imputed cost items are included. This, however, can generate negative returns in many cases, consistent with farmers' behaviour in a situation in which they cultivate small pieces of land using family labour and often try to extract the most from those inputs not purchased at market prices. Cost concept C2 therefore needs to be weighed against alternative concepts in which (1) farmers' family labour cost is not included (CL2), (2) rent on farmers' own land is not included (CR2) and (3) both cost of family labour and rent on owned land are not included (CP2). The use of any of these measures has some justification but may also be disputed. In the prevailing agrarian set-up, commercial profit is often not the motivation driving the farmer, who instead considers the income from family labour or own land incorporated in the returns earned. One basis for such supposition may be the possibility of insignificant or non-positive opportunity cost. While imperfections in the various markets, risk and food security concerns may render the prevailing system a way of life, the above argument cannot be defended in the presence of a rural labour market and particularly a land-lease market where the farmer can earn rent from leasing out land. Use of the alternative measures also makes certain comparisons difficult. For instance, the use of CR2 will make the returns from cultivation in any particular region sensitive to the prevailing land holding structure, an exogenous factor, and a region with greater incidence of landlessness or absentee landownership will record low returns relative to others on account of the higher rental element in cost. Similarly, use of CL2 will mean that a system employing relatively more hired labour will lose out in returns compared to others despite the fact that the landless farm labourers engaged in agriculture gain from employment. Mechanization will tend to reduce returns although the family labour has flexibility to pursue other activities. While the comparison is valid between individual households with different practices, from the standpoint of welfare at the regional level an asymmetry arises from the unequal treatment of rent or wage incomes earned from self-employment and hired-out factors and the returns based on C2 seem to offer a more reasonable and standardized measure for comparison. The concept is more appealing because the chapter seeks to emphasize the commercial prospects for agriculture opened up by trade liberalization. The relevance of the alternative concepts of cost for Indian farm households cannot, however, be underestimated and gains based on CR2, CL2 and CP2 are also calculated. The revenue is taken to be from the sale of the main product only.

For analytical convenience, cost is viewed in two broad groups, traded inputs and non-traded inputs. In the traded category, chemical fertilizer is considered in view of its policy importance in the period of liberaliza-tion. All the other inputs, which are mostly immobile or are exchanged in the local markets, are combined as a composite input. The component inputs are assumed to be minor by themselves, and the group as a whole is not supposed to be affected by trade regime changes directly. The returns or surplus (R) coming to a farmer is measured by the following equation:

$$R = PY - P_x X - P_z Z \tag{5.1}$$

where P and Y are producer price and yield rate of crop, X is a tradable input and Z is the composite non-tradable input, and the subscript denotes the input to which the price refers. The quantity variables are expressed on a per hectare basis and prices are in Rupees (Rs) per kilogram (kg). The equation can also be expressed in the following form:

$$R = PY (1 - p_x \alpha_x - p_z \alpha_z) \tag{5.2}$$

where p is input price relative to product price (relative price) and α is the ratio of input to output (input ratio). While the prevailing input ratio can be calculated readily from current-year data on input and output from COC, such a ratio may not be applicable for a future year. The COC published data are not updated regularly and does not cover the reference year 1998–99. An examination of the data behaviour, however, shows remarkable stability of the ratio α_x for fertilizer during the 1990s at the state level, suggesting the possibility of an approximation from the data. The input ratio is generally technological in character, and its stability largely reflects the technological and agro-climatic status of the state, but the ratio certainly varies across the states and might well vary over a longer stretch of time within a state.[7] The non-traded group is more problematic, since it is heterogeneous in nature and physical input ratios are not obtainable from COC data for most constituent items. In value terms, the ratio expressed by the product $p_z \alpha_z$ shows the same stability under cost concept C2. The approximation of the relation depicted by (5.2) for the reference year can be based on parameters a_x and r_z calculated, respectively, from the average of physical input ratio α_x for fertilizer and value ratio $p_z \alpha_z$ for the non-traded group, anchored on three most recent years for which data is reported, and the ratio is stable. The relation expressing returns approximated for the reference year is therefore:

$$R = PY (1 - p_x a_x - r_z) \tag{5.3}$$

where a_x and r_z are treated as parameters. Underlying (5.3) one can visualize an input–output relation characterizing the region's production practice:

$$X = a_x Y \qquad (5.4)$$

The existence of (5.4) presupposes that under given conditions the major input fertilizer is also the constrained input and it is the availability of fertilizer that helps in deciding yield level while all other inputs adjust. While fertilizer use is influenced by the changing price situation, the explanation for the stability of r_z can be based on the premises that the non-traded input ratios remain stable due to technological conditions and the prices of non-traded inputs simply adjust to output prices when trade brings changes.

The COC reported cost data come with incomplete coverage of states and uneven frequency but nevertheless provide a glimpse of the technology prevailing in the 1990s. Limited by this vital information source, seven states figuring as dominant rice producers are initially selected for study. These are Andhra Pradesh (AP), Haryana (HRY), Orissa (ORS), Punjab (PJB), Uttar Pradesh (UP), Madhya Pradesh (MP) and West Bengal (WB). The input ratio parameters are obtained by averaging over the years 1994–95, 1995–96 and 1996–97 except for UP and HRY, for which the anchor years are 1991, 1992 and 1996.[8]

In the prevailing scenario, domestic demand and supply factors combined with the government's regulatory regimes on both the domestic and external fronts determine the prices faced by farmers (farmgate prices). Farm harvest price is taken to reflect the free-market domestic price fetched in preference to the government administered procurement price. A case of trade liberalization can be considered coming through the price effects on the product and the traded input and reflecting on the relative prices, assuming that under a hypothetical free-trade regime the world market price would prevail. In the case of an exportable crop, the farmer's reference export price would be the FOB price at the port less handling and transport charges from the production centre concerned. This means that farmers in an interior state or a remote centre would find themselves at a disadvantage compared to those in a location near a port. The farmer would gain from the export only if the external price exceeded the prevailing domestic price fetched. For traded inputs, the farmer's price would analogously be the CIF import price at the port plus the handling and transport charges.

The above propositions emphasize the change in the relative price that trade liberalization can bring, but assumes that the crop yield rate is unaffected by the change. In reality, however, trade can impact on returns in at least three ways: (1) direct effect of product price change on revenue and thereby returns, (2) direct effect of a fall or rise in fertilizer price on cost and thereby returns and (3) indirect effect of a change in relative price of input on returns through a change in input use and thereby the yield rate.

The third effect can be captured through an estimated response function of fertilizer use. The COC data offer figures on input use and prices over a number of years in the 1990s between 1990–91 and 1997–98, and across major states that can be pooled for a regression analysis of the following equation showing region-specific effects:

$$X_{st} = b_0 + b_1 p_{xst} + b_2 D_s + b_3 t \tag{5.5}$$

where X is the use of tradable input per hectare, p is the relative price of the same input, D is a region dummy, s is state, t is year and b_i are parameters, of which b_1 is the response. The response parameter is then applied to adjust the given yield rates (Y) by a factor of the inverse of the input ratio parameter:

$$Y_{adj} = Y + \Delta Y \tag{5.6}$$
$$\text{where } \Delta Y = (1/a_x)\, b_1 \Delta p_x$$

The yield adjustment approximation is made subject to the supposition that non-traded inputs will adjust automatically, giving primacy to price changes of fertilizer. There are four estimates of returns per hectare (1) R1, reported yield rates valued at prevailing domestic prices, (2) R2 valued at external price of output and prevailing price of inputs and reported yield rates, (3) R3 valued at external prices of both output and tradable input and reported yield rate and finally (4) R4 valued at prices as in (3) but with yield rates adjusted to price regime. A comparison of free hypothetical trade returns R2, R3 and R4 with the restricted prevailing regime returns R1 indicates the possibility of benefit of trade reaching the farmers and its relative incidence on farmers in various locations, according to distance from port and agricultural prosperity.

In the absence of disaggregated and regionwide cost data on fertilizer trading, average figures of prices and cost provided by the FAI are used, along with regional weights in nutrient consumption to bring in a regional dimension. The non-traded inputs have been subject to far less policy changes, though prices of certain constituents such as irrigation are under review. These prices are assumed to adjust to product prices, so that p_z is considered as same as in the anchor triennium.[9]

The external product price differs from trading port to farmgate as the product goes through an extensive and complex marketing process tracing how hypothetical free-trade farmgate prices are calculated. Farm harvest prices (FHP) reported by the Ministry of Agriculture (MOA) as a time series at a regional level provide the prevailing domestic prices for the reference year. A comparison of the FHP with the external reference prices gives a measure of the protection received by farmers. Likewise, the prevailing and external prices of tradable input fertilizer for the year under consideration can be compared using FAI information.

Price calculations

Fertilizer import price

The farmgate price for imported fertilizer depends not only on the CIF prices and handling and transport charges but such policies as applicable concessions, duties and taxes. The problem is also compounded by lack of published data on costs such as port charges, transportation and handling costs. Even nutrient (N, P, K) data on imports are not reported by DGCIS. However, the FAI provides actual import prices of fertilizers – urea, DAP and MOP – and the average pool handling charges from port to hinterland, which include freight and handling (port and stevedoring). Taking actual consumption of nutrients (N, P, K) as weights, it is possible to arrive at external reference price of fertilizer nutrients in addition to those of disaggregated nutrients. The calculation at the national level is shown in Table 5.7. The varying consumption patterns across agriculturally diverse regions provide a regional dimension to the price through the weights generated. The state domestic and import prices, provided in Table 5A.2, are used in the main analysis.

The ratios of import price to domestic price at both farmgate levels and with consumption weights are taken to measure protection to farmers who are consumers of fertilizer and the values exceeding unity, even at the state levels, suggest that farmers indeed receive a share of protection from higher world prices.

Calculation of farmgate free-trade price of paddy

The hypothetical free-trade producer price, determined by the actual FOB price received by the exporter at the trading port, may be at variance

Table 5.7 Calculation of fertilizer import price (all-India)[a] and an estimate of protection, Rs per tonne, reference year is 1998–99

Fertilizer/nutrient				
Fertilizer[d]	Urea	DAP	MOP	
Import price (US$)	100	220	122	
Import price (Rs)	4224	9250	5132	
Farmgate import price (Rs)[b]	5316	10342	6224	
Domestic sale price (Rs)[c]	3660	8300	3700	
Nutrient	N	P	K	NPK
Import price (Rs)	11557	17961	10374	13031
Domestic price (Rs)[c]	7956	14930	6167	9522
Import price/domestic price[f]	1.45	1.20	1.68	1.37

Notes:
[a] Average exchange rate was Rs 42.07 (for US$).
[b] Farmgate price includes handling charge inclusive of freight at Rs 1,092. No import duty was levied in this year.
[c] Sale price is statutory maximum price of urea under RPS and uniform sale price of DAP and MOP fertilizers.
[d] Fertilizer prices are converted to nutrient prices (see Table 5A.3 for conversion).
[e] Domestic price is sale price which includes concessions (Rs 4,400 for DAP and Rs 3,000 for MOP).
[f] Import price divided by domestic price is a measure of protection to farmers.
For weights see Table 5A.1. The import price for the year is representative, the average of the triennium 1997–2000 being Rs 13.36, somewhat higher than Rs 13.03 for the year as above.
Source: Computation based on FAI data.

with the so-called 'international price' (Chand, 1999) measured by the world average price or the price obtained in a competing country. In fact, the FOB price also varies to an extent from port to port in the country (see Table 5.6) depending on various factors, including the transaction bargains between exporters from the port and the importing country or agency.

As there is considerable overlap among hinterlands, the exporter has to make a conscious choice among alternative ports and this depends not only on the distances to be traversed within and without the country but also the choices of the importers/shippers and the facilities of the ports. Thus there is no clear one-to-one match between the producing centre and the port pair. However, to get a regional picture of the price implications for farmers and the returns the port of reference is important.

This chapter deals with the issue in the following way. (1) For each state, a main market city/town is taken as a reference (hereafter called the 'producing centre'). (2) Trials are conducted for each centre with multiple ports (as in Table 5.5) and the producing centre–port duo which yields maximum returns is taken as the exporter's possible choice. (3) Due consideration is given to the FOB price at the port and other charges involved.

Since international prices are volatile and the rice marketing season is staggered beyond the agricultural year (April–March), the average FOB price of rice in Rupees over the two years 1998–99 and 1999–2000 is considered as the export price. The FOB price of rice in the non-basmati category is obtained from the value and quantity figures reported by DGCIS, by port and by year.

The marketing of rice can be partitioned into three parts: (a) farm to mill, (b) mill to outlet – that is, retailer/ration or fair price shops (FPS)/ portgate – and (c) portgate to ship, and the process is conducted either by private traders or the FCI (or other state agencies) or both. FCI operation has its frequently criticized inefficiencies and obvious economies of scale but much of the former, including large administrative charges and losses in transit, could be avoided if the FCI were to operate in a more competitive setting. While the FCI records and reports cost figures in a systematic way, the private channel is much more heterogeneous, with differing cost structures which are not reported and/or revealed on grounds of competitive advantage. Also the private channel has proved to be 'uncompetitive' of late, with the FCI being the sole supplier to the exporter at the portgate, although the validity of this advantage can no doubt be questioned in a policy environment still partial to the public sector.

Based on the availability and reliability of information, the cost incurred in the farm to mill leg of the journey is taken from FCI sources. These are average figures of relevant items of cost theoretically approximating the cost if FCI were to compete freely in the market with its scale economies and suitable efficiency measures. The procured grain is also custom milled (paddy to rice) at given rates, which are also applicable to the private channel. The other component of FCI cost, involving the huge distribution network, is not relevant in this context. In the mill to port journey gunny (jute) bag cost as reported by the FCI and transport cost from producing centre to the port is included, with the latter derived from average railway freight rates of the regions reported by Indian Railways. This is the less expensive of the two alternatives (railway and roads), and although private traders resort to roads more often this is only in an uncompetitive market. Finally the exporter may incur some cost too, and allow a small margin of around 3 per cent–5 per cent as reported by sources. The processing requirements usually depend on importers' demands. On average, the port charge is about Rs 30.

Table 5.8 and the associated notes show the cost figures used, the reference ports and producing centres and the calculation procedure of the farmgate export price. The ratio of farm harvest price to the FOB price is less than unity in all cases except West Bengal and Haryana, where some protection is indicated and the exportable hypothesis itself does not hold.

Gains at external prices

Supporting numerous studies that noted India's advantage in exporting rice, actual experience in the 1990s found improvement in India's position when trade liberalization and domestic decontrols began to open up the market. The development, however, occurred in a market still distorted by controls and the FCI's dominance. This chapter examines if the actual producers could benefit from exports while the market opens up, given the heterogeneous conditions in which they operated in the reference period. This is done by evaluating returns at prevailing domestic and external reference prices for the reference year and comparing them. The gains come from liberalizations in both output and input markets.

As a starting point, the regional picture in the base scenario of prevailing prices (R1) is considered. Of the seven states under consideration Haryana and West Bengal are the only two where export prices work out as lower than domestic prices a degree of positive protection indicating. Further probes reveal that both states report[10] excessively high farm harvest price (FHP) relative to others, and for West Bengal the input parameters are also high, leading to negative returns at cost C2 in both prevailing and free-trade scenarios (see Table 5.8). These findings suggest that Haryana and West Bengal, though large producers, cannot be considered as exporters of rice. Table 5.9 presents the returns per hectare of the other states, valued at prevailing and external reference prices for different trade regimes. The largest returns, at Rs 3500 per hectare, are reaped by the northern state Punjab, followed by Uttar Pradesh with a moderate return of Rs 925. Andhra Pradesh, Orissa and Madhya Pradesh show lower positive profits. The spatial variation of returns is large given by the CV of 150 per cent.

In the second case, free trade in output markets obviously improves returns (R2) so long as the farmers can get higher prices than possible under controlled conditions. Calculations done in Table 5.8 suggest that FOB prices at relevant ports, adjusted for processing, handling and transport costs still turn out higher than the regional farm harvest prices

Table 5.8 Calculation of farmgate export price and an estimate of protection of rice, reference year is 1998–99

States	Reference producing centre	Reference port	FOB price port[d]	Cost farm to mill[a]	Cost mill to port[b]	Cost port[c]	Cost total	Farmgate export price[f]	Prevailing FH price[e]	Prevailing/ export farmgate
1	2	3	4	5	6	7	8	9	10	11
UP	Lucknow	Kandla	1,147.30	174.57	101.53	77.55	353.65	793.65	645.00	0.81
HR	Karnal	Kandla	1,147.30	174.57	94.89	87.00	356.45	790.85	841.00	1.06
PJB	Amritsar	Kandla	1,147.30	174.57	99.32	81.34	355.23	792.07	723.00	0.91
AP	Vijayawada	Madras	1,275.34	174.57	54.82	79.27	308.66	966.69	726.00	0.75
MP	Raipur	Bombay	1,170.32	174.57	72.74	78.37	325.67	844.65	690.00	0.82
WB	Calcutta	Madras	1,275.34	174.57	112.80	93.42	380.79	894.56	951.00	1.06
ORS	Cuttack	Vishakhapattanam	1,054.40	174.57	58.12	74.11	306.80	747.61	619.50	0.83

Notes:
[a] Cost farm to mill = mandi (market) charges, purchase tax, custody and maintenance (fumigation, storage, etc.), mandi labour, drying, internal movement, interest charge and bank guarantee, milling.
[b] Cost mill to port = gunny (jute) bag + transport. Transport = distance × average railway freight rate of region (north, east, west, south).
[c] Cost port = port charge + processing and margin (5%).
[d] FOB price port = unit value of export of non-basmati rice at given port (average of 1998–2000).
[e] Farm harvest price/FOB price (farmgate level) gives the measure of (dis)protection to farmer. Definitions of cost/price (Rs per 100 kg).
[f] Farmgate export price = FOB price port − cost total.
UP = Uttar Pradesh; HR = Haryana; PJB = Punjab; AP = Andhra Pradesh; MP = Madhya Pradesh; WB = West Bengal.

Source: Computed from DGCIS, FCI, Indian Railways, APEDA, and mapsofindia.com.

Table 5.9 Returns from paddy cultivation valued at prevailing and external prices (Rs/hectare), reference year is 1998–99

State	Prevailing prices of output and input (R1)	External output price and prevailing input price (R2)	External output and tradable input price yield unadjusted (R3)	External output and tradable External input price yield adjusted (R4)
AP	195	766	220	218
ORS	203	321	176	124
PJB	3575	4071	3468	3120
UP	925	1315	1020	906
MP	53	155	24	20
CV	150	121	147	148

Note:
AP = Andhra Pradesh; ORS = Orissa; PJB = Punjab; UP = Uttar Pradesh; MP = Madhya Pradesh.

in all states except Haryana and West Bengal. The other states, especially Andhra Pradesh and Uttar Pradesh would gain from export.

A simultaneous freeing of trade in input fertilizer displays a different picture. Table 5.7 shows that there is an element of protection to farmers[11] and exposing them to free-trade prices raises input costs, bringing down returns (R3) significantly in all states as compared to the free trade in output-only situation. However, the relevant comparison is with the prevailing situation and on this count two states, Andhra Pradesh and Uttar Pradesh make some gains while others lose.

If the impact of price changes on yield rates via input use is also taken into account, the result could be further modified. Based on the esti-mated regression equation (Table 5A.4) which incorporates a trend and region-specific effects, a yield adjustment can be approximated following (5.5), given the change in relative price from prevailing to free-trade regimes and input coefficients as in Table 5A.3. Since the protection from fertilizer pricing outweighs the disprotection from product pricing, the relative price becomes adverse, leading to lower input use, which translates into a fall in yield rates. Taking yield rate adjustment into account, free trade in output and input brings additional gains only to Andhra Pradesh. The modest returns of Madhya Pradesh and Orissa are further truncated. The situation in Uttar Pradesh is not altered greatly and even Punjab sheds returns, revealing its true high-cost structure and dependence on imported inputs. Relative gains in the states from free output trade vary in extent from 13 per cent in Punjab to nearly 300 per cent in Andhra Pradesh, while the gains from free trade in input (with yield adjustment) vary from –63 per cent in Madhya Pradesh to +12 per cent in Andhra Pradesh. The agriculturally lagging states, Madhya Pradesh and Orissa, gain more in percentage terms due to opening of product markets but also lose more from the opening of input market relative to Punjab and Uttar Pradesh. The relative gains in per hectare terms is in reverse order, as portrayed by Figures 5.3 and 5.4, with Andhra Pradesh as the largest gainer from free trade in output and also the smallest

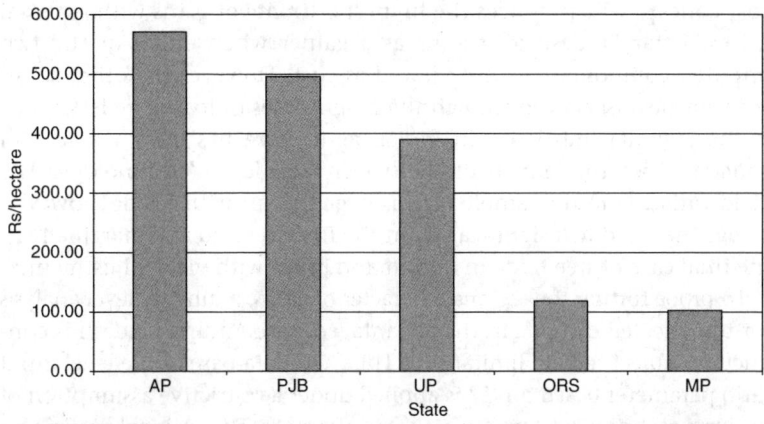

Figure 5.3 Gains from free trade in output, R2 – R1
Notes:
AP = Andhra Pradesh; PJB = Punjab; UP = Uttar Pradesh; ORS = Orissa; MP = Madhya Pradesh.

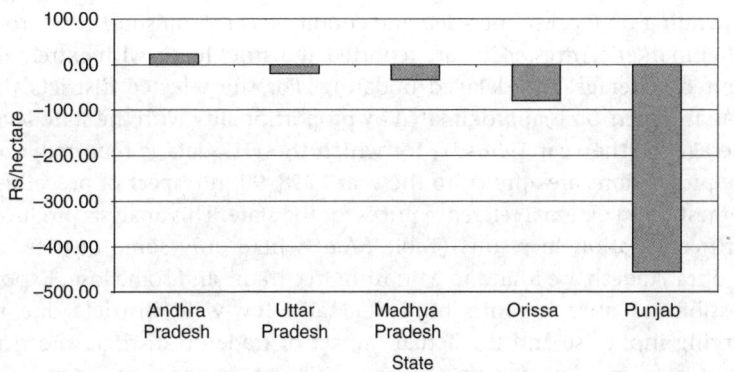

Figure 5.4 Gains from free trade in output and input with yield adjustment, R4 – R1

loser from the input and output market reforms and Punjab as the largest loser from the latter. When alternative cost concepts are considered, the returns from each situation improves, because they incorporate the returns from either or both of the owned inputs. Using similar methodology as the above exercise, these concepts have somewhat differing implications on the relative gains from opening up, as seen in Table 5A.5 reporting the calculated gains. With income from family labour excluded from cost (CL2) the gains for Andhra Pradesh improve and further when rent from own land is also excluded (CR2) so that using cost concept CP2 produces the highest estimate of gains with external prices. Uttar Pradesh also joins as a gainer when either of the two imputed components is not viewed as cost. However the other states continue as losers even though the magnitudes of losses are less.

The regional imbalance in Indian agriculture has been a matter of concern since the launch of the 'Green Revolution' technology. The yield variation in the sample (CV) is large to start with. Trade, however, brings the CV down significantly in the first scenario and marginally in the final case of free trade in output and input with yield adjustment.

To probe further the regional character of gains, a substate-level analysis for ten selected districts in the advantaged state Andhra Pradesh is conducted, subject to data limitations. The COC data-based state-level input ratio parameter based on C2 is applied under a restrictive assumption of uniform technological practices within the state. The regional dimension is captured through three aspects. First, the yield level varies within a state (DES district-level data). The selected districts fall into high-yield rate and low-yield rate categories. Second, fertilizer prices vary through the weights on nutrient use in the differing soil conditions. Third, farmers receive output prices that can be more or less than the state average, depending on local supply–demand conditions and transport costs from other market centres. FHPs, are reported at district levels with extremely limited coverage and delayed updating. For the selected districts the spatial dispersion is approximated by proportionality with the state-level average for the year 1996–97, for which the FHP data is reported, and the proportions are applied to the year 1998–99 in respect of prevailing domestic and external reference prices for the state. This analysis produces further variation in results (Table 5A.6) where only some districts of Andhra Pradesh are found to gain from free trade, and some lose. Export possibilities arise in both high-yield and low-yield districts due to varying input use and the actual impact of trade on districts showing negative gains depends on the elasticities of demand and supply in various districts.

Conclusions

Agricultural development in India is accorded high priority on account of its contribution to national income and its linkage to other sectors. A high rate of agricultural growth was considered to be a precondition for faster employment growth (GOI, 1979) and a regionally disaggregated strategy of agricultural growth was seen as a way to higher employment outcomes as compared to regionally concentrated performance. Rice is the leading product in and across Indian agriculture, covering a large section of poor growers. The presence of comparative advantage in rice, as demonstrated by various studies and the existence of demand in the global market, raises the prospect of rice export, which was amply utilized by the Government of India in the 1990s through its FCI executed price policy with a longer-term aim as an exporter. Such comparative advantage-based exports might imply a frontal attack on rural poverty. This possibility is explored in this chapter with a regional perspective, recognizing that free trade would call for reforms in both external and domestic sectors and opening up both output and input markets.

The study finds that some unequal gain could come from free trade in output markets possibly coming from regional resource advantages specific to rice. Farmers in Andhra Pradesh, Punjab, Uttar Pradesh, Orissa and Madhya Pradesh faced higher export price possibilities than they got in the prevailing regime of controls and would possibly turn out as exporters if the market were fully decontrolled in reference period conditions. However, when the farmer is also exposed to the free market in tradable input this commercial gain is eliminated in all except in one of the seven states considered. If non-paid-out costs of family labour and own land are not viewed as cost, Uttar Pradesh, too, could gain. The tradable and technology-based input fertilizer is not only more expensive to the farmer under free trade than under prevailing situation of government protection, its significance in changing the quality of the immobile resource, land, can take its toll.

Consequently, farmers in most parts of the country are unlikely to gain from rice export in the absence of state protection and the impact on rice exports may not mean much for poverty alleviation. The substate studies expose some heterogeneity of prospects. The analysis highlights the technology factor in competitiveness even in agriculture in a less developed country. When free internal grain movements are taken into account, there may, however, be a price rise in some of the non-exporting states or even districts of a state induced by deficiency (these areas would have to compete with the foreign market) rather than market expansion[12] that may cause political and economic concern and possibly induce rice cultivation in less suitable areas. However, the results of this study show that such a possibility becomes minimal when output and input markets open up. The exportability also needs to take account of other resource costs such as water, required for other crops and purposes and turning scarce in some regions or a conduit to land degradation in others, not considered here. The government would have to continue transfer and public distribution of grains in areas of higher prices for the benefit of the poor.

The present FCI operations leading to a longer-term export policy should be transparent so as not to distort signals and misguide the beneficiary farmers in the longer run. The government can do better incentivizing the farmers to explore other exportable crops, other forms of fertilizers, investing in food security stocks and above all promoting non-crop-based activities in rice-dominated areas which can also structurally improve the profitability of rice.

Appendix 1   Food Corporation of India and Phases of Rice Marketing

Food Corporation of India and private trade

The FCI was established in 1965 under the Food Corporation Act 1964 as a countervailing force to the speculative activities of the private trader and to execute the government's price policy. The large overheads, outdated methods, inadequate storage space and inefficient supervision of the FCI are drawbacks often blamed for mounting subsidies and poor-quality grains. On the defence side, the FCI encountered increasing burdens after the 1970s when favourable weather conditions, a largely open-ended procurement system and frequent rises in support prices built up the FCI's stocks to inordinate levels relative to the desired norms. The FCI also conducts the vital function of food distribution.

The FCI's existence is a politically and economically sensitive issue, and debates hover around the role the FCI might play in the future – whether as a price stabilizing force or a support against distress sales or a guide to resource allocation in agriculture or simply a competing trader in the food grain market.

Rice marketing

Farm to mill

Market arrivals of paddy are staggered over a large part of the year and the paddy is brought to market by bullock carts, though operations and transportation are more mechanized in Punjab and Haryana. The wholesale (state-owned) market is commonly called the *mandi*, set up under the Agricultural Produce Markets Act 1960, managed by a representative committee. The markets often suffer from congestion, lack of electricity, leaky roofs and unpaved roads. Grain brought in bulk is unloaded, visually inspected and auctioned off mostly to private traders but partly to the FCI and other state agents who pay a pre-announced price. The collected grain is transported to the mill.

Mill to port

From the mill the private-channel grain reaches the exporter or the consumer via the wholesale and/or retail markets. The FCI rice is packed in jute bags and transported across the country and distributed through the vast network of privately owned but regulated 'fair price shops' at uniform prices or via employment and poverty-linked programmes. Alternatively, the FCI sells to the exporter and delivers the grain at the portgate. While FCI is able to use cheaper railway wagons for transportation except in hilly areas, the private trader relies more on hired trucks.

Port to ship

The grain is delivered to the exporters comprising either private traders or state trading enterprises at the portgate, and is sometimes subjected to more processing according to importer specifications, especially to bring down the share of broken grains.

Appendix 2   The Retention Price and Subsidy Scheme (RPS) and the Expenditure Reforms Commission (ERC)

The RPS was first adopted in November 1977 for urea, following the suggestions of the High Power Fertilizer Pricing (Marathe) Committee. It aimed to make fertilizer available to farmers at favourable prices on the one hand and to provide adequate incentives to the domestic fertilizer industry on the other. The RPS, later extended to other categories of fertilizer, assures a retention price to the producer to cover their normative cost[13] and at the same time notifies a statutory sale price or farmgate price uniformly throughout the country. The difference, adjusted for freight rate and dealer's margin, is paid as subsidy. With this policy, fertilizer use improved and import dependence in nitrogenous fertilizer (N) and phosphatic fertilizer (P) came down.[14] With a changing economic order, the ERC (set up in 2000) advised a gradual transition to prepare the fertilizer sector to face world market competition by 2006. The RPS is giving way to a group-based concession scheme where the groups are formed on the basis of fuel use and other factors and the existing concessions are to be reduced with time. The farmgate price of urea is to increase 7 per cent per annum, the fuel choice to change towards gas or fuel oil/LNG and distribution to be decontrolled. The ERC also suggests a dual pricing policy to protect the small farmers. The recommendations have been debated and sometimes resisted on both farmer and industry sides.

Appendix 3   Cost of Cultivation Data in India

The 'Comprehensive Scheme for Studying the Cost of Cultivation of Principal Crops in India' (COC) is implemented by the MOA with the basic aim of facilitating the formulation of the government's agricultural price policy. The latest issue, brought out in February 2000, covers the years 1990–91 through 1997–98, though not uniformly. The scheme presents a number of concepts of cost – A1, A2, C2, C2* and C3. The concepts considered for a study would primarily depend on its purpose (Rajaraman and Ghosh, 2002).

Table 5A.1 Cost of cultivation of rice per hectare

State	Years	Value of main product (Rs)	Yield (100kg/hect.)	Cost of family labour (Rs)	Rent on own land (Rs)	Cost C2 (Rs)	Cost CR2 (Rs)	Cost CL2 (Rs)	Cost CP2 (Rs)
AP	1996	20166	47.04	2492	6507	20937	14430	18445	11938
AP	Average	18539	46.63	2049	5893	18874	12982	16826	10933
HRY	1996	19873	43.44	2828	5779	18622	12843	15794	10015
HRY	Average	17987	40.69	1772	3572	13306	9734	11533	7961
ORS	1996	9738	24.18	1905	2623	10310	7687	8405	5782
ORS	Average	9939	27.56	1657	2499	9823	7324	8166	5667
PJB	1996	20961	51.64	1102	5948	17967	12019	16865	10917
PJB	Average	19054	49.84	1216	5218	16247	11029	15031	9813
UP	1996	13557	34.02	2244	3075	11301	8225	9057	5981
UP	Average	9937	30.87	1543	2140	9081	6941	7538	5398
WB	1996	15897	37.20	3091	4583	16930	12347	13839	9256
WB	Average	13387	33.02	2511	3967	13963	9996	11453	7485
MP	1996	9936	22.61	1649	2816	9989	7173	8340	5524
MP	Average	8773	22.01	1321	2478	8742	6264	7421	4943

Note:
Cost CR2 = C2 less rent on owned land; CL2 = C2 less cost of family labour; CP2 = C2 − CR2 − CL2.
AP = Andhra Pradesh; HRY = Haryana; ORS = Orissa; PJB = Punjab; UP = Uttar Pradesh; WB = West Bengal; MP = Madhya Pradesh.

Table 5A.2 Fertilizer nutrient consumption and prices, by states

| State | Consumption of fertilizer nutrients (000 tonnes) | | | | Farmgate price NPK (Rs/tonne) | | Import price/domestic price [b] |
	N	P	K	NPK	Import [a]	Domestic	NPK
AP	1,284.26	560.47	163.19	2,007.92	13,248.47	9,757.57	1.36
UP	2,447.87	557.57	86.09	3,091.53	12,679.11	9,164.38	1.38
MP	738.16	448.37	39.21	1,225.74	13,861.77	10,450.15	1.33
HRY	662.67	171.77	3.95	838.39	12,863.54	9,376.83	1.37
PJB	1,081.06	275.47	18.74	1,375.27	12,823.68	9,328.95	1.37
WB	579.69	305.77	192.48	1,077.94	13,162.42	9,615.04	1.37
ORS	194.58	60.38	44.21	299.17	12,674.75	9,099.46	1.39
India	11,353.78	4,112.15	1,331.53	16,797.46	13,031.04	9,521.82	1.37

Notes:
[a] Import price includes average CIF price and handling charges.
[b] Import price/domestic price is presented as a measure of protection to farmers.
AP = Andhra Pradesh; UP = Uttar Pradesh; MP = Madhya Pradesh; HRY = Haryana; PJB = Punjab; WB = West Bengal; ORS = Orissa.
Source: FAI, Table 7.

Table 5A.3 Parameters underlying calculation of returns

State	Input coefficient (fertilizer) a_x [a]	Input coefficient (others) $p_z a_z$ [b]	Fertilizer price domestic (Rs/kg)	Fertilizer price imported (Rs/kg)	Paddy price[c] domestic (Rs/kg)	Paddy price export (Rs/kg)	Paddy yield (kg/hect.)
AP	0.0379	0.9138	9.76	13.25	4.84	6.44	4,128
HRY	0.0437	0.6591	9.38	12.86	5.60	5.27	3,359
ORS	0.0223	0.9239	9.10	12.68	4.13	4.98	1,818
PJB	0.0365	0.7724	9.33	12.82	4.82	5.28	4,728
UP	0.0288	0.8646	9.16	12.68	4.30	5.29	2,904
WB	0.0209	0.9848	9.62	13.16	6.34	5.96	3,383
MP	0.0278	0.9286	10.45	13.86	4.60	5.63	1,386

Notes:
[a] a_x = input coefficient of traded input.
[b] $p_z a_z$ = input coefficient of non-traded input (value terms).
[c] Prices are farmgate level.
AP = Andhra Pradesh; HRY = Haryana; ORS = Orissa; PJB = Punjab; UP = Uttar Pradesh; WB = West Bengal; MP = Madhya Pradesh.

Table 5A.4 Estimated regression equation for fertilizer use, for yield adjustment[a]

Dependent variable = FRT

Variables	Constant	Time	P-f	R^2	N.
Parameter	116.75	3.76	−35.25	0.72	36
	$(2.73)^b$	(1.42)	(1.80)		
Shifts					
East	28.11				
	(1.35)				
South	137.31				
	(5.79)				
North	105.54				
	(6.69)				

Notes:
[a] Estimated linear regression equation.
[b] Figures in parentheses are t-statistics (Data: COC).

Table 5A.5 Gains in returns at external prices from paddy cultivation estimated with alternative cost concepts, gains in Rs/hectare

State	Cost CP2	Cost CL2	Cost CR2	Cost C2
AP	2754	725	2052	23
HRY	−3202	−2252	−2731	−1780
ORS	−553	−268	−364	−79
PJB	−567	−477	−546	−456
UP	403	157	226	−19
WB	−4040	−1598	−2497	−55
MP	−2	−22	−13	−33

Notes:
Cost CR2 = C2 less rent on owned land; CL2 = C2 less cost of family labour; CP2 = C2 − CR2 −CL2.
AP = Andhra Pradesh; HRY = Haryana; ORS = Orissa; PJB = Punjab; UP = Uttar Pradesh; WB = West Bengal; MP = Madhya Pradesh.

Table 5A.6 Gains in returns at external prices from paddy cultivation: districts of Andhra Pradesh

Yield category	District	Yield rate 100 kg/hectare	Share in area (%)	R2 – R1 Rs/hectare	R4 – R1 Rs/hectare
High-yield	West Godavari	5,055	10.57	637.631	–16.1668
High-yield	Karimnagar	4,859	5.98	652.486	7.67603
High-yield	Guntur	4,818	7.59	699.318	77.3473
High-yield	Prakasam	4,817	3.38	689.615	68.1984
High-yield	Krishna	4,656	9.62	590.737	–9.34029
Low-yield	Medak	3,705	2.85	473.461	–17.0329
Low-yield	Vizianagaram	3,513	3.16	475.762	18.6099
Low-yield	Srikakulam	3,023	4.55	387.153	–1.97703
Low-yield	Mahbubnagar	2,982	3.40	400.398	10.628
Low-yield	Visakhapatnam	2,076	2.75	275.441	1.54937

Notes

1. India's comparative advantage in basmati rice is well documented. This variety constitutes only 1 per cent of total rice produced in the country and grows only in limited areas in northwest India.
2. The ratio of the 1998–99 price level to the average price level of 1991–92 to 1998–99 is 0.93 with respect to fertilizer (NPK) price. The corresponding ratio exceeds 1.20 for the unit value of rice exports and also the nominal exchange rate (Rs/US dollars).
3. The nominal protection coefficient (NPC) is defined as the ratio of domestic price to border price, where border or reference price is adjusted for relevant transport and handling charges.
4. This has somehow moved the power of pricing more to the oil companies under the public sector (*Fertilizer News*).
5. The discovery of gas reserves in India by a private company now brings new promises of self-sufficiency to the fertilizer industry which is in any case moving towards gas as a feedstock.
6. Part of the rice trade is also conducted via the land port of Petrapol in West Bengal since India's close neighbour Bangladesh has appeared as a major importer in recent years. Sourcing has, however, not often been from the state due to restrictions on movement (source data is not available). The trade is affected by economic as well as non-economic considerations of bilateral relations.
7. The relation between input and yield can be captured by an overall production function requiring adequate data. The COC data as published give narrow coverage of inputs and a relatively small sample for estimation of a reliable yield function.
8. For Uttar Pradesh, this is the last triennium reported by COC whereas for Haryana the coefficient of fertilizer use for the year 1994–95 turns out

inordinately high relative to other years. In all cases, the coefficients show stability over the years in the 1990s.

9. Some of the prices have in fact been rather rigid and with further decontrol and greater market orientations, the present prices of non-traded inputs may even over adjust so that the free-trade relative price of non-traded input is likely to increase, implying a negative effect on returns.

10. The FHP reported by MOA is inordinately high for Haryana. The price used in this study is therefore projected on the basis of COC-reported post-harvest price for 1997–98 using the growth in wholesale price of paddy in the state during the period 1997–98 to 1998–99, also reported by COC. Even this modified price is high and indicates protection. Cultivation of basmati variety in Haryana is also a possible source of inconsistency.

11. The RPS also confers a protection to the domestic fertilizer industry so that the producer price in domestic market is actually higher than the import price, which is itself found to be higher than what the farmer pays.

12. States are often categorized as 'surplus' or 'deficit' in terms of their normative grain needs and a reasonable level of price, and identified by movements in the public sector channel. Among the seven dominant rice-producing states examined, public procurements fall short of distributions in the eastern states Orissa and West Bengal, the largest producer.

13. This is cost plus a 12 per cent post-tax return at an output level of 85–90 per cent of rated capacity.

14. Potassic fertilizers (K) are imported, as domestic production is not commercially viable on account of lack of raw materials and low demand. Though urea manufacture relies on indigenous naptha and fuel oil, these products being essentially petro-products, imports are still important. Rock phosphate for P is a domestically scarce resource.

References

Becker, C. M., A. Mitra and E. Balseca (2002) *Competitive Cities*, Background Study for the Inter American Development Bank.

Bhagwati, J. N., A. Panagariya and T. N. Srinivasan (1998) *Lectures on International Trade*, London: MIT Press.

Chand, R. (1999) 'Liberalisation of Agricultural Trade and Social Welfare', *Economic and Political Weekly*, 25 December.

Datta, S. K. (1997) 'Why Does India Need a Total Perspective on Rice Exports?', in B. M. Desai (ed.), *Agricultural Development Paradigm for Ninth Plan under New Economic Environment*, New Delhi: Oxford University Press and IBH Publishing Co.

Fertilizer Association of India (FAI). (various years) *Fertilizer Statistics*, New Delhi. *Fertilizer News* (various years).

Food and Agricultural Organisation (FAO) (1998) *Trade Yearbook*, Geneva: FAO.

Food Corporation of India (FCI) (various years), *Annual Report*.

Ghosh, N. (2002) 'Infrastruture, Cost and Labour Income in Agriculture', *Indian Journal of Agricultural Economics*, 57(2), 153–68.

Government of India (GOI) (1979) *Studies on the Structure of Indian Economy and Planning for Development*, Delhi: Planning Commission PPD.

———— (1998–99) *Indian Railways Year Book*. New Delhi: Indian Railways.

————— (2000) *Comprehensive Scheme for Studying the Cost of Cultivation of Principle Crops in India.* New Delhi: Department of Agriculture and Cooperation, Ministry of Agriculture.

————— (2002) *Economic Survey 2001–2002,* New Delhi.

————— (various) *Agricultural Statistics at a Glance.* New Delhi: Department of Economics and Statistics, Ministry of Agriculture.

————— (various) *Bulletin on Food Statistics.* New Delhi: Department of Economics and Statistics. Ministry of Agriculture.

————— (various) *Farm Harvest Prices.* New Delhi: Department of Economics and Statistics. Ministry of Agriculture.

————— (various) *Foreign Trade Statistics of India.* Kolkata: Directorate General of Commercial Intelligence and Statistics.

————— (various) *Reports of the Commission for Agricultural Costs and Prices.* New Delhi: Department of Agriculture and Cooperation, Ministry of Agriculture.

————— (various) *Agricultural Situation in India.* New Delhi: Department of Economics and Statistics, Ministry of Agriculture.

Gulati, A. (1989) 'Input Subsidies in Indian Agriculture', *Economic and Political Weekly,* 24 June.

Gulati, A. and S. Narayanan (2000) 'Demystifying Fertilizer and Power Subsidies in India', *Economic and Political Weekly,* 4 March.

Gulati, A., P. Sharma and S. Kahkonen (1996) *The Food Corporation of India: Successes and Failures in Indian Foodgrain Marketing,* IRIS Working Paper 18, Center for Institutional Reform and Informal Sector, University of Maryland, College Park.

Gulati, A., A. Sharma, K. Sharma, S. Das and V. Chhabra (1994) *Export Competitiveness of Selected Agricultural Commodities.* New Delhi: National Council of Applied Economic Research

Krishna, R. (1963) 'Farm Supply Response in India–Pakistan: A Case Study of Punjab Region', *Economic Journal,* 73.

Kumar, P. (1997) *Farm Size and Marketing Efficiency in Agriculture – An Analysis of Selected Markets and Crops in Haryana,* PhD thesis, New Delhi: JNU.

Mellor, J. W. and R. Ahmed (1988) *Agricultural Price Policy for Developing Countries,* New Delhi: Oxford University Press.

Nouroz, H. (2001) *Protection in Indian Manufacturing.* London: Macmillan/Palgrave.

Rajaraman, I. and N. Ghosh (2002). 'Revenue Estimates for a Crop Specific Agricultural Tax'. *Economic and Political Weekly,* 30 March.

Rao, C. H. H. (2001) 'WTO and Viability of Indian Agriculture', *Economic and Political Weekly,* 8 September.

Schultz, T. W. (1964) *Transforming Traditional Agriculture,* London: Yale University Press.

Sharma, A., N. Ghosh and P. Kumar (2001) *A Policy Model for Open Market Operations of Wheat in India,* New Delhi: National Council of Applied Economic Research.

Sidhu, D. S. (1998) *Marketing of Rice and Wheat in India,* Background Working Paper, Washington, DC: World Bank, mimeo.

Tyagi, D. S. (1990) *Managing India's Food Economy,* New Delhi: Sage.

Vyas, V. S. (2001) 'Agriculture: Second Round of Economic Reforms', *EPW* 36(10).

Weigend, G. (1958) 'Some Elements in the Study of Port Geography', *Geographical Review,* 48(2): 185–200.

World Bank (1999) *India Foodgrain Marketing Policies: Reforming to Meet Food Security Needs,* Rural Development Sector Unit, South Asia Region, Washington, DC World Bank.

6

The Value of Agricultural Tariff Rate Quotas to Developing Countries

Cathie Laroche Dupraz and Alan Matthews

Introduction

The use of tariff rate quotas (TRQs) was legitimized as a market-access instrument in the Uruguay Round Agreement on Agriculture (AoA). TRQs are defined by three characteristics: the quota volume, the in-quota tariff and the over-quota tariff (which is the MFN tariff). Only one of these characteristics is binding at any one time. The motivation behind this instrument was to guarantee minimum levels of market access and to safeguard current levels of access in the face of the high MFN tariffs resulting from tariffication; 1371 TRQs were notified by 37 countries to the WTO as a result of the Uruguay Round (G/AG/NG/5/7).[1]

However, various problems have been identified in the implementation of TRQs (de Gorter and Sheldon, 2000; Skully, 2001). A majority of TRQs are not being filled and thus minimum access commitments are not being met (G/AG/NG/5/7). While there may be market explanations for this lack of demand, quota underfill may be attributable to the administrative methods employed to implement TRQs. TRQs also generate rents, and the allocation procedures to distribute those rents distort trade and can be subject to political influence (Abbott and Morse, 1999; Abbott, 2002). Thus, whether and in what ways TRQ access should be extended is a subject of some interest in the Doha negotiations on further agricultural trade liberalization (Matthews and Laroche Dupraz, 2001).

A number of countries made proposals to improve the administration and size of TRQs in the Special Session on Agriculture at the start of the Doha negotiations. Exporting countries called for increases in TRQs to improve market-access opportunities. The United States, for example, proposed that these should be substantially increased by annual increments over a fixed period and their functioning improved, including dealing with unfilled quotas. For this purpose, it proposed to base the reduction of in-quota duties on the historical performance of TRQ fill rates: the lower the fill rate, the deeper the duty cut. An automatic trigger mechanism was suggested to reduce in-quota duties in response to falling fill rates (G/AG/NG/W/58). The Cairns Group also called for substantial increases in all tariff quota volumes (G/AG/NG/W/54). Canada proposed that, where tariff peaks remain after a further round of MFN tariff reductions, new TRQs could be opened in order to guarantee a minimum level of market access (G/AG/NG/W/12). The European Union was noticeably silent on the issue of increasing TRQs, but did propose rules and disciplines to increase the transparency, the reliability and the security of TRQ management in order to ensure that the concessions already granted were fully realized (G/AG/NG/W/90).

Developing countries also called for a substantial increase in TRQs and for the simplification of their administration. One group of developing countries wanted arrangements to ensure that new suppliers from developing countries had equal access to allotments within TRQs and called for the mandatory filling of quotas, in developed countries, before imports took place at the above-quota level (G/AG/NG/W/37). India called for the stricter application of the MFN principle in allocating TRQs but with special preference being given to developing countries having less than US$1,000 *per capita* income (G/AG/NG/W/102). Nigeria called for tariff quotas to be made global, and that where bilateral quotas existed, global quotas should be in addition to these bilateral quotas and allocated to countries that were not covered by them (G/AG/NG/W/130). The Small Island Developing States (SIDS) proposed that certain percentage increases in minimum access TRQs should be allocated at a zero in-quota tariff to SIDS. They also proposed that specific duty-free TRQs outside minimum access quotas should be provided to SIDS (G/AG/NG/W/97). Mauritius, as a significant TRQ beneficiary, was concerned to maintain the value of trade preferences and wished to maintain a meaningful difference between in-quota and over-quota tariffs (G/AG/NG/W/96).

A number of previous papers set out to estimate the value of improved TRQ access, focusing in particular on whether the TRQ volume, the in-quota tariff rate or the over-quota tariff is the binding constraint on improved access (Elbehri *et al.*, 1999; OECD, 2002). This chapter differs from those earlier papers in two main ways. First, we have a specific focus on the value of TRQ access to developing countries, whether under global or bilateral quotas. As a preliminary and necessary step to understanding the implications of increasing TRQs, we ask how developing countries have benefited from existing TRQs, using the EU market as a case study. Second, we estimate the value of current TRQ access to developing countries in the EU market at the tariff-line level, using a graphical, partial equilibrium, approach. The previous modelling approaches adopted a high level of commodity aggregation, which led to difficulty in implementing TRQs, which are usually applied at the detailed tariff-line level. The drawback of our approach is that it does not take into account behavioural responses and the possibility of regime switching as prices and quantities change.[2] The advantage, however, is that operating at the tariff-line level allows us to retain the maximum amount of disaggregation in the data.

Given this objective to shed light on the value to developing countries of existing TRQ access to the EU market, the chapter proceeds in three steps. In the next section, graphical analysis is used to identify the potential nature of the welfare gains from TRQ access under a variety of assumptions regarding the binding nature of the TRQ and the competitiveness of developing-country suppliers. This analysis extends the traditional analysis of TRQs by considering not just less-than-perfectly-elastic supply but also multiple sources of supply with different cost functions. The value of TRQs is defined as consisting of the new market access which TRQs created (and the export surplus gained on these additional exports) plus the size of quota rents generated which accrue to developing countries. It seems to be widely accepted that little new market access was created by TRQs, which were mainly used to maintain existing trade flows, often originating in preferential agreements. This chapter concentrates on estimating the value of rents accruing to developing countries. A number of different indicators are defined, including the value of the preference margin, the value of rents created, the value of rents appropriated by exporters and the welfare gain due to the rents appropriated by exporters.

Then we apply this analysis to quantify the value of TRQ access to the EU market. The size of the various indicators is measured and their distribution by commodity sector and by exporter grouping is quantified and discussed. The penultimate section summarizes the results and conclusions from the analysis and evaluates the TRQ proposals in the draft Modalities presented by the Chairman of the Agriculture Negotiating Group to the parties in March 2003 in the light of these findings, and the final section concludes.

The value of TRQs

This section presents a graphical analysis of the welfare impact of TRQs for exporting countries. It extends the conventional analysis not only by assuming less-than-infinitely-elastic supply curves but by explicitly taking multiple sources of supply into account, where these export supply sources have different underlying costs of production. Three situations are considered:

- The TRQ is open to all suppliers (global TRQ)
- The TRQ is fully reserved to preferred suppliers, and preferred suppliers are more competitive than others (bilateral TRQ)
- The TRQ is fully reserved to preferred suppliers, but preferred suppliers are less competitive than others (bilateral TRQ).

In each situation, the impact of the TRQ depends on whether it is binding or not, and whether there are in addition over-quota imports or not. The focus is on the export surplus and level of rents created in each case. For ease of presentation, it is assumed that any rents created are appropriated by the exporting country. In practice, whether this occurs or not will depend on the way in which the TRQ scheme is managed. We distinguish between two concepts, the preference margin (strictly, the unit preference margin) and the quota rent (strictly, the unit quota rent). The unit preference margin is defined as the difference between the over-quota tariff (T) and the in-quota tariff (t). The unit quota rent, where it exists, depends on the way the quota Q is filled and whether an over-quota supply exists or not. It is defined as the difference between the domestic market price in the importing country (P) and the supply price of the exporting country (P').

We distinguish a total of eleven different cases. To illustrate the concepts, three typical cases are presented in graphical format. We begin with the situation of a global quota where there is underfill and no MFN supply. In Figure 6.1, D represents the excess demand curve of the importing country. Two suppliers, or groups of suppliers, are represented with different levels of competitiveness. We suppose that S^1 is more competitive than S^2. Supplies from these countries face the in-quota tariff t and the tariff-laden supply curves are represented by S_t^1 and S_t^2, respectively. The domestic price P is determined by the intersection between D and S_t^{1+2} which is the horizontal summation of the two tariff-laden supply curves. Because S_t^{1+2} not limited by Q the TRQ is not entirely filled. There is no quota rent. The import market shares Q_t^1 and

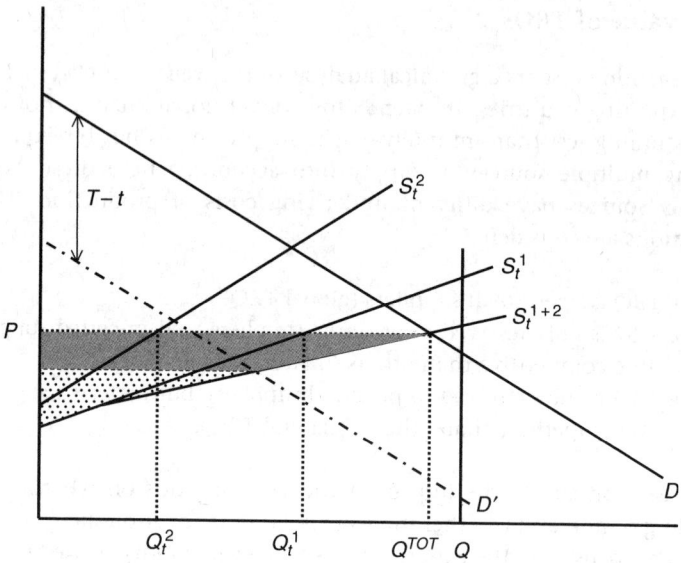

Figure 6.1   Welfare effects of a global TRQ with underfill

Q_t^2 are determined according to the respective competitiveness of S_t^1 and S_t^2. In this case, a TRQ improves the market access of all suppliers.

Under the TRQ regime, in-quota suppliers benefit from an export surplus represented by both the dotted and grey areas. To the left of S_t^1, it is the export surplus of S^1 and, to the right, it is the export surplus of S^2. These export surplus measures would have been smaller in the absence of the tariff quota.

It is possible to assess graphically the gain of export surplus for in-quota suppliers due to the TRQ. This is the difference between the export surplus under the TRQ regime (dotted and grey areas) and the export surplus which would occur without any quota and under a simple MFN tariff T. Without a TRQ, and with only a tariff T in place, we can use S_t^1 and S_t^2 to represent S_T^1 and S_T^2 to determine market equilibrium by using the excess demand curve D', which is D moved horizontally downwards by the amount $(T-t)$. Figure 6.1 shows the export surplus of exporters equivalent to the dotted area in this situation. Thus the gain of export surplus due to the TRQ is represented by the grey area.

If, instead, we had assumed that the quota was exactly binding so that the domestic price was formed by the intersection of the quota volume Q with the excess demand curve D, then we would observe the creation of quota rent. However, in the absence of over-quota imports, the unit value of the quota rent (the difference between the domestic price P and the import price P') would be smaller than the preference margin (equal to $T-t$). Exporters would continue to benefit from an additional export surplus. If the quota were binding and over-quota imports occurred, two further changes would be observed. First, the unit value of the quota rent ($P-P'$) would equal the preference margin ($T-t$). This is because the domestic market price would now be set by the cost of imports paying the over-quota tariff T. Second, the quota rent would now constitute the entire economic gain for exporters arising from the TRQ because the export surplus would be unchanged compared to a situation without the TRQ.

The second situation, shown in Figure 6.2, is a bilateral quota awarded to relatively competitive suppliers which is underfilled and where there is no MFN supply. As before, the total import demand of the importing country is shown as D. Taking into account the coexistence of several exporting suppliers and the specific allocation of the TRQ to one of them, we introduce a residual demand curve, shown as D_{RES}, which is the remaining demand after taking into account the supply which

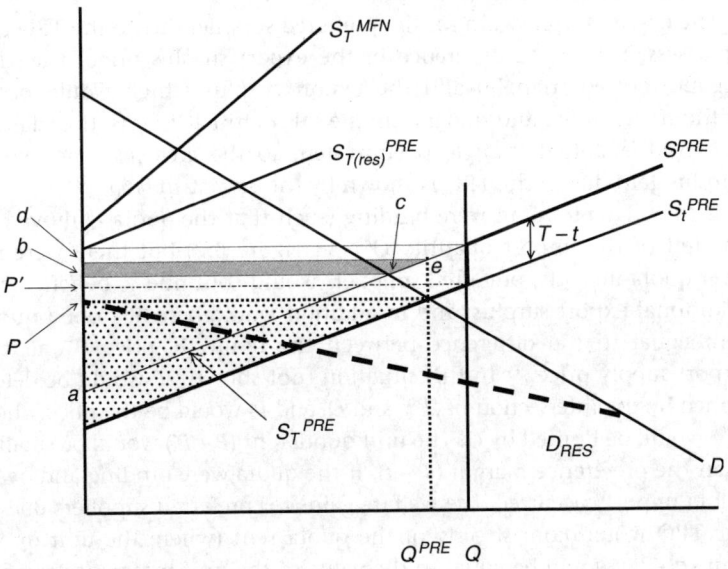

Figure 6.2 Welfare effects of a bilateral TRQ awarded to a more-competitive supplier with underfill

enjoys the preferred access offered by the TRQ. For each price level, $D_{RES} = D - S_t^{PRE}$ where S_t^{PRE} is the supply curve of the preferred supplier burdened with the in-quota tariff. We define further the curve $S_{T(res)}^{PRE}$ as the over-quota supply of the preferred country which is available to meet the residual import demand after consumption of the import tariff quota Q. Finally, S_T^{PRE} is the supply curve of the preferred country which would operate in the absence of the reserved TRQ. There is a vertical distance $(T - t)$ between S_T^{PRE} and S_t^{PRE}.

Under the TRQ regime, preferred supply is represented by a two-step curve $S^{PRE} = S_t^{PRE} + S_{T(res)}^{PRE}$, where S_t^{PRE} is the preferred supply under the in-quota tariff t regime and $S_{T(res)}^{PRE}$ is the preferred supply under the over-quota tariff T regime. The two steps of the curve S^{PRE} are parallel but vertically distant from each other by $(T-t)$ up to the quantity level Q. When the quota is non-binding, the domestic price P is determined by the intersection between D and S_t^{PRE}. At this price, the preferential TRQ is not entirely filled by S_t^{PRE}. There is no over-quota supply and no quota rent. Due to the reduced tariff, preferred supply benefits from an improvement in market access compared to a situation without the TRQ. The export surplus of preferred supply is represented by the dotted area which would be smaller in the absence of the additional market access facilitated by the TRQ.

The export surplus gain for the preferred supplier due to the TRQ can be assessed. It is the difference in the export surplus under the TRQ regime (dotted triangle) and the export surplus which would occur without any quota and under a simple MFN tariff T, that is, the triangle *abc*. As the dotted triangle is equivalent to the area *ade*, the export surplus gain due to the TRQ is shown by the grey strip *bced*.

If the bilateral quota were binding (such that the quota Q moved to the left of the import quantity Q^{PRE} in Figure 6.2) but there were no over-quota imports, preferred suppliers would continue to benefit from additional export surplus, and in addition would benefit from a quota rent equal to the difference between the domestic price P and the export supply price P'. In this situation (not shown), P would be determined by the intersection of S^{PRE} and D, and P' would be the price where S^{PRE} would be limited by Q. The unit quota rent $(P - P')$ would be smaller than the preference margin $(T - t)$. If the quota were binding and over-quota imports occurred, the welfare gains for preferred suppliers due to the TRQ would consist only of the quota rent (where the unit quota rent $(P - P')$ would be equal to the value of the unit preference margin $(T - t)$). Export surplus would be unchanged compared to the situation in the absence of the TRQ.

The final illustrative situation shown in Figure 6.3 is the case of a bilateral quota where the preferred suppliers are less competitive than other suppliers, as shown by the respective positions of the export supply curves S_T^{PRE} and S_T^{MFN}. As before, we present the case where the bilateral TRQ is underfilled and there is no MFN supply. D_{RES} is the residual import demand curve given the level of preferential exports at each price. This curve does not intersect S_T^{PRE}. The domestic price P is determined by the intersection between D and S_t^{PRE}. At this price, the bilateral TRQ is not entirely filled by S_t^{PRE} which supplies the quantity $Q^{PRE} < Q$. There is no over-quota supply and no quota rent. However, the implementation of the TRQ clearly opens market access for preferred supply. S_t^{PRE} is present in the import market and enjoys an export surplus (dotted area) which would not exist in absence of the TRQ. In the case where the quota is binding but there are no over-quota imports, quota rent is created in addition to the additional export surplus, although the size of the unit quota rent $(P - P')$ is less than the unit preference margin $(T - t)$. Where the quota is binding and over-quota imports take

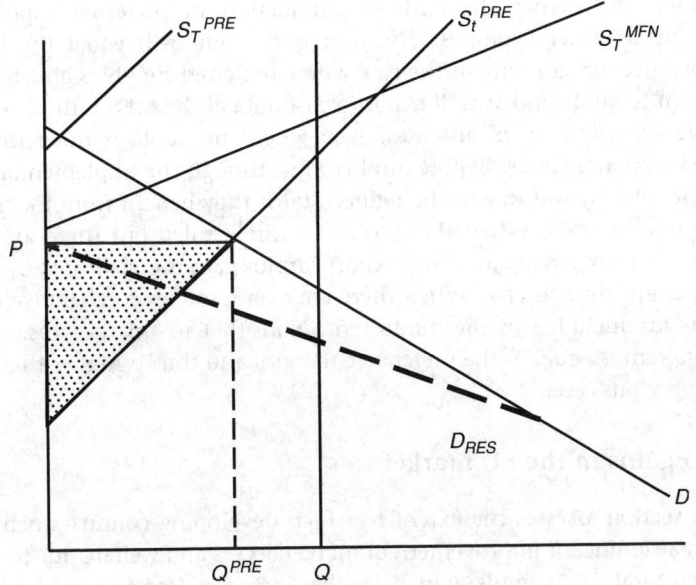

Figure 6.3 Welfare effects of a bilateral TRQ awarded to a less-competitive supplier with underfill

place, the results diverge slightly from those shown for the case where the bilateral quotas are allocated to the most competitive suppliers. In the situation where they are allocated to the less competitive suppliers, export surplus will continue to be created unless the preferred suppliers are sufficiently competitive to be able to supply some of those over-quota imports; only in this situation will there be no additional export surplus and the value of the unit quota rent $(P - P')$ will be equal to the unit preference margin $(T - t)$. Perhaps the more usual situation is that the uncompetitive supplier will be unable to export at the over-quota tariff. In this case, export surplus will be generated on the exports encouraged by the lower in-quota tariff but the size of the unit quota rent will be smaller than the unit preference margin.

Table 6.1 summarizes the results of the graphical analysis for eleven different cases in terms of the nature of the welfare gains for exporters due to the implementation of the TRQ compared to a situation of a simple MFN tariff. As expected, quota rents are zero where the TRQ is not binding (fill rate less than 100 per cent). A key insight from the eleven cases is that only in exceptional circumstances is the quota rent likely to be the same as the preferential margin, and in the majority of cases it is considerably less. Where a quota rent exists, it will be the smaller, the higher the costs of production of preferred suppliers relative to other suppliers. The unit quota rent will equal the unit preference margin only in the case where preferred supply is able to fill the entire quota and as well export over-quota at the MFN tariff.

We observe that, in all cases, even when the quota is not entirely filled, exporters enjoy export surplus gains though the implementation of the TRQ. This is due to the reduced tariff they benefit from for their in-quota imports. When the quota is entirely filled but there are no over-quota exports, part of the export surplus gain is constituted by the quota rent they receive. When there are over-quota exports, all welfare gains are included in the quota rent. Note that in this last case, the quota rent is equal to the preference margin, and thus is higher than in the previous case.

TRQ gains in the EU market

This section assesses the extent to which developing countries benefit from a significant improvement of market access and welfare due to the agricultural TRQs implemented by the European Union compared to a simple MFN tariff regime. The European Union is used as a case study to keep the scope of the empirical work manageable and on the assumption

Table 6.1 Welfare gains for exporters due to the implementation of the TRQ

	Unit rent r	Welfare gains (1)
(1) TRQ imports reserved to preferred countries[a]		
(A) Preferred supply is more competitive		
(a) Preferential TRQ not 100% filled	0	ES
(b) Preferential TRQ 100% filled, no over-quota supply, no MFN supply	$r = (P - P') < (T - t)$	ES, rent
(c) Preferential TRQ 100% filled, positive over-quota supply, no MFN supply	$r = (T - t)$	Rent
(d) Preferential TRQ 100% filled, positive over-quota supply, positive MFN supply	$r = (T - t)$	Rent
(B) Preferred supply is less competitive		
(e) Preferential TRQ not 100% filled, no MFN supply	0	ES
(f) Preferential TRQ 100% filled, no MFN supply, no over-quota supply	$r = (P - P') < (T - t)$	ES, rent
(g) Preferential TRQ not 100% filled, positive MFN supply	0	ES
(h) Preferential TRQ 100% filled, positive MFN supply		
–no over-quota supply	$r = (P - P') < (T - t)$	ES, rent
–positive over-quota supply	$r = (P - P') = (T - t)$	Rent
(2) No specific allocation of TRQ		
(i) TRQ not 100% filled	0	ES
(j) TRQ 100% filled, no over-quota supply	$r = (P - P') < (T - t)$	ES, rent
(k) TRQ 100% filled, positive over-quota supply	$r = (T - t)$	Rent

Note:
[a] Compared to a regime of a simple MFN tariff, the implementation of a TRQ gives to the in-quota exporter(s) the following possible welfare gains:
– ES: gains of export surplus (excluding rent)
– Rent: gains via quota rent
– ES, rent: rent and extra export surplus.

that many of the findings based on EU data may be replicable more widely. The evaluation concerns the quota rent amounts and their sharing out between exporters. The evaluation of other welfare gains in terms of exporter surplus (excluding rents) and its sharing out between exporters is not explicitly measured.

Background

The European Union has opened 87 separate TRQs arising from the AoA.[3] In its notifications to the WTO, the European Union distinguishes between current access and minimum access quotas.[4] Current access quotas were designed to safeguard historical quantities imported under special arrangements, whereas minimum access quotas were designed to fulfil the minimum access obligations of the AoA, 44 of the EU TRQs are current access quotas, 36 are minimum access quotas, while the remaining six are non-tariffed product quotas (these quotas were opened for products which did not have to undergo tariffication to convert non-tariff barriers (NTBs) to tariffs).

Tariffs under the EU current access quotas are much lower than the respective over-quota tariff. Bureau and Tangermann (2002) estimate that, on average, for the 50 quotas under current access and for non-tariffed products, the in-quota tariffs showed a reduction of 80 per cent compared to the over-quota tariff at the beginning of the implementation period. Since the in-quota tariffs remained unchanged over the implementation period while the over-quota tariffs were reduced by an average of 36 per cent, these authors estimate that in-quota tariffs for current access quotas would be about one-third of the corresponding over-quota rate by 2001.

For TRQs under minimum access, the EU applied a relatively uniform reduction. Most in-quota tariffs have been set at 32 per cent of the over-quota MFN initial (base) tariff. Exceptions include milled rice, durum and quality wheat, which are subject to a zero in-quota tariff and high-quality meat where there is a much lower in-quota tariff set compared to the very high MFN tariff. As these in-quota tariffs were not scheduled to change over the implementation period, they are closer to 40 per cent of the out-of-quota tariff by the end of the implementation period (Bureau and Tangermann, 2002).

The European Union used current access quotas to maintain previously existing preferential access arrangements. Of the 44 current access TRQs, 14 are allocated to a particular list of countries. Several of these quotas list developing countries as beneficiaries (including China which was not a WTO member when the EU Schedule was submitted). Some of these quotas are allocated to ACP countries as a result of the Lomé Convention (now the Cotonou Agreement). This includes four quotas for sheep, goats and mushrooms as well as the 1.2 million tonne quota of sugar. Others are allocated to Central and Eastern European (CEE) countries. The EU Schedules mention that, for 18 out of the 36 minimum access quotas, the European Union may count against these quotas preferential imports from CEE countries under the Europe Agreements. This is the case for pigmeat (five quotas), poultry (three quotas), dairy products (seven quotas) and processed eggs (three quotas). However, neither the quantities admitted under quota nor the eligible countries are specified in the Schedule itself.

Table 6.2 shows the importance of EU trade under these TRQs in value terms during the period 1997–99, categorized by major commodity groupings. Data on the size of TRQs and the amount of trade under TRQs are supplied by the European Union in volume terms based on licence data in its annual returns to the WTO, but these data do not indicate from where imports imported under TRQs originate. To derive the value estimates in Table 6.2, two simplifying assumptions are made. The first is that TRQ trade is shared among exporting countries in the same proportion as their shares of the corresponding HS8 tariff line to which the TRQ applies.[5] An exception is made for current access TRQs where bilateral allocations are made to specific countries. It is assumed that these bilateral allocations are first filled before the proportionate rule is applied. Second, it is assumed that the unit value of HS8 trade to which a TRQ applies can also be used to value trade within the TRQ. These assumptions imply that imports entering the EU market under TRQs are broadly representative, in terms of source and quality, of all imports under a HS8 tariff line.[6]

Three indicators of the importance of TRQ trade in total EU agricultural imports are shown in Table 6.2.[7] The first is the actual value of imports in the HS8 tariff lines where TRQs have been opened and their importance relative to total imports (shown in column (3)). The drawback of this measure is that, for some of these tariff lines, considerable trade takes place outside the TRQ so that it exaggerates the importance of TRQ trade. A second indicator estimates the potential value of TRQ trade. This is done by multiplying the eligible or maximum TRQ quantities by the unit value of trade in the HS8 tariff line to which they apply (column (4)). The third indicator is similar to the second, except that notified imports under each TRQ are used instead of the eligible TRQ volumes to measure the actual value of trade (column (6)). The difference between actual and potential imports can be defined as the fill rate (shown in column (8)).

Compared to a total value of EU agricultural imports of ECU 51.3 billion over these years, ECU 8.7 billion were in HS8 tariff lines for which TRQs were opened. The potential value of trade under these TRQs was ECU 6.1 billion, but the actual value averaged ECU 4.9 billion, or a fill rate, defined in value terms, of just over 80 per cent. TRQ trade is most important in the fruit and vegetables sector (reflecting the importance of the banana TRQs allocated to Latin American suppliers), closely followed by the live animals and meat sector and then sugar. TRQs are

142

Table 6.2 Relative importance of TRQ products and TRQ imports, by main commodity, average 1997–99

	Total imports (1)	of which: imports of HS8 products[a] covered by TRQs (2)	As percentage of total (3) = (2)/(1)	Potential value of TRQ imports (4)	As percentage of total imports (5) = (4)/(1)	Actual value of TRQ imports (6)	As percentage of total imports (7) = (6)/(1)	Ratio of actual to potential TRQ imports, i.e. fill rate (8) = (6)/(4)
	(mECU)	(mECU)	(%)	(mECU)	(%)	(mECU)	(%)	(%)
Live animals and meat	4,011	2,060	51.4	1,844	46.0	1,462	36.4	79.3
Dairy	999	547	54.7	502	50.2	357	35.7	71.2
Fruit, vegetable and nuts	11,296	3,108	27.5	2,372	21.0	1,977	17.5	83.3
Tropical products	8,176	0	0.0	0	0.0	0	0.0	...
Cereals and milling products	1,587	1,325	83.5	460	29.0	358	22.6	77.9
Oils and oilseeds	7,890	0	0.0	0	0.0	0	0.0	...
Sugar and sugar confectionery	1,117	717	64.2	718	64.3	718	64.3	100.0
Other processed foods and drink	16,198	946	5.8	230	1.4	57	0.3	24.6
Total	51,275	8,703	17.0	6,125	11.9	4,928	9.6	80.5

Note:
[a] HS8 products are products at the 8-digit level of the Harmonized System of tariff classification.

not significant for trade in tropical products, oils and oilseeds or processed foods nor, except to a very limited extent, for trade in cereals and
milling products or dairy products. Actual TRQ trade accounted for just
under 10 per cent of all EU food and agricultural imports during this
three-year period.

In the context of this chapter, what is interesting is the extent to
which developing countries have been able to make use of the EU TRQs.
Table 6.3 shows the distribution of TRQ trade between regions based on
the assumptions specified above. Globally, developing countries account
for 62 per cent of TRQ trade by value and developed countries for the
remaining 38 per cent. This is close to the proportions provided by each
region in total EU agricultural imports. In absolute terms, TRQs are
most important for developing countries in the fruit and vegetable,
meat and sugar sectors. Developing countries make little use of TRQs in
the dairy, cereal or processed foods sectors. In regional terms, the value
of TRQ trade is most important for Latin American countries, followed
by the non-LDC ACP countries (whose TRQ trade is accounted for almost
entirely by the beef and sugar protocols under the Lomé Convention).

Table 6.3 Usage of EU TRQs, by country grouping, average 1997–99, million ECU

	Live animals and meat	Dairy	Fruit, vegetables and nuts	Cereals and milling products	Sugar	Other processed foods	Total
Total	1,512	356	1,977	292	718	56	4,911
Total [a]LDC non-ACP	0	0	0	0	1	0	1
Total LDC ACP	1	2	0	3	47	0	54
Total ACP non-LDC	104	1	13	6	529	0	654
Total non-LDC Asia	12	6	298	20	11	2	348
Total non-LDC Latin America	474	2	1,247	116	110	4	1,954
Total non-LDC Maghreb, Middle East	1	4	20	0	3	0	27
Total developing countries	593	16	1,578	145	701	6	3,038
Total developed or in transition countries	919	341	398	147	17	51	1,874

Note:
[a] LDC = Least-developed countries.

It is noteworthy that the LDCs obtain almost no benefit from TRQs because their exports are concentrated in agricultural products which have low or zero MFN tariffs.

Welfare effects of EU TRQs

To calculate the rents accruing to developing countries on TRQ trade, the first step is to calculate the preference margin. The results are shown in Table 6.4. What is striking is that the estimated preference margin of ECU 4.0 billion is not that much smaller than the value of actual TRQ trade of ECU 4.9 billion in those years; in fact, for some important commodities, the preference margin actually exceeds the value of trade. The key reason for this is that the unit price received by the exporting countries is smaller than the unit preference margin. The graphical analysis in the previous section showed that rents must exist if the TRQ is binding, as is the case with bananas. Thus these data provide *prima*

Table 6.4 Preference margin on EU TRQ trade, average 1997–99, million ECU

	Live animals and meat	Dairy	Fruit, vegetables and nuts	Cereals and milling products	Sugar	Other processed foods	Total
Total LDC non-ACP	0.0	0.0	0.0	0.0	0.5	0.0	0.5
Total LDC-ACP	1.1	1.0	0.3	3.6	34.1	0.0	40.0
Total ACP non-LDC	59.1	1.0	3.1	1.8	381.1	0.0	446.0
Total non-LDC Asia	6.0	1.7	380.9	16.1	8.2	0.0	413.0
Total non-LDC Latin America	342.9	1.0	1,483.2	130.3	79.8	0.2	2,037.4
Total non-LDC Maghreb, Middle East	0.5	1.2	3.5	0.5	1.3	0.1	7.1
Total developing countries	409.7	5.8	1,871.0	152.3	505.1	0.3	2,944.1
Total developed or in transition countries	688.7	188.1	20.6	142.3	12.3	39.4	1,091.3
Total	1,098.3	193.9	1,891.6	294.5	517.4	39.7	4,035.5

Note:
LDC = Least-developed countries.

facie evidence that exporters are unable to appropriate the full value of the TRQ rent which arises.

The preference margin represents the absolute maximum potential rent which can be extracted on existing TRQ trade.[8] Thus it is worth analysing the potential beneficiaries in more detail. Fruit, vegetables and nuts (46.9 per cent), live animals and meat (27.2 per cent) and sugar (12.8 per cent) are the main contributors to the preference margin. Globally, developing countries appear to be the principal potential beneficiaries, accounting for 73 per cent of the total, while developed countries benefit from the remaining 27 per cent. Among developing countries, Latin American countries would be the largest potential beneficiaries, with 50.5 per cent of the global preference margin, explained by their strong position in the fruit and vegetables and meat sectors. Next in line are the non-LDC ACP countries with 11.1 per cent of the preference margin, but their position is explained totally by their exports of sugar under the Lomé Convention. 10.2 per cent of the global preference margin is attributed to Asian non-LDC countries, concentrated on the fruit and vegetables sector. Other developing countries obtain almost no potential benefit from the operation of TRQs.

The factors influencing the change in the preference margin over the 1997–99 period can be analysed. Logically, the preference margin is the product of the TRQ volume, the fill rate and the unit preference margin. Overall, the value of the preference margin has been falling, from ECU 4.4 billion to ECU 3.7 billion. TRQ volumes have, if anything, slightly increased over this period, particularly for meat and dairy products. Fill rates show more volatility. There are many instances where fill rates have fallen, but on average they have increased slightly over the period. Thus the main contributor to the fall in the value of the preference margin is the fall in the unit preference margin, that is, the difference between the over-quota MFN rate and the in-quota rate. This follows directly from the AoA commitments under which MFN tariff bindings were gradually reduced by an average of 36 per cent over the six-year period 1995–2000. Because this commitment did not apply to the TRQ in-quota rates, the unit value of the preference margin has declined.

The preference margin overstates the actual rent created because it makes no allowance for whether a TRQ is binding or not. Where a TRQ is not binding, no rent is created. To allow for statistical and marketing problems, a TRQ is treated as binding if the fill rate exceeds 90 per cent. Based on this rule, the distribution of created rent is shown by commodity sector in Figure 6.4 and by exporter region in Table 6.5. The value of rent created by EU TRQs is shown as ECU 2.7 billion, or

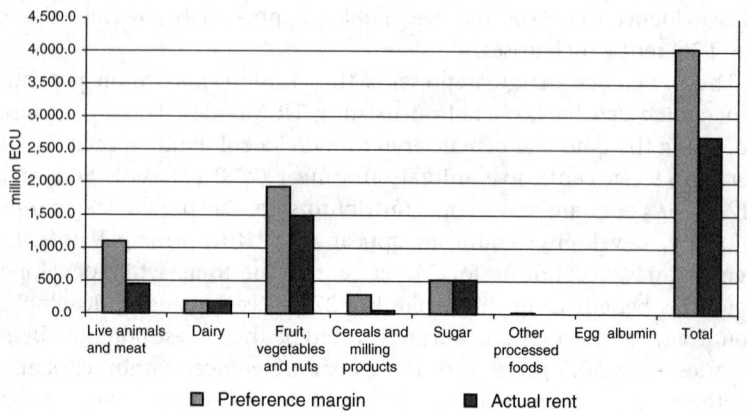

Figure 6.4 Assessed rent versus preference margin by commodity sector, annual average, 1997–99, millon ECU

Table 6.5 Rent created in EU TRQs, average 1997–99, million ECU

	Live animals and meat	Dairy	Fruit, vegetables and nuts	Cereals and milling products	Sugar	Other processed foods	Total
Total LDC non-ACP	0.0	0.0	0.0	0.0	0.5	0.0	0.5
Total LDC ACP	1.0	1.0	0.0	0.2	34.1	0.0	36.3
Total ACP non-LDC	59.0	1.0	0.0	1.5	381.1	0.0	442.6
Total non-LDC Asia	2.3	1.1	0.2	15.5	8.2	0.0	27.3
Total non-LDC Latin America	317.7	0.8	1,480.7	5.8	79.8	0.0	1,884.8
Total non-LDC Maghreb, Middle East	0.4	1.1	0.5	0.3	1.3	0.0	3.5
Total developing countries	380.4	4.9	1,481.4	23.3	505.1	0.0	2,395.1
Total developed or in transition countries	69.4	183.9	10.8	27.7	12.3	0.0	304.1
Total	449.8	188.8	1,492.2	51.0	517.4	0.0	2,699.2

Note:
LDC = Least-developed countries.

67.5 per cent of the value of the preference margin. Most rent is created in the fruit and vegetables sector, followed by live animals and meat and then sugar. For all products together, the share of rent created on exports from developed countries falls to 11.3 per cent (compared to a preference margin share of 27 per cent). The implication is that TRQs are more frequently binding on exports from developing countries than from developed countries. Within the group of developing countries, rent is also more concentrated than the preference margin. 70 per cent of the rent is created on exports from Latin American countries (compared to 50.5 per cent of the preference margin). The share of the rent created by exports from the non-LDC ACP countries increases to 16.4 per cent, compared to 11 per cent for the preference margin. The non-LDC Asian countries now join the other developing-country regions whose exports do not create any significant rents.

The final step in estimating the value of EU TRQs to developing countries is to assign these created rents either to importers or to exporters. The division of rents depends on the arrangements made to administer the quotas. These arrangements are specified in the EU returns to the WTO Committee on Agriculture.[9] The division of rents proposed for alternative administrative arrangements is an elaboration of a scheme initially suggested by Elbehri *et al.* (1999), and is shown in Table 6.6.

Table 6.6 Division of rents, by TRQ import arrangement

	Import arrangement	% rent for importers	% rent for exporters
a	No specific allocation to supplying countries, only import licences required	100	0
b	No specific allocation to supplying countries, no import licences, documents for release for free circulation required	50	50
c	No specific allocation to supplying countries, import licences + certificate of authenticity required	50	50
d	No specific allocation to supplying countries, no import licences, certificates of authenticity issued by exporting country required	0	100
e	Specific allocation to supplying countries, only import licences required	50	50
f	Specific allocation to supplying countries, import licences + certificate of authenticity (or IMA1) required	50	50
g	Specific allocation to supplying countries, import licences + export licences or document required	50	50

Based on these rules, the value of the rents estimated to accrue to developing countries is shown in Table 6.7. Two observations can be made about Table 6.7. First, the value of TRQ rents appropriated by exporters is only 43 per cent of the rents created and only 29 per cent of the value of the preference margin. Second, rents appropriated by exporters are even more concentrated than either rents created or the preference margin. Fully 92 per cent of the exporter-appropriated rents are gained by developing countries, with a value of ECU 1.1 billion. Nearly all of this is accounted for by just two commodity sectors, fruits and vegetables and sugar. Furthermore, 78 per cent accrue to Latin American exporters with a further 19 per cent accruing to the non-LDC ACP group (arising entirely from their Lomé Convention sugar quotas).

The final step in the argument is to consider the sustainability of the trade positions which have emerged under the EU TRQs. The empirical analysis to this point has implicitly assumed that different countries

Table 6.7   Value of rent estimated to accrue to developing countries on EU TRQ trade, average 1997–99, million ECU

Rent	Live animals and meat	Dairy	Fruit, vegetables and nuts	Cereals and milling products	Sugar	Other processed foods	Total
Total LDC non-ACP	0.0	0.0	0.0	0.0	0.3	0.0	0.3
Total LDC ACP	0.1	0.3	0.0	0.1	17.0	0.0	17.5
Total ACP non-LDC	16.7	0.2	0.0	0.7	190.6	0.0	208.2
Total non-LDC Asia	0.1	0.0	0.1	7.7	4.1	0.0	12.0
Total non-LDC Latin America	57.7	0.3	740.3	2.9	39.9	0.0	841.1
Total non-LDC Maghreb, Middle East	0.0	0.3	0.2	0.1	0.0	0.0	0.7
Total developing countries	74.6	1.0	740.6	11.6	251.9	0.0	1,079.7
Total developed or in transition countries	18.7	55.9	5.3	6.8	5.7	0.0	92.5
Total	93.3	56.9	745.9	18.4	257.7	0.0	1,172.2

Note:
LDC = Least-developed countries.

have similar cost structures and that all export at the average EU unit import price. In fact, there is evidence that exporters taking advantage of TRQs have very different cost structures. As shown previously, this has an important implication for the evaluation of the rents appropriated by exporters. For high-cost exporters, TRQs may be a way of opening market access rather than creating rents. These countries may not be competitive in the absence of the preferential access provided behind high MFN tariffs. The 'rents' appropriated by these countries may simply be absorbed by higher production costs, and the value of TRQ access may be confined to the export surplus value created on these exports. For low-cost exporters, on the other hand, the rents represent an additional transfer to the export surplus earned on their TRQ exports.

To gain an indication of the competitive position of TRQ exporters, the FAOSTAT database has been used to calculate for each exporting country and each product the unit export price, defined as the export value divided by the export volume. Each country's unit export price is then compared to the world unit export price for that product (calculated by the same method, and using an average of the 1997–99 period) to determine if the country is a high-cost or low-cost producer of that commodity. Countries are grouped into the regional groupings used in the other tables in this chapter and average export prices for broad sectoral commodity groups calculated for each country.[10] The results are presented in Table 6.8.

Despite the computational caveats, a number of clear messages emerge from Table 6.8. In each case, Latin American unit export prices are below world unit export prices. Latin American countries are clearly competitive exporters to the world market. The rents identified as accruing to them in Table 6.7 are probably actual rents and they would be in a position to maintain these export flows were trade liberalization to take place.

On the contrary, for the ACP countries export unit prices for those products where they apparently enjoy a rent transfer (sugar and meat, in particular) are above the world unit export prices for those products. It seems reasonable to assume that the rent transfers to these countries are absorbed by higher production costs and thus do not represent a net welfare gain to these economies.[11] The removal of the specific bilateral TRQs from which many of these countries benefit would probably have negative effects on their ability to retain their market shares.

Finally, for Asian countries, their export unit values are in general below world unit export values, except for the product group where

Table 6.8   Average export prices, average 1997–99, US$/t

	Live animals and meat[a]	Dairy	Fruit, vegetables and nuts	Cereals and milling products	Sugar	Other processed foods
LDC non-ACP	6,080	1,215	362	175	362	81
LDC ACP	2,177	1,066	462	166	364	74
ACP non-LDC	2,451	1,170	506	173	371	238
non-LDC Asia	1,886	1,201	271	254	249	500
non-LDC Latin America	1,806	1,417	339	138	214	514
non-LDC Maghreb, Middle East	1,745	1,415	379	268	269	1,045
Total developing countries	1,857	1,330	343	197	243	471
Developed or in transition countries	1,630	1,632	532	136	287	538
World	1,836	1,514	443	157	287	667

Note:
[a] Live animals are not taken into account because prices are not in the same unit as meat.
LDC = Least-developed countries.
Source: FAOSTAT.

they are supposed to benefit from a rent (cereals and milling products). The same remarks apply to these countries as to the ACP group.

Results and discussion

The justification for TRQs in the AoA was that they maintained or created market access in the face of the very high MFN tariffs created by tariffication. One element of the welfare benefit accruing to exporters able to take advantage of these TRQs is the additional export surplus they earn on TRQ exports. But TRQs when they are binding also create rents, and in many cases it is the rent element which becomes the most significant benefit of TRQ access. The previous analysis has focused on the value of the rent transfers created by the EU TRQ arrangements.

Around 10 per cent of the European Union's agricultural imports by value enter under TRQ arrangements, and developing countries account for over 60 per cent of these imports. The preference margin on these TRQ imports amounted to ECU 4.0 billion annually over the period 1997–99. Globally, developing countries are the largest potential beneficiaries of this preference margin with access to 73 per cent of the total, while developed countries could benefit from the remaining 27 per cent.

The value of the preference margin, and thus the associated rents, has been falling as the tariff reductions mandated under the AoA took effect. This illustrates the vulnerability of relying on preferential access schemes to generate gains for developing countries when multilateral trade liberalization is taking place concurrently.

This preference margin translates into rent creation only if the TRQ is binding; rent creation was estimated at ECU 2.7 billion annually over the same period. TRQs are more frequently binding in the case of developing countries; hence the rent created on imports from developing countries accounts for 89 per cent of the total rents created, compared to 11 per cent arising from imports from developed countries. Even among imports from developing countries, rent creation is highly concentrated, with 70 per cent of the total generated on imports from Latin American countries.

A striking finding is that the value of the preference margin is very close to the actual value of TRQ imports into the European Union and, for some important commodities, the preference margin exceeds the value of trade. This is *prima facie* evidence that exporters are unable to appropriate the full value of the TRQ rents which arise. The formal analysis confirmed that the majority of this rent (57 per cent) was appropriated by import agents as a result of the way TRQs are administered in the European Union. Only ECU 1.2 billion was appropriated by exporting countries, almost entirely by developing country exporters (ECU 1.1 billion of the total).

Most of this rent transfer accrued to Latin American exporters of fruits and vegetables, while nearly all the remainder accrued to ACP sugar exporters. EU TRQs are irrelevant to LDCs and to the countries of the Middle East and the Maghreb. They are of limited significance to Asian and ACP non-LDC countries, but these countries do not appear to be competitive enough to benefit from an actual rent transfer in the context of binding TRQs. Instead, the main function of their TRQ access appears to be to secure a market foothold, which otherwise they would have difficulty in maintaining.

In the light of these findings, the possible impact of the TRQ proposals contained in the revised Harbison draft of the Modalities for the Doha agricultural trade negotiations in March 2003 (TN/AG/W/1/Rev.1) can be evaluated. The Harbison draft will be superseded by others in the negotiations, but is nonetheless useful to illustrate the likely effects of key negotiating proposals. Two of the elements of his proposals are (i) that further increases in TRQ access should be confined to existing TRQs that appear in members' schedules, thus ruling out the extension of TRQs to new products, and (ii) that additional market access opportunities provided by the expansion of tariff quotas should be on an MFN basis. There appears to be a general agreement that TRQ volumes should be expanded; the Harbison draft suggests that volumes should equate to 10 per cent of current domestic consumption (suggested as the three-year period 1999–2001 or the most recent three-year period for which data are available), although some flexibility is provided. Member states could opt to bind the TRQ volume at a lower level (8 per cent is suggested) for up to one-quarter of the total number of tariff quotas concerned, provided that the volumes for a corresponding number of tariff quotas are expanded to 12 per cent. There would be no requirement to reduce in-quota tariffs.[12] The expansion of TRQs would take place in equal instalments over five years. In addition, a series of detailed proposals to improve TRQ administration has been tabled.

Special and differential treatment (SDT) is provided in two forms. First, the increase in obligations will be less onerous for developing countries. Generally, the final bound TRQ volumes for notified TRQs will be expanded to 6.6 per cent of domestic consumption over a period of ten years. For up to one-quarter of the total number of TRQs concerned, a developing country member could opt to bind the TRQ volume at 5 per cent of domestic consumption, provided that the volumes for a corresponding number of TRQs are expanded to 8 per cent. Second, there will be no requirement to expand TRQ access for products designated as 'special products [SP]'. These are agricultural products which developing countries could designate at the HS4- or 6-digit level as being special products with respect to food security, rural development and/or livelihood security concerns.

Two comments can be made on these proposals in the light of our findings. First, the emphasis on increasing TRQ volumes rather than reducing in-quota tariffs is sensible from a developing-country perspective. The main argument for reducing in-quota tariffs is to deal with low fill rates, on the assumption that the in-quota tariff is the main impediment to exporters taking advantage of the TRQ access. It also helps to create additional export surplus in cases where the quota is not binding. However, lack of demand or administrative or licensing restrictions may be more important causes of underfill, in which case reform of these procedures would be a more effective way of addressing the problem. For TRQs with high fill rates and where quotas are binding, the main effect of reducing in-quota tariffs would be to transfer tariff revenue into quota rent. But, as the empirical analysis showed, very little of the quota rent created accrues to developing-country exporters at the present time. In the absence of changed procedures, they are unlikely to benefit much from seeking to change this aspect of the Harbison draft.

Second, the proposal that only existing TRQs will be increased and that additional access will be on an MFN basis implies that the existing distribution of the benefits of TRQ access to the EU market in favour of Latin American suppliers will be not only maintained but reinforced. Not only are they dominant suppliers for the existing TRQs, but as relatively competitive global producers they are likely to be able to compete for a larger share of the increased global quotas made available. The Harbison proposals, or indeed any improvements in TRQ access unless specifically skewed in their direction, have little relevance to the LDCs or low-income developing countries.

Conclusions

This chapter has used a graphical, partial equilibrium, approach to estimate the value of the welfare gains to developing countries arising from the TRQ access to the EU market granted in the Uruguay Round. It is not implied that these welfare gains emerged as a result of the Uruguay Round. Under the AoA, the European Union opened both current access and minimum access TRQs. Only the minimum access TRQs represented new market opening commitments. The graphical analysis was used to show that the welfare gains take two forms: (i) increased export surplus on additional market access, and (ii) quota rents created when the TRQ is binding. We have assumed that the main value of TRQs to developing countries is the additional quota rent they can capture, and we have implemented a methodology to quantify the value of these rents captured as a result of TRQ access to the EU market.

The results can be interpreted for policy purposes in two ways. First, because rents accrue as a result of differences between over-quota (MFN) tariffs and in-quota tariffs, they indicate the size of the potential welfare losses to developing countries on TRQ access arising from a reduction of MFN tariffs. These losses, of course, must be offset against the gains obtained from easier access to export markets arising from reciprocal MFN tariff reductions. Second, the scale of rents accruing to developing countries helps to establish their possible interest in a further expansion of TRQs in the Doha Round of multilateral trade negotiations.

On the first point, the overall rent accruing to developing-country exporters on average annually over the 1997–99 period in the EU market amounts to just over €1 billion, of which just €225 million accrues to non-Latin American developing-country exporters (on the assumption that ECU1 in the late 1990s equals €1 today). These are the most likely non-competitive producers whose access to the EU market is sustained by bilateral TRQs, and who thus would be most vulnerable to further reductions in MFN tariffs on TRQ commodities. The great bulk of this arises in the case of ACP sugar exports under the Lomé Convention (now the Cotonou Agreement) and underlines the need for special measures to address the adjustment difficulties created for these countries by the process of multilateral trade liberalization. To the extent that, by definition, mechanisms must be in place to ensure that developing-country exporters can capture a (high) proportion of the rent created in these instances, then a reduction in in-quota tariffs, where they are currently positive, would be an effective means of providing some temporary compensation for the erosion of quota rents through MFN tariff reductions. Specifically in the case of ACP sugar exports to the European Union, this is not a practical option as the *de facto* tariff levied on TRQ imports is already zero. However, it may be a useful instrument in other countries where preferential TRQ access is provided. An alternative proposal which might be relevant in some cases might be to introduce specific changes in the licensing rules designed to ensure a greater transfer of the quota rents to developing-country exporters, for example, by requiring export certificates supplied by the exporting country. While the WTO *Bananas* case made clear that this cannot be done on a discriminatory basis, it may have some potential as a compensatory mechanism to offset a loss of quota rents arising from further trade liberalization. A drawback of the proposal is that any attempt to compensate countries through TRQs risks creating a constituency in favour of maintaining high levels of MFN tariffs and thus the value of their TRQ access, as shown by the Mauritius proposal to the Special Session on Agriculture.

The second point addresses the importance of extending TRQs in the Doha Round and their use as a development instrument. Latin American suppliers of fruits and vegetables (bananas are the main product in this group) appear to be able to appropriate significant rents from TRQ access, and this might encourage them to seek extensions of this access in the current negotiations. However, their very competitiveness which enables them to appropriate rents means that they would also benefit from further MFN tariff reductions. The fact that TRQ preferences by definition will be temporary, as their value will be eroded by successive rounds of MFN tariff reductions, argues against spending their limited negotiating capacity in that direction.

The argument for the ACP and, to a lesser extent, Asian economies is a different one. Extending TRQ access for these countries has the danger that building up markets whose value depends on continued protection would encourage resources in these countries to move into sectors which are not sustainable in the longer run. On the other hand, these countries are vulnerable to moves either to reduce or eliminate their preferences or to multilateralize those TRQ quotas from which they currently benefit. Ways must be found to protect their interests in the negotiations. To the extent that increasing TRQ volumes is a relatively non-contentious issue, this could bring some benefits to competitive developing-country suppliers, particularly if it meant that the TRQ was no longer binding. In the longer run, however, the main benefit to developing countries will come from a reduction in over-quota tariffs. It will be important for developing countries not to lose sight of this fact in an attempt to obtain rather marginal gains for poverty alleviation through tinkering with the TRQ system.

Notes

1. WTO official documents are identified by their document code and can be downloaded from the WTO website, www.wto.org.
2. Regime-switching occurs where there is a change in the particular TRQ characteristic which is binding.
3. The quota for rum and taffia, which was added in July 1997 resulting from an agreement between the European Union and the United States on spirituous beverages, has not been included in this analysis.
4. Formally, it is the European Communities (EC) which has acceded to the WTO but to avoid confusion we refer to the European Union throughout this chapter.
5. In TRQ notifications, covered products are classified by tariff item numbers which follow the 8-digit level of the Harmonized System (HS).
6. To the extent that TRQ rents accrue to exporters, the unit value of TRQ imports should be higher than the unit value of non-TRQ HS8 imports by the value of the unit rent which accrues to exporters. As TRQ imports cannot be separately distinguished from non-TRQ imports, the average value of HS8 imports to which this situation applies will be slightly raised, and thus the size of the unit preference margin (defined above) will be underestimated. The importance of this error will depend on the relative shares of TRQ and non-TRQ imports in individual tariff lines, and in the size of the unit quota rent which the exporter can appropriate.

   A third, more technical assumption is required in some limited cases to apportion TRQ volumes which straddle HS8 tariff lines to those individual tariff lines. This was done on the basis of the relative size of the overall trade in each of the HS8 tariff lines affected.
7. Agricultural imports are defined as the sum of HS Chapters 1 to 24 less fish and fish products (Chapter 3). The AoA in addition covers a small number of

    additional products in HS Chapters 25 and above which are not included in Table 6.2 (see AoA, Annex 1).

8. With 100 per cent fill rates, using the actual TRQ volumes rather than the notified TRQ imports would give slightly higher estimates of the preference margin. For the three individual years 1997, 1998 and 1999, the potential preference margin would have amounted to ECU 5.4 billion, 4.9 billion and 4.4 billion, respectively, compared to the actual preference margin of ECU 4.4 billion, 4.3 billion and 3.7 billion calculated on the basis of notified imports.

9. WTO, 14 June 2001, Committee on Agriculture, Addenda to table MA1 Notifications: General Council Decision, WT/L/384 [G/AG/N/EEC/1, EEC/3, EEC/14 & EEC/15].

10. Measurement problems arise in this exercise. The FAOSTAT product classification corresponds approximately but not exactly with the HS4 classification, and the FAOSTAT country classification does not correspond exactly to the EU's COMEXT trade database. In aggregating countries and products into groups, not all countries export each product and the product composition of a region's exports may be different. The figures shown in Table 6.8 should be taken as indicative of the relative competitiveness of each region in producing the products shown in the table.

11. Note that we are using the unit export prices of ACP countries to the world market and not just to the European Union in Table 6.9. It is possible that EU export prices are inflated by the rent transfer, and thus the higher export prices on EU exports would not necessarily imply low competitiveness (see n.6). While the use of unit export prices on world exports is intended to mitigate this effect, the exports of many ACP countries are highly concentrated on the EU market, so contamination from this rent transfer effect cannot be ruled out.

12. Exceptions to this would be a requirement that (i) the in-quota duty would be zero for tropical products, whether in primary or processed form, and for products of particular importance to the diversification of production from the growing of illicit narcotic crops, or crops whose non-edible or non-drinkable products, while being lawful, are recognized as being harmful for human health, and (ii) that in-quota tariffs should be reduced in respect of TRQs where fill rates on average in the most recent three years for which data are available have been less than 65 per cent.

References

Abbott, P. (2002) 'Tariff Rate Quotas: Failed Market Access Instruments?', *European Review of Agricultural Economics*, 29(1): 109–30.

Abbott, P. and B. A. Morse (1999) 'TRQ Implementation in Developing Countries', Paper presented at the WTO/World Bank conference on Agriculture and the New Trade Agenda from a Development Perspective, Geneva, 1–2 October.

Bureau, J. C. and S. Tangermann (2002) 'Tariff Rate Quotas in the EU', *Agriculture and Resource Economics Review*, 29(1): 70–80.

De Gorter, H. and I. Sheldon (eds) (2000) *Issues in Reforming Tariff-Rate Import Quotas in the Agreement on Agriculture in the WTO*, Commissioned Paper 13, International Agricultural Trade Research Consortium.

Elbehri, A., M. Ingco, T. Hertel and K. Pearson (1999) 'Agricultural Liberalisation in the New Millenium', Paper presented at the WTO/World Bank conference on Agriculture and the New Trade Agenda from a Development Perspective. Geneva, 1–2 October.

Matthews, A. and C. Laroche Dupraz (2001) 'Agricultural Tariff Rate Quotas as a Development Instrument', *Economie Internationale*, 87: 89–106.

OECD (2002) *Agricultural and Trade Liberalisation: Extending the Uruguay Round Agreement*, Part 1, 'Tariff Rate Quotas and Tariffs in OECD Agricultural Markets: A Forward-Looking Analysis', Paris: OECD.

Skully, D. W. (2001) 'The Economics of TRQ Administration', Technical Bulletin 1893, Economic Research Service, US Department of Agriculture, Washington, DC.

Part III
Manufacturing

7
Industrial Tariffs, LDCs and the Doha Development Agenda

Marc Bacchetta and Bijit Bora

Introduction

Non-agricultural market access (NAMA) is often referred to as the 'core business' of the WTO, since the original tariff negotiations that formed the basis of the General Agreement on Tariffs and Trade (GATT) were on non-agricultural products. Successive rounds of tariff negotiations since 1947 have resulted in the current world average applied tariff for non-agricultural products of 9.4 per cent and an average bound rate of 29.4 per cent. In comparison the similar figures for tariffs on agricultural products, which were negotiated multilaterally for the first time only during the Uruguay Round negotiations are 17.9 per cent for applied tariffs and 62 per cent for bound tariffs. Therefore, the current round of negotiations on NAMA reflects a situation of fairly low tariffs in general. But, as will be shown, not all tariffs are at insignificant levels.

The Doha Ministerial Declaration[1] states that the negotiations on non-agricultural products should aim in particular at the reduction or elimination of tariff peaks, high tariffs and tariff escalation, in particular on products of export interest to developing countries, and that product coverage shall be comprehensive and without *a priori* exclusions. The Declaration also states that the agreed negotiation modalities will include appropriate studies and capacity-building measures to assist least-developed countries (LDCs) to participate effectively in the negotiations.

Several published studies have provided a partial overview of the post-Uruguay Round non-industrial tariff landscape.[2] They all reach the same general conclusions regarding the current market-access situation. First, developed countries have bound all or most of their non-agricultural tariffs. Second, on average, their bindings are low but certain products, such as textiles and clothing, leather and footwear or fish, and fish products, stand out as having higher tariffs than others, with a higher tariff dispersion, tariff escalation and tariff peaks. These peaks and high tariffs affect particularly developing countries and LDCs as they protect products which are of particular export interest to developing countries. Third, most developing countries have either bound their tariffs at relatively high levels or they have bound only a limited number of tariff lines. Fourth, developing countries' applied tariff rates are often far below their bound levels. Fifth, LDCs benefit from preferences granted by developed countries. But developed countries also grant preferences to certain developing countries and to other developed countries as part of regional trade agreements (RTAs).

This chapter aims at further clarifying the current tariff landscape and in particular the situation regarding non-preferential tariffs. It builds upon past results and elaborates on three specific areas. First, the residual protection in developed country markets in the form of peaks and escalation. Second, the high level of tariffs in developing countries and in some regions the limited coverage of tariff bindings. Third, the LDCs and the international call for more effective non-reciprocal market access. This, of course, is combined with the fact that as a group these countries have very low levels of bindings.

Market access: unfinished business?[3]

There is a number of ways to view the issue of market access, and the question of to what degree it is unfinished business. For example, Bora (2002a) estimates that the share of world imports that enter markets duty-free is 55 per cent. This estimate includes imports that enter under most-favoured-nation (MFN) tariffs and preferential tariffs, including non-reciprocal arrangements. Using this figure as a benchmark one could interpret the issue of market access as being either more than 50 per cent complete – or, for some perhaps, work that progressed well beyond its usefulness to developing countries (Rodrik, 2001).

An alternative view of market-access issues would be to place them within the institutional context of the degree to which tariff lines are bound at zero within the WTO. In that respect Bora's (2002a) 55 per cent estimate of duty-free trade was obtained using applied tariffs, not bound tariff rates, which are the instruments that are negotiated within the WTO. The pattern, coverage and distribution of bound tariffs can vary quite significantly from that of applied tariffs for a given member

(WTO, 2001). Therefore, market access in the context of bound rates could be interpreted as not only duty-free lines with applied rates at zero, but also lines that are bound at zero. Since this chapter examines the issues confronting negotiators the primary focus will be on the institutional view, or bound rates, although we do discuss applied rates.

The first question addressed here is where WTO members stand with regard to their objective of achieving a substantial reduction of tariffs and eliminating discriminatory treatment in the area of non-agricultural tariffs. Two indicators are used to respond to that question. The first is the total number of MFN bound duty-free tariff lines for a sample of members divided by the corresponding total number of lines.[4] The second indicator is the value of imports under MFN bound duty-free tariff items for a sample of members divided by the corresponding value of total imports.[5]

Our overall result is that approximately 6 per cent of the total number of non-agricultural items in our sample of WTO members' tariff schedules are bound duty-free. This small number of duty-free items, even though they account for one-third of the value of world trade in industrial products, confirms that there is still a lot to be done in multilateral tariff negotiations.[6]

For the first indicator, we found significant differences between developed and developing countries on the one hand and between different regions of the world on the other. The Quad countries in our sample have between one-quarter and one-half of their tariff items bound duty-free, which accounts for between 30 and 40 per cent of their imports. Developing countries, with the exception of Hong Kong, Macau, Singapore and the Republic of Korea have generally bound between 0 and 5 per cent of their items at zero. This limited number of duty-free lines accounts for up to 30 per cent of non-agricultural imports in some cases.

In the case of bound duty-free import shares for individual countries, important differences between members in developing Asia and in Latin America can be identified. The share of imports of bound duty-free items in total imports is on average about one-third for newly industrialized Asian economies while it is close to zero for most Latin American economies. This difference is partly linked to the fact that most Asian economies participate in the Information Technology Agreement[7] while only three Latin American countries have signed this Agreement.

Combining these two indicators shows that the issue of market access for industrial products can be considered unfinished business. However, where are the pressure points in the context of the current negotiations?

Do these differ across members? These two questions are examined in the next section.

The current situation

In this section, we take up the issue of market access across three broad classifications of markets: developed countries, developing countries and LDCs. In the context of the first two groups, given the difficulties in examining data across all developed and developing members, and the concentration of world imports, the approach that we have taken is to examine in detail market access into leading importers' markets. In 2000, the largest import markets accounting for a total of 85 per cent of world imports were the Quad countries (the United States, European Union, Japan and Canada), followed by China, Hong Kong, Mexico, the Republic of Korea, Chinese Taipei, Singapore, Switzerland, Malaysia, Australia, Thailand, Brazil, Turkey, India and Poland. The framework that we shall use is based on the mandate provided by para. 16 of the Doha Ministerial Declaration. The focus is on areas which will require significant negotiating effort, such as the coverage of tariff bindings, peaks, escalation and products of interest to developing countries.

General landscape

Before proceeding with this analysis it should be noted that there are other measures beyond tariffs and non-tariff measures that may impede market access. One of these is the complicated structure of import regimes employed by some members. Market access can be improved if import regimes are simple and transparent. In this regard, Table 7.1 provides basic tariff statistics on bound tariffs for the 15 largest importers except China and Chinese Taipei, for which comparable information is not available. Column (1) of Table 7.1 indicates the number of tariff lines in the tariff schedule of various members. The variance in the figures is quite surprising. Most members have tariff schedules in the range of 5,000–8,000 lines, which is already quite significant. However, a few members, such as Turkey, Malaysia, Mexico and Brazil have more than 10,000 lines. Turkey has triple the number of India's tariff lines.

A second indicator of simplicity and transparency is the percentage of lines that are non-*ad valorem*. The problems caused by non-*ad valorem* lines in the agriculture sector are well known. In industrial products the stand out cases are Thailand, with 19.7 per cent of its lines as non-*ad valorem*, and Switzerland, with 82.8 per cent. Japan, Malaysia and the United States also have some non-*ad valorem* lines.

Table 7.1 Bound tariffs on industrial products:[a] scope of bindings, simple averages, standard deviations and tariff peaks

Import markets	Total number of tariff lines	Share of bound tariff lines[b]	Share of bound duty-free tariff lines	Share of unbound duty-free tariff lines	Share of non-ad valorem tariff lines	Simple average bound tariff	Std dev.	Share of tariff lines with duties more than three times the average	Share of tariff lines with duties above 15%
	(1)	(2)	(3)	(4)	(5)	(6)	(7)	(8)	(9)
NORTH AMERICA									
Canada	6,261	99.6	34.5	0.1	0.3	5.2	5.0	5.8	5.8
United States	7,872	100.0	39.4	0.0	4.2	3.9	5.6	7.5	3.5
LATIN AMERICA									
Brazil	10,860	100.0	0.5	0.0	0.0	30.0	7.4	0.0	97.4
Mexico	11,255	100.0	0.0	0.0	0.0	34.8	3.4	0.0	99.3
EUROPE									
European Union	7,635	100.0	26.9	0.0	0.5	4.1	4.0	2.6	1.5
Poland	4,354	95.8	2.2	0.0	0.0	10.4	5.2	1.2	13.3
Turkey	15,479	36.3	1.4	0.8	0.1	42.6	36.7	3.5	73.9
Switzerland	6,217	98.9	17.2	0.0	82.8	1.8	4.6	8.7	0.3

Table 7.1 (Continued)

Import markets	Total number of tariff lines	Share of bound tariff lines[b]	Share of bound duty-free tariff lines	Share of unbound duty-free tariff lines	Share of non-ad valorem tariff lines	Simple average bound tariff	Std dev.	Share of tariff lines with duties more than three times the average	Share of tariff lines with duties above 15%
	(1)	(2)	(3)	(4)	(5)	(6)	(7)	(8)	(9)
ASIA									
Australia	5,520	95.9	17.7	0.2	0.8	14.2	14.7	6.3	25.3
Hong Kong, China	5,110	23.5	23.5	76.5	0.0	0.0	0.0	0.0	0.0
India	4,354	61.6	0.0	0.4	1.1	58.7	33.3	0.1	97.8
Japan	7,339	99.2	47.4	0.4	3.5	3.5	6.0	5.2	1.8
Korea, Rep. of	8,882	90.4	11.6	0.0	0.2	11.7	9.6	1.4	19.1
Malaysia	10,832	61.8	1.6	2.8	3.2	17.2	13.4	0.4	58.3
Singapore	4,963	65.5	15.2	33.8	0.2	4.6	4.8	0.5	0.2
Thailand	5,244	67.9	0.0	1.2	19.7	27.5	10.6	0.1	87.1

Notes:
[a] Excluding petroleum.
[b] All shares are expressed as a percentage of the total number of industrial tariff lines (column (1)) .

Source: WTO (2001).

In terms of bindings, column (2) of Table 7.1 shows that while developed countries have bound most of their tariffs, Turkey has bound far less than half of its tariff lines and several Asian countries have bound only between 60 and 70 per cent of their tariff lines. Except for Hong Kong and Singapore, developing countries also have a higher simple average bound tariff and more dispersion, as measured by the standard deviation, than the developed countries.

Column (3) of Table 7.1 presents data in the context of measuring the openness and predictability of the trading system, in the context of tariffs. It indicates that the Quad members have the largest share of bound duty-free lines. Japan leads the way with 47.4 per cent followed by the United States (39.4 per cent), Canada (34.5) and the European Union (26.9). Although Singapore and Hong Kong have bound less lines as a percentage when compared to members of the Quad, this can be explained by the fact that they have a higher share of lines that are duty-free. Hong Kong has more than three-quarters of its lines duty-free, while the comparable figure for Singapore is about 50 per cent.

There is also a wide variance in the structure of tariffs for members in our sample. The simple average bound rate for the Quad members, Hong Kong, Singapore and Switzerland is less than 5.2 per cent, although it should be pointed out that the figure for Switzerland does not take into account non-*ad valorem* lines. The highest averages are in India and Turkey, which also have the highest standard deviations. Furthermore, when comparing their tariff structure and taking 15 per cent as a benchmark, members with high national averages also have a high percentage of lines above that benchmark. On the other hand, the Quad members have both low averages and low percentages of lines above 15 per cent.

While Table 7.1 provides useful information in a general context, it also masks a number of key issues in both the context of industrial policy and in multilateral negotiations. Therefore, the level of bindings is now examined at a more disaggregated level. Table 7.2 shows the simple average of bindings at the MTN category level.[8] Four categories of products stand out as having higher tariff averages than the others in both developed and developing countries.[9] Those are: textiles and clothing; leather, rubber, footwear and travel goods; transport equipment; and fish and fish products. In eight out of our 15 sample countries, textiles and clothing has the highest tariff average of all categories, while in four others, the highest average is in the fish and fish products category. Table 7.3 shows that those sectors are also the ones with the largest share of lines with bindings above 15 per cent.

Table 7.2 Bound tariffs on industrial products: simple averages, by country and MTN category

Import markets	Wood, pulp, paper and furniture	Textiles and clothing	Leather, rubber, footwear and travel goods	Metals	Chemicals and photographic supplies	Transport equipment	Non-electric machinery	Electric machinery	Mineral products and precious stones and precious metals	Manufactured articles not elsewhere specified	Fish and fish products
	(1)	(2)	(3)	(4)	(5)	(6)	(7)	(8)	(9)	(10)	(11)
NORTH AMERICA											
Canada	1.3	12.4[a]	7.6	2.8	4.5	6.8	3.6	5.2	3.1	4.2	1.8
United States	0.6	8.9	8.4	1.8	3.7	2.7	1.2	2.1	3.3	3.0	2.2
LATIN AMERICA											
Brazil	27.7	34.9	34.7	33.4	22.7	33.6	32.6	31.9	33.5	33.5	33.4
Mexico	34.0	35.0	34.8	34.7	35.2	35.8	35.0	34.1	34.4	34.6	35.0
EUROPE											
European Union	0.7	7.9	4.8	1.6	4.8	4.7	1.8	3.3	2.4	2.7	11.8
Poland	8.0	13.1	11.9	9.9	8.7	16.1	8.9	9.7	6.9	11.6	16.3
Turkey	40.5	80.3	79.9	30.4	29.0	25.8	23.7	26.6	39.4	43.3	26.2
Switzerland	2.1	4.6	2.0	1.1	1.5	2.2	0.6	0.7	1.5	1.3	0.5
ASIA											
Australia	7.0	28.8	17.5	4.5	9.2	15.1	9.1	13.3	7.0	7.0	0.8
Hong Kong, China	0.0	0.0	0.0	0.0	0.0	0.0	0.0	0.0	0.0	0.0	0.0
India	56.4	87.8	67.8	58.3	44.1	53.9	36.2	44.8	47.2	72.4	68.6
Japan	1.2	6.8	15.7	0.9	2.4	0.0	0.0	0.2	1.0	1.1	6.2
Korea, Rep. of	4.8	18.2	16.7	7.7	6.7	24.6	11.1	16.1	10.4	11.4	19.1
Malaysia	19.8	20.7	19.1	14.2	15.4	29.8	10.9	14.1	14.7	12.6	14.5
Singapore	3.1	7.8	3.4	3.2	5.0	4.4	4.3	4.9	1.2	1.2	9.8
Thailand	21.3	29.2	34.1	25.6	29.3	38.5	23.4	30.5	25.9	29.5	12.5

Note:
[a] **Bold numbers** are values above the national average.
Source: WTO (2001).

Table 7.3 Bound tariffs on industrial products: tariff peaks (share of tariff lines above 15%, by country and MTN category), percentage of total tariff lines in each category

Import markets	Wood, pulp, paper and furniture	Textiles and clothing	Leather, rubber, footwear and travel goods	Metals	Chemicals and photographic supplies	Transport equipment	Non-electric machinery	Electric machinery	Mineral products and precious stones and precious metals	Manufactured articles not elsewhere specified	Fish and fish products
	(1)	(2)	(3)	(4)	(5)	(6)	(7)	(8)	(9)	(10)	(11)
NORTH AMERICA											
Canada	0.5	30.6	17.1	0.0	0.0	7.9	0.0	0.0	1.1	1.6	0.0
United States	0.0	13.0	14.9	0.2	0.0	3.1	0.0	0.0	2.4	1.2	1.1
LATIN AMERICA											
Brazil	91.1	100.0	100.0	98.5	96.8	99.3	82.8	97.5	93.6	99.2	97.2
Mexico	96.0	99.8	100.0	99.3	99.8	96.2	100.0	99.4	97.4	99.6	100.0
EUROPE											
European Union	0.0	0.0	11.2	0.0	0.0	3.9	0.0	0.0	0.0	0.1	21.8
Poland	0.0	42.2	32.9	0.2	1.7	26.2	0.0	7.2	6.9	15.5	36.4
Turkey	81.6	94.5	88.5	78.5	50.6	77.1	68.1	62.7	72.5	72.5	99.0
Switzerland	0.0	0.7	0.0	0.1	0.8	0.5	0.0	0.0	0.3	0.0	0.0
ASIA/PACIFIC											
Australia	1.0	73.3	37.2	4.2	0.2	14.8	8.4	20.2	5.7	4.4	0.0
Hong Kong, China	0.0	0.0	0.0	0.0	0.0	0.0	0.0	0.0	0.0	0.0	0.0
India	98.4	99.3	99.3	95.9	97.1	95.1	98.8	100.0	94.9	98.3	100.0
Japan	0.0	0.3	39.0	0.0	0.0	0.0	0.0	0.0	0.0	0.0	0.0
Korea, Rep. of	5.5	37.2	35.8	6.6	4.7	40.3	8.1	42.6	14.9	13.4	82.5
Malaysia	92.2	80.4	53.3	35.8	43.8	58.5	27.1	36.8	31.7	31.9	29.0
Singapore	0.0	0.0	0.0	0.0	0.0	8.0	0.0	0.0	0.0	0.0	0.0
Thailand	68.8	93.0	94.7	82.0	96.0	72.9	98.9	97.6	68.3	88.6	31.0

Source: WTO (2001).

Table 7.4 shows that in several of the sample countries, the four sectors identified as having the highest bindings have lower shares of unbound tariffs. Several countries have bound only a limited proportion of lines in the transport equipment category. Thailand, for instance, has bound less than a quarter of its transport equipment lines. Similarly, in the textiles and clothing category, Turkey has bound only 11 per cent and India 26 per cent of tariff lines, while Poland has bound only 13 per cent of the tariff lines in fish and fish products.

While developed countries, most transition economies and most Latin American countries have bound all, or almost all, of their industrial tariff lines, most African and Asian countries have bound only a limited number of tariff lines. Table 7.5 shows the distribution of binding coverage across countries, respectively, for Africa, Asia and Latin America. In Africa, the distribution of binding coverage is concentrated in the extremes. More than half the countries have bound less than half their tariff lines. As can be seen in column (1), 14 out of a total of 41 African countries have bound less than 10 per cent of their industrial tariff lines. Of those, 11 have even bound less than 5 per cent of their lines. At the same time, 11 countries have bound between 90 and 100 per cent. In Asia, one-third of the 21 countries in our sample have consolidated less than half their lines and only nine countries have consolidated more than 90 per cent of their lines. In Latin America, the situation is strikingly different, with only four out of 32 countries with a binding coverage of less than 90 per cent.

Moreover, we know that applied tariffs in developing countries are often far below the level of bindings. For those two reasons, it is important to consider both the bound and the applied tariffs.[10] Our investigation of the tariff structures of leading importers thus continues with an examination of their applied MFN tariffs. Simple applied tariff averages at the MTN category level are presented in Table 7.6 for 15 of the 18 leading importers.[11] Textiles and clothing have the highest or the second highest tariff average in all countries except Poland and Chinese Taipei, where they rank third. More generally, for all countries in our sample, the two sectors with the highest applied tariff averages across categories are among the four sectors identified as the most protected based on their bindings. Moreover, as can be seen from Table 7.7, in about half the countries in our sample the sector with the largest proportion of lines with tariffs above 15 per cent is textiles and clothing. In most of the other countries, including the European Union, the largest share of peaks is found in the fish and fish products category. For Japan, the largest share of peaks is in the leather, rubber, footwear and travel goods category.

Table 7.4 Bound tariffs on industrial products: scope of bindings, by country and MTN category

Import markets	Wood, pulp, paper and furniture	Textiles and clothing	Leather, rubber, footwear and travel goods	Metals	Chemicals and photographic supplies	Transport equipment	Non-electric machinery	Electric machinery	Mineral products and precious stones and precious metals	Manufactured articles not elsewhere specified	Fish and fish products
	(1)	(2)	(3)	(4)	(5)	(6)	(7)	(8)	(9)	(10)	(11)
NORTH AMERICA											
Canada	100.0	100.0	100.0	100.0	100.0	**93.7**	100.0	100.0	98.2	100.0	100.0
United States	100.0	100.0	100.0	100.0	100.0	100.0	100.0	100.0	100.0	100.0	100.0
LATIN AMERICA											
Brazil	100.0	100.0	100.0	100.0	100.0	100.0	100.0	100.0	100.0	100.0	100.0
Mexico	100.0	100.0	100.0	100.0	100.0	100.0	100.0	100.0	100.0	100.0	100.0
EUROPE											
European Union	100.0	100.0	100.0	100.0	100.0	100.0	100.0	100.0	100.0	100.0	100.0
Poland	100.0	99.4	100.0	100.0	99.6	**57.4**	99.4	100.0	99.4	95.7	**4.7**
Switzerland	100.0	100.0	100.0	100.0	95.2	100.0	100.0	100.0	**93.0**	100.0	100.0
Turkey	33.7	**11.3**	29.8	18.5	56.1	61.2	60.2	57.6	24.3	41.1	**13.1**
ASIA/PACIFIC											
Hong Kong, China	93.2	**2.4**	24.0	54.2	5.8	5.1	16.8	4.2	39.7	20.9	100.0
India	61.5	**26.0**	48.6	56.5	88.8	70.5	92.4	87.3	71.6	39.3	**13.1**
Japan	92.8	100.0	100.0	100.0	100.0	100.0	100.0	100.0	100.0	100.0	**87.0**
Korea, Rep. of	92.2	99.7	82.3	99.3	95.5	62.7	94.6	64.4	92.0	95.3	**35.8**
Malaysia	**20.0**	94.8	87.0	49.8	72.9	39.5	89.0	77.5	65.1	84.0	43.0
Singapore	96.0	78.0	33.5	64.1	98.7	11.6	62.0	53.2	14.6	27.2	98.5
Thailand	85.9	94.4	**45.6**	54.3	54.6	24.3	88.2	57.0	**43.8**	68.7	92.3
Average	85.0	80.4	76.7	79.8	84.5	68.4	86.8	80.1	76.1	78.1	72.5

Note:
Bold numbers are values above the national average.
Source: WTO (2001).

Table 7.5 Distribution of binding coverage in Africa, Asia and Latin America

Binding coverage (%)	African countries (41)		Asian countries (21)		Latin America (32)	
	Number (1)	(%) (2)	Number (3)	(%) (4)	Number (5)	(%) (6)
≤5	11	26.8	1	4.8	0	0.0
5 < binding coverage ≤ 10	3	7.3	1	4.8	0	0.0
10 < binding coverage ≤ 20	1	2.4	2	9.5	1	3.1
20 < binding coverage ≤ 30	4	9.8	1	4.8	2	6.3
30 < binding coverage ≤ 40	3	7.3	1	4.8	0	0.0
40 < binding coverage ≤ 50	0	0.0	1	4.8	0	0.0
50 < binding coverage ≤ 90	2	4.9	5	23.8	1	3.1
90 < binding coverage < 100	11	26.8	8	38.1	8	25.0
= 100	6	14.6	1	4.8	20	62.5
Total	41	100.0	21	100.0	32	100.0

Source: WTO (2001).

Non-*ad valorem* lines are present in certain countries and certain MTN categories.[12] Thailand has the highest shares of non-*ad valorem* tariff lines with no *ad valorem* equivalent: over 30 per cent in wood and furniture, textile and clothing and leather and travel goods. The shares of Chinese Taipei in fish and fish products, the United States in not elsewhere specified articles, Thailand in chemicals and photographic supplies and in mineral products and precious stones and metals are over 15 per cent.

Sector-specific landscape

Having identified the most protected sectors, we will now go one step further and examine the structure of tariffs in those sectors. We proceed in two steps. First, we identify which sectors, at the 4-digit level, have the highest tariffs, and then we examine the importance of these sectors for developing countries.

Fish and fish products

In the fish and fish products category, small subsets of 4-digit subgroups are clearly affected by higher tariffs, than other subgroups. The European Union applies the highest tariffs to fish and fish products in all Quad countries. Two out of 13 products face tariff rates higher than 15 per cent. Japan ranks the second highest tariffs in the fish and fish

Table 7.6 Applied tariffs on industrial products: simple averages, by country and MTN category[a]

Import markets	Wood, pulp, paper and furniture	Textiles and clothing	Leather, rubber, footwear and travel goods	Metals	Chemicals and photographic supplies	Transport equipment	Non-electric machinery	Electric machinery	Mineral products and precious stones and precious metals	Manufactured articles not elsewhere specified	Fish and fish products
	(1)	(2)	(3)	(4)	(5)	(6)	(7)	(8)	(9)	(10)	(11)
NORTH AMERICA											
Canada (2000)	2.1	10.6	6.6	2.6	3.4	5.3	1.8	2.4	2.1	2.9	1.5
United States	1.1	9.4	6.4	2.3	4.0	2.7	1.3	2.0	3.4	2.3	2.2
LATIN AMERICA											
Brazil	13.1	19.8	15.8	14.1	10.0	18.6	13.5	15.3	9.9	16.3	12.3
Mexico (2000)	15.4	24.0	20.7	15.6	11.5	17.3	13.2	16.1	15.2	17.9	27.1
EUROPE											
European Union	2.3	8.6	4.9	2.4	4.6	4.7	1.7	2.8	2.4	2.5	12.2
Poland (2000)	8.5	14.0	12.7	11.0	8.5	19.4	7.9	8.3	7.9	10.5	18.3
Turkey (1999)	3.1	15.3	8.0	5.6	4.8	5.7	1.8	2.8	2.5	2.4	49.8
ASIA											
Australia	3.5	12.3	6.8	3.5	1.9	5.5	3.4	3.4	1.9	1.6	0.1
China	9	18	15	7	8	16	10	11	10	11	19
India	29.6	30	32	32.2	34.4	37.2	25	26	29	29	35
Japan (2000)	1.9	8.5	11.6	1.6	2.5	0.0	0.0	0.2	1.0	1.2	5.9
Korea, Rep. of	5.6	9.8	8.8	6.2	7.3	5.9	6.3	5.7	6.0	6.7	16.9
Malaysia (2000)	2.4	15.3	12.8	10.7	5.8	50.7	6.3	10.9	11.6	7.3	4.2
Chinese Taipei	4.8	10.1	6.2	6.0	3.9	14.1	4.9	5.6	4.5	4.7	27.1
Thailand (1999)	32.1	69.2	58.1	23.2	32.1	54.3	32.8	41.2	28.8	41.2	59.0

Note:
[a] For the year 2001 except where otherwise indicated in parenthesis.
Source: WTO Integrated Data base.

Table 7.7 Applied tariffs on industrial products: tariff peaks (share of tariff lines above 15%, by country and MTN category)[a]

Import markets	Wood, pulp, paper and furniture	Textiles and clothing	Leather, rubber, footwear and travel goods	Metals	Chemicals and photographic supplies	Transport equipment	Non-electric machinery	Electric machinery	Mineral products and precious stones and precious metals	Manufactured articles not elsewhere specified	Fish and fish products
	(1)	(2)	(3)	(4)	(5)	(6)	(7)	(8)	(9)	(10)	(11)
NORTH AMERICA											
Canada (2000)	0.6	41.9	18.8	0.0	0.0	6.3	0.0	0.0	0.8	1.6	0.0
United States	0.0	16.8	9.1	0.0	0.0	5.7	0.0	0.0	2.9	0.4	1.1
LATIN AMERICA											
Brazil	36.2	92.8	60.0	48.1	26.6	54.2	23.2	60.1	21.0	65.8	16.3
Mexico (2000)	40.5	87.7	62.5	45.0	23.5	60.4	40.3	56.8	45.4	58.6	93.5
EUROPE											
European Union	0.0	0.0	10.4	0.0	0.0	6.2	0.0	0.0	0.0	0.0	23.4
Poland (2000)	0.4	44.6	33.9	0.2	1.5	28.0	0.1	10.6	7.3	13.7	35.7
Turkey (1999)	0.2	10.9	30.5	8.6	0.0	13.2	0.0	0.0	1.2	0.2	96.4
ASIA											
Australia	0.0	24.2	2.4	0.0	0.1	0.0	0.0	0.0	0.0	0.0	0.0
China (1997)	36.1	87.4	50.0	12.8	18.0	53.1	33.7	34.5	28.3	52.5	71.6
India (1997)	83.9	99.9	82.9	91.3	96.2	84.4	98.3	96.5	88.4	99.1	16.8
Japan (2000)	0.0	2.2	30.8	0.0	0.0	0.0	0.0	0.0	0.0	0.0	0.0
Korea, Rep. of	0.0	0.0	5.8	0.0	0.0	0.0	0.0	0.0	0.0	0.0	68.6
Malaysia (2000)	8.9	44.2	42.1	35.2	19.4	64.8	20.9	32.3	32.5	20.1	12.8
Chinese Taipei	2.2	11.3	1.1	0.0	0.2	37.3	2.3	1.2	0.6	1.5	60.7
Thailand (1999)	40.1	62.6	64.2	60.6	79.6	76.7	99.9	91.8	54.8	85.4	85.1

Note:
[a] For the year 2001 except where otherwise indicated in parenthesis.
Source: WTO Integrated Data base.

products category. Among each of the Quad countries, prepared or preserved fish, and prepared or preserved crustaceans and molluscs (1604 and 1605) clearly stand out as being affected by the highest tariffs in this category. Together with fish or crustaceans' extracts and juices (1603), these products are also the most protected in most of the emerging economies in our sample.

Prepared or preserved fish (1604), the subgroup with the highest average tariff in all Quad countries except for Japan where it has the third highest level, is the second most important import product from developing countries in Quad countries. By far the main import of Quad countries from developing countries in this category is crustaceans (0306). Tariffs on imports of crustaceans are relatively high in the European Union but they are not among the highest in other Quad countries.

Tariffs on fish and fish products in Quad countries clearly exhibit escalation. This can be illustrated with the example of crustaceans. Comparing tariffs on live, fresh, frozen, or dried crustaceans with tariffs on prepared or preserved crustaceans shows that the latter are higher than the former in the Quad countries. This may contribute to discourage the processing of crustaceans in developing countries. It is interesting to note that in the case of crustaceans, escalation is far less important in emerging economies than in the Quad (Table 7.8).

Leather, rubber, footwear and travel goods

This category includes rubber and rubber products from natural rubber in primary forms to tyres and articles of hard rubber; leather and leather products; and footwear in leather, plastics, textiles or rubber.

Three categories (6401, 6402 and 6404) out of 39 have tariff averages above 15 per cent in three of the four Quad countries. All three correspond to specific types of footwear. The two other footwear subgroups (6403 and 6405) are also affected by higher tariffs in two Quad countries. Japan differs to some extent from the other Quad countries in that it also has peaks on different sorts of leather, furskins and articles of furskin, as well as on several other products. In most emerging countries in our sample, tariffs on footwear are among the highest in the category, even if they do not always stand out as much as in the Quad countries.

The bulk of Quad countries' imports from developing countries in this product category are footwear with uppers of rubber or plastics (6402), footwear with uppers of leather (6403) and footwear with uppers of textile (6404). As already mentioned, those are the subgroups with the highest tariffs. Other products imported in large quantities

Table 7.8   Applied average tariffs on live, fresh, chilled or frozen crustaceans (0306) and prepared or preserved crustaceans (1605)

Import markets	Applied average tariffs on 0306 and 1605			
	Live, fresh, chilled or frozen crustaceans (0306) (a)	*Prepared or preserved crustaceans (1605) (b)*	*Tariff escalation (b) − (a)*	*Escalation rate: $\frac{(b) - (a)}{(a)}(\%)$*
Developed countries				
European Union	11.0	17.6	6.6	60.1
Japan	3.8	7.9	4.2	110.9
United States	1.3	2.6	1.4	109.6
Canada	2.7	3.2	0.5	18.3
Emerging economies				
China	23.9	24.4	0.4	1.8
Korea, Rep. of	19.4	20.0	0.6	2.9
Poland	28.5	41.4	12.9	45.4
Brazil	12.5	18.5	6.0	48.0
Malaysia	5.4	2.9	−2.5	−46.8
Mexico	28.2	23.0	−5.2	−18.4
Turkey	55.0	57.1	2.1	3.8
Chinese Taipei	28.1	31.8	3.7	13.1
India	15.0	45.0	30.0	200.0

include articles of apparel and clothing accessories of leather (4203), tyres (4011), natural rubber (4001), articles of vulcanized rubber (4015 and 4016) and bovine or equine leather (4104). While natural rubber is exempted in all Quad countries, articles of rubber have positive tariffs, which are in some cases even higher than average. Tariffs on bovine leather are relatively high, in particular in Japan but, except in Japan, they are lower than tariffs on leather apparel and accessories and much lower than tariffs on footwear. As Table 7.9 shows, tariffs on leather and leather products are also escalating in emerging economies. We see that tariffs on leather clothing accessories (4203) and leather footwear (6403) are higher than those on leather (4104) in most countries in Table 7.9.

Textiles and clothing

Trade in textiles and clothing products will continue to be subject to a special regime under the multilateral trade rules until 1 January 2005. Until that time a significant share of world trade in textiles and clothing is still distorted by the complex set of quantitative restrictions inherited

Table 7.9 Tariffs on leather (4104), leather clothing accessories (4203) and leather footwear (6403)

Simple average tariffs				HS 4-digit			
	4104 (a)	*4203 (b)*	*(b) – (a)*	*$\frac{(b)-(a)}{(a)}$(%)*	*6403 (c)*	*(c)–(a)*	*$\frac{(c)-(a)}{(a)}$(%)*
Australia	2.5	11.7	9.2	366.8	11.7	9.2	366.8
Canada	2.4	10.8	8.4	355.3	14.2	11.9	500.0
European Union	5.1	6.6	1.5	29.6	7.7	2.7	52.5
Japan	21.8	13.9	–7.8	–36.0	25.6	3.9	17.7
Poland	6.6	23.0	16.4	248.5	12.0	5.4	81.8
Turkey	5.2	6.5	1.3	25.7	21.7	16.5	319.5
United States	3.1	7.5	4.4	141.1	5.7	2.6	83.2
Brazil	9.7	22.5	12.8	132.4	23.0	13.3	137.6
China	8.8	25.0	16.3	185.7	25.0	16.3	185.7
India	0.0	45.0	45.0	–	45.0	45.0	–
Korea, Rep. of	5.0	13.0	8.0	160.0	13.0	8.0	160.0
Malaysia	0.0	9.2	9.2	–	7.5	7.5	–
Mexico	11.0	27.7	16.7	151.5	34.8	23.8	216.2
Chinese Taipei	1.3	10.0	8.8	700.0	4.7	3.5	277.6

from the Multifibre Agreement (MFA). The Uruguay Round Agreement on Textiles and Clothing (ATC) sets out provisions to be applied by members during the transition period. Only on 1 January 2005 will the textiles and clothing sector be completely integrated into the GATT 1994 and all quantitative restrictions eliminated.

The quantitative restrictions, however, should not conceal the high tariffs with which they cohabit. As was shown above, in most of the leading merchandise importers, the textiles and clothing sector is among the few categories with the highest bound and applied tariff averages, and the largest number of tariff peaks. The ATC does not address the issue of tariff protection. The complete integration of the textiles sectors into the GATT, by eliminating the quantitative restrictions, will only bring the tariffs to the forefront.

The textiles and clothing category includes more than 150 4-digit subgroups, which is considerably higher than the three other categories we are investigating. A detailed examination of the tariff structures of the countries in our sample is thus beyond the scope of this chapter. The tariff structures of our sample countries, however, have a certain number of characteristics in common. First, with the notable exceptions of India and Turkey, all countries apply higher tariffs to clothing than to textile products. Some countries, such as Poland, Brazil and Mexico, apply the same higher tariff to all clothing products, while others impose higher but non-uniform tariffs on clothing products. Second, in most cases, the dispersion of tariffs across 4-digit subgroups in the textiles sector is significant. In absolute terms, inter-group dispersion is the highest in Malaysia, Thailand and Turkey. Among developed countries, it is the highest in Australia, Canada and the United States, where tariff averages range between 0 and more than 15 per cent.

Table 7.10 shows the pattern of tariff escalation of both Quad countries and emerging economies of textiles imports, eight of them being leading importers of textiles products.[13] It lists tariffs for textile products, both the raw materials and the highly processed products. For example, the first pair of products is the tariff rate for garneted stock of wool or of fine or coarse animal hair (5104), which is lower than that for yarn of wool or fine animal hair put up for retail sale (5109). Jute is a product of interest to LDCs. Natural fibres of jute (5303) is among the very few products with zero applied tariffs in the four Quad countries. However, woven fabrics (5310) of jute are exempted only in some of the Quad countries. Unprocessed synthetic textiles (5404, 5405) have lower tariffs in most countries than tariffs for more processed synthetic textiles such as 5606 and 5609. Synthetic staple fibres, not carded, combed or otherwise processed for spinning (5503) has lower tariffs than woven fabrics of synthetic staple fibres, containing 85 per cent or more by weight of synthetic staple fibres (5512) in 14 of the countries listed here, the only exception being Poland. Furthermore, this escalation pattern is very clear in the last two examples. Garments (6210), made up of fabrics under heading (5903), applies higher tariffs than textile fabrics impregnated, coated, covered or laminated with plastics (5903). And garments (6113) displays higher protection levels than one of its raw materials, rubberized textile fabrics (5906). The fact that tariffs on clothing are higher than tariffs on textile products offers sufficient evidence of the presence of tariff escalation.

Most imports of clothing products from developing countries in the four Quad countries are concentrated in a small number of 4-digit subgroups. Those include jerseys, pullovers and similar articles, knitted or crocheted (6110); women's or girls' suits, ensembles, jackets, etc. (6204); T-shirts (6109) and men's or boys' suits (6203). These products do not stand out as having higher or lower tariffs than other clothing products in the Quad countries. Similarly, a small number of 4-digit subgroups accounts for the lion's share of imports of textiles products from developing countries into the four Quad countries. Those include trunks, suitcases, cases, bags and the like (4202), and bed linen, table linen,

Table 7.10 Tariff escalation on textile products: applied tariffs on textiles and clothing products

Import markets	Wool		Jute		Synthetic fibre		Artificial filament		Synthetic staple		Textile fabrics coated with plastic		Rubberized textile fabrics	
	Stage 1	Stage 2	Stage 1	Stage 2	Stage 1	Stage 2	Stage 1	Stage 2	Stage 1	Stage 2	Stage 1	Stage 2	Stage 1	Stage 2
European Union	0.0	5.0	0.0	4.0	4.6	6.6	3.8	5.8	5.1	8.9	9.2	12.6	6.5	10.3
United States	–	4.5	0.0	0.1	4.7	9.0	6.6	4.0	3.2	14.0	4.8	6.2	3.5	6.1
Japan	0.0	3.5	0.0	14.0	8.0	7.2	4.2	5.2	7.1	8.6	4.2	12.4	5.5	10.6
Canada	0.0	9.5	0.0	4.7	4.8	4.8	9.5	17.5	2.5	9.6	5.9	12.5	8.3	10.2
Mexico	13.0	18.0	13.0	13.0	16.6	17.0	16.0	15.5	12.9	18.0	17.3	35.0	18.8	35.0
China	11.5	20.0	8.0	19.0	23.0	24.0	17.0	27.0	17.4	35.7	22.0	33.5	23.0	35.0
Korea, Rep. of	1.0	8.0	2.0	8.0	8.0	8.0	8.0	8.0	8.0	10.0	10.0	13.0	8.0	13.0
Australia	0.0	5.0	0.0	0.0	5.0	2.5	5.0	10.0	0.0	15.0	12.5	16.5	7.5	13.0
Poland	3.0	9.0	0.0	13.1	6.0	9.0	6.0	9.0	13.1	9.0	9.0	19.7	9.0	19.7
Turkey	0.0	39.8	0.0	4.0	5.1	38.7	38.0	58.0	5.8	9.5	10.0	13.0	44.3	10.5
Thailand	30.0	40.0	30.0	80.0	30.0	40.0	30.0	35.0	30.0	–	50.0	100.0	40.0	100.0
Brazil	8.5	18.5	10.5	17.8	15.0	20.5	14.5	20.5	13.3	16.5	18.5	22.5	18.5	22.5
Norway	0.0	6.5	0.0	0.0	0.0	7.6	0.0	0.0	0.0	4.8	6.6	13.8	3.8	8.6
Malaysia	0.0	0.0	0.0	0.0	10.0	0.0	10.0	5.0	1.0	15.0	30.0	20.0	0.0	20.0
New Zealand	0.0	7.0	0.0	0.0	0.0	7.5	0.0	7.5	0.0	0.0	5.3	19.0	1.8	19.0
India	25.0	45.0	15.0	45.0	45.0	45.0	45.0	45.0	35.0	45.0	45.0	45.0	45.0	45.0
Chinese Taipei	0.0	7.5	0.0	5.0	3.0	9.7	3.0	11.7	1.3	8.3	8.8	12.5	12.8	12.5

Source: WTO (2001).

toilet linen and kitchen linen (6302).[14] Tariffs affecting linen are significantly higher than those affecting trunks and bags.[15] In summary, tariffs on clothing are higher than tariffs on textiles products but dispersion across subgroups is higher among textiles than among clothing.

Transport equipment

The last category of products which we consider here is transport equipment. Transport equipment includes not only cars, trucks and buses and their components, but also railways and tramways, bicycles and boats. Except in Malaysia (where it has the highest tariff average and largest share of peaks of all non-agricultural MTN categories), and in Japan (where it is not protected by tariffs at all), transport equipment is generally less protected than textiles and clothing or leather but more than most other categories. One characteristic of tariff protection of transport equipment for the largest importers is that even if there is some overlap, they do not all have their tariff peaks on the same products. The European Union imposes higher tariffs on bicycles (8712) and motor vehicles including buses, cars and trucks (8702, 8703 and 8704) as well as on chassis fitted with engines for motor vehicles (8706). The United States imposes higher tariffs on railway and tramway passenger coaches and goods wagons (8605 and 8606), as well as on trucks (8704) and bicycles (8712). The other leading importers generally impose higher tariffs on buses, cars, and trucks. The difference between developing countries in Asia is striking. While the highest tariff on transport equipment in Korea is 10 per cent on buses, Thailand imposes tariffs of 120 per cent and more on buses and cars, and Malaysia and China have peaks at, respectively, 100 and 80 per cent on cars.

The most important product from developing countries for Canada, the European Union and the United States is by far cars. In the case of Japan, however, imports of bicycles exceed imports of cars. Trucks rank second for the United States but not for the European Union, where they come only third after vessels for the transport of persons or goods (8901).

The degree of tariff escalation depends on the products and on the countries. In the case of bicycles, tariffs on parts are lower than tariffs on bicycles in Canada, the European Union and the United States as well as in four emerging countries.

Least-developed countries

There are also explicit references to market-access issues for LDCs in the Doha Ministerial Declaration. The language that is used builds on the commitments that were made at the Third United Nations Conference on Least Developed Countries (14–20 May 2001, Brussels). Of particular importance in this regard is the commitment to the 'objective of duty-free, quota-free market access for LDCs'. Furthermore, market-access issues have been given a specific mandate in the work programme of the Sub-Committee on LDCs.[16]

In 1999, 97 per cent of imports originating from LDCs entered the European Union duty-free (UNCTAD, 2001). While this figure is impressive when compared to figures for the other Quad countries, which are approximately 50 per cent, what is notable is the number of HS6 lines in which LDCs had non-zero exports to the Quad markets. The European Union, with the most open market, imports the largest diversity of products from LDCs. In 1999 it imported products from LDCs across 2222 HS6 lines. In comparison, a similar number for the other Quad countries ranged from 545 to 946. This strong evidence shows that if a market is open, it allows countries to diversify their export structure.

The European Union has further opened its markets to LDCs by allowing all imports into their market, except arms, duty-free, although the transition period is longer for bananas, rice and sugar. Other developed countries, have also opened their markets, but the task of complete duty- and quota-free market access for products originating from LDCs will not be easy. Table 7.11 examines duty-free imports into developed products of non-oil, and non-arms products originating from LDCs. It is based on Indicator 37 for the Millennium Development Goals (MDGs) and shows that the trend for duty-free access for products from LDCs is not particularly encouraging. Since 1996 the trend has been negative. Furthermore, these data shows that for these products the market-access treatment for LDCs is not significantly different than that for products from other developing countries. The data are for 2001 and do not include a number of recent initiatives, most notably the EU Everything But Arms (EBA) initiative and the US Africa Growth Opportunity Act.[17]

Table 7.11 Duty-free imports into developed countries from developing countries and LDCs, 1996–2001, per cent

	1996	1997	1998	1999	2000	2001
Excluding arms						
Developing countries	54.8	50.5	49.9	57.2	62.8	65.7
LDCs	71.5	67.2	77.7	77.1	75.4	75.3
Excluding arms and oil						
Developing countries	56.8	51.5	49.9	58.1	65.1	66.0
LDCs	81.1	75.5	75.0	73.6	70.5	69.1

In addition to these market opening initiatives on the part of the developed countries there is the issue of whether or not other markets for LDC products should also be opened. Bora (2002b) estimates that 34 per cent of LDC exports go to LDC countries. Yet, many of these countries do not offer preferential schemes for LDC products. To see the impact of the absence of such schemes, consider the pattern of protection facing fish and fish products, which are the fifth largest export product of LDCs. Table 7.12 shows that preferences can have a significant impact on the pattern of protection. There is no effect on the already high (relative) tariffs in the developing countries, whereas with the exception of Japan the remaining Quad members all have zero duties.

Modalities for negotiations

The mandate for NAMA, as provided in para. 16 of the Doha Ministerial Declaration, clearly states that an objective for the negotiations is 'to reduce, or as appropriate, eliminate tariffs, including the reduction or elimination of tariff peaks, high tariffs, and tariff escalation, as well as non-tariff barriers, in particular on products of export interest to developing countries'. Ministers also mandated that the product coverage for the reduction of tariffs should be 'comprehensive'.

In achieving these aims, the text recognizes that the negotiations shall 'take fully into account the special needs and interests of developing and least-developed countries, including through less than full reciprocity in reduction commitments, in accordance with the relevant provisions of Article XXVIIIbis of GATT 1994 and the provisions in paragraph 50 [of the Ministerial]'.

The work programme for the negotiations envisaged a common understanding on a possible outline of modalities by the end of March 2003 with a view to reaching an agreement on those modalities by 31 May 2003. Neither of these deadlines was met, which implied that any agreement would have to be reached at the Fifth Ministerial Conference. As is well known, that meeting ended in failure with no agreement whatsoever. At the time of writing the status of the negotiations is unclear. However, in order to place things into perspective the process needs to be better understood. It started with the Chair of the Negotiating Group on Market Access who tabled a paper on possible elements for Modalities. The subsequent stage was a proposal by the Chair of the General Council and the last stage was the text proposed by the Minister of Trade for Mexico, Mr Ernesto Derbez, in his capacity as Chair of the Fifth Ministerial Conference.

Table 7.12 Pattern of MFN and preferential tariffs facing LDC exports of fish and fish products in selected markets

HS 4-digit	European Union		Japan		United States		Canada		China		Korea, Rep. of		Thailand		India	
	MFN	LDC	MFN	LDC	MFN	LDC	MFN	LDC	MFN	LDC	MFN	LDC	MFN	LDC	MFN	LDC
Live fish (0301)	6.8	0	2.3	2.3	0.0	0	0.0	0	11.7	11.7	10.0	10.0	60.0	60.0	15	7.5
Fish, fresh or chilled (0302)	12.9	0	4.9	4.9	0.8	0	0.1	0	17.9	17.9	20.0	20.0	60.0	60.0	15	7.5
Fish, frozen (0303)	13.6	0	4.4	4.4	0.7	0	0.1	0	18.5	18.5	10.0	10.0	60.0	60.0	15	7.5
Fish fillets and other fish meat (0304)	10.2	0	4.4	4.4	0.7	0	0.0	0	30.0	30.0	14.0	14.0	60.0	60.0	55	7.5
Fish, fit for human consumption (0305)	13.3	0	9.8	9.8	1.7	0	0.3	0	27.6	27.6	20.0	20.0	60.0	60.0	15	7.5
Crustaceans (0306)	11.0	0	3.8	3.8	1.3	0	2.7	0	23.9	23.9	18.5	18.5	60.0	60.0	15	7.5
Molluscs (0307)	7.2	0	7.4	7.2	0.4	0	0.5	0	21.9	21.9	18.9	18.9	60.0	60.0	15	7.5
Natural sponges of animal origin (0509)	2.6	0	1.8	0	3.0	0	0.0	0	15	15	9.5	9.5	35.0	35.0	15	7.5
Fats and oils of fish (1504)	3.9	0	2.3	1.6	0.8	0	3.2	0	21.7	21.7	3.5	3.5	10.0	10.0	35	35
Extracts of aquatic invertebrates (1603)	6.4	0	10.8	0	4.3	0	4.5	0	25.0	25.0	30.1	30.9	30.0	30.0	40	20
Prepared/preserved fish (1604)	18.4	0	9.2	0	5.2	0	5.4	0	25.0	25.0	20.0	20.0	30.0	30.0	40	20
Aquatic invertebrates prepared or preserved (1605)	17.6	0	8.0	0	2.6	0	3.2	0	24.4	24.4	20.0	20.0	30.0	60.0	40	20

The negotiating issues in NAMA can be classified into two broad categories: level of ambition and less than full reciprocity. The level of ambition relates to the degree of market-access opening. In this respect, there are two issues. The first is the level of cuts in applied rates, or what is usually defined as 'effective' market access. The second is the binding coverage of tariffs.

As noted earlier, there is a clear and unambiguous difference in the average applied rates of developed and developing countries. The average applied rate for seven[18] developed countries is 3.5 per cent, with Australia having the highest average at 4.6 per cent and Norway the lowest at 1.7 per cent. In contrast, the major developing country markets have averages that are sometimes two to three times higher – for example, Brazil (14.9 per cent), China (11.3 per cent), Egypt (19.4 per cent) and India (30.5 per cent).

These very different tariff profiles and also different economic structures and stages of developments combine to deliver differing levels of ambition and aspirations among the WTO members. For example, the United States has proposed the complete elimination of duties on non-agricultural products. At the same time a number of developing countries has suggested that their current tariff profiles were achieved too quickly and would require additional time before considering further liberalization.

Increasing the level of binding coverage for tariffs on non-agricultural products is the second issue in the context of ambition. Unlike agricultural products, the binding coverage of non-agricultural products is not required to be 100 per cent. Some members have low levels of binding coverage, whereas others have nearly 100 per cent. An ambitious negotiating agenda would be one which results in binding parity for agricultural and non-agricultural products.

The level of ambition, as defined by the degree of applied cuts and the coverage of bindings, is therefore the first fundamental issue to be addressed by negotiators. The second fundamental issue is operationalization of the provision for 'less than full reciprocity' (LFR). The mandate for such a provision is clear. The degree and nature of lower obligations for developing countries has to be defined. In the NAMA context, LFR is broadly defined as developing countries taking on fewer obligations than developed countries – for example, lower tariff reductions, and/or longer implementation periods for these reductions. As an extreme, LFR could also be interpreted as a complete exemption from any obligations.

Another dimension of LFR is the level of binding coverage. Since some developing countries have bound less than 100 per cent of their non-agricultural tariff lines and binding is considered to be a concession, LFR could be interpreted as maintaining less than 100 per cent binding coverage.

The most pressing issue facing participants in the negotiations, at this point, is to obtain an agreement on modalities for negotiations. The chair of the Negotiating Group on Market Access released a paper, under his own responsibility, entitled 'Draft Elements of Modalities for Negotiations on Non-Agricultural Products' (TN/MA/W/35). The paper covered tariff reductions, non-tariff barriers (NTBs) and appropriate studies and capacity-building. His proposal for tariff reductions was based on two core approaches: a formula and elimination of tariffs in certain sectors.

The chair proposed a non-linear formula to be applied on a line-by-line basis. A key property of the proposed formula was that it cut higher tariffs by greater amounts than lower tariffs (hence non-linear). The percentage cuts by each member were envisaged to be different since they were based on the calculated average of a member's bound tariff schedule: the higher the tariff average, the lower the cut for a given tariff. Similarly members with low tariff averages would be required to make larger tariff cuts.

The second approach is the elimination of tariffs in broadly defined sectors of export interest to developing countries, with the precise definition of the sectors to be decided by the participants in the negotiations. The proposed sectors are: electronics and electrical goods; fish and fish products; footwear; leather goods; motor vehicle parts and components; stones, gems and precious metals; and textiles and clothing. The path to reach the zero tariffs in any agreed sector would be different for developed and developing countries. Without specifying time periods, the chair proposed a single period for developed countries and three periods for developing countries. In the first period, tariffs are reduced to at least 10 per cent and then retained at that level for the second period. The tariffs are eliminated only at the end of the third period. The phasing down of tariffs during the first and third periods are through equal annual reductions.

In addition to the formula and sectorial tariff elimination the chair proposed supplementary modalities, such as request and offer and sectorial harmonization and elimination. He also proposed that participants should consider the elimination of low duties.

LFR is incorporated into the chair's proposal in a number of ways. First, through the formula where certain developing countries have recourse to a higher coefficient and hence lower tariff cuts. Second, by having access to different longer and different phases for the elimination of tariffs in the sectorial component of the modalities. Third, through longer periods for the implementation of tariff cuts. Fourth, developing countries that have not bound 100 per cent of their tariff lines are given the possibility to leave at least 5 per cent of their lines unbound, provided that these unbound lines cover less than 5 per cent of their imports. Fifth, the exemption of LDCs from any tariff reductions.

The chair of the General Council adopted the same framework for tariff reductions that was proposed by the chair of the Negotiating Group on Market Access. However, due to the fact that the Fifth Ministerial Conference was faced with a decision on modalities as opposed to negotiating a specific formula, the text that was forwarded to Cancún was of a general nature (Job 03/150 Rev.1). It suggested only the use of a 'non-linear' formula and sectoral tariff elimination. Despite these generalities, there was no consensus to agree to the proposal.

Lack of agreement to the text, however, needs to be interpreted cautiously. As is well known, the Ministerial failed when the chair called the meeting to a close based on his assessment of no possible agreement on a decision regarding modalities for negotiations on the Singapore issues. In essence, the text on non-agriculture was not tested. For that matter, neither was the text on agriculture. Nevertheless, the prevailing opinion of many was that considerable progress had been made in Cancun on the non-agriculture text that could have resulted in a satisfactory text for all members. However, we shall never know if that would have been possible.

Although members are continuing to discuss how to proceed with the post-Cancún process, there is an emerging consensus that the architecture for modalities as set out by the chair could be used as a framework for negotiations. Specific issues such as the functional form of the formula to be used (if at all) and the product coverage and participation in any sectorial initiative could be negotiated at a later stage.

Conclusions

The negotiating mandate for the Doha Development Agenda is both broad and comprehensive. This chapter has tried to focus on the basic mandate given to negotiators in the area of tariffs and trade in industrial products. Although there have been quite a few studies that have identified the general parameters for the negotiations, this chapter has tried to extend the analysis further by taking advantage of more detailed data on bound tariffs.

With respect to developed-country markets, the key issue is how to tackle the residual protection arising from low overall levels of protection. We have identified a number of products at the 4-digit level where issues of peaks and escalation need to be addressed. For developing countries there are two issues – their high levels of tariffs and the limited coverage of bindings for some members. These, however, do not preclude issues of peaks and escalation such as those that we have identified as problems in developed-country markets. Finally for LDCs the issues are the degree of effective non-reciprocal market access granted by developed countries, the very high levels of protection they face in developing-country markets and the role that high levels of protection are playing as industry policy instruments in their economies.

Notes

1. Para. 16 of the Declaration states:

   We agree to negotiations which shall aim, by modalities to be agreed, to reduce or as appropriate eliminate tariffs, including the reduction or elimination of tariff peaks, high tariffs, and tariff escalation, as well as non-tariff barriers, in particular on products of export interest to developing countries. Product coverage shall be comprehensive and without *a priori* exclusions. The negotiations shall take fully into account the special needs and interests of developing and least-developed country participants, including through less than full reciprocity in reduction commitments, in accordance with the relevant provisions of Article XXVIIIbis of GATT 1994 and the provisions cited in paragraph 50 below. To this end, the modalities to be agreed will include appropriate studies and capacity-building measures to assist least-developed countries to participate effectively in the negotiations.

2. See for instance Finger, Ingco and Reincke (1996); OECD (1999); Bacchetta and Bora (2001, 2002); Supper (2001); WTO (2001); Cernat, Laird and Turrini (2002).

3. This section is based on Bacchetta and Bora (2002), which contains the detailed tables used in the analysis.

4. Bound duty-free lines were here defined as all those 6-digit HS subheadings for which all bound rates were duty-free.

5. The shares were calculated for a sample of 71 WTO members for which trade data and bound rates were available. These countries account for about 80 per cent of total world imports. The calculations are also close at the 6-digit level.

6. For the most recent years.

7. The Ministerial Declaration on Trade in Information Technology Products (ITA) was concluded by 29 participants at the Singapore Ministerial conference in December 1996. The ITA provided for participants to eliminate duties completely on IT products covered by the Agreement by 1 January 2000.

8. See WTO (2001) for definitions of the product categories.

9. These four categories also turn out to have the highest standard deviation vand the highest share of high tariffs in most of our sample countries, (see WTO, 2001).
10. Further investigation of tariff bindings will be possible with the Consolidated Tariff Schedules (CTS) database.
11. Data for Switzerland were not available, and Hong Kong and Singapore were dropped because their applied tariffs are all at zero. On the other hand, applied tariffs were available for China and Chinese Taipei, two countries for which information on bindings were missing.
12. Generally speaking, non-*ad valorem* tariffs are much more frequent in the agricultural sector (Bacchetta and Bora, 2002).
13. The leading importers of clothing also include Switzerland and Russia. But Switzerland is excluded here because comparable data are not available. Russia is excluded here because it is not a member of the WTO. Hong Kong, China, which pursues a free-trade policy, figures among both the leading importers of textiles and clothing.
14. Subgroup 8708, which corresponds to parts and accessories of motor vehicles, also accounts for a significant amount of imports from developing countries. Only one 6-digit subgroup of 8708, however – that is, safety belts (8708.21) – enters the definition of textiles products.
15. The data have not been presented, but are available upon request.
16. In para. 42 of the Doha Ministerial Declaration, WTO members committed themselves 'to the objective of duty-free, quota-free market access for products originating from LDCs' and 'to consider additional measures for progressive improvements in market access for LDCs'.
   'The Work Programme shall therefore include:
   • identification and examination of market access barriers, including tariff and non-tariff barriers for the entry of LDCs' products into markets of interest to them;
   • annual reviews in the Sub-Committee, of market access improvements, of any market access measures undertaken by members, and including the identification of reported market access barriers to LDCs' products in markets of interest to them. These reports will be on the basis of factual annual studies by the WTO Secretariat; and
   • examination of possible additional measures for progressive and predictable improvements in market access, in particular the elimination of tariff and non tariff barriers to export products from LDCs and further improvement of preferential access schemes such as the GSP schemes.'

   Reports on this work will be submitted annually to the Committee on Trade and Development. These reports will be designed to highlight LDC concerns in the context of negotiations taking place in other bodies of the WTO, but in full recognition of the integrity of the mandates of those bodies. The first report was to be submitted after the Sub-Committee's last meeting of 2002 to allow for concrete follow-up action in 2003.
17. Initial figures for 2002 provided by the Office of the United States Representative indicates that 92 per cent of US imports from AGOA-eligible countries enter the United States duty-free under various preference programmes.

18. Australia, Canada, the European Union, Japan, New Zealand, Norway and the United States.

References

Bacchetta, M. and B. Bora (2001) 'Post Uruguay Round Market Access Barriers for Industrial Products', *Policy Issues in International Trade and Commodities*, Study Series 1, Geneva: UNCTAD.

———— (2002) 'Industrial Tariff Liberalisation and the Doha Development Agenda', Paper presented at the WTO Tariff Seminar, May, forthcoming as a WTO Discussion Paper.

Bora, B. (2002a) 'Market Access Issues: What's at Stake?', Paper presented to the WTO Public Symposium, 29 April, Geneva: WTO, mimeo.

———— (2002b) 'LDC Market Access Issues and the Doha Development Agenda', Geneva: WTO, mimeo.

Cernat, L., S. Laird and A. Turrini (2002) 'Back to Basics', Geneva: UNCTAD, mimeo.

Finger, M., M. Ingco and U. Reincke (1996) *The Uruguay Round: Statistics on Tariff Concessions Given and Received*, Washington, DC: World Bank.

OECD (1999) *Post Uruguay Round Tariff Regime: Achievements and Outlook*, Paris: OECD.

Rodrik, D. (2001) 'Global Governance of Trade as if Development Really Mattered', New York: United Nations Development Program.

Supper, E. (2001) 'Is There Effectively a Level Playing Field for Developing Country Exports?', *Policy Issues in International Trade and Commodities*, Study Series 1, Geneva: UNCTAD.

UNCTAD (2001) *Duty and Quota Free Market Access for LDCs: An Analysis of Quad Initiatives*, Geneva and London: UNCTAD and Commonwealth Secretariat.

WTO (2001) *Market Access: Unfinished Business*, Geneva: WTO.

8
Developed-Country Trade Barriers and the LDCs: The Economic Results of Freeing Trade*

Jon D. Haveman and Howard J. Shatz

Introduction

In the work programme laid out by the Doha Ministerial Declaration of 20 November 2001 (WTO, 2001), the assembled trade representatives committed themselves 'to the objective of duty-free, quota-free market access for products originating from LDCs [Least Developed Countries]'.[1] Through a large number of programmes, the *Triad* economies of the European Union, Japan, and the United States already offer broad duty-free and preferential treatment to developing countries. Some, such as the Generalized System of Preferences programme (GSP), are decades-old. Others, such as the US African Growth and Opportunity Act (AGOA), the EU Everything But Arms (EBA) Initiative and Japan's 99 Per Cent Initiative, are just getting started.

The drive to grant substantial trade preferences to the LDCs, however, is relatively new. Although there is no formal system for identifying countries as 'developing', the 'least developed countries' are selected by the United Nations Economic and Social Council, based on a number of criteria and confirmed by a vote of the UN General Assembly. First created in 1971, the list is updated every three years, and there are now 49 UN-designated LDCs.

An initiative to improve market access for the LDCs was broached in the WTO's Singapore Ministerial Declaration of 1996.[2] At the WTO's Seattle Ministerial of 1999, the European Union formally proposed duty-free access for essentially all LDC exports. This and other efforts resulted in the Doha commitment.

In this chapter, we confront the Doha commitment directly, by investigating episodes of unilateral trade liberalization for goods of poor countries and projecting the effect on LDC exports were the Triad economies to eliminate tariffs on all LDC goods. Although Triad tariff barriers against LDC products have fallen dramatically in recent years, many remain, especially against certain products in which LDCs specialize.[3]

To understand trade liberalization and changing trade patterns, we describe the programmes previously instituted by the Triad to ease restrictions on trade of the poorest countries, provide formal estimates of the effect of these programmes and then project the effect of moving to a zero-tariff world for LDC goods. Examples of previous programmes include the GSP, offered by all three Triad economies; the Caribbean Basin Economic Recovery Act (CBERA), the Caribbean Basin Trade Partnership Act (CBTPA), the Andean Trade Preferences Act (ATPA) and the AGOA, offered by the United States; and successive iterations of benefits for former colonies in Africa, the Caribbean and the Pacific (ACP), offered by the European Union. Table 8.1 shows programmes uniquely offered by the United States and the European Union.

This chapter has six sections, and we will go on to describe the GSP, and discuss regional non-reciprocal Triad preference programmes. We then review the impact of four US programmes – CBERA, CBTPA, ATPA and AGOA – on developing country exports. The next section then uses econometric analysis to attack two key questions. The first asks: how have current preference programmes affected LDC exports to the Triad economies? The second asks: how will LDC exports to the Triad economies

Table 8.1 US and EU preferences programmes

A US preference programmes

Programme	Relevant dates and notes
Caribbean Basin Economic Recovery Act (Caribbean Basin Initiative)	Enacted 5 August 1983, extended and expanded in 1990; no expiry date
Andean Trade Preferences Act	Enacted 4 December 1991 with expiration set for 3 December 200; extended (retroactively) and expanded in 2002 through 31 December 2006
Caribbean Basin Trade Partnership Act	Enacted 18 May 2000; preferences expire 30 September 2008 or with the entry into force of a Free Trade Area of the Americas
African Growth and Opportunity Act	Enacted 18 May 2000; preferences expire 1 October 2008

Sources: United States Congress (2000, 2002) and United States General Accounting Office (2001).

Table 8.1   (Continued)

B   *EU preference programmes*

Programme	Relevant dates and notes
Yaoundé I	Signed 1963, effective 1964
Yaoundé II	Signed 1969, effective 1971
Arusha	
ACP–EC[a] Convention of Lomé I	Signed 1975, effective 1976–80
ACP–EC Convention of Lomé II	Effective 1981–85
ACP–EC Convention of Lomé III	Effective 1986–90
ACP–EC Convention of Lomé IV	Effective 1991–2000
Revised Convention of Lomé IV	Signed 1995, amended Lomé IV
ACP–EC Partnership Agreement, the 'Cotonou Agreement'	Signed 23 June 2000, effective 20 years
'Everything But Arms' Council Regulation	Effective 5 March 2001

Note:

[a] ACP refers to the African, Caribbean and Pacific countries; EC refers to the European Community.

Sources: European Union (1995–2002); European Union (2001); United States General Accounting Office (2001); and Agreements Office, The Council of the European Union (2003).

expand if all tariff barriers against them are removed? This is the heart of the Doha proposal.

The first non-reciprocal preference programme: the GSP

The GSP was proposed at the first session of the United Nations Conference on Trade and Development, held in March–May 1964. Later that year, a committee of the GATT proposed a GATT amendment to allow members to grant trade preferences to developing countries.[4] The amendment was necessary because such a preference programme violates the GATT's most-favoured-nation (MFN) clause, which requires all signatory trading partners to receive benefits equal to the most favourable benefits offered any trading partner. The amendment, known as the 'enabling clause', was approved for a limited period of 10 years in 1971, giving birth to GSP programmes, and then was made permanent in 1979. At least 18 economies currently offer or have offered a GSP programme.[5]

Although helping to expand developing-country exports, the GSP has come under criticism for a number of reasons.[6] Originally, the programmes offered benefits for only a limited range of products, and they still hold some products sacred – the European Union limits agricultural goods, the United States limits textiles and apparel and Japan limits footwear and prepared food. Rules of origin are sometimes complex, making it difficult for exporters to meet programme requirements. The programmes also sometimes cap the quantity of developing-country exports that can receive benefits, so it is possible for a country to be too successful. Finally, there is some evidence that such unilateral preference programmes stunt trade liberalization in developing countries themselves.[7]

The GSP in the Triad

The United States first approved a GSP programme in the Trade Act of 1974 with the programme taking effect on 1 January 1976. It was intended to last only until 1985, but remains in place today. In their reports on the bill, both the US House of Representatives and the US Senate said they instituted the programme to enhance economic development, economic diversification and exports of LDCs.[8] Benefits included duty-free treatment for designated commodities and designated countries.

The commodity list set the standard for future US trade programmes until the Trade and Development Act of 2000 (discussed later). In particular, it excluded certain textile and apparel items, watches, import-sensitive electronic items, import-sensitive steel products, some footwear and import-sensitive glass products.[9] It also established competitive need limits, under which a product from a particular country would come off the GSP list if its exports to the United States hit a certain value. The initial beneficiary list included 98 independent countries and 40 non-independent countries and territories, among which were 26 of the 27 then-UN-designated LDCs, excluding Uganda.[10] However, the initial programme contained no special benefits for the LDCs.

The Trade and Tariff Act of 1984 authorized the President to waive competitive needs limits on LDCs, known under US trade law as 'least developed beneficiary developing countries'. In 1985 President Reagan designated 32 such countries – most, but not all of the UN-designated LDCs. LDCs gained more benefits in 1997 when President Clinton named about 1,770 additional items duty-free exclusively for them.

Under the rules of its GSP, the United States can exclude countries on a number of grounds, such as having a communist government, harbouring terrorists, or belonging to an organization that withholds vital supplies from the world economy. This has led to the exclusion of LDCs at times, including Afghanistan in 1980 and the Central African Republic and Myanmar in 1989. Laos and Sudan are among those currently excluded.

The European Union (then the European Economic Community, EEC) was the first economy to implement a GSP after approval of the GATT enabling clause. Unlike the US programme, the EU programme does not offer duty-free market access on all goods. Instead, the programme in its current revision designates goods as 'non-sensitive' and 'sensitive', the latter of which compete more directly with European producers. Non-sensitive goods enter at zero duty, and sensitive goods enter at reduced duty compared to the MFN rate.[11] Although not all GSP products enter duty-free, the EU eliminated quotas and quantitative restrictions on these products in 1995.

The EU GSP provided more favourable treatment for LDCs from the beginning. It now offers more favourable benefits to a number of different types of countries based on promotion of labour rights, protection of tropical forests, or combating of drug production and trafficking. The most favourable arrangements are reserved for LDCs.

The European Union has expanded benefits for LDCs over at least the last three revisions of its programme. In each case, the benefits apply to all UN-designated LDCs. The latest expansion is the EBA Initiative, effective from 1 March 2001, in which the European Union allows duty-free and quota-free access to all products except arms and ammunition. Bananas, rice and sugar are also excluded, although trade in these three goods is to be liberalized in stages by the end of 2009.[12] Rules of origin, documentation and other requirements of the GSP programme still apply, although unlike other GSP benefits, the EBA programme has no expiration date.

Japan first offered its GSP in 1971 for 10 years and has since extended it through 2011.[13] The current iteration of the programme offers benefits on a positive list of 226 agricultural products and all industrial products, except for a negative list of 105 items. Tariffs on agricultural products range from zero to a reduction of the MFN rate, and tariffs on industrial products are zero except for items designated 'sensitive'. These items have a value or quantity ceiling, and tariffs are zero or a reduction of the MFN rate.[14]

The programme as of April 2002 includes 149 countries and 15 territories and grants LDC benefits to all but two of the 49 UN-designated LDCs – Comoros and Djibouti have not applied for benefits under the programme. In addition, the Democratic Republic of Congo and Zambia are not scheduled to receive benefits on refined copper until 2005.

Japan was early in giving special benefits to LDCs, extending preferences in April 1980. These benefits include duty-free treatment to all products covered by the GSP and the elimination of import ceilings. As of 1 April 2001, Japan went even further with its 99 Per Cent Initiative, in which it added about 360 items duty-free and quota-free to the GSP list exclusively for LDCs.[15] New products include all textile and apparel items. By Ministry of Economics, Trade and Industry estimates, this increased to 99 per cent (from around 94 per cent) the share of industrial products granted duty-free, quota-free access from LDCs. Furthermore, the initiative covered all UN-designated LDCs, including those not in the regular GSP programme at the time.[16]

Triad regional non-reciprocal preference programmes

US programmes

The oldest region-specific US unilateral preference programme is the CBERA, passed in 1983 and popularly known as the Caribbean Basin Initiative (CBI). Since then, the United States added the ATPA in 1991, and in 2000, the Caribbean Basin Trade Partnership Act (CBTPA) and the AGOA.

Preferences for the Caribbean[17]

CBERA was approved to help the region develop economically and diversify its exports. The programme provided duty-free access for all products not specifically excluded. However, many goods for which the Caribbean countries had a comparative advantage were excluded, including a wide variety of footwear, textiles and apparel. The United States amended the programme in 1990 with CBERA II, which made it permanent and improved benefits with tariff reductions for some leather goods and duty-free treatment on imports made completely from US components. The programme again, however, excluded textiles and apparel.

The last change to preferential programmes for the Caribbean came with the CBTPA, Title II of the Trade and Development Act of 2000. This programme essentially extended benefits equivalent to the benefits Mexico gained from the reciprocal North American Free Trade Agreement (NAFTA). Most importantly, the CBTPA included a range of textile and apparel products, although with rules-of-origin requirements.

Nearly all the countries of the Caribbean, including those of Central America, participate in the Caribbean programmes, as shown in Table 8.2A. The original CBERA designated 27 countries as eligible (Aruba did not exist separately in 1983) and 24 eventually became beneficiaries. President Clinton designated the same 24 as beneficiaries under the CBTPA.[18] Haiti, the only LDC in the Western Hemisphere, has been a beneficiary from the beginning.

Preferences for the Andean Nations[19]

ATPA was enacted on 4 December 1991, with the stated purpose of promoting economic development and export diversification to provide alternatives to the production of drug crops. The act provided preferences similar to those under the CBERA, duty-free access for all products except footwear, textiles, apparel, tuna, petroleum, watches and watch parts and sugars and similar products, and was set to last 10 years. It has been extended through the end of 2006, and the extension broadened the goods eligible for preferences. Most importantly, it included apparel under certain conditions, and tuna, although not tuna packed in cans.

The original act extended eligibility to four of the five members of the Community of Andean Nations – Bolivia, Colombia, Ecuador and Peru. Bolivia and Colombia became beneficiaries in 1992, and Ecuador and Peru in 1993. The bill excluded Venezuela from eligibility, and in the run-up to renewal, both the Andean Community and the government of Venezuela unsuccessfully sought Venezuela's inclusion.[20] None of the beneficiaries is an LDC.

Table 8.2   Eligible countries for US preferences programmes[d]

A   Caribbean trade preference eligible countries

Anguilla[a]	Guyana
Antigua and Barbuda	*Haiti*
Aruba	Honduras
The Bahamas	Jamaica
Barbados	Montserrat
Belize	Netherlands Antilles
British Virgin Islands	Nicaragua
Cayman Islands[a]	Panama
Costa Rica	Saint Kitts and Nevis
Dominica	Saint Lucia
Dominican Rep.	Saint Vincent and the Grenadines
El Salvador	Suriname[a]
Grenada	Trinidad and Tobago
Guatemala	Turks and Caicos Islands[a]

Notes:
[a] Non-beneficiary countries; these four countries have not requested beneficiary status.
Source: Office of the United States Trade Representative (1999).

B   African growth and opportunity eligible countries

Angola[b]	*Liberia*[b]
Benin	*Madagascar*[c] (6 March 2001)
Botswana[c] (27 August 2001)	*Malawi*[c] (15 August 2001)
Burkina Faso[b]	*Mali*
Burundi[b]	*Mauritania*
Cameroon[c] (1 March 2002)	Mauritius[c] (19 January 2001)
Cape Verde[c] (28 August 2002)	*Mozambique*[c] (6 February 2002)
Central African Republic	Namibia[c] (3 December 2001)
Chad	*Niger*
Comoros[a]	Nigeria
Democratic Republic of Congo	*São Tomé and Príncipe*
Republic of Congo	*Rwanda*[c] (4 March 2003)
Côte d'Ivoire	*Senegal*[c] (23 April 2002)
Djibouti	Seychelles
Equatorial Guinea[b]	*Sierra Leone*
Eritrea	*Somalia*[a]
Ethiopia[c] (2 August 2001)	South Africa[c] (7 March 2001)
Gabon	*Sudan*[a]
Gambia	Swaziland[c] (26 July 2001)
Ghana[c] (20 March 2002)	*Tanzania*[c] (4 February 2002)
Guinea	*Togo*[b]
Guinea-Bissau	*Uganda*[c] (23 October 2001)
Kenya[c] (19 January 2001)	*Zambia*[c] (17 December 2001)
Lesotho[c] (23 April 2001)	*Zimbabwe*[b]

Notes:
[a] Non-beneficiary countries. These three countries have not requested beneficiary status.
[b] Non-beneficiary countries. These seven countries have been reviewed but not yet been granted beneficiary status.
[c] Textile and apparel beneficiary, with date of textile and beneficiary status in parentheses. Countries in italics are currently UN-designated LDCs, Botswana was an LDC from 1971 to 1994.
[d] Information is current as of the end of 2002.
Source: Office of the United States Trade Representative with the Assistance of the Trade Partnership (2000); Office of the United States Trade Representative (2001b, 2002), *Federal Register* (various issues).

Preferences for Africa[21]

The third region to receive unilateral US preferences is Africa, under AGOA, Title I of the Trade and Development Act of 2000. AGOA sets a new standard for US programmes in several different ways. First, it locks in GSPs for beneficiary countries for eight years. Otherwise, GSPs are renewed annually. It also adds 1,835 new products to the GSP list especially for AGOA beneficiaries. In addition, it removes the competitive needs limits that apply throughout the GSP programme. Finally, it includes benefits for textiles and apparel, provided beneficiaries show they have procedures in place to prevent transshipments and meet rules-of-origin requirements, creating two tiers of beneficiaries.

The law named all sub-Saharan African (SSA) countries as eligible, and 34 became beneficiaries on 2 October 2000. Table 8.2B shows eligible countries and their beneficiary status. In 2001, the first full year of the programme's operation, 11 countries were named textile and apparel beneficiaries, with at least five more named in 2002.

In the Caribbean and Andean programmes, all eligible countries that requested beneficiary status eventually gained it. This is not so in the Africa programme. As with all unilateral US programmes, eligible countries must request beneficiary status and must fulfil certain requirements, such as making progress toward establishing or having established a market-based economy, having policies to reduce poverty, combat corruption and protect worker rights, and helping combat terrorism.[22] Accordingly, only 22 of the 34 UN-designated African LDCs currently receive AGOA benefits. Of these, 10 have gained textile and apparel benefits.

EU programmes

The European Union has provided preferences to its former colonies in ACP almost since the beginning of its formation. These efforts have included two Yaoundé Conventions, the Arusha Convention, four Lomé Conventions and now the Cotonou Agreement.[23] As these agreements evolved, they included some and then all ACP LDCs, but never any Asian LDCs. The final Lomé Accord included all ACP LDCs for the first time.

Yaoundé I and II in 1963 and 1969, respectively, between the EEC and former African colonies gave commercial advantages on industrial items along with financial assistance. Arusha in 1969 gave separate benefits to three East African states, all previously under British rule or administration.

The accession of the United Kingdom to the EEC in 1973 led to the Lomé Convention (Lomé I) of 1975, which expanded membership to African and Caribbean former British colonies. In addition to preferences that made almost all exports duty-free, the Convention included a commodity export earnings stabilization scheme known as STABEX. Although agreed to by the GATT, there was some feeling among GATT members that the ACP trade preferences were not entirely GATT-legal. These concerns continued throughout the life of the Lomé Conventions.[24] Lomé II, signed in 1979 and effective in 1981, added a new system for ACP mineral and mining exports, known as SYSMIN. Lomé III, signed in 1984 and effective in 1986, and Lomé IV, signed December 1989 and updated mid-term in 1995, broadened country coverage.

The newest agreement, the ACP–EC Partnership Agreement, also known as the Cotonou Agreement, represents a significant break with the unilateral preferences of the past. Faced with issues about whether preferences to the ACP nations but not to other developing countries violate the WTO accords, the EU will phase out these preferences and instead institute Economic Partnership Agreements (EPAs) with different regional groupings of the ACP countries by 2008 at the latest. These agreements effectively will be reciprocal free-trade agreements (FTAs) rather than unilateral preference programmes.[25]

The Cotonou Agreement includes 39 LDCs. They will not be affected by the requirement for EPAs and can retain their Lomé benefits. Furthermore, under the EBA GSP, the LDC Cotonou signatories will have duty-free access for all products regardless of Cotonou terms.

US programmes and developing-country export enhancement

Preference imports from developing countries comprise a small share of all US imports. As shown in Figure 8.1, between 1989 and 2001 regional US programmes and the GSP covered only 1.8 per cent–3.8 per cent of US imports. They covered between 2.6 per cent and 9.4 per cent of all non-dutiable imports during the same period. The trend of the non-dutiable share has been downward since 1993, probably because of an expansion of goods coming in duty-free from all countries as a result of the Uruguay Round Agreements. Growth of trade under these preferences has been volatile, rising with the creation of new benefits under CBTPA and AGOA, as shown in Figure 8.2.

Among the Caribbean beneficiaries, total trade under the programmes has boomed since 1989, the first year of available data. Table 8.3A shows US imports from the Caribbean beneficiary countries for 1989, 2000 and 2001. While total US imports from the 24 countries rose more than 200 per cent between 1989 and 2001, total preference trade – CBERA, CBTPA and GSP – rose more than 500 per cent. For the four non-beneficiary eligible countries, in contrast, US imports fell by almost 60 per cent during the same period, from US$383 million to US$160 million. Much

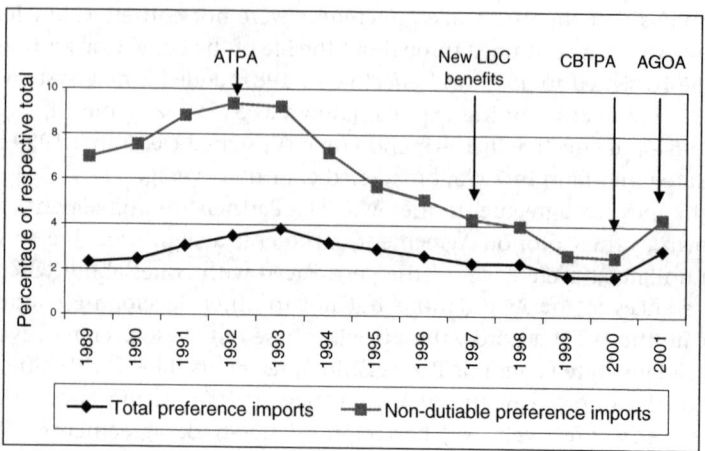

Figure 8.1   US preference imports relative to total US imports,[a] 1989–2001
Notes:
[a] Total preference imports are shown relative to total imports, and non-dutiable preference imports are shown relative to non-dutiable total imports. Imports are imports for consumption. Preference imports include all imports entering under the GSP, the ATPA, the CBERA, the CBTPA, and the AGOA.
Arrows show the year each new programme started.
New LDC benefits apply to the GSP programme.
Source: United States International Trade Commission (undated).

of the increase from beneficiaries stems from the CBTPA. Imports under this programme rose from essentially zero in 2000 to US$5.6 billion in 2001.

Use of the CBERA and CBTPA programmes is broader on a country basis than the use of AGOA or even ATPA, as will be seen. In 2001, nine of the 24 beneficiary countries were each responsible for at least 1 per cent of US imports under the programme. Still, use of the programme is quite concentrated, with the Dominican Republic and Honduras accounting for almost 50 per cent of programme imports, as shown in Table 8.3B.

The two largest commodities imported under the Caribbean programmes were both apparel items, as shown in Table 8.3C. In large part, these were not eligible for preferences under the GSP or even CBERA. However, the new preferences did not increase overall exports of these items much; rather, they shifted the items from dutiable to non-dutiable or reduced-dutiable categories. The total value of these imports stayed more or less steady between 2000 and 2001, but the non-dutiable value rose markedly. Despite the apparel results, the preference programmes

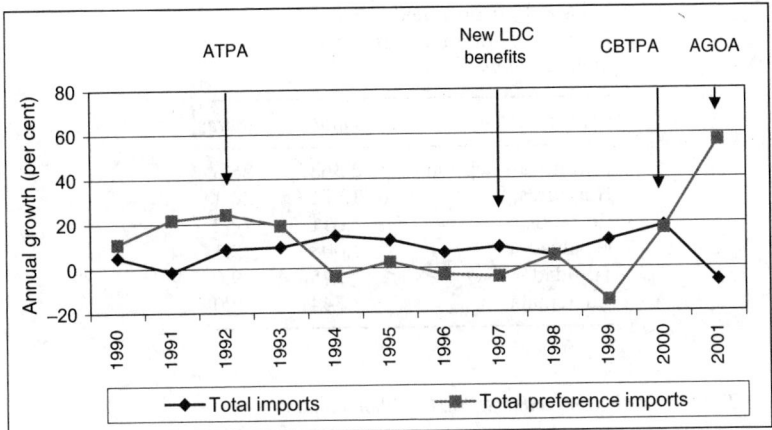

Figure 8.2   Growth rate of US total imports and US preference imports[a]

Notes:

[a] Imports are imports for consumption. Data for each year show the growth rate from the previous year. For example, the figure for 1990 shows 1990 imports relative to 1989 imports. Preference imports include all imports entering under the GSP, the ATPA, the CBERA, the CBTPA, and the AGOA.

Arrows show the year each new programme started.

New LDC benefits apply to the GSP programme.

Source: United States International Trade Commission (undated).

Table 8.3   Trade performance under the Caribbean programmes

A   *Imports from the 24 beneficiary eligible countries, 1989–2001, million dollars[a]*

	Value			Percentage change	
	1989	2000	2001	1989–2001	2000–01
Total US imports	6,637	22,161	20,679	211.6	−6.7
of which:					
CBERA, CBTPA and GSP	1,331	2,994	8,478	536.9	183.1
CBERA imports	915	2,635	2,706	195.7	2.7
CBTPA imports	0	157	5,593	NA	3,462.3
GSP imports	416	202	179	−57.0	−11.5
Non-dutiable imports	3,455	14,139	15,089	336.7	6.7
of which:					
CBERA, CBTPA and GSP	1,331	2,710	7,941	496.6	193.0
CBERA imports	915	2,351	2,623	186.6	11.6
CBTPA imports	0	157	5,140	NA	3,173.5
GSP imports	416	202	179	−57.0	−11.5

Table 8.3   (Continued)
B   *Top   Caribbean   beneficiaries,   2001, million dollars*

Country	Value	Share
Dominican Republic	2,363	28.5
Honduras	1,671	20.1
Costa Rica	1,011	12.2
El Salvador	1,008	12.1
Trinidad	745	9.0
Guatemala	744	9.0

C   *Top five Caribbean products, 2001, million dollars[b]*

Commodity	Value	Share	Percentage change from 2000
Knitted apparel (HS 61)[c]	2,936	35.4	0.6
Non-knitted apparel (HS 62)	2,257	27.2	−2.9
Mineral fuels and oils (petroleum) (HS 27)	436	5.3	−13.8
Edible fruit and nuts (HS 8)	332	4.0	−11.6
Electrical machinery and equipment (HS 85)	307	3.7	−1.8

Notes:
[a] Imports are imports for consumption.
[b] In Panel C, percentage change represents change in value of total imports, not just CBERA and CBTPA imports.
[c] HS stands for Harmonized System, the international tariff code system.
Source: United States International Trade Commission (undated).

appear to have spurred increased imports rather than a shift in the categorization of goods. Imports of many of the top preference items either rose, or fell less than, total imports from beneficiaries between 2000 and 2001.

As with CBERA and CBTPA imports, ATPA imports have boomed. Table 8.4 shows trade in 1991, the year before the programme started, and 2001, for the four ATPA beneficiaries. Total imports rose 92.5 per cent, while preference imports (ATPA and GSP) rose 278 per cent. All of this rise can be attributed to ATPA, since GSP imports actually fell 62.5 per cent. And although some of the ATPA rise may be attributed to shifts of products from the GSP to ATPA, this can form only a small portion. GSP trade in 1991 totalled US$492 million, while ATPA trade in 2001 totalled US$1.6 billion.

Table 8.4 Trade performance under the Andean Trade Preferences Act, 1991 and 2001

A *Imports from the four beneficiary countries, million dollars[a]*

	1991	2001	Percentage change
Total US imports	4,969	9,569	92.5
of which:			
ATPA and GSP	492	1,859	278.0
ATPA imports	0	1,675	NA
GSP imports	492	184	−62.5
Non-dutiable imports	2,599	5,770	122.0
of which:			
Non-dutiable ATPA and GSP	492	1,836	273.5
Non-dutiable ATPA imports	0	1,652	NA
Non-dutiable GSP imports	492	184	−62.5

B *Top Andean beneficiaries, 2001, million dollars*

Country	Value	Share
Colombia	718.0	42.9
Peru	686.3	41.0
Ecuador	216.3	12.9
Bolivia	54.0	3.2

C *Top five Andean products, 2001, million dollars[b]*

Commodity	Value	Share	Percentage change from 1991
Copper (HS 74)[c]	440	26.3	728.3
Live trees and plants (cut flowers) (HS 6)	383	22.9	85.9
Dyes and paints (HS 32)	195	11.7	2,276.6
Pearls, gems, precious metals (HS 71)	153	9.1	−13.5
Vegetables (HS 7)	78	4.7	1,223.4

Notes:
[a] Imports are imports for consumption.
[b] In Panel C, percentage change represents change in value of total imports, not just ATPA imports.
[c] HS stands for Harmonized System, the international tariff code system.
Source: United States International Trade Commission (undated).

ATPA benefits are quite concentrated in the top two countries, as shown in Table 8.4B. Colombia and Peru accounted for more than 80 per cent of all ATPA imports. However, they also accounted for more than 80 per cent of total GDP of the four countries. Compared to their share of GDP, Colombia's use of the programme is low (GDP share of 51.1 per cent), Peru's use is high (GDP share of 33.1 per cent), Ecuador's use is about equal to its GDP (GDP share of 11.0 per cent) and Bolivia's use is low (GDP share of 4.9 per cent).

ATPA benefits are concentrated among four main product groups – copper, live trees and plants (cut flowers), dyes and paints and precious metals. Table 8.4C shows the top five products. A large number of these top products are resource-based, either agricultural products or metal- and mining-based products. Finally, overall imports in nearly all the top product groups grew more than total US imports from these countries.

AGOA, the newest regional preference programme, has given a tremendous boost to duty-free trade from Africa, as shown in Table 8.5A. While GSP imports totalled US$600 million from AGOA beneficiaries in 2001, down from US$704 million the year before, AGOA imports totalled almost US$8.2 billion, making almost 50 per cent of all imports from these countries duty-free. In contrast, the non-beneficiary countries saw their non-dutiable imports fall by almost 9 per cent from 2000 to 2001, largely because of decreased US GSP imports.

However, AGOA benefits are even more concentrated among countries and products than are Caribbean or ATPA benefits, as shown in Parts B and C of Table 8.5. The two top countries, Nigeria and Gabon, accounted for more than 87 per cent of all AGOA imports, and only six of the 35 countries eligible throughout 2001 accounted for at least 1 per cent of AGOA imports. The top product was crude petroleum, which accounted

Table 8.5 Trade performance under the African Growth and Opportunity Act, 2000 and 2001

A   *Imports from the 35 beneficiary eligible countries, million US dollars*[a]

	2000	*2001*	*Percentage change*
Beneficiary eligible countries			
Total US imports	18,321	17,573	–4.1
Non-dutiable imports	9,207	14,247	54.7
of which:			
AGOA and GSP	704	8,179	1061.1
AGOA imports	0	7,579	NA
GSP imports	704	600	–14.8

B   *Top African beneficiaries, 2001*

Country	Value	Share
Nigeria	5,688	75.0
Gabon	939	12.4
South Africa	417	5.5
Lesotho[d]	130	1.7
Republic of Congo	129	1.7
Madagascar	92	1.2

C   *Top African products, 2001*[b]

Commodity	Value	Share	Percentage change from 2000
Mineral fuels and oils (petroleum) (HS 27)[c]	6,827	90.1	−3.3
Vehicles (HS 87)	241	3.2	138.8
Knitted apparel (HS 62)	212	2.8	17.6
Non-knitted apparel (HS 61)	143	1.9	62.2
Iron and steel (HS 72)	79	1.0	−37.4

Notes:
[a] Imports are imports for consumption.
[b] In Panel C, percentage change represents change in value of total imports, not just AGOA imports.
[c] HS stands for Harmonized System, the international tariff code system.
[d] Countries in italics are currently UN-designated LDCs.
Source: United States International Trade Commission (undated).

for 96.6 per cent of all Nigeria AGOA exports and 100 per cent of all Gabon AGOA exports. Despite the dominance of oil, AGOA has opened the way for apparel exports to the United States. In 2000, almost no apparel exports from AGOA beneficiaries were duty-free. However, in 2001, almost 38 per cent were duty-free, almost entirely because of AGOA. Total AGOA-beneficiary exports in the two apparel tariff categories rose 34.7 per cent between the two years.

The implications of Triad LDC preferences

Triad preferences have done a great deal to expand exports from LDCs, yet lower barriers have the potential to expand the demand for LDC goods even more. This section provides estimates of the increase in LDC exports to Triad countries resulting from unilateral preference programmes offered through 2000. These include the GSP for all three Triad economies, CBERA for the United States, and the Lomé ACP preferences for the

European Union.[26] The figures are based on 2000 trade and tariff data, so they are an understatement of the benefits to developing countries because preference programmes have become more generous in the years since. However, they still provide a reasonable indication of the impact of these programmes on LDC exports to Triad countries.

Following an assessment of the trade benefits derived from existing preferences, this section then provides estimates of the increase in LDC exports to Triad economies that would result from making the preferences comprehensive, or setting tariffs on imports from LDCs equal to zero. This exercise shows the effects of eliminating the remaining barriers. The largest benefits are projected to come from increased exports to the United States, although exports to the European Union and Japan should also increase.

Methodology

The methodology used is closely related to that introduced in Haveman, Nair-Reichert and Thursby (2003). In a framework of monopolistic competition, goods are differentiated by both country of origin and by whether they are produced domestically or are imported. For example, from the perspective of a US consumer, the degree of differentiation between goods produced in Japan and an LDC is comparable to that between goods from Japan and the European Union, but the degree of differentiation between any of these goods and those produced in the United States is the same. In essence, the model assumes that imports from any pair of foreign countries are better substitutes for one another than they are for domestically produced products.

The framework incorporates multiple tariff effects. The first, the *trade-reduction effect*, provides a measure of the elasticity of substitution between domestic and foreign goods. This effect arises from the general increase in import prices that results from the imposition of a tariff on goods from any or all countries. Consumers are assumed to engage in two-stage budgeting. In the first stage, consumers allocate their expenditures for each good to domestic and foreign purchases. As the price of imports rises, expenditures allocated to imports fall for all imports of a particular good. This means that the imposition of a tariff, whether on goods from one country or goods from all countries, will reduce imports from all countries.

The second tariff effect is the *trade-diversion effect*. This effect accounts for the redistribution of expenditures away from imports from countries that face relatively high tariffs, the second stage of the budgeting process. Once overall expenditures are allocated between domestic and foreign purchases, they must be allocated across varieties of imports. In the current context, this effect permits LDC tariff preferences to increase LDC exports relative to exports from other countries. The trade-diversion effect is expected to be larger than the trade-reduction effect, since the elasticity of substitution between foreign sources is generally larger than that between domestically produced goods and imports.

The results presented below are based on the analysis of highly detailed bilateral trade data. Regressions are run separately on the imports of each Triad member. The unit of observation for the dependent variable is a bilateral trade flow on a commodity basis between the European Union, the United States, or Japan and a single foreign country.[27] The analysis includes imports from approximately 240 economies. Further, coefficient estimates are generated independently for each 3-digit Standard Industrial Classification (SIC) industry. That is, the universe for each regression is a single 3-digit 1987 US SIC industry, made up of individual observations on bilateral trade flows at the 6-digit Harmonized System (HS) level. Different trade-reduction and trade-diversion effects are therefore estimated for each of 165 SIC groupings for each of the Triad members. These estimates are generated independently of one another and are produced by a TOBIT regression framework that permits the analysis to incorporate the informational content of the zero-flow observations in the data. The vast majority of bilateral trade observations at the 6-digit HS level are zeros.

In addition to these variables, the regressions include year dummies, because the observations include trade flows from multiple years: 1993, 1995, 1996, 1998, 1999 and 2000. Data for 1994 and 1997 are unavailable. Also included is a set of indicator variables for the income level of the exporter, and GDP for the exporter crossed with income level.[28] The estimating equation also includes controls for distance between importer and exporter, whether or not the same language is predominant in both countries, and whether or not the countries share a land border, along with an indicator for the presence of non-tariff barriers (NTBs) to trade or specific tariffs.

The estimating equation can be written as:

$$\ln M_{I,j,t,h} = \alpha + \beta_1 \ln TAUBAR_{I,t,h} + \beta_2 \ln TDIVER + \beta_3 NTM_{I,j,t,h}$$
$$+ \beta_4 SPEC_{I,j,t,h} + (\beta_5 + \beta_6 \ln GDP_{j,t})^* \sum_{l=1}^{4} \beta_{6+l} INC_{I,j,t}$$
$$+ \beta_{11,t} YEAR_t + \beta_{12} \ln(DISTANCE_{I,j}) + \beta_{13} BORDER_{I,j}$$
$$+ \beta_{14} LANGUAGE_{I,j} + \varepsilon_{I,j,t}$$

where the dependent variable, ln $M_{I,j,t,h}$ is imports by country I from country j of commodity h in year t. Here, I indicates one of the United States, the European Union, or Japan, j is one of 240 potential exporters, t is one of the years listed above and h is a 6-digit HS product line within a specific 3-digit SIC industry. TAUBAR is the trade-reduction effect, calculated as the trade-weighted average tariff that country I imposes on imports of commodity h from all countries in year t. TDIVER is the trade-diversion effect and is the difference between the actual tariff imposed on imports by I from j of product h in year t and the average tariff that country I imposes on all countries but j.[29] β_1 and β_2 are expected to be negative with $\beta_2 > \beta_1$.

Table 8.6 summarizes coefficient estimates and hence the trade-reduction and diversion effects that are estimated. US imports are both more sensitive to the imposition of tariffs – the trade-reduction effect is bigger – and the presence of preferences – the trade-diversion effect is bigger – than are imports to other Triad economies. EU trade is the least sensitive. This means that US trade contracts the most in response to the imposition of a tariff, and more readily alters its pattern of imports in response to the imposition of preferences. In each of the three Triad economies, the trade-diversion effect is larger than the trade-reduction effect, which provides a simple check on the validity of the coefficient estimates. Recall that the reduction effect is a direct indication of the elasticity of substitution between domestically produced goods and foreign products while the diversion effect is highly correlated with the elasticity of substitution between foreign varieties. As was stated earlier, the latter effect is expected to be greater than the former. As is common with regressions at this level of detail, the predicted sign on the coefficient estimates of the control variables is not always obtained, but in all cases the predicted sign is more common than is an incorrect sign.

Table 8.6 Summary of tariff effects on Triad trade,[a] standard deviations of the coefficient estimates are in parentheses

	Mean coefficient estimates	
	Trade reduction	*Trade diversion*
US	−8.3 (32.2)	−19.4 (25.9)
EU	−3.3 (21.4)	−8.5 (16.2)
Japan	−7.8 (17.8)	−13.1 (21.7)

Notes:
[a] For more on the commodity distribution of these types of estimates, see Haveman *et al.* (2003).

The figures presented in Table 8.6 may be interpreted as follows. For the United States, on average, a 1 per cent increase in the average tariff imposed on imports reduces imports by 8.3 per cent. Further, a 1 per cent tariff preference leads to a 19.4 per cent increase in trade for the exporter in question. These numbers are reasonably large, suggesting significant benefits for LDCs from the unilateral preference programmes.

In the following subsections, the coefficient estimates are used first to estimate the amount of LDC exports to Triad countries attributable to tariff preferences, and then to forecast the increase in LDC exports that might result from the elimination of all tariffs only on the imports of LDC products.

Estimating the trade implications of existing preferences

Triad preference programmes have provided large boosts to LDC exports. Table 8.7 provides both an indication of the importance of LDC trade in overall Triad imports and an estimate of the increase in observed trade flows attributable to the existence of tariff preferences. Columns (1) and (2) of the table simply present actual data. Columns (3) and (4) present counterfactual results generated from the coefficient estimates presented above. The figures in column (3) are predictions of the amount of trade that would not have occurred were all beneficiaries of Triad unilateral preference programmes subject to MFN tariffs.

Of the three members, the European Union imports more from LDCs than do either of the others, in both value terms and as a percentage of

Table 8.7   Triad LDC imports and preferences programmes in force, 2000

Triad member	Total imports, 2000 (US$ billion)	Imports from LDCs, 2000 (US$ billion)	Imports from LDCs resulting from preferences (US$ billion)	Change in LDC imports (%)
	(1)	*(2)*	*(3)*	*(4)*
US	1,058.2			
All LDCs		4.6	0.4	10.5
CBERA[a]		0.3	0.03	13.7
EU	614.3			
All LDCs		9.2	2.8	14.0
ACP		5.8	0.7	45.5
Japan	234.2	0.8	0.3	65.1

Note:
[a] Haiti is the only LDC affected by the CBERA programme.

total trade. The United States imports about half as much, while Japan's imports from LDCs are a distant third, at less than US$1 billion. The Triad's LDC imports due to unilateral preferences follow a similar pattern. The European Union has experienced the largest effect, with trade increases of US$2.8 billion, followed by the United States, US$0.4 billion and then Japan, at US$0.3 billion. However, as a percentage of LDC imports, Japan's programme does the most to expand trade, with preferences increasing trade by 65 per cent. The EU programmes are in the middle, raising trade by 45 per cent, while US programmes have provided only a 10.5 per cent boost to imports from LDCs.

The preferences as implemented affect slightly different sectors in the three country groups. Preferences from the United States in the mineral products and mechanical machinery sectors account for more than half of the increased imports. EU preferences also increase trade in the mechanical machinery sector, but the preferences also result in a significant expansion of textile imports, which is not the case for the United States. Japanese preferences expand imports in the textiles, wood and wood products, and headwear and footwear sectors.

This pattern of benefit reflects the design of the various programmes. The EU programmes are deep and broad, in the sense that all 2-digit HS sectors receive coverage and preferences are generally extended to the vast majority of products within a sector. Exceptions include some agricultural and food trade. The Japanese and US programmes are likewise broad, but significantly less deep, meaning that there are preferences in most sectors but that in most cases preferences do not extend to all products in each sector.

Also reflective of this pattern is the number of countries that benefits from the preference schemes. The EU and Japanese programmes provide benefits in excess of a 10 per cent increase in exports to 26 and 25 countries, respectively. In fact, the EU programmes are estimated to be responsible for a doubling of exports from seven countries, while the Japanese programme is estimated to be responsible for a doubling of exports from nine countries. For the European Union, the seven include (in descending order) the Solomon Islands, the Maldives, Lesotho, Bangladesh, Cambodia, Laos and Madagascar. Of these, the Maldives, Bangladesh, Cambodia and Laos benefit only from the EU GSP programme, not its ACP preferences. For Japan, the nine countries include (in descending order) Mauritania, Gambia, Cambodia, Mozambique, Nepal, Bangladesh, the Solomon Islands, Madagascar and Senegal.

The US programmes have led to export increases of more than 10 per cent for only 15 countries, of which five experienced more than a doubling of exports as a result of these programmes. These five were Togo, Burkina Faso, Benin, Angola and Equatorial Guinea. For the last two countries, imports were more than 40 times what they would have been in the absence of preferences. There is no overlap between the top US beneficiaries and the top EU and Japanese beneficiaries, but there is considerable overlap between the EU and Japanese beneficiaries – Bangladesh, Cambodia, Madagascar and the Solomon Islands.

Concerning commodities, approximately 70 per cent of the increase in total EU imports from LDCs is in Textiles and Textile Articles, the imports of which increase by about 136 per cent under the two EU preference programmes. The bulk of the increase in Japanese imports – almost 68 per cent – is in the Animals and Animal Products sector, the imports of which almost triple due to the Japanese GSP. Almost half of the import expansion for the United States is in the Mineral Products sector, the imports of which more than triple under the US preference programmes. About 29 per cent of the US expansion comes in the Textiles and Textile Articles sector, but this represents only a 3.7 per cent increase in the imports of these products.

The distribution and effect of preferences indicates why US imports from LDCs under the preference programmes expand so little compared to EU or Japanese imports. Although the United States provides broad tariff preferences to LDCs – tariffs are eliminated on 48 per cent of the tariff lines with positive MFN tariffs – the goods for which a preference is not granted are both the goods in which LDCs possess a strong comparative advantage and goods with some of the highest applied tariffs. These are primarily Textiles and Textile Articles, including apparel.[30] In contrast, the European Union and Japan have granted significant preferences in textiles and apparel, but have failed to provide free access in their own sensitive sectors, those related to agricultural and general food production. As a result, Vegetable Products imports increase very little in both the European Union and Japan under their preference programmes, although Animals and Animal Products imports increase a great deal.

Estimating the trade implications of the removal of existing preferences

Although exports from LDCs have benefited a great deal from preferences, there is still much room for trade liberalization, as recognized in the plans for the Doha Round of multilateral trade negotiations. As of 2000, the United States maintained significant barriers to imports from LDCs, with an import-weighted average tariff in excess of 5.3 per cent. The remaining barriers in the European Union and Japan were much lower, at 0.02 and 1.8 per cent, respectively. As a result, the elimination of all tariffs on imports from LDCs by the Triad members would be expected to expand exports the most for US partners and the least for EU partners. Table 8.8 provides evidence.

While Table 8.7 reported the implications of restoring MFN tariffs to LDCs, Table 8.8 predicts the effects of eliminating the remaining tariffs on Triad imports of LDC goods. Again, this is accomplished by applying the results of the regression analysis in forecasting counterfactual trade flows for the year 2000.

The remaining tariffs on US imports from LDCs clearly pose the most significant impediment to LDC exports. The projections indicate that LDC exports would have been almost US$7 billion, or 148 per cent, higher in 2000 than was observed had the United States levied no tariffs on imports from LDCs. These increased imports are highly concentrated in the textiles, footwear and transportation equipment sectors. The remaining EU barriers, on the other hand, are relatively few and their elimination would lead to a 2.6 per cent expansion in imports from LDC countries. Predictably, agricultural and food-related sectors are responsible for nearly all of this increase. Japan represents the middle ground, with a projected increase in imports from LDCs of approximately 69 per cent. However, this represents an increase in imports from LDCs of only US$0.6 billion, the vast majority of which is in the animal and animal products sector.

More countries stand to benefit from the further elimination of tariffs by the United States and Japan than by the European Union. For the

Table 8.8   Changes in Triad imports from LDCs as a result of eliminating all tariffs on LDC exports, 2000

Triad member	Total imports, 2000 (US$ billion)	Imports from LDCs, 2000 (US$ billion)	Imports from LDCs resulting from enhanced preferences (US$ billion)	Change in LDC imports (%)
US	1,058.2			
All LDCs		4.6	6.8	147.9
CBERA		0.3	0.5	162.3
EU	614.3			
All LDCs		9.2	0.2	2.6
ACP		5.8	0.0	0.1
Japan	234.2	0.8	0.6	69.3

United States, 19 countries are projected to experience a 10 per cent or greater expansion of exports, 12 of which would see exports more than double. The same is roughly true for Japan with 21 countries expanding exports by more than 10 per cent and with exports more than doubling for 10 of those countries. For the United States, the magnitudes are quite significant. The country experiencing the largest gain in value terms is Bangladesh, for which exports could be expected to increase by US$4.0 billion, or 168 per cent. For Japan, the largest gainer is Mauritania, for which exports expand by US$0.2 million, or 198 per cent.

The gains if the United States and Japan were to institute zero-tariff regimes on LDC trade would be even more broad-based than indicated above, because there is little overlap among the top gainers. Only the Maldives is projected to more than double exports to both the United States and Japan, by 177 per cent to the former and 157 per cent to the latter.

Exporters to the European Union could expect only modest gains, with just two countries, Senegal and São Tomé and Príncipe, experiencing double-digit growth. For both countries it is projected that exports would have been almost 70 per cent higher had preferences been comprehensive in 2000. Senegal is the largest gainer in value terms, with exports projected to increase by US$0.2 million.

By industry, exports to the United States have been the most significantly hindered in the Textiles and Textile Articles sector. Had preferences been comprehensive in 2000, US imports of these products from LDCs would have been almost three times larger, increasing from less to US$3.6 billion to almost US$9.9 billion. This expansion of US imports in textiles and apparel accounts for approximately 90 per cent of the total export gains from zeroing out tariffs on goods imported from LDCs. Other sectors growing significantly include Footwear and Headgear, Prepared Foodstuffs and Hides and Skins, all of which are projected to grow more than 150 per cent.

For Japan, 80 per cent of the gains come in the Animals and Animal Products sector, in part stemming from a projected 152 per cent increase in the imports of these products. This sector is also responsible for most of the gains under Japan's GSP as of 2000, suggesting that although LDCs have gained important benefits already, barriers are still high. Although the Animals and Animal Products sector is the only one in which Japanese imports would more than double, substantial gains also occur in imports of Mineral Products (47 per cent), Wood Pulp and Products (31 per cent) and Textiles and Textile Articles (12 per cent).

As in Japan, Animals and Animal Products imports would provide the bulk of the gains – a little more than 61 per cent of the increase – in EU imports from LDCs. However, EU imports from LDCs in this sector would increase by only 19 per cent, reflecting the generous preferences already offered by the European Union. Other industries that would experience significant increases in imports are Animal or Vegetable Fats and Oils (46 per cent) and Prepared Foodstuffs (25 per cent), reflecting EU barriers to agriculture-based trade.

Although the current preference schemes do provide large benefits to many LDCs, these projections indicate that there are significant gains to be had from further expansion of these programmes. Existing preferences have increased Triad imports from LDCs to the tune of US$3.5 billion. However, this number is less than half the LDC exports that could be had from totally freeing trade with LDCs. Should these programmes be made comprehensive, exports from LDCs to Triad members would be expected to grow by approximately US$7.6 billion, US$6.8 billion of which would be destined for the United States.

Conclusions

Significant discussion took place between the time when the idea of a GSP-type programme was introduced at UNCTAD-I in 1964 and the passage of the enabling clause in 1971 allowing such programmes to be GATT-legal. Those seven years of work resulted in programmes that have had significant expansionary effects regarding LDC exports, as shown by the estimates of the previous section. Certainly the programmes were not perfect. Benefits were concentrated among a minority of countries, and difficult rules of origin and other procedures have kept many exporters from taking advantage of the programmes.

One key difficulty with the GSP and other unilateral preference programmes has been product coverage, and this was recognized in the WTO's Singapore Ministerial in 1996. Since then, the European Union has gone a long way towards removing all tariff barriers against LDC trade, while Japan has also increased benefits and the United States has taken selective steps. However, as the projections of this chapter show, there are still large trade expansionary gains to be had from fulfilling the Doha Ministerial goal of zero tariffs on all LDC imports. This is especially true of US imports from LDCs.

Certainly this cannot solve all development issues. Within trade policy alone there are still issues of rules of origin, capacity-building, trade infrastructure and LDC tariffs limiting imports from the rest of the world. However, the elimination of barriers should increase LDC exports a great deal. They will still remain a small portion of overall trade, however, limiting any disruptive effects they may have on the Triad economies.

Notes

* The authors thank participants at a UNU-WIDER project meeting for useful comments, project director Basudeb Guha-Khasnobis for initial feedback on the project and Eli Miloslavsky for research assistance.
1. Para. 42, page 9, available at http://www.wto.org/english/thewto_e/minist_e/min01_e/mindecl_e.pdf.
2. Inama, Roffarello and Musollino (2001).
3. Haveman and Shatz (2003).
4. United States International Trade Commission, Office of Industries and Office of Economic Research (1978).
5. The earliest such preference programmes actually were offered well before the passage of the enabling clause – by the USSR in 1965 and by Australia in 1966. Australia gained a GATT waiver for its programme (United States International Trade Commission, Office of Industries and Economic Research, 1978).
6. Inama, Roffarello and Musollino (2001).
7. Özden and Reinhardt (2002).
8. United States International Trade Commission, Office of Industries and Office of Economic Research (1978).
9. United States International Trade Commission, Office of Industries and Office of Economic Research (1978: 7).
10. Executive Order No. 11888, 24 November 1975 (United States International Trade Commission, Office of Industries and Office of Economic Research, 1978: 8–9).
11. European Union (1999, 2002).
12. Council Regulation 416/2001 (European Union 2001a, 2001b).
13. Customs and Tariff Bureau, Ministry of Finance (2001) and Ministry of Foreign Affairs (2002).
14. Sensitive items include 1,181 products in 81 product groups.
15. Ministry of Economics, Trade and Industry (2000) and Ministry of Foreign Affairs (undated).
16. However, Comoros and Djibouti have not applied for benefits under the Initiative.
17. Much of the institutional detail described in this section is from Office of the United States Trade Representative (1999, 2000) and United States Congress (2000).
18. The White House, Office of the Press Secretary (2000).
19. Institutional background in this section is drawn largely from Office of the United States Trade Representative (2001a).
20. Venezuela was originally excluded because the drug trade was less significant there than in the other Andean countries, because it had a far higher *per capita* GDP than the other countries and because a large share of its

exports to the United States is petroleum, which is excluded from the Act (Federal Information Systems Corporation, Federal News Service, 1991).
21. Institutional background for this section is drawn from United States Congress (2000); Office of the United States Trade Representative with the Assistance of the Trade Partnership (2000); United States Customs Service (2001); and Office of the United States Trade Representative (2001b, 2002).
22. Office of the United States Trade Representative with the Assistance of the Trade Partnership (2000: 20–3).
23. Much of this material is from European Union (undated), along with European Centre for Development Policy Management (2001a, 2001b).
24. General Agreement on Tariffs and Trade (1977, 1983, 1989, 1994). Under GATT rules, preference schemes for developing countries could not discriminate against developing countries not party to the scheme (European Centre for Development Policy Management, 2001a).
25. European Centre for Development Policy Management (2001b).
26. The US ATPA includes no LDCs.
27. Observations are excluded in the event that the importer does not import the item from any country or the exporter does not export the item to any country.
28. Income levels are low-income, lower-middle-income, upper-middle-income and high-income, as determined by the World Bank. Crossing GDP with income levels allows the influence of GDP on a country's export potential to vary across income categories. Results indicate that this specification is preferred to one that holds the effect of GDP constant.
29. The detailed tariff data are drawn from extracts of the UNCTAD-TRAINS project. See http://www.eiit.org/protection for more information. *TDIVER* takes into consideration all tariff preferences, not just those for LDCs.
30. See Haveman and Shatz (2003) for more on the nature of the existing preferences programmes.

References

Agreements Office, The Council of the European Union (2003) *Agreements* Website, available at http://ue.eu.int/accords/default.asp?lang=en, updated 8 January.
Customs and Tariff Bureau, Ministry of Finance (2001) *Customs Administration in Japan 2001*, Tokyo: The Bureau.
European Centre for Development Policy Management (2001a) 'Cotonou Infokit: From Lomé to Cotonou', Infokit 13, Maastricht: ECDPM, January.
———— (2001b) 'Cotonou Infokit: Regional Economic Partnership Agreements', Infokit 14, Maastricht: ECDPM, January.
European Union (undated) *New ACP–EU Agreement*, Web document, available at http://europa.eu.int/comm/development/cotonou/index_en.htm.
———— (1995–2002) 'The Lomé Convention', web document, Brussels: European Union, available at http://europa.eu.int/comm/development/cotonou/lome_ history_en.htm.
———— (1999) 'Vademecum: Guide to the European Union's Scheme of Generalised Tariff Preferences', Web document, available at http://europea.eu.int/comm/trade/pdf/guide_tariffpref.pdf.
———— (2001) 'Partnership Agreement Between the Members of the African, Caribbean and Pacific Group of States of the One Part, and the European Com-

munity and its Member States, of the Other Part' (ACP/CE/en 1), Brussels: European Union.

————— (2001a) 'Council Regulation (EC) No. 416/2001 of 28 February 2001 amending Regulation (EC) No. 2820/98 applying a multiannual scheme of generalized tariff preferences for the period 1 July 1999 to 31 December 2001 so as to extend duty-free access without any quantitative restriction to products originating in the least developed countries', Brussels, *Official Journal of the European Communities.*

————— (2001b) 'Generalised System of Preferences: Council Regulation amending the GSP so as to extend duty and quota free access to least-developed countries (LDCs)', Brussels: European Union, available at http://europa.eu.int/comm/ trade/miti/devel/eba4_sum.htm, March.

————— (2002) 'User's Guide to the European Union's Scheme of Generalised Tariff Preferences', Web document, available at http://europea.eu.int/comm/ trade/miti/devel/gspguide.htm, April.

Federal Information Systems Corporation, Federal News Service (1991) 'USIA Foreign Press Center Briefing. Topic: US Trade Policy, Latin America, and the Uruguay Round', Briefer: Myles Frechette, Assistant US Trade Representative, Moderator: Clint Wright, 19 December.

Federal Register (various issues), Washington, DC: US Government Printing Office.

General Agreement on Tariffs and Trade (1977) *GATT Activities in 1976*, Geneva: GATT, April.

————— (1983) *GATT Activities in 1982.* Geneva: GATT, April.

————— (1989) *GATT Activities in 1988.* Geneva: GATT, June.

————— (1994) *GATT Activities in 1993.* Geneva: GATT, August.

Haveman, J. D., U. Nair-Reichert and J. Thursby (2003) 'How Effective are Trade Barriers? An Empirical Analysis of Trade Reduction, Diversion and Compression', *Review of Economics and Statistics*, 85(2): 480–85.

Haveman, J. D. and H. J. Shatz (2003) 'Developed Country Trade Barriers and the Least Developed Countries: The Current Situation', Paper prepared for the UNU-WIDER project on *The Impact of the WTO Negotiations on Least Developed Countries.*

Inama, S., L. M. Roffarello and M. Musollino (2001) 'Improving Market Access for the Least Developed Countries', (UNCTAD/DITC/TNCD/4), Geneva: United Nations, May.

Ministry of Economics, Trade and Industry (2000) 'Policy Information: 99% Initiative on Industrial Tariffs for Products from Least Developed Countries (LDCs)', web document, available at http://www.meti.go.jp/english/information/ data/cLDC01e.html, 13 December.

Ministry of Foreign Affairs (undated) *Japan and the Least Developed Countries: Beyond One Dollar A Day*, Tokyo: MOFA.

————— (2002) *Japan's GSP*, web document, available at http://www.mofa.go.jp/ policy/economy/gsp/, April.

Office of the United States Trade Representative (1999) *Third Report to the Congress on the Operation of the Caribbean Basin Economic Recovery Act, 1 October 1999*, Washington, DC: USTR.

————— (2000) 'Fact Sheet on Caribbean Basin Trade Partnership Act and Country Designations', Washington, DC: USTR.

————— (2001a) *Third Report to the Congress on the Operation of the Andean Trade Preference Act, 31 January 2001*, Washington, DC: USTR.

———— (2001b) *2001 Comprehensive Report of the President of the United States on US Trade and Investment Policy Toward Sub-Saharan Africa and Implementation of the African Growth and Opportunity Act*, Washington, DC: USTR, May.

———— (2002) *2002 Comprehensive Report on US Trade and Investment Policy Toward Sub-Saharan Africa and Implementation of the African Growth and Opportunity Act*, Washington, DC: USTR.

Office of the United States Trade Representative with the Assistance of the Trade Partnership (2000) *African Growth and Opportunity Act Implementation Guide October 2000*, Washington, DC: USTR.

Özden, Ç. and E. Reinhardt (2002) 'The Perversity of Preferences: GSP and Developing Country Trade Policies, 1976–2000', Emory University, Atlanta, 24 May, manuscript.

United States Congress (2000) 'Trade and Development Act of 2000', Public Law 106–200, 106th Congress, 18 May.

———— (2002) 'Trade Act of 2002', Public Law 107–210, 107th Congress, 6 August.

United States Customs Service (2001) *What Every Member of the Trade Community Should Know About: The African Growth and Opportunity Act. An Informed Compliance Publication*, Washington, DC: Customs, May.

United States General Accounting Office (2001) 'Appendix II: US and EU Nonreciprocal Trade Preference Programmes', in *Comparisons of US and European Union Preference Programmes*, Report GAO-01–647, Washington, DC: GAO, June.

United States International Trade Commission (undated) *Dataweb* Electronic Database, available at http://www.usitc.gov (Version 2.5.0).

United States International Trade Commission, Office of Industries and Office of Economic Research (1978) *Study of the Effects of the Generalized System of Preferences on US Trade in the Programme's First Year of Operation* (Staff Research Study 12), Washington, DC: The Commission, March.

The White House, Office of the Press Secretary (2000) 'To Implement the United States–Caribbean Basin Trade Partnership Act', Washington, DC: The White House, 2 October.

World Trade Organization (2001) 'Ministerial Declaration: Adopted on 14 November, 2001 (WT/MIN(01)/DEC/1, 20 November 2001)', Ministerial Conference, Fourth Session, Doha, 9–14 November.

9

The EU Everything But Arms Initiative and the LDCs*

Lucian Cernat, Sam Laird, Luca Monge-Roffarello and Alessandro Turrini

Introduction: preferences as a development policy instrument

In recent years there have been increased pressures to help the poorest nations through aid, debt relief and trade initiatives. At the first Ministerial Meeting of the WTO in Singapore in 1996, the then Director-General of the WTO, Renato Ruggiero, declared his intention to press WTO members to afford tariff and quota-free entry to imports from the least developed countries (LDCs) to the markets of the developed countries. This initiative bore fruit in 2000, when the EU Trade Commissioner, Pascal Lamy, announced the intention to grant duty-free and quota-free access for all goods (with the exception of arms) originating in LDCs – its 'Everything But Arms' (EBA) initiative, under which it proposed to reduce to zero all tariffs on imports from LDCs except arms and to free such imports from any quantitative restriction. Other developed countries have made similar proposals, including the US African Growth and Opportunities Act (AGOA), but in terms of the value of trade the EU proposal is the most important. This chapter evaluates the EU proposal, using *ex ante* trade simulation techniques, and draws some tentative conclusions.

The notion of providing trade preferences for development purposes has its origins in Prebisch and Singer's work on the secular decline in the terms of trade for agricultural commodities and the perception that only manufacturing could provide stability and jobs in developing countries.[1] The Prebisch–Singer hypothesis led to two important policy prescriptions: sectoral intervention favouring import-competing manufacturing industry (import-substitution industrialization), and the idea of creating non-reciprocal tariff preferences to foster manufactured exports from the developing countries. In the latter case, the Generalized System of Preferences (GSP) is the most extensive and explicit expression of an attempt to use trade preferences as a tool of development, but today there are a number of other schemes, limited to subgroups of developing countries, with varying product coverage and preferential arrangements. Juridically, preferences for LDCs form a subset of the GSP, while other unilateral preferences depend on explicit waivers of WTO rules.

Statistics demonstrate that relatively few countries have captured the main benefits of GSP.[2] Across the major schemes, there is a strong representation of East Asian countries and India. China is the leading beneficiary in the schemes of Canada, the EU and Japan, but is excluded from the US scheme. Brazil is the major Latin American beneficiary, while South Africa is the leading African beneficiary (North African countries being covered by other preferential schemes in the EC where they might otherwise be larger suppliers than South Africa). However, there are no LDCs among the top 20 GSP plus LDC suppliers to the Canadian market. Bangladesh is the only LDC in the top 20 of such suppliers to the EC, and Mauritania is the only LDC in the top 20 of such suppliers to Japan (mainly phosphates). Angola and the Democratic Republic of the Congo (diamonds) are among the top 20 suppliers to the US market. This weakness in the trade performance of the LDCs is a key explanation for the EBA initiative.

EU preferential market-access arrangements for LDCs

The European Union is the single most important market for LDC exports. Over 50 per cent of LDC exports were sold in 2000 on the EU market, compared to 37 per cent in 1999. In 2000, the European Union took around 70 per cent of LDC agricultural exports. Among the 49 LDCs, 15 are dependent on this market, as over 50 per cent of their exports are directed there. The orientation of LDC exports towards the EU market is partly explained by the relatively low tariff barriers faced in the European market under its various preferential regimes (Table 9.1).[3] Out of total LDC exports, 44.7 per cent received preferential market access and prior to EBA implementation only 3 per cent of existing LDC exports faced a tariff into the European Union. Out of the 49 LDCs included in the GSP scheme for LDCs 39 LDCs have also benefited from preferential market access under the ACP regime. For non-ACP LDCs,

Table 9.1 European Union: major imports from LDCs, 2000

HS6 code[a]	Description	Total EU imports (US$000)	Share of LDCs in total EU imports (%)	MFN tariff[b] (%)	LDC tariff[b] (%)
090500	Vanilla	22, 666	84.80	6.00	0
260500	Cobalt ores and concentrates	110, 753	83.06	0	0
330126	Essential oils and resinoids	3, 281	77.75	1.15	0
130120	Gum arabic	28, 780	77.35	0	0
230500	Residues and waste from the food industry	20, 321	76.25	0	0
530310	Vegetable textile fibres	2, 276	76.14	0	0
430130	Raw furskins	10, 999	72.66	0	0
530710	Vegetable textile fibres	18, 075	72.23	0	0
530390	Vegetable textile fibres	253	64.43	0	0
260600	Aluminium ores and concentrates	367, 985	63.16	0	0
090700	Cloves	3, 075	61.14	8.00	0
560729	Twine, cordage, ropes and cables	2, 602	60.26	12.00	0
030333	Fish	5, 003	58.56	7.50	0
410310	Raw hides and skins	3, 852	58.07	0	0
150810	Crude oil	115, 519	55.67	3.20	0
630510	Sacks and bags	23, 209	55.18	3.00	0
121299	Oil seed, oleagi fruits	31, 335	53.60	0	0
120300	Oil seed, oleagi fruits	42, 742	51.96	0	0
110319	Groats and meal	43	44.19	–	–
530720	Vegetable textile fibres	55, 126	44.03	0	0
120720	Cotton seeds	38, 576	42.02	0	0
530410	Vegetable textile fibres	25, 755	41.93	0	0
710210	Diamonds	225, 661	41.92	0	0
030339	Fish	9, 450	41.67	11.25	0
030759	Octopus	252, 975	39.96	8.00	0
081090	Edible fruits and nuts	107, 523	37.02	5.60	0
030270	Livers and roes	5, 032	36.86	10.00	0
240310	Tobacco	1, 795	36.66	74.90	0
530890	Vegetable textile fibres	2, 303	36.56	3.87	0
620530	Not knitted apparel	536, 965	35.92	12.00	0

Notes:
[a] 30 HS6 categories with highest import share from LDCs.
[b] Tariff data refers to *ad valorem* tariffs only.
Source: UN Comtrade and UNCTAD TRAINS Data base.

however, since 1998 the preferential market access for LDCs in the European Union has been enhanced so as to provide them with ACP-equivalent market access. Yet, there were still notable differences between the two preferential regimes.[4]

The pre-EBA market access for LDCs

Over time, the EU GSP scheme for LDCs has undergone a considerable number of changes. For some products, the scheme granted duty-free entry. For other products, preferences for a given product were expressed as a percentage reduction of the most-favoured-nation (MFN) duty rates. This percentage depended on a given product's 'sensitivity', which is determined by the situation of the sector manufacturing the same product in the Community. According to its degree of sensitivity, each product was classified as belonging to one of four groups (1) very sensitive products, for which the MFN preferential margin is 15 per cent; (2) sensitive products, for which the MFN preferential margin is 30 per cent; (3) semi-sensitive products, for which the MFN preferential margin is 65 per cent; (4) non-sensitive products, which enter the EU market duty-free.

Since 1995, the European Union has eliminated all quantitative limitations. Yet, its GSP scheme maintained the 'graduation mechanism' under which the benefit of the scheme is phased out for specific sectors or countries that have reached a degree of competitiveness where they increased their exports even without enjoying GSP treatment.[5] Moreover, as with other preferential arrangements, the EU GSP scheme contained safeguard measures that could suspend or withdraw the preferential market access. Also, as mentioned above, in 1998 the European Union improved the GSP scheme for LDCs to grant them a similar level of market access as that enjoyed by ACP countries.[6]

However, although the pre-EBA LDC market access to the European Union had a wide coverage of products, more than 900 agricultural products (at HS 8-digit level) were subject to *ad valorem* or specific duties. Table 9.2 provides a selection of products with the highest number of dutiable lines faced by LDCs exports in 2000 to the European Union, prior to the implementation of the EBA initiative.

The EBA initiative

The EBA proposal was enacted by the Council Regulation No. 416/2001 of 28 February 2001, amending EC Regulation No. 2820/98 applying a multiannual scheme of generalized tariff preferences for the period 1 July 1999 to 31 December 2001, so as to extend duty-free access without

Table 9.2 Selected LDC exports facing tariffs in the European Union, by major product category, 2000

Product code HS 2-digit	Description	Number of dutiable lines at HS 6-digit
11	Malt, starches, wheat gluten	29
02	Meat and edible meat offal	27
04	Dairy products; birds' eggs; natural honey	20
19	Flour, starch, pastry products	15
17	Sugars and sugar confectionery	14
10	Cereals	12
22	Beverages, spirits and vinegar	11
08	Edible fruit and nuts	10

Source: UNCTAD.

any quantitative restrictions to 919 agricultural products originating in the LDCs. More than 50 per cent of the liberalized tariff lines covered meat and dairy products, beverages and milled products (Table 9.3). The EBA entered into force on 5 March 2001.

It should be noted that while the preferences for developing (LDC and non-LDC) countries under the GSP scheme are subject to periodic renewal, the special arrangements provided for in the EBA initiative (modifying the GSP) with regard to market access for LDCs were to be maintained for an unlimited period of time. Not being subject to periodic renewal, the EBA initiative takes a step further in reducing the uncertainty of preferential market access for LDCs although, unlike the negotiated EU–ACP arrangements, it can be modified unilaterally by the European Union.

All the products included in the initiative are agricultural products – in contrast with the original GSP which, in line with the Prebisch–Singer thesis, focused on manufactured products. Products such as fruits and vegetables, meat, beverages and dairy products are now granted duty-free and quota-free access to the EU market. Only three products have not been liberalized immediately: bananas, rice and sugar. Their phase-in periods for full market access are as follows:[7]

- **Bananas** – duties will gradually be eliminated, by a 20 per cent annual reduction, starting on 1 January 2002. All duties will be eliminated from 1 January 2006.
- **Rice** – full liberalization will gradually be phased in between 1 September 2006 and 1 September 2009. Duties will be reduced by

Table 9.3   EBA: the distribution of liberalized products, by sectors, HS 2-digit

HS 2 code	Description	LDCs export share in the EU market, 2000 (%)[a]	Number of liberalized products (8-digit level)[b]	Percentage of liberalized tariff lines [b]
02	Meat and meat products	0.007	173	18.82
04	Dairy products	0.008	166	18.21
22	Beverages, spirits and vinegar	0.033	103	11.21
11	Milled products	0.005	77	8.38
20	Preparation of vegetables and fruits	0.054	74	8.05
10	Cereals	0.114	48	5.22
17	Sugars and sugar confectionery	1.269	45	4.9
19	Preparation of cereals	0.005	38	4.13
01	Live animals	0.111	30	3.26
23	Residues and waste from food industry	0.089	30	3.26
16	Preparation of meat, fish or crustaceans	0.799	28	3.05
08	Fruits	0.460	25	2.72
07	Vegetables	0.496	19	2.07
18	Cocoa and cocoa preparations	0.478	19	2.07
21	Miscellaneous edible preparations	0.013	12	1.31
15	Fats and oils	0.201	10	1.09
38	Miscellaneous chemical products	0.004	8	0.87
35	Albumins and enzymes	0.043	6	0.65
29	Organic chemicals	0.035	5	0.54
12	Oil seeds	1.212	3	0.33
	Total	0.175	919	100

Sources: [a] WITS (www.witsys.com).
[b] Based on information available from the European Commission, at www.europa.eu.int/comm/trade/pdf/ebaprodlist.pdf.

20 per cent on 1 September 2006, by 50 per cent on 1 September 2007 and by 80 per cent on 1 September 2008. During the transition period, LDC rice can be exported duty-free to the European Union within the limits of a tariff quota. The initial quantities of this quota shall be based on best LDC export levels to the European Union in the recent past, plus a growth factor of 15 per cent. The quota will grow

every year, from 2,517 tonnes (husked-rice equivalent) in 2001/2002 to 6,696 tonnes in 2008/2009.

- **Sugar** – similar arrangements are provided for sugar. Full liberalization will be phased in between 1 July 2006 and 1 July 2009. During the transition period, LDC raw sugar can be exported duty-free to the European Union within the limits of a tariff quota, which will be increased from 74,185 tonnes (white-sugar equivalent) in 2001/2002 to 197,355 tonnes in 2008/2009. The provisions of the ACP–EC Sugar Protocol will remain valid.

The adoption of the EBA had to meet certain conditions imposed by other international trade arrangements where the European Union was signatory: the WTO agreements and the ACP preferential trade arrangements. The EBA was adopted as an amendment to the existing GSP scheme in order to benefit from the compatibility with the WTO rules of the current GSP scheme. The basis for the EBA under the WTO is para. 2(d) of the Enabling Clause of 1979, which allows for special treatment to be granted for LDCs in the context of any general or specific measures in favour of developing countries. The EBA had only not to be WTO-compatible but also in line with the ACP regime. The Lomé Convention required the European Union to grant non-discriminatory market access to all ACP countries. However, the EBA initiative would have granted more preferential market access to ACP LDCs than that enjoyed by ACP non-LDCs. Therefore, in the Cotonou Agreement that superseded the last Lomé Convention, Article 174(2)(b) of the Lomé Convention (imposing non-discrimination among ACP states) was eliminated. Thus, the European Union can offer better market access to LDC ACP states without extending it to non-LDC ACP countries, as the above-mentioned article would have required.

Apart from the extension of duty- and quota-free market access to all products (with the exceptions of arms) originating in LDCs the EBA brings only few changes in the general rules administering the existing GSP scheme. Of these, one of the more important changes is that, unlike the EU GSP scheme that is subject to renewal and revision, the EBA has no time limitation. On the other hand, the EBA also introduces new provisions allowing the European Union to introduce safeguard measures when massive increases in imports of products originating in the LDCs arise in relation to their usual levels of production and export capacity. Specific safeguard measures apply especially with regard to sensitive products (bananas, sugar and rice), if imports of these products cause 'serious' disruptions to the European Union. The European

Commission will review the functioning of the EBA in 2005, when amendments can be introduced, if necessary.

Furthermore, under Article 28 of the above-mentioned regulation, MFN duties on a product may be reintroduced where that product originating from a developing country is imported on terms which cause or threaten to cause 'serious difficulties' to a Community producer of like or directly competing products, taking account of any reduction in market share of Community producers, reduction in their production, increase in their stocks, closure of their production capacity, bankruptcies, low profitability, low rate of capacity utilization, employment, trade and prices.

The EBA initiative modifies the GSP scheme by adding to the reasons for the possible temporary withdrawal of preferences a 'massive increases in imports into the Community of products originating in LDCs in relation to their usual levels of production and export capacity'.[8] This addition will allow the Commission to 'react swiftly when the Communities' financial interests are at stake'.[9] The post-EBA GSP scheme also contains an extra paragraph in Article 28 allowing for the suspension of the preferences provided by this regulation for rice, sugar and bananas, 'if imports of these products cause serious disturbance to the Community markets and their regulatory mechanisms'.[10] The Commission announced that whenever LDC imports of rice, sugar or bananas exceed, or are likely to exceed, the preceeding year's level by more than 25 per cent, then it will automatically examine whether the conditions for applying GSP safeguard measures are met.[11]

It remains to be seen whether the EBA modifications to the GSP safeguard scheme will in practice work to frustrate market access for LDCs or to provide a genuine escape mechanism where severe market disturbances result from the newly granted LDC preferences.

The economics of non-reciprocal trading arrangements

The larger part of current preferential trade is associated with the existence of regional agreements, under GATT Article XXIV, whereby countries reciprocate mutual trade concessions. The EBA initiative is an example of a non-reciprocal, preferential trade arrangement, falling within the framework of the WTO's Enabling Clause. Under these arrangements, 'beneficiary' or preference-receiving countries do not have the obligation to reciprocate to 'donor' or preference-granting countries. What distinguishes the EBA from other unilateral preference schemes (excluding GSP) is a lower degree of discrimination. Although GSP is supposed to be 'generalized' and 'non-discriminatory', in practice GSP arrangements often provide, for each sector, differential treatment of beneficiary countries. By contrast, under the EBA all LDCs are to be given equally duty-free, quota-free access to the market of the EU donor countries in all sectors but arms.[12]

A relatively simple way to think about the effects of preferential trade arrangements is to refer to a partial equilibrium three-country, one-product framework. Viner (1950) and more recently Panagariya (1998) have shown that, under standard assumptions, granting non-reciprocal preferences is more likely to generate gains in the beneficiary country, losses in the donor country, to have negligible effects on third countries and to produce a dead-weight loss on aggregate.[13] The major welfare effects are associated with easily identifiable and measurable trade flows. In particular, the gains to the beneficiary country are associated with its export expansion, while the losses in the donor country are associated with the amount of third-country imports displaced.

However, there are some major caveats concerning this standard analysis. First, the result that trade creation is nil for the donor country after granting preferential market access depends crucially on the assumption that the supply curve for the rest of the world is perfectly elastic. Second, it assumes a single homogeneous good, justifying the assumption of the supply curve of the rest of the world being perfectly flat. When goods originating from different countries are imperfect substitutes and the supply by both beneficiary and third countries is perfectly elastic, a policy of preferential, non-reciprocal liberalization may either increase or lower world welfare (UNCTAD, 2002). Third, general equilibrium effects are neglected and no conclusion is possible as to whether non-reciprocal trade arrangements are likely to improve or worsen the allocation of resources.

To address some of these problems with the classical analysis, in the next section we simulate the granting of unilateral preferences by the European Union for LDCs under non-infinite supply conditions, non-homogeneous goods (the 'Armington' assumption) and, in part of the analysis, we also move to a general equilibrium framework.

Assessing the impact of EBA

First, we assess the aggregate worldwide distribution of gains and losses of the EBA initiative, focusing on the LDCs and on third non-beneficiary developing countries, using a computable general equilibrium (CGE) simulation model (GTAP). Second, we explore detailed country and sectoral effects using a partial equilibrium simulations (based on the SMART model – see below).

The aggregate impact

The experiment, the model and the data

First, we look at the effects of the policy on each country's welfare, and on their sectoral trade and production patterns, by simulating the complete removal of both tariff and non-tariff barriers (NTBs) faced by LDCs in the EU market. Welfare changes are further decomposed in to their allocative effects and the terms of trade component. Our policy experiment is similar to those found in Ianchovichina, Mattoo and Olarreaga (2001), UNCTAD (2001) and Trueblood and Somwaru (2002). The model used for the CGE simulations in the present study is that developed under the GTAP, as described in Hertel (1997). Since the EBA initiative is likely to impact mainly the agricultural sector, the standard static, perfect competition, constant returns to scale version of GTAP is adopted. However, there are some important differences between the previous literature and the CGE experiments performed in this chapter. These differences are further discussed below.

While our policy experiment is similar to that of other studies mentioned earlier, the results cannot be fully compared across these studies, for several reasons. First, the database used in the simulations is that available in GTAP Database Release No. 5 (GTAP5), with a 1997 base year. Second, we modified the basic protection data available in GTAP5 to take into account the pre-EBA preference margins available to LDCs in the EU market, using data from the UNCTAD TRAINS database (see Table 9.4 for the protection data used). Third, the beneficiary countries of the EBA initiative are all LDCs, whereas in Ianchovichina, Mattoo and Olarreaga (2001) preferential market access is targeted to sub-Saharan African (SSA) countries only. Fourth, the versions of the GTAP database used in the different studies differ (GTAP4 in Ianchovichina, Mattoo and Olarreaga, 2001; GTAP5 Pre-Release 3 in UNCTAD, 2001; GTAP5.0.1 in Trueblood and Somwaru, 2002; and a modified version of GTAP5 in the present study) and the product/sectoral aggregation also varies. Finally, the treatment of pre-EBA preferences is different.

To facilitate analysis, we aggregated the basic 66 GTAP regions into 18 regional groups. LDCs are disaggregated into Bangladesh, Malawi, Mozambique, Tanzania, Uganda, Zambia and rest of SSA (see Tables 9.4 and 9.6). Because of data constraints, not all LDCs can be singled out in our CGE simulations in order to assess their benefits from the EBA, so that the results should be seen only as indicative. The original 57 sectors available in GTAP5 have been aggregated into 21 new sectors (see Tables 9.4 and 9.6).

Table 9.4 Protection rates applied in the European Union on merchandise trade

	NAFTA	China	Japan	Rest of Asia	Latin America	Rest of developed countries	Transition economies	Rest of Africa	Malawi
Paddy rice	64.9	64.9	64.9	64.9	64.9	64.9	64.9	64.9	61.7
Cereals	51.3	45	45.1	48.7	41.2	60	47	50.9	28.6
Vegetables, fruits and nuts	14.5	14.5	14.5	14.5	14.5	14.5	14.5	14.5	2.2
Oil seeds	0	0	0	0	0	0	0	0	0
Sugar cane, sugar beet	251.4	251.4	251.4	251.4	251.4	251.4	251.4	251.4	0
Natural fibres	0	0		0	0	0	0	0	0
Crops	3.1	3.1	3.1	3.1	3.1	3.1	3.1	3.1	0
Livestock, animal products	16.9	7.6	32.6	7.9	7.8	8	16.9	9	2.7
Forestry	3	0.9	0.1	1.5	3.1	0.1	0.1	3.5	0
Fishing	8.9	3.3	1.4	4.1	10.5	0	9.1	12	0
Coal, oil, gas and minerals	1.8	5.1	3.5	2.1	0.6	0	1.5	0.4	0
Meat and meat products	69.7	34.1	61.1	34.6	65.3	79	38.1	77.5	5.7
Vegetable oils and fats	11.4	11.4	11.4	11.4	11.4	11.4	11.4	11.4	0.2
Dairy products	86.9	66.9	87.5	53	76.3	87.6	84.9	39.7	35.1
Processed rice	87.4	87.4	87.4	87.4	87.4	87.4	87.4	87.4	87.4
Sugar	76.4	76.4	76.4	76.4	76.4	76.4	76.4	76.4	68
Other food products	28.8	28.8	28.8	28.8	28.8	28.8	28.8	28.8	0.3
Beverage and tobacco products	8.3	8.3	8.3	8.3	8.3	8.3	8.3	8.3	0.1
Textiles, apparel and leather	8.8	10.5	8.7	10.5	6.7	0.7	10.9	11.4	0
Other manufactures	3.3	4.5	5.1	4	2.9	0.1	4	2.8	0

Table 9.4 (Continued)

	Zambia	Mozambique	Tanzania	Uganda	Rest of SSA	Bangladesh	Middle East	Rest of the world	Total
Paddy rice	61.7	61.7	61.7	61.7	61.7	61.7	64.9	64.9	1081
Cereals	28.5	28.6	28.6	28.6	29.1	37	51.1	47.2	697
Vegetables, fruits and nuts	14.5	2.2	2.2	2.2	2.2	2.2	14.5	14.5	173
Oil seeds	0	0	0	0	0	0	0	0	0
Sugar cane, sugar beet	224	223.7	223.7	223.7	223.7	246.4	251.4	251.4	3879
Natural fibres	0	0	0	0	0	0	0	0	0
Crops	0	0	0	0	0	0	3.1	3.1	30.9
Livestock, animal product	3.7	4.3	3.5	3.1	3	6.3	14.4	11.6	159
Forestry	0	0	0	0	0	0	4.2	0.1	16.5
Fishing	0	0	0	0	0	0	9.7	8	66.9
Coal, oil gas and minerals	0	0	0	0	0	0	0.4	2.3	17.7
Meat and meat products	5.3	5.9	6	11.1	8.2	13.4	45.7	54.5	615
Vegetable oils and fats	0.2	0.2	0.2	0.2	0.2	0.2	11.4	11.4	116
Dairy products	32.7	27.8	24.7	1.6	17.3	34.6	42.9	75.2	875
Processed rice	87.4	87.4	87.4	87.4	87.4	87.4	87.4	87.4	1485
Sugar	68	68	68	68	68	74.9	76.4	76.4	1247
Other food products	0.3	0.3	0.3	0.3	0.3	0.3	28.8	28.8	290
Beverage and tobacco products	0.1	0.1	0.1	0.1	0.1	1.3	8.3	8.3	85.1
Textiles, apparel and leather	0	0	0	0	0	0	11.1	11.5	90.8
Other manufactures	0	0	0	0	0	0	4	3.8	34.5

Two points are worth noting about the sectoral data. First, the EU MFN protection is concentrated in agriculture and food (with particularly high rates – between 50 and 200 per cent – in rice, sugar, cereals, dairy products and meat). Textiles and clothing also receive considerable MFN protection, with rates around 10 per cent. Second, prior to the EBA, imports of textiles and in manufacturing from LDCs enjoyed duty-free treatment, while in agriculture and food preference margins in favour of LDCs varied considerably across product categories. In dairy and meat products, vegetables and fruits, vegetable oils and fats and other food products preference margins are quite high, well above 50 per cent. Conversely, preference margins are very tight in rice, sugar and cereals.

Simulation results

As one might expect, all beneficiary countries gain from the EBA initiative in welfare terms, while the donor (the European Union) loses slightly from the initiative (Table 9.5). The results also show that some world

Table 9.5 Welfare changes, 1997 US$ million

Regions	Allocative effects[a]	Terms of trade effects[a]	Total
NAFTA	0.2	−17.9	−26.4
EU	−24.0	−186.9	−212.3
China	−0.7	8.6	4.2
Japan	−2.9	−14.9	−24.3
Rest of Asia	−5.8	−11.6	−20.9
Latin America	−0.4	−4.1	−7.7
Rest of developed countries	4.2	4.3	7.6
Transitions economies	2.4	2.4	3.9
Rest of Africa	−2.4	−5.8	−8.5
Malawi	10.0	23.6	31.6
Zambia	−5.3	34.2	27.4
Mozambique	1.1	2.9	6.7
Tanzania	12.9	28.3	52.2
Uganda	0.2	1.1	1.7
Rest of SSA	35.8	119.0	174.1
Bangladesh	0.2	1.4	2.0
Middle East	4.1	14.4	18.1
Rest of the world	−0.8	−0.6	−2.3
Total	28.8	−1.5	27.2

Note:
[a] A number of GTAP welfare decomposition effects are not reported, so the allocative and terms of trade effects do not add up to the total.

regions stand to lose, while others gain. In the aggregate, the world net gains from the EBA initiative are positive.

In absolute terms (equivalent variation in US$ million) the biggest gain accrues to the rest of SSA, while the greatest loss occurs for the European Union. Uganda and Bangladesh are the beneficiary countries whose gains are estimated to be the lowest. Among third countries, those that reap positive gains are the rest of developed countries (mainly Oceania and EFTA countries), transition economies and the Middle East. Conversely, NAFTA and Asian countries are those that suffer the biggest losses.

Overall, the results point to an improvement in allocative efficiency, and this explains the gain at the worldwide level. Allocative gains are especially evident for LDCs. A shift towards agricultural goods and food production (which face the highest pre-EBA levels of protection in the European Union) induces a better exploitation of comparative advantages in these countries. On the other hand, the European Union loses in terms of efficiency, which may be interpreted as a typical consequence of trade diversion: the preferential liberalization targeted to LDCs displaces more efficient imports originating from third countries. However, the bulk of welfare changes for individual countries are associated with terms of trade effects. Not surprisingly, all beneficiary countries benefit from increased prices for their exports to the EU market and this causes an improvement in their terms of trade. Conversely, the EU terms of trade fall as a result of higher import prices from LDCs. As far as third countries are concerned, Japan and NAFTA countries incur a particularly strong negative terms of trade effect, while the Middle East and China receive a considerable gain associated with an improvement in the terms of trade. In general, the welfare changes due to terms of trade effects are quite small for third countries. This is because the world share of LDCs exports is too small for EBA to cause a significant negative twist in the terms of trade of competing exporters.

The greatest percentage increases in exports by beneficiary countries are paddy rice, sugarcane, sugar and processed rice (Table 9.6). In SSA LDCs, sugar exports may even become ten times higher after the EBA. In general, we also see that cereals and diary products become increasingly exported by beneficiary countries. The rise in vegetable and fruit exports is substantial only for Zambia, Bangladesh and the rest of SSA, while that in meat and meat products is concentrated in Uganda and the rest of SSA. Some export industries for LDCs that do not benefit from the EBA may contract. This is particularly the case for textiles and clothing from Bangladesh and services from Mozambique where prior protection was very low. This explains why total exports from Bangladesh

233

Table 9.6 Exports, percentage changes

	NAFTA	EU	China	Japan	Rest of Asia	Latin America	Rest of developed countries	Transition economies	Rest of Africa	Malawi
Paddy rice	-0.57	-2.25	-0.81	1.32	-1.33	-0.67	-0.43	-0.21	0	30.16
Cereals	-0.01	-0.09	-0.02	0.19	-0.02	-0.01	0.01	-0.03	0.68	32.1
Vegetables, fruits and nuts	-0.02	-0.12	0.05	0.01	0.01	-0.07	0.03	-0.07	-0.11	-8.68
Oil seeds	0.02	0.05	0.03	0.02	0.06	0.02	0.05	0.03	0.16	-8.94
Sugar cane, sugar beet	-0.04	-69.69	-0.46	-32.44	-25.41	-25.03	0.74	-1.04	-27.33	31.24
Natural fibres	0.2	0.34	0.23	0.29	0.24	0.27	0.23	0.19	0.35	-7.37
Crops (nec)[a]	0.25	0.42	0.28	0.27	0.28	0.29	0.33	0.45	0.4	-9.09
Livestock, animal products	-0.01	0	-0.04	-0.01	0	-0.02	-0.04	-0.08	-0.03	-4.73
Forestry	0.1	0.18	0.11	0.19	0.16	0.18	0.1	0.13	0.16	-16.15
Fishing	-0.01	-0.04	-0.01	0	0	0.01	-0.01	0.02	-0.01	-16.23
Coal oil gas and minerals	0.03	0.03	0.02	0.03	0.01	0.04	0.02	0.01	0.02	-10.46
Meat and meat products	-0.01	0.01	-0.02	-0.01	-0.01	-0.02	-0.02	-0.03	-0.03	-5.3
Vegetable oils and fats	0	0.03	-0.01	-0.06	0.02	0	0	-0.03	-0.02	-11.71
Dairy products	-0.03	0.01	-0.03	-0.02	-0.02	-0.02	-0.03	-0.04	0.02	74.16
Processed rice	-0.67	-6.04	-0.67	-2.62	-0.38	-1.2	-0.39	-2.15	0.01	-5
Sugar	-1.17	-5.23	-0.8	-1.23	-1.07	-1.37	-0.18	-1.47	-7.72	468.7
Other food products	-0.01	0.05	-0.01	-0.01	-0.02	-0.02	-0.04	-0.04	0.01	-11.58
Beverage and tobacco products	-0.06	0.07	-0.06	-0.05	-0.06	-0.06	-0.1	-0.07	0.13	-18.66
Textiles, apparel and leather	0	0.03	0	0.01	0.01	0.02	0	0.01	0.03	-20.62
Other manufactures	0	0.02	-0.01	0	0	0.01	-0.01	-0.01	0.13	-18
Services	0.01	0.02	0.07	0.01	0.01	0.02	0.01	0.01	0.01	-10.14

Table 9.6 (Continued)

	Zambia	Mozambique	Tanzania	Uganda	Rest of SSA	Bangladesh	Middle East	Rest of the world
Paddy rice	139.2	199.8	243.16	266	363.4	23.35	-0.93	-0.98
Cereals	28.8	6.02	66.33	12.31	30.77	35.59	-0.06	-0.02
Vegetables, fruits and nuts	49.46	-1.63	-7.67	4.15	5.87	7.3	-0.12	0.1
Oil seeds	-19.75	-1.25	-8.84	-0.45	-1.6	-0.23	0	0.08
Sugar cane, sugar beet	403.7	816.5	1063.1	2808	1266	1085	-29.91	-13.63
Natural fibres	-16.86	-1.23	-5.42	-0.23	-1.24	0.24	0.3	0.33
Crops (nec)[a]	-18.74	-1.98	-7.94	-0.15	-1.17	0.15	0.3	0.37
Livestock, animal products	-14.66	4.16	-7.06	4.84	5.71	2.29	-0.1	-0.02
Forestry	-11.41	-2.75	-12.21	-0.65	-1.04	0.05	0.18	0.12
Fishing	-11.64	-2.42	-14.09	-0.88	-1.38	-0.18	-0.04	-0.01
Coal oil gas and minerals	-4.3	-1.83	-7.04	-0.41	-0.49	-0.04	0.01	0.03
Meat and meat products	-5.77	-1.51	3.8	45.64	21.65	-0.04	-0.02	0
Vegetable oils and fats	-16.38	-1.78	-7.08	0.43	-0.47	0.13	0	-0.01
Dairy products	24.84	-1.9	59.93	2.05	12.1	56.12	-0.03	-0.01
Processed rice	212.3	379.3	471.02	158	452	385.4	-0.88	-2.04
Sugar	429	19.35	680.47	293	391.7	264.7	-1.25	-8.52
Other food products	-10.5	-1.26	-7.15	0.22	-0.34	0.35	-0.05	-0.03
Beverage and tobacco products	-18.49	-2.95	-12	-0.83	1.91	-0.14	-0.04	-0.04
Textiles, apparel and leather	-13.17	-3.37	-11.84	-0.92	-1.92	-0.17	-0.01	0.03
Other manufactures	-8.65	-2.13	-8.9	-0.45	-1.35	-0.11	-0.01	0.03
Services	-5.17	-1.64	-6.59	-0.35	-0.87	-0.07	0	0.01

Note:
[a] nec: Not elsewhere classified.

remain almost unchanged and those of Mozambique even fall slightly on aggregate. As for the European Union, the export increase is associated with resources shifting away from agriculture into export-oriented industries.

Overall, results indicate that the EBA policy has a positive impact of LDCs exports and welfare, coupled with losses for the EU and third countries of a smaller magnitude. LDCs exports appear to increase by almost US$300 million per year, nearly half a percentage point from the baseline value. Compared with those found in other studies, our simulations show smaller export and welfare gains for beneficiary countries. This is due to the fact that the database used is referred to a more recent benchmark (this is a difference with respect to Ianchovichina, Mattoo and Olarreaga, 2001 and UNCTAD, 2001) and because pre-EBA LDC preferences in the EU market are taken into account (a major point of departure from Trueblood and Somwaru, 2002). As found in previous studies, the impact of the EBA appears to be very concentrated in few sectors, in particular sugar and rice.

The results also suggest that concerns about the possible impact of the EBA on the EU Common Agricultural Policy (CAP) are ill founded. It had been argued by many domestic producer groups that the EBA, by eliminating tariffs and tariff quotas on products that are subject to CAP provisions, would increase imports to such an extent that it would make CAP support measures ineffective (Agra Europe, 2001). Despite these concerns, several factors suggest that the impact of the EBA on European agriculture and the CAP budget will be, if not minimal, at least manageable. An impact study conducted by the European Commission on the effects of the EBA on several agricultural markets shows that, depending upon the preliminary assumptions used, the extra-budgetary costs are between 1.5 and 2.6 billion Euro (EC, 2000a). This would represent an increase by approximately 3–7 per cent of the 1999 CAP budget, but even this looks rather large in the light of our results.

It is important to stress that the analysis refers to a long-run scenario, and adjustment issues are neglected. Moreover, no account is taken of institutional aspects, such as stringent rules of origin that might prevent LDCs from taking advantage of the EBA.

The EBA initiative: who wins and who loses?

One concern voiced during the adoption of the EBA by the European Union was the potentially significant trade-diversion effects that adoption of the proposal could have on other developing countries, ACP countries in particular (Page and Hewitt, 2002). The current section seeks to expand the results obtained in the previous one, in particular to focus on the possible impact of the EBA at the most disaggregated level in terms of both countries and products, with a special focus on the three sensitive products included in the EBA: rice, sugar, and bananas.

The model, data and scenarios

The model used to estimate the various effects of the EBA is the SMART model. SMART is a simple *ex ante* partial equilibrium model, measuring the first-round impact of trade policy changes.[14] Unlike the general equilibrium analyses, the model does not account for economywide effects of trade liberalization or inter-industry effects. However, the advantage of partial equilibrium models is the very detailed level of analysis. Working at this disaggregated level the SMART model allows considerable precision in identifying sensitive products and countries affected by the EBA.

The most important effects estimated by the model are the *trade-creation* and *trade-diversion* effects. The *trade-creation effect* results from the changed level of domestic demand for imports from a particular trading partner caused by the changed price of the imported good after the tariff change or relative to the price of the domestically produced substitute. It is assumed that the price change would fully reflect the tariff change – that is, the benefits of the tariff change would be passed on to consumers. Effects capture the increase in imports by donor countries (exports by beneficiaries) resulting from the tariff cut and the corresponding decrease in domestic prices (which are assumed fully reflect the tariff changes). *Trade diversion* measures the extent to which imports from preference-receiving countries will substitute current imports from third countries, as a result of changes in relative import prices after tariff reductions. Imports from alternative foreign suppliers are assumed to be imperfect substitutes and export supply elasticities are not assumed to be infinite (although this is a default value in the modelling system, as described below).

To estimate the trade-creation and trade-diversion effects, the model uses a number of variables (imports, exports, applied and bound MFN and preferential tariffs, elasticity of import demand with respect to domestic price, price elasticity of export supply, Armington elasticities) mainly from the UNCTAD-TRAINS data base, supplemented by UNCTAD's GSP database.[15] The scenarios included testing the impact of the EBA under different assumptions, taking into account the importance of LDC trade re-orientation, as suggested by other studies.[16] It is assumed that all LDCs benefit from duty-free and quota-free market access, without taking into account other trade regulations that might impede their market access in the European Union.

Scenario (1): no LDC trade re-orientation

Scenario (1) of the EBA effects on LDCs, the European Union and third countries assumes that LDCs are able to export all their products covered by the EBA with duty- and quota-free market access. This scenario also assumes that the improved market access in the European Union will have no impact on trade flows between LDCs and third countries.

Scenario (2): LDC trade re-orientation

A shortcoming of most modelling approaches is their path-dependent logic. In particular, these methodologies imply that the absence of trade flows between two partners in the base period, for example, because of the presence of a non-tariff measure or prohibitively high tariff, means that there will be no trade either in the estimated period. One approach is to circumvent this limitation by running a simulation using LDC exports to world markets rather than to the European Union alone. The reasoning behind this simulation is that certain LDCs may face restrictions on their current access to the European Union but, under the EBA, would be able to divert some of their existing exports from lower-priced markets to the European Union to take advantage of the preferential margin introduced by the EBA and the substantial price differential between EU domestic and world prices. An important example is sugar, where EU prices are 160 per cent higher than world prices. This sector will be looked at in greater detail later.

Therefore, scenario (2) assumes that LDC exports to the world of products liberalized by the EBA will actually be re-oriented towards the European Union, in order to take advantage of preferences and price wedges between EU domestic prices and world market prices. For sensitive products under a transition period of duty-free tariff rate quotas (sugar, rice and bananas), this scenario estimates the impact of the EBA at the end of the transition periods.

Results

Although the EBA extends duty and quota-free market access for LDCs in more than 900 tariff lines, the SMART estimates from scenario (1) suggest that, based on current exports, LDCs will be able to take advantage of this enhanced market access for only 124 products at tariff-line level. Under more optimistic assumptions that LDCs will be able to shift existing exports from third countries to the EU market (scenario (2)), the number of products (at tariff-line level) that are likely to benefit from the EBA rises to 622. The expected increase in sugar exports is by far the most important to emerge at the end of the transition period. The results from scenario (1) (Figure 9.1) suggest quite clearly that the EBA rather than being 'everything but arms' could be better labelled 'nothing but sugar'.

Our estimates also show that, under scenario (1), only a handful of LDCs would see total trade at tariff-line level increased by more than US$100,000, which is a combination of trade creation- and trade-diversion effects, positive or negative, as the case may be (see the figures in Cernat, *et al.*, 2003, which illustrate these scenarios in detail). Malawi, the biggest winner, stands to increase its cane sugar exports by more than US$25 million. Other African LDCs (Madagascar, Tanzania, Zambia) are likely to see their cane sugar exports increase by between US$5 and US$10 million. The only Asian LDC that shows exports increases at tariff-line level by more than US$100,000 is Myanmar. The SMART estimates also suggest that Sudan is likely to see significant increases in its exports of molasses (product code 1703) and cereals (grain sorghum, product code 1007).

Unsurprisingly, the largest losers from negative trade diversion, in absolute values, are the current major ACP sugar exporters (Mauritius, Aruba, Fiji, Guyana). There is also a relatively large loss from trade diversion for the United States in grain sorghum. However, two of the sensitive sectors identified by the European Union (rice and bananas) do not seem to face particularly large trade effects, compared to sugar.

The SMART estimates suggest that, in the case of rice exports, apart from modest export increases in certain rice products for Madagascar, Lao PDR and Mozambique, other LDCs will not have any probable improvements in their market shares in the European Union. This moderate increase in rice exports from LDCs seems to come at the expense of current rice exports from Thailand and the United States. A similar analysis for bananas suggests that the largest total trade effect is likely to occur for Rwanda (US$147,000), while the reductions in current exports through trade diversion would be fairly evenly distributed between Latin and Central American producers (Costa Rica, Ecuador, Colombia, Panama) (Figure 9.2).

Once the possibility of re-orientation of LDC exports from third markets to the European Union is taken into account (scenario (2)), the EBA shows a more diverse potential impact of the patterns of LDC exports to the European Union. Apart from sugar and molasses – which remain key – live sheep, sheep meat, powder milk and cream, bananas, maize,

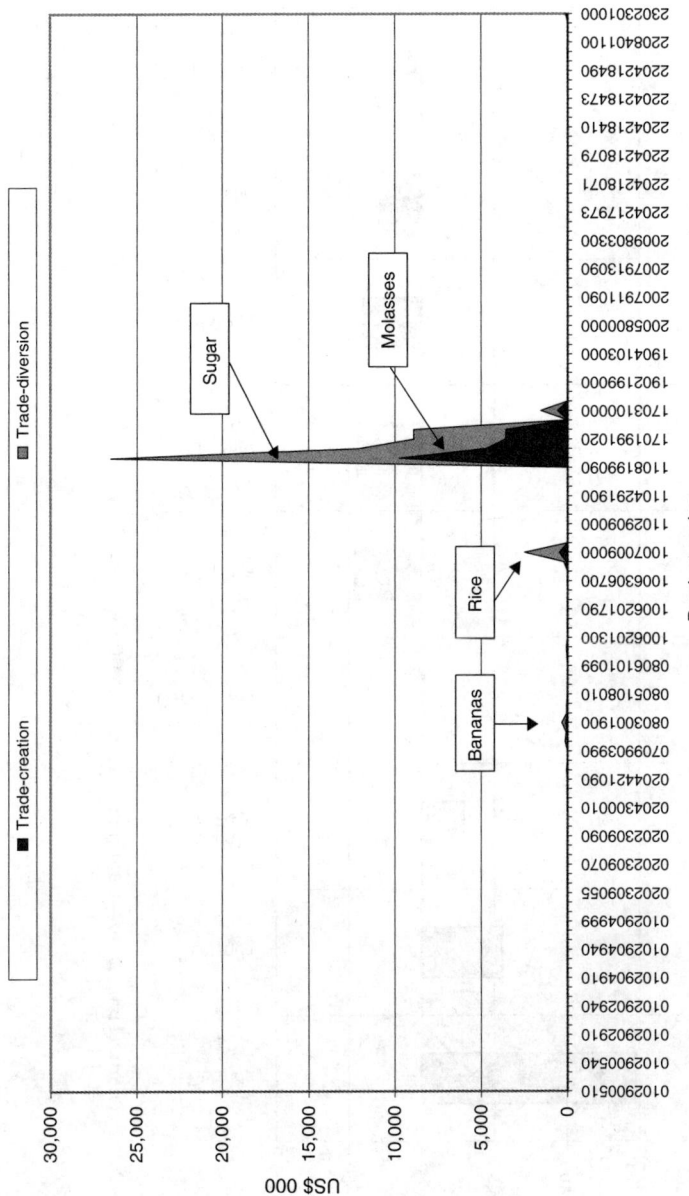

Figure 9.1 EBA scenario (1): trade-creation and trade-diversion effects, US$ 000

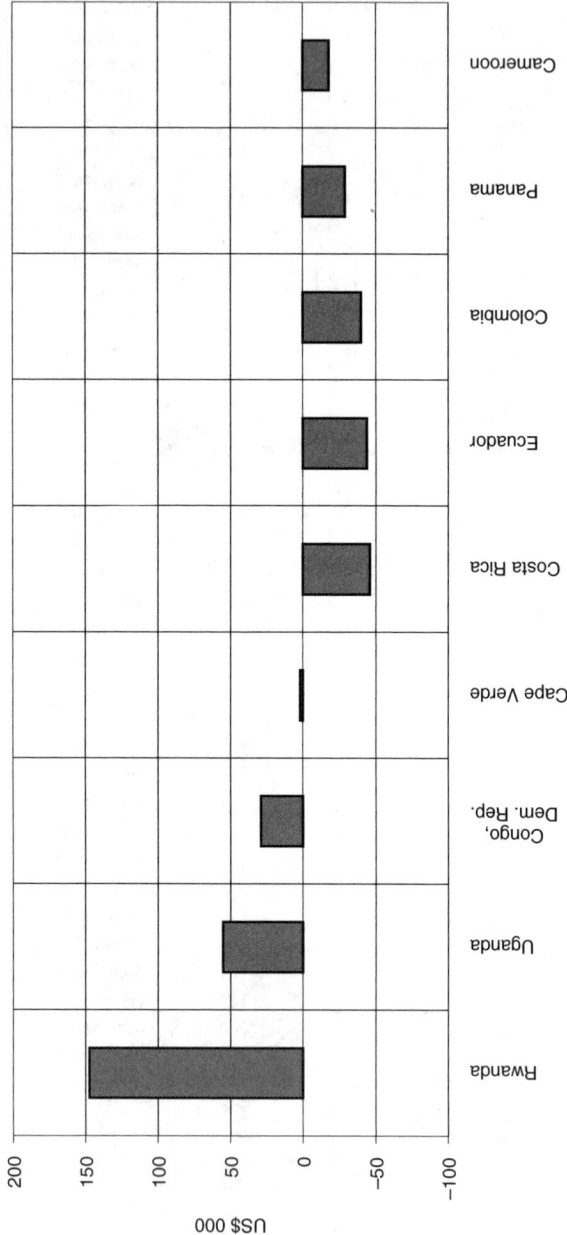

Figure 9.2 Scenario (1): bananas – total trade effects, US$ 000

broken rice, grain sorghum, wheat flour, rum and tafia are other products in which relatively high export changes can occur (Figure 9.3). Two other important products for LDCs, apart from sugar, are wheat bran (product code 2302301000) and broken rice (product code 1006400010). In the case of wheat bran, the Democratic Republic of Congo and Tanzania appear to benefit the most from the EBA provisions. For broken rice, Togo and Niger seem able to almost double their current exports, should a trade re-orientation occur and EBA provisions permit such a steep increase in imports of rice from LDCs.

In terms of beneficiary countries, Sudan emerges as the largest winner with a relatively large variety of products (sugar, cereals, live animals), followed by Malawi and Mozambique, which remain largely dependent on their increases in sugar exports. Overall, however, the number of beneficiary countries that manage to increase their exports substantially at tariff-line level increases significantly. Fourteen LDCs are able to reap overall positive trade effect bigger than US$500,000. Sudan, Tanzania and Niger have relatively more diversified trade effects, while Nepal and the Democratic Republic of Congo are likely to benefit from significant trade effects in only one tariff line. Somehow surprising is the modest presence of Asian LDCs among the major beneficiaries of the EBA. Previous studies have identified Asian LDCs as those that enjoy less favourable market access than ACP LDCs and, by this token, the EBA should have brought them relatively more gains. However, according to the simulation results, the only Asian LDC that could potentially benefit from the EBA to a significant degree is Myanmar.[17]

Also, under scenario (2), the list of negatively affected countries becomes more diverse than under scenario (1). Apart from ACP countries negatively affected in their sugar exports, other preference-receiving countries (for example, Hungary, Romania, Bulgaria, Poland) appear as net losers from trade diversion, particularly in live animals. However, if one takes into account the indirect protection on vegetables, fruits, meat and diary products as well as other food products introduced by complex sanitary and phytosanitary (SPS) measures – by many LDC standards – that their exports must meet before entering the European Union, the increase in LDC exports for processed agri-food products may well turn out to be smaller than our estimates.[18]

In the case of sensitive products (sugar, rice, bananas), under scenario (2) larger gains and losses are distributed to a larger pool of countries, when compared to scenario (1). In the case of sugar, under scenario (2) Mozambique and Madagascar would benefit the most, together with

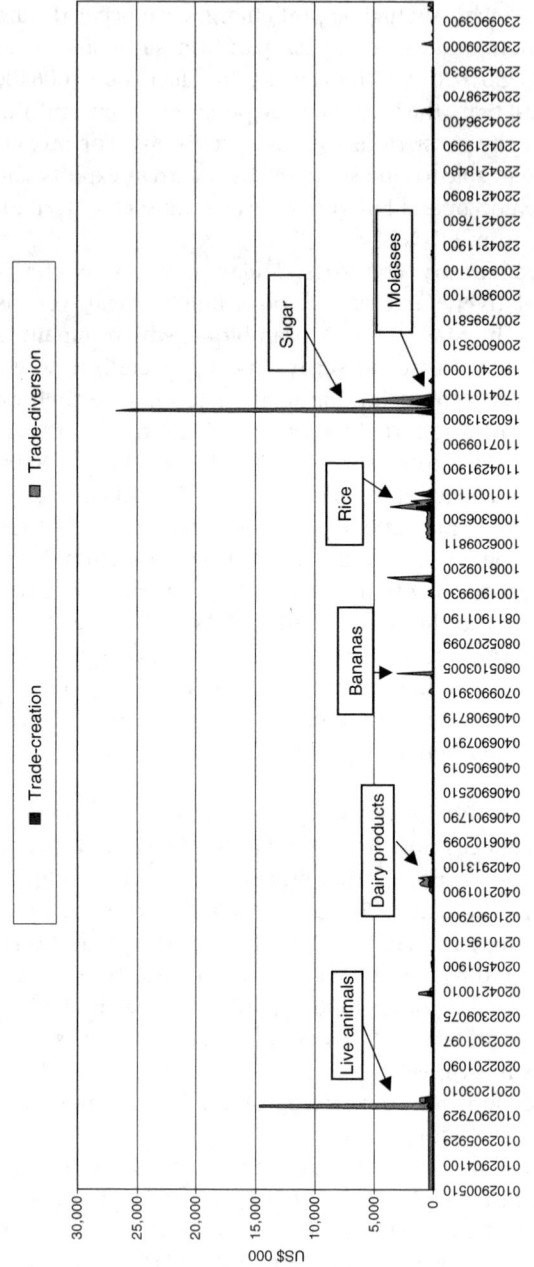

Figure 9.3 Scenario (2): trade-creation and trade-diversion effects, US$ 000

Malawi. Other African LDCs (Tanzania, Zambia, Burkina Faso) would also increase their sugar exports by more than US$5 million.

Under scenario (2) not only the distribution of negative and positive trade effects across countries would be different but the order of magnitude for the estimated effects also changes considerably. Under scenario (1) the major beneficiary was Madagascar, with less than US$150,000 in total trade effects. If rice world exports from LDCs are re-allocated to the EU market, Myanmar, Togo and Niger would become the major beneficiaries of the EBA with total trade effects more than 20 times higher than those under scenario (1). A similar effect is obtained for bananas (Figure 9.4). Under scenario (2), Yemen becomes the major beneficiary with trade effects almost 20 times higher than those of the largest beneficiary under scenario (1) (Rwanda). As a result of this, under scenario (2), market share erosion becomes more significant particularly for some non-LDC ACP (Cameroon, Côte d'Ivoire) and Latin and Central American banana producers (Costa Rica, Ecuador, Colombia, Panama).

Sensitive products: the special case of sugar

While the analyses showed only modest overall effects on the volume of imports into the EU market, it seems that the impact in the sugar sector in particular may be more marked, and concern has been expressed by EU sugar producers and the main ACP sugar exporters.[19] Both are concerned that LDC exports may displace their own production, but the fears of the ACP seem much more soundly based. In order to assess the real magnitude of these concerns, this section provides some additional insights on the issue, including the mechanisms regulating the EU sugar regime.[20]

The EU market for sugar is perhaps one of the most outstanding examples of extensive market regulations and state intervention aimed at ensuring high and stable prices for sugar producers and refineries. The main elements of the Common Market Organization of Sugar (CMOS) relevant for our purposes are:

- Domestic production quotas (divided in sugar quotas A, B and 'sugar C')
- The intervention price acting as a minimum guarantee price (through Paying and Intervention Agencies)
- Export refunds or subsidies
- Import duties and preferential imports.

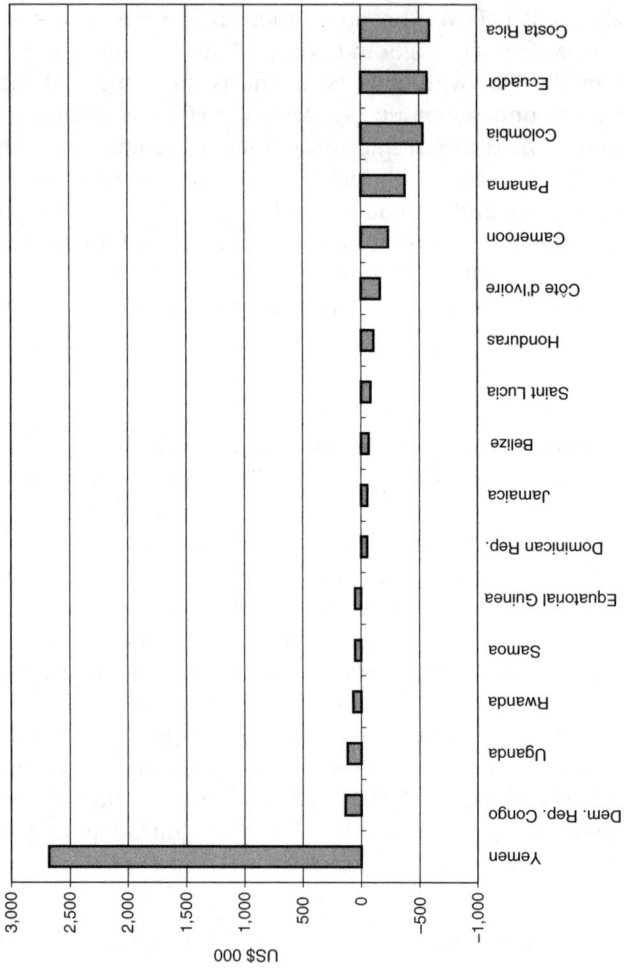

Figure 9.4 Scenario (2): bananas – total trade effects, US$ 000

Domestically, EU countries and producers are given production quotas for sugar A and B,[21] and only these quotas are entitled for price support. In addition, when exported outside the European Union, the sugar produced under these quotas is also granted a refund[22] (or subsidy) roughly equal to the difference between the international and domestic (EU market) prices. Although the European Union is prepared to pay the intervention price to buy quotas of white sugar offered to intervention agencies (when internal EU prices fall below a trigger price), this has happened only once in the last 20 years (in Germany) and for small quantities. In fact, domestic prices for sugar have always been well above the support price, with no need for sugar producers, to revert to this kind of support. Therefore, the cost of this system is largely borne by EU consumers (by paying higher prices) rather than by direct funds from the EU budget. In addition, exporting surplus sugar quotas with the support of export refunds appears to be a more attractive option for sugar producers than selling sugar to an Intervention Agency at the intervention price. So export refunds rather than domestic support price has been the main financial support for sugar producers.

Member states are free to produce sugar above quota levels, but this 'C sugar' must be entirely exported outside the EU market and it does not receive any support in terms of export refunds.

In the context of the WTO Agreement on Agriculture (AoA) and recognizing the probable negative impact that subsidized exports might have in depressing international prices for sugar (outside the EU market), the European Union has made commitments to reduce the total quantity of sugar that can be exported with the support of exports refunds and the total amount of export refunds. Once these limits are reached, the European Union is expected to reduce quotas so as to eliminate the surplus of quota sugar.

Besides regulating the prices and quantities of sugar being produced with the European Union, another pillar of the EU sugar regime to sustain internally high prices for sugar is a strict policy on imports. Market access conditions for sugar in the European Union are indeed extraordinarily stringent, *de facto* preventing any imports of sugar other than those provided in the context of the existing preferential trade arrangements (see below). In fact, although duties on sugar have been bound and, over time, gradually reduced in accordance with the AoA,[23] following the end of the implementation period (2000/2001), their levels remain prohibitive. In addition, given the depressed prices for sugar recorded during the recent years in the international markets, since 1995 the European Union has made regular use of the special safeguard measure under Article 5 of the AoA, allowing the imposition of extra duty on sugar imports. The resulting combination of these two duties has, therefore, made sugar imports possible only through preferential tariffs quotas, with hardly any importation of non-preferential sugar actually taking place. The European Union permits the importation of raw sugar on a preferential basis under four different trade arrangements (including the EBA):

(1) 'Preferential sugar' originating in ACP countries and India

Under the Sugar Protocol 3 of the EU/ACP Partnership Agreement (previously Lomé), the Community undertakes, for an indefinite period of time, to purchase and import on a duty-free basis and at guaranteed price[24] specific quantities of cane sugar (raw or white equivalent, see Table 9.7), originating in 17 ACP countries. Under the EC–India Agreement, similar treatment is provided to 10,000 tonnes of sugar from India per year.

Table 9.7 Sugar quotas allocation under the EC–ACP and EC–India preferential sugar regimes, quantities expressed in metric tons of 'white-sugar equivalent' for delivery in each 12-month period

Barbados	50,312
Belize	40,348
DR Congo	10,000
Fiji	163,600
Guyana	157,700
Côte d'Ivoire	10,000
Jamaica	118,300
Kenya	5,000
Madagascar	10,000
Malawi	20,000
Mauritius	487,200
Christopher and Nevis	15,000
Swaziland	116,400
Tanzania	10,000
Trinidad-Tobago	69,000
Uganda	5,000
Zimbabwe	30,000
All ACP	1,294,700
India	10,000
Total	1,304,700

(2) 'MFN' sugar

Despite its misleading name, 'MFN' sugar is actually a preferential tariff quota of raw sugar (82,000 tonnes) granted by the European Union to Cuba (68 per cent), Brazil (28 per cent) and a few other countries. It comes from a previous obligation contracted by Finland within the GATT. Once Finland joined the EC, this obligation was carried over by the European Union. Such raw sugar is subject to a reduced customs duty of ECU 98 per tonne and its price is freely negotiated without the support of a minimum guaranteed price. Nevertheless, because of the high EU price for sugar, it is very likely that the price paid for this sugar is well above international price and in line with what it is received by EU domestic producers.

(3) EBA sugar

As mentioned before, under the EBA the full liberalization of sugar (HS heading 17.01) for LDC exporters will be phased in between 1 July 2006 and 1 July 2009 by gradually reducing the Community MFN tariff to zero. In the meantime, LDC raw sugar (HS code 17.01.11.10) can be exported duty-free within the limits of a tariff quota, which will grow from 74,185 tonnes (white-sugar equivalent) in 2001/2002 to 197,355 tonnes in 2008/2009 (July–June marketing year).

Imports of sugar from LDCs–ACP benefiting from the ACP–EC Sugar Protocol (Madagascar, Malawi, Tanzania, Uganda) are excluded from the above calculations so as to uphold the viability of this Protocol for these LDC/ACP Countries. For the EBA sugar, the European Union guarantees that the refiners pay a minimum purchase price equal to the intervention price with some adjustments.[25]

(4) Special preferential sugar (SPS)

The final quotas of sugar allowed to enter in the EU market come under the name of special preferential sugar (SPS). These additional tariff quotas have been created with a view to ensuring adequate supplies of raw sugar to seven refineries of certain EU members, namely Portugal, the United Kingdom, Finland and France, where their forecast maximum supply needs (MSN) cannot be met by alternative supplies of raw sugar.

More specifically the preamble of Council Regulation 1260/2001 states that: 'these quantities ... are to be determined ... , once all available raw and cane sugar of community origin and preferential raw sugar and raw sugar originating in countries benefiting from tariffs quotas under trade concessions granted by the Community have been refined.'

In other words, the MSN are calculated taking into account all the available balances from Community sugar, the 'preferential sugar', the MFN sugar and now it would appear also from the EBA sugar. MSN are supposed to be initially filled with imports of raw sugar from the French Overseas Departments (FODs). If the balance shows that the amounts available will be still insufficient to meet the maximum needs, additional duty-free (or highly reduced) tariff quotas, called SPS, are created.[26] For this sugar, EU refineries are due to pay a minimum purchase price equal to the guaranteed price.[27]

Article 39 of Regulation (EC) No. 1260/2001 provides that SPS imports during the 2001/02–2005/06 marketing years shall be allocated only among those states with which the Community has concluded preferential supply agreements. As during the previous five-year period (1995/96–2000/01), at present such agreements have been concluded[28] only with the ACP states party to the Sugar Protocol and India.

Given as constant the number and capacity of the EU refineries[29] and being the Community sugar regulated by fixed quotas, as is the case for 'preferential sugar', MFN sugar and now EBA sugar, the only variable quantity for calculating the SPS has been (and still is) the imports from the FODs. Therefore, the variance over time of SPS tariff quotas has been *de facto* very limited.

Implications for traditional sugar exporters

The transitional period

Bearing in mind the functioning of this system, in the transitional period a number of factors might affect the current market access conditions currently enjoyed by traditional raw cane sugar exports. Some are directly linked to the EBA, while others are independent from it.

The first relates to the commitments undertaken by the European Union in the context of the WTO to reduce the total quantity of sugar that can be exported with the support of exports refunds, and the total amount of these export refunds. In this regard, the European Union has already reduced (and probably will again in the future) its domestic quotas and, accordingly, the MSNs by a similar percentage. Not to mention either the forthcoming enlargement of the European Union that will bring in additional sugar supplied from acceding countries, or more commitments to reduce subsidies coming from current negotiations at the WTO within the Doha Work Programme. In all cases, SPS quotas are bound to be affected.

Second, it appears that the EBA sugar quotas are to be taken into account as an additional component, together with the Community balances of sugar, the 'preferential sugar' and the MFN sugar, in determining the MSNs. As the resulting additional quotas (the SPS) are created only when all available raw cane and beet sugar originating in the Community origin and in other countries benefiting from sugar preferences have been already refined, the EBA sugar, by increasing supply, will undoubtedly reduce the MSNs. Given the yearly increase of the EBA sugar quotas, it is reasonable to expect that the quantity of SPS available will decrease over time as MSNs are gradually and increasingly filled.

Third, the current countries entitled to SPS preferential quotas are only those parts of the EU/ACP Protocol 3 and India, with which the European Union has signed an agreement. The regulation leaves the door open for negotiating similar arrangements with other countries. If such agreements were to be effectively signed between the European Union and LDCs (or other countries), SPS quotas' shares available to traditional sugar exporters would be reduced even further.

Finally, a dispute opened up by two WTO members against the EU sugar regime, and in particular on its export subsidies, if successfully pursued, could significantly affect all components of this intertwined system. The parties are still trying to settle the matter amicably, but this is also a first legal step to contest the system.

The longer period

Some analyses claim that, following the transitional period, LDC sugar would eventually substantially erode the current market share enjoyed by ACP countries such as Mauritius and Fiji, that are dependent on preferential market access for their sugar.

The patterns of LDCs' different sugar exports in 2000 to the European Union are presented in comparative perspective in Table 9.8. The table presents the top exporters of cane sugar (product code 1701), beet sugar (product code 1702) and molasses (product code 1703). Only 11 LDCs figure among top 50 sugar exporters in all categories, six of them (Malawi, Madagascar, Tanzania, the Democratic Republic of Congo, Zambia, Myanmar) being specialized in cane sugar exports, two in other sugars (Sierra Leone and Bangladesh), while Sudan, Senegal and Mozambique are among the top 25 exporters of molasses (product code 1703). The most important LDC exporters are Malawi, with cane sugar exports worth US$20.9 million, and Madagascar, with US$10,6 million. However, even these LDCs account for less than 4 per cent of total EU cane sugar imports. Senegal and Bangladesh together account for less than 0.01 per cent of the EU market for other sugar (product code 1702).

Table 9.8 European Union: top sugar exporters and their market share, 2000, US$ 000

Rank	Cane sugar (1701)			Beet sugar (1702)			Molasses (1703)		
	Country	Value (US$ 000)	Market share (%)	Country	Value (US$ 000)	Market share (%)	Country	Value (US$ 000)	Market share (%)
1	Mauritius	207,645	24.59	Israel	19,508	49.63	Pakistan	64,748	33.28
2	Fiji	110,104	13.04	Canada	15,168	38.59	India	20,199	10.38
3	Guyana	108,305	12.82	United States	14,360	36.53	Poland	17,684	9.09
4	Jamaica	76,756	9.09	Turkey	3,698	9.41	Egypt, Arab Rep.	16,014	8.23
5	Swaziland	75,177	8.90	Mexico	3,673	9.35	United States	14,698	7.55
6	Trinidad and Tobago	29,675	3.51	Hungary	1,357	3.45	Sudan	9,993	5.14
7	Barbados	25,785	3.05	Slovak Rep.	895	2.28	Cuba	8,263	4.25
8	Cuba	23,753	2.81	Argentina	739	1.88	South Africa	7,265	3.73
9	Belize	23,677	2.80	South Africa	638	1.62	Morocco	7,128	3.66
10	Zimbabwe	22,685	2.69	Japan	571	1.45	Mexico	4,167	2.14
11	Malawi	20,970	2.48	Switzerland	540	1.37	Guatemala	3,606	1.85
12	Brazil	19,113	2.26	New Zealand	312	0.79	Lithuania	3,603	1.85
13	Aruba	17,400	2.06	Côte d'Ivoire	284	0.72	Mauritius	3,193	1.64
14	Côte d'Ivoire	13,230	1.57	China	233	0.59	Iran, Islamic Rep.	2,941	1.51
15	Madagascar	10,600	1.26	Bulgaria	207	0.53	Senegal	2,252	1.16
16	St Kitts and Nevis	8,354	1.26	Thailand	190	0.48	Slovak Rep.	1,759	0.90
17	Tanzania	7,864	0.99	Norway	172	0.44	Syrian Arab Rep.	1,277	0.66
18	Congo, Rep.	7,109	0.93	Costa Rica	85	0.22	Latvia	996	0.51
19	Zambia	5,393	0.84	Brazil	64	0.16	Guyana	723	0.37

#	Country			Country			Country		
20	*Myanmar*	3,366	0.64	Indonesia	56	0.14	Turkey	705	0.36
21	United States	2,907	0.40	Czech Rep.	54	0.14	Macao	664	0.34
22	South Africa	2,880	0.34	Lebanon	35	0.09	Venezuela	620	0.32
23	Bahamas, The	2,862	0.34	Saudi Arabia	34	0.09	Mozambique	503	0.26
24	Poland	2,453	0.34	Sri Lanka	28	0.07	Russian Federation	418	0.21
25	Paraguay	1,916	0.29	Pakistan	27	0.07	Ethiopia (excludes Eritrea)	368	0.19
26	Netherlands Antilles	1,872	0.23	Slovenia	23	0.06	Slovenia	235	0.12
27	Norway	1,570	0.22	Singapore	20	0.05	Algeria	143	0.07
28	Czech Rep.	1,471.	0.19	Malaysia	18	0.04	Austria	111	0.06
29	Turkey	1,181	0.17	Hong Kong, China	17	0.04	Brazil	96	0.05
30	Kenya	1,044	0.14	Korea, Rep.	16	0.04	Norway	67	0.03
31	Switzerland	974	0.12	Sierra Leone	15	0.04	Paraguay	25	0.01
32	El Salvador	912	0.12	Australia	15	0.04	Thailand	21	0.01
33	India	859	0.11	Latvia	13	0.03	Costa Rica	18	0.01
34	Argentina	837	0.10	India	10	0.03	Czech Rep.	17	0.01
35	Costa Rica	822	0.10	Poland	10	0.03	Singapore	12	0.01
36	United Arab Emirates	410	0.10	Jamaica	9	0.02	China	10	0.01
37	Colombia	405	0.05	Iceland	8	0.02			
38	Croatia	390	0.05	United Arab Emirates	7	0.02			
39	Hungary	384	0.05	Malta	7	0.02			
40	Philippines	300	0.05	Papua New Guinea	6	0.02			

Table 9.8 (Continued)

Rank	Cane sugar (1701)			Beet sugar (1702)			Molasses (1703)		
	Country	Value (US$ 000)	Market share (%)	Country	Value (US$ 000)	Market share (%)	Country	Value (US$ 000)	Market share (%)
41	China	281	0.04	Trinidad and Tobago	6	0.02			
42	Ecuador	234	0.03	Bangladesh	6	0.02			
43	Estonia	216	0.03	Nicaragua	6	0.01			
44	Bulgaria	164	0.03	Colombia	4	0.01			
45	Sri Lanka	61	0.02	Morocco	4	0.01			
46	Australia	55	0.01	Ukraine	3	0.01			
47	Thailand	48	0.01	Cyprus	3	0.01			
48	Slovak Rep.	44	0.01						
49	Guatemala	37	0.01						

Note:
LDCs are in italics.
Source: WITS – Comtrade.

Set against these figures, the fears expressed by the EU sugar lobby of a massive rise in LDC exports of sugar products appear to be puzzling.

First, the ability of LDCs to erode the market share of EU domestic sugar producers seems quite limited, based on the trade-creation estimates from our simulation in all scenarios.

Second, even for the most important sugar product of interest to LDCs and non-LDC ACP countries – cane sugar – the partial equilibrium estimates situate the increase in LDC cane sugar exports (products in tariff lines from section 1701) between roughly US$34 million (scenario (1) with no LDC trade re-orientation) and US$64 million (scenario (2)). Scenario (2) took into account the potential additional exports of LDCs based on a re-orientation of their current world exports of sugar. While it is true that the expansion in LDC sugar exports is achieved to a large extent at the expense of other non-LDC ACP exporters, this is far from a major market share reshuffle between LDCs and other ACP countries. For instance, the EC (EC, 2000a: 16) assumes that LDC exports of sugar can rise to around 2.7 million tonnes over three years. Our partial equilibrium estimates place this export increase rather between 50,000 and 100,000 tons, based on EU domestic prices similar to those used by the EC study.[30]

For instance, according to the SMART estimates under scenario (1) (Table 9.9), the largest ACP sugar exporters such as Mauritius and Fiji would see their current level of exports reduced by 5 and 2.4 per cent, respectively. More drastic market share reduction could arise for smaller exporters of preferential sugar to the European Union, such as the Netherlands Antilles (more than 50 per cent), Aruba (25 per cent) and India (15.3 per cent), who enjoy similar market-access conditions as ACP countries.

Under LDC trade re-orientation (scenario (2)), several other LDCs will see their current exports significantly increased (Table 9.10) and the number of countries negatively affected expand considerably. It has to be noted however that under scenario (2) the distribution of gains and losses is more dispersed. A number of factors, not accounted for under the SMART simulations, are nevertheless likely to limit to a large extent such major redistributions of current market shares. The main factor is the limited ability of LDCs to supply the EU market with increased exports of sugar. The second major constraint stems from the implicit safeguards mechanisms included in the EBA, both during and after the expiration of the transition periods.

Some LDCs may face further unforeseen trade barriers. Mozambique, for instance, did not benefit from either the ACP Sugar Protocol or SPS

Table 9.9 Scenario (1): cane sugar – export changes

Country	Scenario (1) percentage change in current exports
Malawi	81.5
Zambia	78.9
Tanzania	78.0
Myanmar	55.3
Madagascar	51.5
Barbados[a]	−1.0
South Africa[a]	−1.7
Swaziland[a]	−2.4
Jamaica[a]	−2.4
Guyana[a]	−2.4
Fiji[a]	−2.4
United States	−3.4
Mauritius[a]	−5.0
Brazil	−7.9
Côte d'Ivoire[a]	−11.1
Paraguay	−11.7
India	−15.3
Aruba	−24.9
Netherlands Antilles	−53.3

Note:
[a] Non-LDC ACP countries.

Table 9.10 Scenario (2): cane sugar – export changes, initial levels of exports greater than US$ million

Country	Percentage change in current exports
Somalia	114.4
Myanmar	105.7
Nepal	103.0
Niger	85.5
Malawi	81.8
United Rep. of Tanzania	77.3
Burkina Faso	77.1
Zambia	76.8
Mozambique	74.1
Madagascar	73.1
Sudan	20.3
Ethiopia	14.5
India	−1.4
South Africa[a]	−2.2

United States	-3.6
Mauritius[a]	-4.8
Cuba[a]	-5.4
Philippines	-6.6
El Salvador	-6.6
Kenya[a]	-6.6
Bahamas[a]	-6.6
Congo DR[a]	-6.7
Saint Kitts and Nevis[a]	-6.7
Belize[a]	-6.7
Barbados[a]	-6.7
Trinidad and Tobago[a]	-6.7
Jamaica[a]	-6.7
Swaziland[a]	-6.7
Guyana[a]	-6.7
Fiji[a]	-6.8
Zimbabwe[a]	-7.4
Paraguay	-7.9
Ecuador	-10.0
Brazil	-10.0
Argentina	-11.7
Norway	-12.0
Colombia	-12.1
Costa Rica	-13.1
China	-13.4
Estonia	-14.7
Côte d'Ivoire[a]	-15.6
Hungary	-18.8
Netherlands Antilles	-22.9
Australia	-24.4
Czech Rep.	-24.4
Switzerland	-24.5
Turkey	-24.5
Poland	-24.5
United Arab Emirates	-24.6
Croatia	-24.6
Bulgaria	-24.7
Aruba	-29.1

Note:
[a] Non–LDC ACP countries.

Agreement and consequently could not export cane sugar (product code 1701) to the EU market under the pre-EBA preferential treatment for LDCs. Under the assumptions of scenario (2) allowing for a re-orientation of exports from third countries to the European Union, Mozambique could potentially export cane sugar worth of around US$16.6 million, an increase of more than 74 per cent of its total sugar exports. However, the EBA stipulates that before the end of the transition period in 2009, LDCs are allocated duty-free quotas based on an annual 15 per cent increase of their historical market share in the European Union. For Mozambique, however, unless other arrangements are negotiated bilaterally, this means that the country will be unable to export any cane sugar until 2009. Other LDCs are in a similar position.

Even though there are still a number of constraints in place, there are some other factors that could work in favour of increased LDC exports. For instance, in order to take advantage of the EBA, a re-allocation of LDC sugar consumption from domestic sugar to imported sugar from third countries could occur. Our estimates (under both scenarios (1) and (2)), however, did not factor in such potential increases in exports. Nor did they take into account any potential increase in supply capacity of LDCs as a result of the preferential market access offered by the EBA.[31] In the longer term, as long as CAP policies maintain a price differential between EU domestic prices and world prices, both of these effects are likely to occur as LDC producers will have strong incentives to increase exports to the European Union further.

Conclusions

The idea of trade preferences is to contribute to development through the expansion of exports from beneficiary countries by generating increased investment, growth and employment, and the diversification of the production base away from a heavy reliance on the production of primary commodities. Indeed, the relative success of those countries that have been able to diversify into manufactures seems to lend support to this basic premise. On the other hand, LDCs have remained heavily dependent on commodities and have seen their share of world trade decline. The idea of the EBA initiative and similar programmes is to try to lift the trade performance of the LDCs and, hence, their overall economic development.

Improved non-preferential (MFN) market-access opportunities, bound within a WTO multilateral negotiations, would also be helpful and would be more secure than unilaterally granted preferences. However, in sensitive sectors, there would be heavy resistance to such general liberalization. Moreover, it may well be that the enhanced trade opportunities would be snapped up by other developing countries with greater supply capacity, as has happened in the GSP. In the longer term, progressive MFN liberalization is inevitable, but the temporary competitive 'edge' provided by preferences may help the LDCs and other developing countries catch up with the more developed countries.

Two disadvantages of preferences are, first, that the preferences may induce beneficiaries to specialize in activities in which they may never become competitive and, second, that they create vested interests opposed to multilateral trade liberalization. Inappropriate specialization may be particularly acute where preferential access entails economic transfers arising from privileged access behind high non-tariff barriers (NTBs), as has been the case, for example, with certain agricultural preferences. Not only is the reversal of reliance on such high rent transfers likely to prove extremely painful unless it is carefully managed over an extended period, but the preferences themselves have perpetuated mono-cultural dependence rather than promoting diversification of the production base.

Experience shows that GSP and other unilateral preference schemes have had only moderate success in generating significant export opportunities that have been captured by the more advanced developing countries. Of course, improvements could be made to the various preferential schemes, as has been recognized by the donors themselves. Greater simplicity and stability of coverage, improved rules of origin, more transparent competitive needs exclusions and so on are factors. It is recognized that the simplicity and stability of the Japanese scheme has contributed to a relatively higher share of preferential trade in total imports and high utilization of the scheme. In this sense, the apparent simplicity and absence of restrictions in the EBA initiative imply that it could be important in generating new trade from the world's poorest countries, whose commodity-oriented exports have done badly in recent years by comparison with other countries.

Overall, our study shows moderate, but useful, welfare and trade gains from the EBA initiative, with the largest gains being recorded for SSA. The gains are likely to be concentrated in relatively few sectors, and our analysis highlights the significance of improved access to the EU sugar market as the single most important source of change. The effects on the European Union itself are minimal, but the increased market access for LDCs comes mostly at the expense of other preference-receiving countries (ACP countries, in particular), although again the trade-diversion effects are in most cases minor and widely distributed.

However, the analysis does not fully account for NTBs affecting trade flows that may preclude LDCs from increasing their exports to the extent predicted by our analysis. In addition, in the longer term, for many items, supply-side factor constraints rather than limitations on market access may be the more important constraints and need the urgent attention of the international community. Even the most generous market-access enhancements alone may not be sufficient to strengthen the links between trade and development in the poorest countries in the world.

Notes

* The views expressed in the chapter are those of the authors, and do not necessarily represent the views of the organizations for which they work nor the member states of those organizations.

1. For an early history, see 'The History of UNCTAD 1964–84', New York, United Nations, 1985 (Document UNCTAD/OSG/286).
2. WTO document WT/COMTD/W/93, 5 October 2001.
3. For a general description of the EU GSP scheme, including the EBA initiative, see, for instance, UNCTAD (2002).
4. See UNCTAD (2001: 17) for further details on the products for which non-ACP LDCs were receiving less preferential market access, compared to ACP LDCs in the pre-EBA GSP scheme for LDCs.
5. Further details can be found in the UNCTAD Handbook on the EU GSP Scheme, available at http://www.unctad.org/gsp/.
6. See Council Regulation (EC) No. 602/98 of 9 March 1998, extending the coverage of Regulations (EC) No. 3281/94 and No. 1256/96 concerning Community schemes of generalized tariff preferences for the benefit of the LDCs (*Official Journal* L 080 1998: 1–16).
7. The information provided below is based on data available from the European Commission, at http://www.europa.en.int/comm.
8. Article 1:4 of Council Regulation No. 416/2001 of 28 February 2001.
9. Para. 13 in the preamble of Council Regulation No. 416/2001 of 28 February 2001.
10. Article 1:5 of Council Regulation No. 416/2001 of 28 February 2001.
11. Statement of the European Commission of 1 March 2001. See also the reports available at http://w.sugartraders.co.uk/archive.htm and http://www.eurinco.co.uk/trade/eba_rev2.htm.
12. This is not the case of the US scheme that provides duty-free and quota-free treatment for African countries, some of which are not LDCs, while excluding non-African countries.
13. This is elaborated in the WIDER Discussion Paper 2003/47 version of this Chapter (Cernat *et al.*, 2003).
14. For a technical description of the model, methodology, data and uses, see Laird and Yeats (1990).
15. See Laird and Yeats (1990) for a full description of the data sources and for the series of equations and identities from which the trade-creation and trade-diversion effects reported in the simulations are derived.
16. On the possible re-orientation of LDC exports as a result of the EBA, see EC (2000a, 2000b).
17. However, since 1997 Myanmar has been temporarily excluded from GSP treatment for alleged forced labour practices and therefore does not benefit

from the EBA initative. See Council Regulation No. 552/97 of 24 March 1997 (*Official Journal* L 85, 27 March 1997).

18. See, for instance, the case of shrimp exports from Bangladesh provided in UNCTAD (2001: 108–9).
19. See, for instance, the impact study carried out by the Sugar Traders Association of the United Kingdom, available at http://www.sugartraders.co.uk/eba_impact_study.pdf.
20. For a more detailed analysis on the EU sugar regime and its impact on developing countries, see Oxfam (2002).
21. A and B sugar quotas differ, *inter alia*, on the level of the minimum price guaranteed – see Council Regulation (EC) No. 1260/2001 of 19 June 2001.
22. Export refunds are equal to the intervention price plus the storage levy, plus the FOB minus the sugar world price. Sugar contained in food and drinks also qualifies for export refunds.
23. A 20 per cent reduction from a base rate of 524 ECU/tonne to the current 419 ECU/tonne in six annual steps.
24. In principle, preferential sugar is entitled to receive the same price support granted to domestic sugar (under quotas) where an importer buyer is not willing to pay the guaranteed prices. In practice, given the high prices in the EU market, this has never happened.
25. Article 4 of the Commission Regulation (EC) No. 1381/2002 of 29 July 2002.
26. For example in the year 1998/99, the SPS quota was set at 334,000 tonnes of white sugar equivalent (Council Regulation 1375/98 and Commission Regulation 440/99).
27. Commission Regulation (EC) No. 1096/2002 of 24 June 2002.
28. Council Decision 2001/870/EC; *Official Journal* L 325, 8 December 2001, p. 21; and Article 35, of Council Regulation (EC) No. 1260/2001; *Official Journal* L 178/1, 30 June 2001.
29. Indeed a penalty might be levied to refineries that import more than the set MSN.
30. Our results are in line with other studies that predicted more modest increases in sugar exports from LDCs – see for instance Oxfam and IDS (2001).
31. Sudan, with sales of over 240,000 metric tonnes now mainly to COMESA, is one such case; its Kenana plant is the world's largest integrated sugar producer.

References

Agra Europe (2001) 'EBA Treaty will Force Further CAP Reforms', *Agra Europe*, 9, 1–3.

Cernat, L., S. Laird, L. Monge-Roffarello and A. Turrini (2003) 'The EU's Everything But Arms Initiative and the Least-developed Countries', WIDER Discussion Paper DP2003/47, Helsinki: UNU-WIDER.

European Commission (EC) (2000a) 'EU Trade Concessions to Least Developed Countries – Everything But Arms Proposal: First Remarks on the Possible Impacts on the Agricultural Sector', Report by the European Commission Directorate for Agriculture, available at http://europa.eu.int/comm/commissioners/fishler/eba_en.pdf.

———— (2000b) 'EU Trade Concessions to Least Developed Countries – Everything But Arms Proposal: Possible Impacts on the Agricultural Sector', Report by the

European Commission Directorate for Trade, available at http://europa.eu.int/comm/trade/pdf/eba_ias.pdf.

Hertel, T. (1997) *Global Trade Analysis: Modeling and Applications*, Cambridge: Cambridge University Press.

Ianchovichina, E., A. Mattoo and M. Olarreaga (2001) 'Unrestricted Market Access for Sub-Saharan Africa: How Much is it Worth and Who Pays?', CEPR Discussion Paper 2820.

Laird, S. and A. Yeats (1990) *Quantitative Methods for Trade Barrier Analysis*, New York, Macmillan and NYUP.

Oxfam (2002) 'The Great EU Sugar Scam', Oxfam Briefing Paper 27, London, 25 August.

Oxfam and IDS (2001) *The Impact of the EU's 'Everything but Arms' Proposal: A Report to Oxfam*, London, January.

Page, S. and A. Hewitt (2002) 'The New European Trade Preferences: Does the "Everything But Arms" (EBA) Help the Poor?', *Development Policy Review*, 20(1): 91–102.

Panagariya, A. (1998) 'Rethinking the New Regionalism', in J. Nash and W. Takacs, (eds), *Trade Policy Reform. Lessons and Implications*, Washington, DC: World Bank.

Trueblood, M. and A. Somwaru (2002) 'Trade Liberalization and the Least Developed Countries: Modeling the EU's Everything but Arms Initiative', Paper presented at the 2002 Conference on Global Economic Analysis, Taipei.

UNCTAD (2001) *Duty and Quota Free Market Access for LDCs: An Analysis of Quad Initiatives*, London and Geneva: United Nations Conference on Trade and Development and the Commonwealth Secretariat.

———— (2002) *Handbook on the Scheme of the European Community*, UNCTAD/ITCD/TSB/Misc.25/Rev.2, Geneva.

Viner, J. (1950) *The Custom Union Issue*, New York: Carnegie Endowment.

10

Export Subsidies: Theory, Evidence and the WTO Agreement on Subsidies*

Rajeev Ahuja

Introduction

The WTO Agreement on Subsidies and Countervailing Measures (SCM Agreement) framed in the Uruguay Round governs the conduct of member countries with respect to export subsidies. An important aspect of the current provisions of the Agreement is that while export subsidies are prohibited for the developed countries, certain developing countries have been exempted from the prohibition on such subsidies for non-agricultural products.[1]

The Agreement has been in operation since 1995. Many member countries consider a review of its provisions to be necessary. Accordingly, the ministerial declaration mandates that the Doha Round will aim at clarifying and improving disciplines under the Agreement.[2] Many developing countries consider the Agreement to be iniquitous to their interest and have been seeking improvements and refinements in certain provisions.

The rationale for export subsidies has undergone a significant change for countries such as Brazil and India that having pursued an import-substitution development strategy during the 1960s, 1970s and much of the 1980s, are now liberalizing trade. While the rationale earlier was to offset the bias against exports inherent in the import substitution strategy, the rationale now is to promote exports *à la* South Korea that successfully pursued an export promotion strategy after the 1960s.

While the evidence on the link between export promotion strategy and higher economic growth is strong enough, the same unfortunately cannot be said for export subsidies and export performance. It is difficult to disentangle the effects of export subsidies on exports, as the latter depend on a host of other factors such as macroeconomic policy, exchange rate, foreign direct investment (FDI), infrastructure facilities and so forth. In essence, both the domestic supply factors and the external demand conditions influence export performance of a country. Nevertheless, the limited available evidence, on balance, suggests a significant positive relationship between subsidies and exports, provided such subsidies are selective and focused to achieve the objective.

This chapter is organized as follows: in the next section we bring out the important differences in the provisions of the SCM Agreement as applicable to different countries, and the improvements and clarifications that developing member countries are seeking. In the following section we examine the role of export incentives in Brazil, India and South Korea with a view to bringing out the underlying motivation for their introduction as well as to understand their role in export promotion. We then review the theory and evidence in the literature on the effect of export subsidies on export performance. The conclusions are drawn in the final section.

WTO Agreement on Subsidies and Countervailing Measures[3]

The SCM Agreement that has been tightened in the Uruguay Round deals with two distinct but related issues. These concern the multilateral disciplines (set of rules) on the provision of subsidies that a member nation must follow, and the countervailing measures to neutralize the adverse effect of subsidized imports.

Multilateral discipline on subsidies

Not all export incentives are regarded as subsidies under the SCM Agreement. The SCM Agreement defines what constitutes a *subsidy*. A measure is defined to be a subsidy if it contains the following three elements: (1) it is a financial contribution, (2) the contribution is by a government or any public body within the territory of a member and (3) the contribution confers a benefit.

A financial contribution could take the form of direct transfers or of price/income support. Direct transfers could take the form of grants, loans and equity infusion when the government provides for loan guarantees. A government is deemed to have made a financial contribution if revenue otherwise due to the government is not collected. Examples include fiscal incentives in the form of direct tax exemptions or where a government provides for goods and services other than general infrastructure, or purchases goods on favourable terms. A government may either itself carry out these functions or may entrust these to any private agency. The Agreement provides examples of measures that represent a financial contribution. It is important to note that remission or drawback of duties on the inputs used in the production of exports is *not* considered a financial contribution, and so also a government's financial contribution for general infrastructure such as rail, roads, ports and so on. Hence these do not qualify as a subsidy. However, *excess* of remission or drawback is considered to be a financial contribution and, as we shall see later, is also considered a subsidy.

A financial contribution by itself does not necessarily constitute a subsidy. The financial contribution must confer *benefit* to the recipient. An important point to note is that a subsidy is not defined with reference to its cost to the government. It is defined with reference to the market – that is, to a commercial benchmark. The same is true for the calculation of countervailing duties.

Government provision of equity capital, for example, is considered a benefit if an investment decision is considered inconsistent with the usual investment practice of private investors. Similarly, a government loan or a loan guarantee is considered a benefit if the amount a firm actually pays is less than the amount that the firm would have paid if the same facility were to be available on a commercial basis from the market. Government provision of equity capital, for example, does not confer any benefit if the decision made is consistent with the usual investment practice of private investors in the territory of that member.

Even if a measure is shown to be a subsidy, it cannot be subjected to SCM Agreement disciplines unless it is provided *specifically* to an enterprise or industry or group of enterprises or industries. Subsidies that are provided *specifically* to an enterprise distort the allocation of resources within an economy. On the contrary, subsidies that are widely available are presumed to be non-distortionary. Thus subsidies that are *specific* alone are subjected to the SCM Agreement disciplines.

Turning to multilateral disciplines on *export subsidies*, such subsidies are prohibited for developed-country members. If any developed-country member is found to be giving an export subsidy, it can be straightaway taken to the Dispute Settlement Body (DSB) of the WTO by any member country.[4] However, the provisions differ with respect to developing countries. For the developing countries listed in Annex VII,[5] export subsidies are not prohibited but are actionable. That is, if export subsidies are found to be causing injury to the domestic industry of the importing member country, the importing country can impose countervailing duties or take the member to the DSB. For developing-country members not listed in Annex VII (referred as 'other' developing-country members), a period of eight years, from the date of entry into force of the WTO Agreement, is given for the removal of such subsidies, with a two-year grace period. This eight-year period ended on 31 December 2002.[6]

Since both Korea and Brazil have *per capita* income greater than US$1000, they are outside the group of countries listed in Annex VII of the SCM Agreement.[7] They fall under the category of 'other' developing countries and are therefore allowed a period of eight years for the removal of export subsidies. On the other type of prohibited subsidy (import substitution or local content subsidy), Brazil and Korea, like all developing country members, were required to withdraw any programme that encouraged the use of domestic goods over imported goods within a five-year period ending 1 January 2000.

Countervailing measures

Countervailing measures are a unilateral remedy applied by a member country in accordance with the criteria laid down in the SCM Agreement. To be able to impose countervailing duty the member country must establish the following three substantive aspects: (1) that the imports are subsidized, (2) that an injury is caused to the domestic industry of the importing country, and (3) that there exists a causal link between the subsidized imports and the injury. The procedure for conduct and imposition of CVDs is well laid out in the Agreement.

All countervailing duties normally have a life of not more than five years. If there is a change in the extent of subsidy or in the injury to domestic industry, a case can be made for the review of CVDs within a reasonable period of time. If no review takes place within five years all CVDs must automatically terminate, and in any case for the imposition of CVDs has to be made afresh.

Developing country members whose exports are subject to counter-vailing duty investigations are given special and preferential treatment. An investigation regarding a product originating in a developing country member are immediately terminated if:

- the subsidy level does not exceed *de minimis* level which is 1 per cent for a developed-country member, 2 per cent for an 'other' developing-country member and 3 per cent for an Annex VII country member (if an 'other' developing-country member eliminated export the subsidy prior to the expiry of the eight-year period the *de minimis* level would be 3 per cent, instead of 2 per cent); or
- the volume of subsidized exports represents less than 4 per cent of the total imports of the like product in the importing member country,

unless imports from developing-country members, whose individual shares of total imports represent less than 4 per cent, collectively account for more than 9 per cent of total imports of the like product in the importing member.

To sum up this section, we find that not all export incentives qualify as subsidies as under the SCM Agreement. For example, remission/ refund of taxes/duties on the inputs used in exports is not considered to be a subsidy. While for developed member countries export subsidies are prohibited, certain developing countries (such as India) are allowed to give subsidies but such subsidies are actionable if they cause adverse effects on the domestic industry of the importing country. 'Other' developing countries (such as Brazil and South Korea) have to phase out all export subsidies within a certain time period.

Improvements and clarifications[8]

Many developing countries consider the Agreement to be iniquitous to their interests and have been seeking changes in certain provisions. Some of the important changes being sought are listed below.

Inclusion of capital goods in the definition of inputs consumed

The Agreement in its current form allows for remission/refund of taxes/ duties only on the inputs used in export production but not on the capital goods. This treatment is considered to be against the principle of fiscal neutrality, which has been the guiding principle behind the remission/refund of indirect duties/taxes on the inputs consumed in the production process.[9] It is argued that even though capital goods are not physically incorporated in the final product in the same manner as some of the other inputs, remission/refund of taxes paid on such inputs must be allowed under the current provisions of the Agreement. Remission/refund is allowed even on inputs such as energy, fuels, catalysts and the like, that are not physically incorporated but not on capital goods used in export production. Capital goods do undergo reduction in value due to their use, which is accounted for in the form of depreciation.

Non-refund of duties on imported capital goods used in export production is viewed as iniquitous to the interest of developing countries who impose customs duties on capital goods imports for protecting domestic industry but, more importantly, for revenue purposes.[10] Developed countries, on the other hand, impose few or negligible duties on capital goods imports. At present, member countries countervail remission of duties on capital goods imports for export production.

Aggregate and generalized rates of duty remission

The existing rules in the Agreement require information about the exact amount of inputs consumed in the production process for duty drawback. Members must have regard to the fact that a rule that requires separate verification for every unit is impracticable and unfair to countries having a large number of small and medium enterprises (SMEs). In India, for example, small-scale industries account for some 40 per cent of manufacturing production and over 35 per cent of exports. Given the preponderance of these units in developing countries, India therefore proposes that whenever an averaging procedure is developed fairly and systematically and used to determine the amount payable to the exporter on account of remission of indirect taxes or import duties, there must be a presumption that a reasonable and effective verification system is in existence.

Export credit

Brazil and India have asked for a review of disciplines on export credit in the SCM Agreement. According to them, the current disciplines on credit do not take into account differences among the members. This has introduced asymmetry in the capacity of member countries to compete on an equal footing as far as providing export credit is concerned. In international purchases, closing a deal often depends not just on price and quality parameters but also on the length of repayment and interest rate charged. Given the fact that cost of fund is different for different member countries, those that have a high interest rate are at a disadvantage in extending credit to buyers of goods. To remove this disadvantage, if the member countries lower the cost of export credit, it should not be regarded as a subsidy. Furthermore, given that developing countries have higher cost of credit compared to developed countries, the former can never meet the terms offered by the latter. Although the OECD export credit arrangement that has been grand-fathered in the agreement is available to developing countries, it is of limited utility to them.[11]

International competitiveness

Under the current subsidy provisions, a developing country is pro-hibited from giving an export subsidy to a commodity if its share in total world exports of that commodity touches 3.25 per cent per cent in two consecutive calendar years. In that case, the country is deemed to have become internationally competitive in that commodity, and it must therefore withdraw all export subsidies given to the commodity. Some developing countries consider a two-year period to be too short to judge competitiveness, and want this period to be raised to at least five years. Furthermore if, subsequent to its becoming internationally competitive, a country's share falls below this threshold, developing countries propose that there be an automatic withdrawal of the prohibition provision.

Other changes to the existing provisions of the Agreement that the developing countries are seeking are: raising the *de minimis* level for initiating countervailing action, excluding a developing country from the Annex only after its GNP has been above the level for a continuous period of three years and not just a one-time attainment as at present (similarly true in defining the international competitiveness of a product) and restricting countervailing duties (CVDs) only to the amount by which the subsidy exceeds the *de minimis* level. Besides, there are certain areas where the Agreement does not provide any (or enough) guidance on how to go about calculating CVDs or on the use of benchmarks.[12]

Export incentives: a brief perspective

One of the important lessons learned in the late twentieth century was that trade orientation matters. Developing countries that pursued outward orientation experienced higher economic growth compared to those that adopted an import-substitution strategy (Krueger, 1980; Moreira, 1995). Outward orientation did not mean a 'hands-off' approach of governments or minimal government intervention. In fact, it was significant both in countries that adopted an import-substitution development strategy as well as in those that pursued an export promotion strategy. One of the forms that this intervention took was through export incentives. In the past, export subsidies have been used widely by both sets of countries. However, the rationale behind these incentives, their extent and form vary, depending on the country's trade orientation, its economic structure (including fiscal structure), overall resource availability, export potential, price elasticity of exports and so on. We briefly examine below the role these incentives played in Brazil and India that adopted an import-substitution strategy, and in South Korea that is considered to be the quintessence of an outward oriented strategy.

Import-substitution development strategy: Brazil and India

Both Brazil and India had some export incentives in place in the 1950s. They used these incentives extensively to increase exports from the early 1960s onwards, and they did help in reducing the anti-export bias inherent in the strategy they pursued. Furthermore, both these countries embarked on major trade reforms in the early 1990s. We briefly chart below the role that these incentives played in promoting exports from each of these countries.

Brazil[13]

Brazil, within its import-substitution strategy, tried promoting exports through several incentives and through a crawling peg exchange rate regime that protected the real exchange rate from inflation. Early attempts to promote exports from Brazil can be traced to the 1950s, when limited tax incentives were given to exporters. However, it was not until the early 1960s when the government realized the need to promote exports. This realization came when Brazil ran into balance of payment problems and needed to import intermediate inputs and primary products that it could not produce domestically. Thereafter, in order to promote exports the Brazilian government started giving several export incentives such as tax exemptions. Exemption of federal value-added tax, called the tax on industrial production (IPI), was given in 1965. In 1967, states followed suit and exempted exports from state value-added tax, called ICMS. These incentives, together with others, did help increase exports from the country, particularly in the early and mid-1970s, the oil crisis notwithstanding.[14] These incentives specifically benefited manufactured exports.

In response to the external shocks of the early 1980s, the Brazilian government further enhanced export incentives and sharply devalued the currency. This gave a fillip to manufactured exports from Brazil, leading to their seven-fold increase. This improved their share in total exports – from 24.1 per cent in 1974 to 49.6 per cent in 1987. Between 1973 and 1987, total exports registered a growth of 11.9 per cent per annum.

According to Pinheiro and Moreira (2000), export subsidies in Brazil averaged 50 per cent of the value of manufactured exports during the 1970s and 1980s and were rather costly and failed to turn exports into 'more than just a poor alternative to domestic policies'.[15] By the end of the 1980s, manufactured exports accounted for less than 10 per cent of manufactured output. Also, manufactured exports remained highly concentrated: in 1990, 53 companies accounted for about 44 per cent of all manufactured exports from Brazil.

During the 1970s and 1980s, even though the government provided several incentives to exporters, the import-substitution policy restricted competition through high tariffs that made production for the domestic market more lucrative than production for export. Brazil's heavy reliance on foreign firms, particularly in capital-intensive sectors, is also considered to be a factor that restricted the access of its exports to the markets of developed countries. The macroeconomic problems in the 1980s, lack of long-term investments for technological upgrading and a lack of strategic vision to focus on products in which it had a comparative advantage, led to the decline of the competitiveness of Brazilian exports in the international market after the mid-1980s.[16] This was reflected in its declining share in important markets such as the United States, Japan and Germany.

During 1985 and 1990, macroeconomic problems, particularly inflation, made it difficult for the government to support export promotion programmes. The prevailing economic conditions forced the Brazilian government to embark on an economic liberalization and reforms programme. In the early 1990s, the Brazilian government started economic reforms comprising trade reforms, privatization and deregulation. Trade reform on the import side saw removal of most non-tariff barriers (NTBs) in 1990, and the announcement of a tariff reduction programme which brought the average nominal tariff down from 32.2 per cent in 1990 to 14.2 per cent in 1993.

On the export side, subsidies were eliminated and incentives reduced to a minimum. Pinheiro, Giambiagi and Moreira (2001) report that these incentives fell from an average of 3.1 per cent of GDP in 1981–4 to 1.3 per cent in 1990–91. However, the government continued to exempt tax on exports and also strengthened export financing schemes. Trade reforms also saw the establishment of Mercosur: a market with Argentina, Uruguay and Paraguay, having a common external tariff (CET) implemented from 1 January 1995.[17] With financial liberalization, the Brazilian economy also started to become financially more integrated with the world economy.

After the launching of reforms in the early 1990s, the earlier rationale for export incentives, namely to offset export bias, which was so strong in the 1970s and 1980s, was no longer valid. Moreover, the growing pressure on the government to keep its fiscal position in control necessitated the Brazilian government to terminate several of its export promotion programmes that had been adopted in the 1970s and 1980s. Some of the important subsidy programmes that were terminated were: preferential working capital financing for export (terminated from

30 August 1990), over-rebate of state value-added tax on goods destined for exports, preferential financing to exporters if they maintained certain minimum level of deposit of foreign exchange (20 September 1988), financing for the storage of merchandise destined for exports, income tax exemption for export earnings (12 April 1990), preferential financing for trading companies (31 August 1990), and preferential medium- and long-term financing for manufactured exports (15 October 1990).

Trade reform enabled exporters to access modern capital goods and inputs at international prices. This, coupled with structural changes, exposed Brazilian producers to competitive pressures, particularly from foreign imports. This led to higher productivity growth and greater specialization, and also gave Brazilian firms stronger incentives and better conditions to penetrate international markets. Brazilian trade more than doubled (from US$52 billion to US$114 billion) between 1990 and 1997 but it still had high export concentration. In 1997, about 250 large Brazilian companies accounted for about 85 per cent of Brazil's total exports. Of course, export growth achieved in the decade between the late 1980s and the late 1990s was much lower (5.7 per cent per annum) than what had been achieved during the prior decade.

In 1997, the Brazilian government announced with the Export Promotion Programme the explicit objective of doubling exports by 2002. The programme was designed to increase exports through the joint effort of the public and the private sector. Under this programme new sectors were identified that would receive special attention from the government in gaining markets in other countries.[18] The SMEs in the export business were given special attention. The second half of the 1990s also saw rebuilding of the export financing system on a market-friendly basis. Despite the reduction of trade bias a substantial gap between internal and external markets prevailed until the devaluation in 1999.[19] At present, even though Brazil has terminated many of its export incentives, a few such programmes are still in place. The most well known is Preferential Export Financing under the PROEX programme.

Preferential Export Financing under the PROEX programme was established in June 1991 to substitute for another programme, called FINEX. Its objective is to support Brazilian exports of goods and services by giving exporters the financial conditions of the international market. This programme for financing is supported by the national Treasury resources. It is operated in two systems: PROEX-Financing and PROEX-Equalization. The financing is operated exclusively by the Bank of Brazil, acting as the Brazilian Treasury agent, in which it is possible to finance up to 85 per cent of export value. The repayment period varies from 60 days to 10 years, depending on the degree of industrialization required for production. Under PROEX-Financing, loans are given to exporters (supplier's credit) or foreign buyers (buyer's credit). In order to finance 85 per cent of the export value, the PROEX rules demand that at least 60 per cent of components must be Brazilian.

Under PROEX-Equalization, funding is provided by commercial banks that offer loans to exporters or importers of Brazilian goods and services. In this system, the Brazilian Treasury pays part of the expenses in order to equalize the differences between Brazilian and foreign rates. The payment is made through the Bank of Brazil to international or Brazilian banks. The equalization rates are previously determined by the Brazilian Central Bank (BACEN) and vary according to the credit period. The payment is made through the Bank of Brazil to international or Brazilian banks. The equalization is paid in case of suppliers' credit as well as buyers' credit and the credit terms are the same as PROEX-Financing.

In 1999, a WTO panel found PROEX interest equalization payments used to finance the sale of regional aircraft manufactured in Brazil to be a prohibited export subsidy because of the local content requirement condition. The WTO Appellate Body upheld this finding. The government of Brazil modified PROEX to bring it into conformity with WTO subsidy rules, but Canada also challenged the modified scheme in the WTO. The United States intervened in this challenge as a third party and also expressed some concerns about the adequacy of Brazil's implementation of the panel's findings.

Besides direct subsidies, exports may also benefit indirectly from production or domestic subsidies that are given to units located in a region or to those in a particular industry, and sometime even to specific units in a particular industry. Production subsidies take both non-recurring and recurring forms. Non-recurring subsidies are given in the form of equity infusion, debt forgiveness, debt to equity swap and long-term financing, while recurring subsidies are given in the form of fiscal benefits through a variety of exemptions and rebates of indirect taxes such as import duties, federal and state value-added taxes. Production subsidies are especially targeted to selected industries. In Brazil, the four industries that have specifically been given government support are aircraft, automobiles, shipbuilding and steel.

The government has had a significant presence in certain basic industries, especially the steel industry, given special benefits in a variety of ways such as injection of equity, infrastructure support, etc. A number of

Table 10.1   CVD measures in force (as at 31 December 2002), against Brazilian exports

Member countries	Products
Canada	Stainless steel round bar
United States	Brass sheet and strip
	Cut-to-length carbon steel plate
	Carbon and certain alloy steel wire rod
	Iron construction castings

Source: Reports of Countervailing Duty Actions, www.wto.org.

CVD cases has occurred against steel exports from several countries, and therefore government subsidy programmes to the steel industry have come to light (for the list of CVD cases see Table 10.1). Such benefits may actually be common in other industries as well, particularly those in which the government has significant presence.

India

The country neglected its exports during the 1950s and early 1960s. However, a slow growth of exports during 1956–61, made policy-makers aware of the need to promote exports by redressing the bias against exports. Until 1966, there were broadly two types of export incentives: fiscal measures and import entitlement schemes. While the former was meant to neutralize the effect of taxes and duties borne by inputs used in exports, the latter constituted the principal method of export sub-sidization, as the scheme entitled exporters to receive import licences, fetching high import premia, in proportion to exports (Balasubramanyam and Basu, 1990). According to Bhagwati and Srinivasan (1975) the value of exports covered by the entitlement schemes amounted to around 60–80 per cent of total exports from the country. This scheme, along with the fiscal measures, contributed to an export growth that was around 3.7 per cent per annum during 1961–66.

In 1966, there was a major devaluation of the Indian Rupee. The devaluation was accompanied by other measures such as removal of the import entitlement schemes for exporters, abolition of a number of cash subsidy schemes for exports and a significant reduction in import duties. However, the abolition of such measures was short lived as they were re-introduced, although in a modified form. Bhagwati and Srinivasan (1975) estimated that exports incentives given after devaluation to a wide range of non-traditional exports averaged around 50–90 per cent on an effective *ad valorem* basis. The value of exports from the country showed an impressive average growth of 7 per cent during 1966–71. Besides export incentives, there were other favourable factors during this period that aided export growth. Between 1971–72 and 1975–76, the value of exports grew at phenomenal (average) rate of 21 per cent. However, export growth ranged between 5 and 8 per cent between 1976–77 and 1987–88.

The number and scope of such programmes increased between 1960 and 1990.[20] Pursell and Sharma (1996) note that while the existence of the schemes was probably a necessary condition for some of the manufactured exports, these did not compensate for the overall anti-export bias of the trade regime. For example, during the 11 years 1980–81 to 1990–91, it has been estimated that the trade policy induced Rupee overvaluation was about 30 per cent, while an average value of the principal export incentives relative to the FOB value of manufactured exports amounted to only 8 per cent.[21]

In mid-1991, India embarked on economic reforms, of which trade reform was an essential part. Trade reforms included rationalization of exchange rate policy, liberalization of imports, incentives to promote exports and introducing administrative flexibility. These reforms marked a distinct shift in the trade strategy: from import substitution to export promotion. In the 1990s a number of export promotion schemes were put in place with the genuine intention of promoting exports from the country. Export promotion zones, export-oriented units and export houses were given a number of incentives. Easy availability of inputs, including export credit and imported raw material, was ensured. These reform measures had significant positive impacts, raising the exports to GDP ratio from 5 per cent during 1985–90 to 10 per cent in 2000. During the 1990s a number of trade policy changes was made to fine-tune the export promotion schemes. Some of the important trade policy changes were effected to make them WTO-compliant, for example, the removal of quantitative restrictions (QRs). For other policy changes, such as phase-out of tax exemption on export income, it is hard to fathom whether the motivation was fiscal imperative or WTO compliance: probably, both motivations were present. A few export promotion programmes are still in vogue. Some programmes that qualify as subsidies have invited CVDs (see Table 10.2) – exports from India invited the maximum number of CVDs as at 31 December 2002. In early 2002, the government announced a medium-term export strategy to increase the share of country's exports to 1 per cent of world exports by 2006–07. The products and the markets where the country enjoyed competitive advantage were identified.

Table 10.2   CVD measures in force (as at 31 December 2002), against Indian exports

Member countries	Products
Canada	Memorials
	Hot-rolled carbon steel plate
	Hot-rolled carbon steel sheet
	Stainless steel round bar
EU	Antibiotics (broad-spectrum)
	Flat rolled products of iron or non-alloy steel (hot rolled coils)
	Polyethylene Terephthalate (PET)
	PET film
	Polyester textured filament yarn (PTY)
	Stainless steel bars
	Stainless steel wire (≥1 mm diameter)
	Stainless steel wire (<1 mm diameter)
	Sulphanilic acid (AS)
United States	Certain cut-to-length carbon quality steel
	Certain hot-rolled carbon steel flat products
	Sulphanilic acid (AS)
	Polyethylene terephthalate film, sheet, and strip (PET film)
South Africa	Suspension PVC
	Welded galvanized steel pipe
	Wire ropes

Source: Reports of Countervailing Duty Actions, www.wto.org.

Even though the SCM Agreement allows for the refund of duties and taxes borne by the inputs used in export production, the way the refund schemes are designed can qualify it as a subsidy under the SCM Agreement. A refund scheme called DEPB (Duty Entitlement Pass Book) was countervailed precisely for this reason. There are other schemes such as the 'export promotion capital goods' scheme that allows for import of capital goods to be used in export production on concessional terms. Under the current provisions of the Agreement, a duty refund on capital goods is considered to be a subsidy, and the scheme has been countervailed by some member countries. Similarly, exports from India continue to benefit from exemption of tax on export profits even though the phase-out plan for such exemption has already been announced. This scheme is clearly countervailable under the Agreement. The government also provides loan guarantees, primarily to public sector units, on an ad hoc basis; this loan guarantee is not necessarily on the basis of either export performance or on the use of domestic over imported goods. For example, the Steel Authority of India Limited (SAIL) received loan guarantees on several of its outstanding long-term foreign loans from the government and the State Bank of India. The United States countervailed SAIL exports of cut-to-length carbon-quality steel plate.

Export promotion development strategy: South Korea[22]

South Korea quite successfully pursued an export promotion development strategy from the early 1960s, after trying an import-substitution strategy in the 1950s. By laying emphasis on the promotion of labour-intensive light manufacturing where it had comparative advantage, South Korea achieved high export and economic growth: exports increasing 15-fold and GNP quadrupled between 1962 and 1970. The government is considered to have played a crucial role by: actively promoting exports, devaluing the currency (in 1965), improving infrastructure facilities such as ports, power plants and highways and making finance available for exports at lower rate of interest.[23] The government introduced a number of export promotion measures during 1962–72: preferential export credits, tariff exemptions on the imports of intermediate goods used in export production, reductions of taxes on export income, linking import permits and quotas to export performance, exemptions from tariffs and indirect taxes for domestic suppliers of intermediate goods used for export production and accelerated depreciation for fixed assets of major export industries (Sohn, Yang and Yim, 1998). Exporting firms set up their export targets and the government periodically reviewed these targets in its trade promotion meetings.

Two kinds of government support for exporters played an important role in promoting exports. One is financial and tax incentives and the other is psychological support to exporters. Export financing scheme between the early 1960s and the early 1980s effectively switched resources from domestic to export use. Interest subsidies, in terms of a percentage of exports, peaked in 1967 at 17.7 per cent and thereafter started to decline. As for psychological support, especially in the 1960s and 1970s, all Korean exporters received attention from the President, and the successful exporters were regularly honoured (Kim, 1994).

To what extent these measures helped Korea achieve high export growth has remained a controversial and contentious issue. At one extreme, the view is that high export growth would not have been possible without the government's role in export promotion and in providing a stable macroeconomic environment. The other extreme view is that export promotion measures had at best a limited impact in achieving high export growth in Korea. High export growth, according to this view, was the result of policies that encouraged investment in the country (Rodrik, 1995). Both these views relate to 'supply-side' factors. A different view that has also been put forward stresses not so much 'supply-side' factors an 'demand-side' conditions. This view is based on the argument that the impetus for export growth came from external sources, in particular from Japan (Castley, 1995).

Although the basic policy remained in place till the early 1980s the focus in the 1970s shifted from light manufacturing towards heavy manufacturing and chemical industries (HCI). Since the mid-1970s, interest rate subsidies and credit availability for exports became the major export incentive, and also the most important way in which HCI was promoted. Strong emphasis was placed on large enterprises and *Chaebols*. As resources were diverted towards the development of HCI, the light manufacturing and SME industries were adversely affected.

Emphasis on HCI led to unbalanced development. To correct this imbalance, the new government in the early 1980s moved away from an intervention policy and laid renewed emphasis on the export growth that had taken a back seat in the 1970s. During 1980–93 the government pursued a wide range of market liberalization policies, particularly after the late 1980s. It began to deregulate the financial sector and undertook import liberalization that significantly increased trade and current account deficits. Steps also were taken to sever the ties between the government and businesses, but were not very successful as informal ties remained in place. Over the period as a whole, exports as a percentage of the GDP showed a steady increase, from 5.6 per cent during 1962–69 to 21.2 per cent in the 1970s to 31 per cent in the 1980s.

During 1994–97, Korea joined the WTO, APEC and the OECD. It further liberalized trade and modified its trade and industrial policies to make them WTO-consistent. Korea abolished direct export subsidies, eliminating four subsidies that violated WTO regulations in 1998 – reserves for export losses,[24] reserves for overseas market development,[25] facility investment loans provided by the SME foundation fund and tax credit for investment in facilities.[26]

In 1997, the Asian Crisis began in Thailand and spread to Korea, exposing many weaknesses of the economy, particularly the seemingly cosy relationship between the government and the *Chaebols*. Interest rates were increased and banks became more reluctant to lend. This credit crunch caused a recession in Korea, when imports of all kinds of goods declined and exports failed to pick up despite a more than 40 per cent depreciation in the Korean won. A sharp decline in the value of Korean won per dollar led Korea to sign a standby arrangement with the IMF.

Korea used the crisis as an opportunity to carry forward market-oriented reforms, to restructure its trade and industrial policies and to correct several structural weaknesses present in the economy. The government had previously given several tax incentives[27] to achieve specific national economic objectives under the Tax Exemption and Reduction Control Law (TERCL) and the Foreign Investment Promotion Act (FIPA). However, on 1 January 1999 the Act was replaced by the Special Tax Treatment Control Law (STTCL), and in May 1999 the FIPA was also subsumed into STTCL. All tax incentives under STTCL already have 'sunset rules' whereby an incentive comes to an end after the expiry of a certain period, unless it is extended.

Many programmes under TERCL that were deemed to be countervailable have been withdrawn and the tax incentives given under STTCL are non-specific in nature.[28] However, these programmes have yet to be evaluated in CVD investigations. If exports continue to benefit from a government programme that once existed, the benefit from that programme is still countervailed even after the programme has been withdrawn. In the recent CVD investigations, tax incentives under TERCL may be countervailed if the lingering effect of those programmes continues to benefit exports.

The government claims that most of the tax incentives now given under STTCL are based on objective criteria – for example, tax incentives for SMEs are based on the number of employees or the amount of capital or turnover. However, according to the WTO Trade Policy Review, Korea's notification concerning subsidies include numerous tax measures.

Korea also has region-specific subsidies to encourage investments in certain regions or to encourage relocation of industry from large cities to locations outside metropolitan areas. One such programme is designated as special cases of taxation for balanced development among areas. Many government programmes that *prime facie* appeared to be non-specific were, upon closer examination, found to be *de facto* specific. The specificity test becomes the crucial issue here,[29] particularly with programmes that define eligibility criteria (horizontal in scope and neutral in application) in such a way as to benefit only selected industries. Since the mid-1990s, the United States has been the only country that has imposed CVDs against exports from Korea, invariably against steel exports (see Table 10.3).[30]

In the past, the government of Korea has extended a number of production subsidies, and some of these may still be present. Such subsidies

Table 10.3   CVD measures in force (as at 31 December 2002), against Korean exports

Member countries	Products
United States	Certain cut-to-length carbon quality steel
	Corrosion-resistant carbon steel
	Stainless steel sheet and strip in coils
	Structural steel beams
	Top-of-the-stove stainless steel cooking ware

Source: Reports of Countervailing Duty Actions, www.wto.org.

are both recurring and non-recurring in nature and ad hoc/discretionary as well as given through well-defined programmes.

The government of Korea had strong control over the financial sector and used it to direct credit. Through the 1990s government continued to wield control, directly or indirectly, over the lending practices of government-owned banks and other domestic banks.[31] It directed credit to specific sectors, often to specific companies. The steel industry was one of the major beneficiaries of such lending. Steel exports from Korea benefited more from production subsidies than from export subsidies; this could be because steel is produced mainly by public sector companies. A government-owned steel company, called POSCO, has benefited in several ways, and steel exports from Korea have therefore been countervailed in some countries. However, production subsidies have not been confined to providing benefits to POSCO alone but have been provided fairly widely and in numerous ways.

Whatever the trade orientation, Brazil, India and South Korea have thus widely used subsidies to promote their exports. While Brazil and India used subsidies to remove an anti-export bias imparted by their import-substitution development strategy, Korea made active use of subsidies to achieve higher export and economic growth. Export subsidies seem to have played a significant role in increasing exports from all three countries, but are now generally in decline in all of them. Even so, a few subsidy programmes are still in place. In Brazil and Korea, exports benefited not just from export subsidies but also from a range of production subsidies that have also been countervailed by member countries. This is certainly true of steel exports from all three countries that have been countervailed by the United States. Production subsidies are given both in discretionary and non-discretionary ways. Government-owned companies, particularly in the steel industry, have received several non-discretionary benefits; Brazil and India now have a more focused approach to promotion of exports.

Export incentives: theory and evidence

The rationale for export promotion comes from the theory of domestic distortions. Protection creates bias against exports, and an equivalent subsidy to export activities can restore neutrality, encourage trade along the lines of comparative advantage and improve economic welfare (Fitzgerald and Monson, 1989). Two other reasons given in the trade literature for an export subsidy are the (i) infant-industry argument and (ii) need to achieve export expansion and diversification that can help a country cope better with external trade shocks. However, these justifications are not necessarily supported by the proponents of free trade, who do not deny the existence of distortions in developing economies but favour their removal *per se* rather than mitigating their effects through subsidies.

More recently, a rationale for export subsidy has come from strategic trade theory, suggesting that in the presence of significant market imperfections in the product or factor market, a country could through a suitably designed policy increase profit and hence welfare. For example, Brander and Spencer (1985) show that export subsidies can help an exporter gain a higher share of a third-country market at the cost of a foreign competitor, thereby improving national welfare net of subsidies. Fitzgerald and Monson (1989) examine various rationales in the literature in giving preferential export credit and export insurance. Market failure in export credit and insurance are the most compelling rationales for giving such preferential treatment. Many countries have actively sought to promote exports through credit and insurance programmes;[32] Fitzgerald and Monson also examine the practice of these programmes in the developed (the United States, United Kingdom, France) and the developing countries (Colombia, India, Korea, Sri Lanka, Turkey, Venezuela). According to them, many of the rationales for such subsidies do not stand up to close inspection.

Many developing countries justify subsidies on the ground of structural weaknesses – lack of basic infrastructure, high credit cost, inflexible labour laws, a low tax base and so on. It takes a long time to remove such distortions or to develop these markets, and they argue that until then developing countries be allowed to use export subsidies. Whatever the rationale, a case for export subsidy must also pass the test of actually benefiting exports. Few studies have tried to measure the effectiveness of subsidies in boosting exports from a country, in many cases this link is assumed to hold. We turn to the empirical evidence on this below.

One of the earlier papers measuring the impact of export incentives on export performance in developing countries was Balassa (1977). The study provided a comparative evaluation of export incentives and their effects on exports and economic performance in 11 major developing countries during 1966–73. The study classifies these countries into four groups, depending on the timing and extent of their export promotion efforts.[33] The inter-country comparisons showed that greater export orientation in the system of incentives tends to be associated with higher export growth and better economic performance. In individual countries, the growth of exports and GNP generally accelerated following the introduction of the export promotion scheme.

Panchamukhi (1978) found the predominant role of government policy variable in explaining the export behaviour of five countries (Sri Lanka, India, Khmer Republic, Malaysia and Thailand) during the late 1960s. Variables representing import duties and export taxes are included among the policy variables. The coefficient of these variables turned out to be positive but not statistically significant. The positive sign was interpreted as indicating the greater positive effect on exports of export promotion measures (such as duty drawback schemes or other compensatory support schemes).

Westphal and Kim (1982) used a cross-section analysis for 92 sectors in Korea for 1968 to examine the impact of export incentives on export growth. They found the impact to be positive and statistically significant. Ffrench-Davis and Pinera (1976)[34] cite several time-series estimates for Colombia which indicate elasticities ranging between 0.7 and 1.3 for non-traditional exports with respect to incentives. However, the statistical significance of these results is found to be low. A study by Nadav Halevi[35] for Israel found elasticity of exports with respect to incentives to be 1.3, based on time-series analysis. However, incentives to exports included both export exchange rates and export subsidies (export exchange rates alone did not have a statistically significant impact).

Milanovic (1986) carried out an analysis of the role of various export incentives, such as export tax rebates, export credits, foreign exchange allocation and real exchange rate, in export promotion in Turkey during 1980–84. According to his analysis, export incentives were instrumental in stimulating the country's export growth during the period. Similarly, Arslan and Wijnbergen (1993) analysed the extent to which export subsidies explained Turkey's export boom over the period 1980–87 and found that subsidies did have a positive and a significant impact on exports. They used the *ad valorem* equivalents of export subsidies and applied two-stage least squares to show that export subsidies in the current period and with two years' lag had a positive and significant impact on log value of proportion of goods exported.

Conclusions

Even though trade theory argues against providing export incentives and favours removing distortions *per se* rather than mitigating their effect through subsidies, the structural weakness of developing countries does provide grounds for permitting them to subsidize exports. Interestingly, in the SCM Agreement export subsidies are not prohibited for certain developing countries. But such subsidies can be countervailed if they cause adverse affect in the importing member country. Most often the effect of export subsidies is expected to work through the price channel, and imposition of CVDs tends to neutralize the gains from subsidies. But the fact is that not all exporters avail themselves of export subsidies, and not all member countries impose CVDs. The limited empirical evidence does suggest a positive, significant influence of such subsidies on exports from a country. Given the limited ability of developing countries to subsidize exports due to their fiscal constraints, a selective and focused programme may be more helpful than a programme that subsidizes exports across the board. Hence, each developing-country member for whom export subsidies are not prohibited must weigh the benefits against the cost of running such a programme in the light of the possibility of some importing member countries imposing CVDs.

'Other' developing member countries, such as Brazil and Korea, have to phase out all their export subsidies within the stipulated time period. Exports from these countries can continue to get the benefit of production subsidies, but such subsidies are actionable. In case of production subsidies, the specificity test becomes important – a government programme may *prime facie* be non-specific (that is, neutral in nature and not seen to be benefiting any particular region or industry) but *de facto* may be specific, in which case it qualifies as a subsidy and hence action can be taken. The limits of specificity have not yet been tested in the WTO jurisprudence.

Many developing countries have sought improvements and clarifications in the SCM Agreement. Now that it is on the agenda of the Doha Round, developing countries can collectively make a case for changes in mutual interest or can 'buy' that option by making concessions elsewhere.

The incidence of CVDs may fall once the improvements and refinements that developing countries are seeking in the SCM Agreement are brought about.

Notes

* I am grateful to Anwarul Hoda for his comments on an earlier draft of this chapter.
1. However, this exemption does not imply immunity from countervailing duty procedures, should the subsidized products cause material injury to domestic industries in importing countries. Indeed, many member countries have imposed countervailing duties against subsidized exports from other member countries.
2. The Declaration enjoins that in this exercise 'the basic concepts, principles and effectiveness' of the Agreement and its instruments and objectives would be preserved and 'the needs of developing and least-developed participants' would be taken into account. In other words, no fundamental change in the Agreement is envisaged.
3. For information in this section we relied on, among other sources, the WTO web site www.wto.org. For analysis of the Agreement in greater detail see Hoda and Ahuja (2003).
4. No injury proof is required in this case.
5. Annex VII countries are the LDC members as well as developing country members with *per capita income* (GNP) less than US$1,000.
6. Under existing provisions, these members can seek extension to the phase-out deadline provided the request is submitted one year prior to the end of the period. If an extension is granted the member has to hold annual consultations with the Committee on SCM to determine the necessity of maintaining subsidies. If no such determination is made the developing member must phase out the export subsidies within two years of the last authorized period. At the Doha Ministerial Meeting it was decided that certain developing countries (whose share of world merchandise export trade was not greater than 0.10 per cent, and total Gross National Income was at or below US$20 billion) would be granted annual extensions through 2007 for export subsidy programmes that involved full or partial exemptions from import duties and internal charges that were in existence not later than 1 September 2001.
7. Brazil has *per capita* GDP of around US$4,200 and Korea of US$9,600. Of course, India, with a *per capita* GDP of around US$400, is among the countries listed in Annex VII of the Agreement.
8. This information has been culled from the country proposals submitted to the WTO and Government of India (2002).
9. To avoid double incidence of tax on exports, an international practice has developed that relates all indirect taxes to the *destination principle* and all direct taxes to the *origin principle*.
10. The proposals of India and Colombia seek inclusion of capital goods in the definition of inputs consumed in the production process.
11. Although a WTO panel ruling on a Brazil–Canada aircraft financing case has raised some questions about, and clarified, the extent of applicability of the

safe haven, there still exist many ambiguities in the interplay between the OECD Arrangement and the WTO Agreement. Besides, there is also a deeper political economy issue of how an agreement amongst fewer than 30 nations (the OECD Arrangement) can exist without reference to an agreement signed by other (WTO) members.

12. This has led to considerable divergence in the practice of some member countries in their interpretation of the Agreement and the use of benchmarks in calculating subsidy margins.

13. For information on Brazil we relied on, among other sources, the working papers (Marahnao, 1998; Cardoso, 2001; Monteiro, 2001; Averbug, 1999; Sucupira and Moreira, 2001) of the Institute of Brazilian Issues, George Washington University. These papers can be downloaded from the web site at http:// www.gwu.edu/~ibi/minerva/pesquisa.html.

14. Because of the high growth rate and low inflation during 1968–73, this period is also referred to as the 'economic miracle'.

15. According to Moreira (1995) these subsidies in the case of Korea – a country widely believed to be an aggressive exporter – were only 20 per cent, on average, during the same period.

16. The 1980s was marked by prolonged crisis with alternate years of growth and recession and high inflation during the late 1980s. For this reason, the 1980s and early 1990s is also referred to as the 'lost decade'.

17. The CET was initially to cover 85 per cent of 9,000 tariff items, and by 2006 to extend to all items.

18. In setting of target and defining a strategy for achieving the target, India is doing in 2002 what Brazil began in 1997.

19. The devaluation was the direct result of the change in exchange rate regime in response to the Asian Financial Crisis in 1997, which was followed by Russia's moratorium in mid-1998.

20. To quote from Pursell and Sharma (1996) 'at least one variant of just about every known scheme was on the books and in principle available'. Such schemes provided both direct and indirect subsidies and included cash compensatory support, replenishment import licences, tax exemption of export income, subsidized export credit and export credit insurance, bonded warehouses, support for export marketing and so on.

21. Excluded from the calculation of these figures are transaction costs, delays and corruption involved in using the various schemes. Tandon (1983) has a good analysis of GOI export promotion schemes before 1980; also see Nayyar (1987).

22. For an excellent monograph on Korea's trade and industrial policies from 1948 to 1998, see Sohn, Yang and Yim (1998). This section is partly drawn from the monograph.

23. According to Sohn, Yang and Yim (1998) firms producing goods for export could borrow at an official interest rate that was lower than the market rate. The difference between these two rates was as high as 8.5 per cent in 1968.

24. A domestic person or a corporation engaged in a foreign exchange earning business was allowed to establish a reserve amounting to the lesser of 1 per cent of foreign exchange earning or 50 per cent of net income for the respective tax year. If certain export losses occurred, these could be offset using money in the reserve fund. Any amount that was not used to offset a loss was to be returned to the income account and taxed over a three-year period, after

a one-year period of grace. All of the money in the reserve would eventually go into an income account and be subjected to corporate tax either when it was used to offset export losses or when the grace period expired and the funds were returned to taxable income. Deferral of taxes owed to the government amounted to an interest-free loan in the amount of the company's tax savings. This programme is an export subsidy as it is contingent upon export performance and confers a financial benefit on its recipient.

25. Similar to the reserves for export losses outlined in n. 24.
26. The companies in Korea were allowed to claim tax credits for various kinds of investments. If the tax credits could be used at the time they were claimed, the company was authorized to carry them forward for use in later tax years. Because Korean companies received a higher tax credit for investments made in domestically produced facilities, investment tax credits received under several Articles constituted an import substitution subsidy.
27. Details about the special depreciation as a tax-deductible cost contingent on exports, and export industry facility loans could not be obtained, so these programmes are not discussed.
28. Various incentives given under TERCL that have been countervailed have not been analysed here.
29. It should also be mentioned that the limits of specificity have not yet been tested in the WTO jurisprudence.
30. From 1 January 1995 to 30 June 2001, the EC had initiated five CVD cases against Korea, but these cases were dropped because the subsidy levels were found to be *de minimis*.
31. Loans from the Korean branches of foreign banks were not subject to the government's control and direction. Therefore such loans did not confer benefits to the recipient of such loans and hence were not countervailed.
32. Export credit is given both as pre-shipment and post-shipment credit. Pre-shipment credit lowers the price of capital while post-shipment lowers the prices of export goods.
33. The first group consists of Korea, Singapore and Taiwan; the second group of Argentina, Brazil, Colombia and Mexico; the third group of Israel and Yugoslavia; the fourth group of India and Chile.
34. Pp. 88–90, as cited in Balassa (1977).
35. The study, published in Hebrew is cited in Balassa (1977). See also Michaely (1976: 30).

References

Arslan, I. and S. Wijnbergen (1993) 'Export Incentives, Exchange Rate Policy and Export Growth in Turkey', *Review of Economics and Statistics*, 75(1): 128–33, available at http://www.bndes.gov.br/english/studies/td91-ing.pdf.

Averbug, A. (1999) 'Brazilian Trade Liberalization and Integration in the 1990s', available at http://www.bndes.gov.br/english/studies/trade.pdf.

Balassa, B. (1977) 'Export Incentives and Export Performance in Developing Countries: A Comparative Analysis', World Bank Staff Working Paper 248.

Balasubramanyam, V. N. and D. Basu (1990) 'India: Export Promotion Policies and Export Performance', in C. Milner (ed.), *Export Promotion Strategies: Theory and Evidence from Developing Countries*, New York: New York University Press.

Bhagwati, J. N. and T. N. Srinivasan (1975) *Foreign Trade Regimes and Economic Development*, New York: Columbia University Press, for the NBER.

Brander, J. A. and B. J. Spencer (1985) 'Export Subsidies and International Market Share Rivalry', *Journal of International Economics*, 18(1–2): 83–100.

Cardoso, L. A. (2001) 'Analysis of Brazilian Export Policies: A Comparison of Some of the Most Important Latin America's Economies', Paper presented at the Institute of Brazilian Issues, Washington, DC: George Washington University.

Castley, R. J. (1995) 'Korea's Export Growth: An Alternate Explanation', available at http://idpm.man.ac.uk/idpm/dispap43.htm.

Fitzgerald, B. and T. Monson (1989) 'Preferential Credit and Insurance as Means to Promote Exports', Washington, DC: International Bank for Reconstruction and Development.

Ffrench-Davis, R. and J. Pinera (1976) 'Colombia Export Promotion Policy', Paper presented at the ECLA/IBRD seminar on Export Promotion Policies, Santiago, Chile, 5–7 November.

Government of India (2002) 'Agreement on Subsidies and Countervailing Measures/ Anti-Dumping Agreement: Proposals on Implementation Related Issues and Concerns', New Delhi: Ministry of Commerce, Government of India.

Hoda, A. and R. Ahuja (2003) 'Agreement on Subsidies and Countervailing Measures: Need for Clarification and Improvement', ICRIER Working Paper 101, Delhi, available at http://www.icrier.res.in/WP101.doc.

Kim, H. Y. (1994) 'The Role of Government in Export Expansion in the Republic of Korea: A Revisit', Asian Development Bank, Economic and Development Resource Center, EDRC Report Series 61.

Krueger, A. O. (1980) 'Trade Policy as Input to Development', *American Economic Review*, 70(2): 288–92.

Marahnao, C. A. (1998) 'Brazilian Foreign Trade and its Role in International Competitiveness', Washington, DC: George Washington University, available at http://www.gwu.edu/~ibi/minerva/Fall1998/Carlos.Maranhao.html.

Michaely, M. (1976) 'Export Promotion in Israel', Paper presented at the ECLA/ IBRD seminar an Export Promotion Policies, Santiago, Chile, 5–7 November.

Milanovic, B. (1986) 'Export Incentives and Turkish Manufactured Exports, 1980–1984', World Bank Staff Working Paper 768.

Monteiro, S. S. M. (2001) 'International Marketing Strategies for Small Firms in a Globalized Economy', Washington, DC: Institute of Brazilian Issues, George Washington University.

Moreira, M. M. (1995) *Industrialisation, Trade and Market Failures: The Role of Government Intervention in Brazil and South Korea*, London: Macmillan.

Nayyar, D. (1987) 'India's Export Performance, 1970–85: Underlying Factors and Constraints', *Economic and Political Weekly*, 22(19–21), Annual Number, May.

Panchamukhi, V. R. (1978) *Trade Policies of India: A Quantitative Analysis*, Delhi: Concept Publishing Company.

Pinheiro, A. C., F. Giambiagi and M. M. Moreira (2001) 'Brazil in the 1990s: A Successful Transition?', Textos Para Discussão do BNDES 91, Rio de Janeiro, November.

Pinheiro, A. C. and M. M. Moreira (2000) 'The Profile of Brazil's Manufacturing Exporters in the Nineties: What Are The Main Policy Issues', Textos Para Discussão do BNDES 80, Rio de Janeiro, June.

Pursell, G. and A. Sharma (1996) 'Indian Trade Policies Since the 1991–92 Reforms', Washington, DC: World Bank, mimeo.

Rodrik, D. (1995) 'Trade Strategy, Exports, and Investment: Another Look at East Asia', NBER Working Paper 5339, Cambridge, MA: NBER.

Sohn, C.-H., J. Yang and H.-S. Yim (1998) 'Korea's Trade and Industrial Policies: 1948–1998: Why the Era of Active Trade Policy is Over?', Korea Institute for International Economic Policy, KIEP Working Paper 98–05.

Sucupira, R. and M. M. Moreira (2001) 'Development, Exports and Trade Finance: Brazil's Recent Experience', in G. Hufbauer and R. Rodriguez (eds), *Exi-Im Bank in the 21st Century: A New Approach?*, Washington, DC: Institute for International Economics.

Tandon, R. (1983) *Some Perspectives on India's Trade Policy*, Allahabad: Chugh Publications.

Westphal, L. E. and K. S. Kim (1982) 'Korea', in B. Balassa *et al.* (eds), *Development Strategies in Semi-Industrial Countries*, Baltimore, MD: Johns Hopkins University Press.

Index

absentee landownership   105
ACP (Africa, Caribbean, Pacific)
   countries   8, 49–50, 59(n7),
   140, 143–51, 154, 155, 156(n11),
   192t, 198–9, 205–6, 209t, 212t,
   220, 222, 223, 235, 246, 246t,
   249, 257, 258(n4)
   LDC   241, 247
   non-ACP   49
   non-LDC   225, 243, 253,
      254n, 255n
   sugar exporters   9, 238, 243
   'wasteful trade-restrictive
      policies'   50
   see also Arusha Convention
ACP–EC Sugar Protocol   225, 247,
   248, 253
Afghanistan   194
Africa   14t, 17, 25, 31(n1), 57–8, 170,
   197–8, 258(n12)
   distribution of binding
      coverage   172t
   exports (percentage changes,
      EBA)   233t
   'rest of'   229t
   welfare changes (EBA)   231t
   see also Sub-Saharan Africa
African Growth and Opportunity Act
   (AGOA, USA, 2000)   8, 23, 51,
   181, 188(n17), 190, 191, 191t,
   195, 197–8, 199–200, 201f,
   204–5, 216(n21–2), 219
   requirements   198
aggregate measure of support
   (AMS)   16
agricultural goods (farm
   products)   10, 39, 39t,
   40, 41t, 66, 161, 193,
   194, 204, 232
   developing country trade with
      OECD (1997)   71t, 72
   duty-free access to EU   222–3
   exports from one developing
      country to another   59(n5)
   international prices   50, 57
   terms of trade   219
   trade specialization indices   68–9t,
      70, 89(n3)

agricultural subsidies/support   17–18,
   25, 30
agriculture   15, 186, 210, 212, 228,
   231
   erosion of tariff preferences   48–52,
      59–60(n7–11)
   global trade   42
   impact of EBA in EU itself   235
   market access   16–19
   non-ad valorem tariffs   164,
      188(n12)
   OECD domestic support and
      developing countries   63–91
   policy implications   57–9
   poverty in low-income
      countries   37–62
   returns from land (India)   92–129
   trade reform   53
   trade liberalization   5–7, 35–157
   Uruguay Round   46
   value of TRQs to developing
      countries   130–57
   world prices   72, 89(n4)
Ahuja, R.   xvii, 282(n3)
aid/aid agencies   4, 52
aircraft   271, 282–3(n11)
albumin   146f
Algeria   251t
allocative efficiency   78, 79t, 82, 83t,
   86, 86t, 232
Amritsar   113t
Andean Trade Preference Act (ATPA,
   USA, 1991)   191, 191t, 195, 196–7,
   200–4, 215–16(n19–20), 216(n26)
Anderson, K.   xvii, 42, 45, 53–4, 59(n6)
Anderson, K., et al. (2001)   40, 60,
   73, 89
   Dimaranan, B.   60, 89
   Francois, J.   60, 89
   Hertel, T.   60, 89
   Hoekman, B.   60, 89
   Martin, W.   60, 89
Andhra Pradesh (AP)   107, 112–17,
   123–6t
Angola   31(n1), 197t, 211, 220
Anguilla   196t
animals and animal products   67t,
   82t, 85t, 211–14, 229–30t, 233–4t

anti-dumping　16, 19, 20t, 51, 59(n10)
anti-export bias　9, 12, 14, 31(n5), 268, 272, 273, 278, 279
Antigua and Barbuda　196t
Anton, J.　77
APEC (Asia-Pacific Economic Cooperation)　276
apparel (clothing/garments)　15, 43t, 44t, 162, 167–72, 173t, 176–80, 185, 188(n13–15), 193, 195–8, 200, 202t, 205t, 205, 213, 221t, 229–30t, 231, 232, 233–4t
see also textiles
area payments　81
Argentina　5, 20t, 67t, 78, 250t, 251t, 255t, 269, 284(n33)
  bilateral trade with OECD　71t, 71
  cereal exports　9
  export specialization　67[–]70
  impact of EU15 wheat MPS reform (simulation)　79t
  impact of OECD domestic support reform (simulation)　83t
  trade specialization indices (1965–98)　68t, 70
  welfare impact of re-instrumentation　86t
  world wheat prices　79t, 80
Armington
  approach　76
  elasticity　236
  trade structure　80
Arslan, I.　280
Aruba　9, 195, 196t, 238, 250t, 253, 254–5t
Arusha Convention　192t, 198
  see also Cotonou Agreement
ASEAN4 (Malaysia, Philippines, Singapore, Thailand)　5, 67t
  bilateral trade with OECD　71t
  impact of EU15 wheat MPS reform (simulation)　79t
  impact of OECD domestic support reform　83t
  trade specialization indices (1965–98)　68t
  welfare impact of re-instrumentation　86, 86t
Asia　38, 52, 143t, 144t, 145–51, 155, 163, 170, 180
  distribution of binding coverage　172t
  'rest of'　229t, 231t, 232, 233t

Asian Financial Crisis (1997)　276, 283(n19)
ATPA　*see* Andean Trade Preference Act
Australia　20t, 66t, 164, 178, 251t, 252t, 255t
  applied tariff rates　184, 189(n18)
  applied tariffs on industrial products　173t, 174t
  bound tariffs on industrial products　166t, 168t, 169t
  farm incomes (simulation)　84
  preference programmes　215(n5)
  PSE　64, 65t
  tariff escalation on textile products　179t
  tariffs on leather　177t
  trade specialization indices (1965–98)　68t, 70
Austria　251t
Averbug, A.　283(n13)

Bacchetta, M.　xvii, 187(n2–3)
Bahamas　196t, 251t, 255t
balance of payments　268
Balassa, B.　280, 284(n34–5)
bananas　49, 51, 141, 144, 154, 181, 194, 223, 225, 226, 235, 238–43, 244f
Bangladesh　60(n10), 127(n6), 210, 211, 213, 220, 228, 230t, 231t, 232, 234t, 235, 249, 252t, 258(n18)
Bank of Brazil　270–1
banks　271, 276, 278, 284(n31)
Barbados　196t, 246t, 250t, 254t, 255t
basmati rice　96, 127(n1), 128(n10)
beef　81, 143
'behind the border' barriers/policies　12, 14–15, 26, 29, 30
Belize　196t, 244f, 246t, 250t, 255t
Bengal famine　94
Benin　197t, 211
Berg, A.　59(n2)
'best endeavours' commitments　23
'better than MFN' treatment (principle)　26
beverages　223t, 223, 224t, 229–30t, 233–4t
  'other processed'　142t, 143, 143t, 144t, 146f, 146t, 148t, 150t
  spirituous　155(n3)
Bhagwati, J. N.　272
Bhavnagar　101t
Blonigen, B.　19

Bolivia 196, 203t, 204
Bora, B. xvii, 162, 182, 187(n2–3)
border barriers 12[–]14, 18
border measures 88
border price concept ('no clear
    definition') 93
Botswana 197t, 197n
Brander, J. A. 279
brass 272t
Brazil 5, 9, 20t, 67t, 164, 220,
    247, 250t, 251t, 254t, 255t,
    261, 262, 265–7, 278, 279,
    281, 284(n33)
aircraft-financing dispute with
    Canada 271, 282–3(n11)
applied tariff rates 184
applied tariffs on crustaceans 176t
applied tariffs on industrial
    products 173t, 174t
bilateral trade with OECD 71t
bound tariffs on industrial
    products 165t, 168t,
    169t, 171t
comprehensive OECD domestic
    support reform
    (simulation) 82
CVD measures in force (2002)
    against 272t
'economic miracle' 283(n14)
GDP 264, 282(n7)
impact of EU15 wheat MPS reform
    (simulation) 79t
impact of OECD domestic support
    reform (simulation) 82, 83t
import-substitution development
    strategy 268–72, 283(n13–19)
'lost decade' 283(n16)
sources 283(n13)
tariff escalation on textile
    products 179t
tariffs on leather 177t
tariffs on textiles and
    clothing, 177–8
termination of export subsidy
    programmes 269–70
trade specialization indices
    (1965–98) 68t, 70
welfare impact of
    re-instrumentation 86t
Brazil: Central Bank (BACEN) 271
Brazil: Treasury 270–1
Brazilian government 268–9, 270,
    283(n18)
British Virgin Islands 196t

Bulgaria 241, 250t, 252t, 255t
Bureau, J. C. 140
Burkina Faso 197t, 243, 254t
Burundi 197t

Cairns Group 60(n13), 131
Calcutta 96t, 101, 101t, 102t, 102,
    103t, 104, 113t
Cambodia/Khmer Republic 210,
    211, 280
Cameroon 197t, 240f, 243, 244f
Canada 20t, 51, 66t, 131, 178, 180,
    250t, 272t, 274t
aircraft-financing dispute with
    Brazil 271, 282–3(n11)
applied tariff rates 189(n18)
applied tariffs on crustaceans 176t
applied tariffs on industrial
    products 173t, 174t
bound tariffs on industrial
    products 165t, 167, 168t,
    169t, 171t
farm incomes (simulation) 84
GSP 220
MFN and preferential tariffs facing
    LDC exports 183t
producer subsidy equivalent and
    components (1987, 2000) 65t,
    65
tariff escalation on textile
    products 179t
tariffs on leather 177t
trade specialization indices
    (1965–98) 68t, 70
Cancún conference (Fifth WTO
    Ministerial Conference, 2003)
    xii, 182, 186
capacities, differential 27–9
capacity-building 45, 161, 185,
    187(n1), 214
Cape Verde 197t, 240f
capital 50, 54, 74, 77, 78t, 82t,
    277, 284(n32)
capital goods 270
inclusion in definition of inputs
    consumed 265–6, 282(n10)
capital subsidy 76, 82, 89(n6)
Cardoso, L. A. 283(n13)
Caribbean 8, 14t
Caribbean Basin Economic Recovery
    Act (CBERA, USA, 1983) 191,
    191t, 195–6, 199, 200f,
    200, 201f, 201t, 202t, 205,
    209t, 212t

Caribbean Basin Trade Partnership Act
(CBTPA, USA, 2000) 191, 191t,
195, 196, 199, 200f, 200, 201f,
201t, 202t
Cayman Islands 196t
CDE functional form 76
Central African Republic 194, 197t
Central America 195, 238, 243
Central Asia 17
Central and Eastern Europe
(CEE) 140
cereals 43t, 44t, 142t, 143, 143t,
144t, 146f, 146t, 148t, 150t,
150, 224t, 229–30t, 231, 232,
233–4t, 238, 241
Cernat, L. xvii, 51, 187(n2)
Cernat, L., et al. (2003) 238,
258(n13), 259
Laird, S. 259
Monge-Roffarello, L. 259
Turrini, A. 259
CEU (Hungary and Poland) 66t
Chad 197t
chaebols 276
Chand, R. 96, 96t
chemical products 224t
chemicals and photographic
supplies 168t, 169t, 171t,
172, 173t
Chen, S. 54
Chennai/Madras 101, 101t, 102t,
102, 103t, 104, 113t
Chhabra, V. 129
Chile 20t, 284(n33)
China 25, 30, 40, 66t, 96, 140,
163, 164, 180, 220, 229t, 250t,
251t, 252t, 255t
applied tariff rates 184
applied tariffs on crustaceans 176t
applied tariffs on industrial
products 173t, 174t
bilateral trade with OECD 71t,
71, 72
exports (percentage changes,
EBA) 233t
impact of EU15 wheat MPS reform
(simulation) 79t
impact of OECD domestic support
reform 82, 83t
inequality 53–4
liberalization, agriculture and
poverty 53–4
MFN and preferential tariffs facing
LDC exports 183t

tariffs on leather 177t
trade specialization indices
(1965–98) 68t, 70
welfare changes (EBA) 231t, 232
welfare impact of
re-instrumentation 86, 86t
WTO accession 38, 53, 54, 82
Chinese Taipei *see* Taiwan
Cirera, X. 59(n2)
civil society 10–11
Clinton, W. J. 193, 196
clothing 39, 40, 41t, 42, 51, 53,
60(n11), 188(n13)
coal 229–30t, 233–4t
cocoa 224t
coefficient of variation (CV) 102,
103t, 112, 114t, 116
coherence 28, 32(n8)
Colombia 20t, 196, 203t, 204, 238,
240f, 243, 244f, 251–2t, 255t, 279,
282(n10), 284(n33)
COMESA 259(n31)
COMEXT trade database
(EU) 156(n10)
commodities 208, 208n, 211
duty-free treatment 193
primary 256
subsidized 18
commodity groups 149
commodity supply 74
common elasticity of substitution
(CES) 74–5
nested-CES production
function 74
common external tariff (CET) 269,
283(n17)
Common Market Organization of
Sugar (CMOS) 243
quotas A, B, C 243, 259(n24)
Commonwealth Secretariat 51,
60(n10–11)
Community of Andean
Nations 196
Comoros 194, 197t, 215(n16)
companies/corporations 48,
283(n24)
export concentration (Brazil)
268, 270
foreign 269
government-owned 278–9
imperfectly competitive 47
import-competing 19
large 276
multinational 11

national 14
producing goods for
    export 283(n23)
    specific 278
comparative advantage 18, 30,
    42, 50, 51, 52–3, 92, 95, 96,
    117, 127(n1), 195, 211, 232,
    269, 275, 279
'sensitive' products 24
competition 15, 46, 269, 270
    foreign 279
    imperfect 9, 47
    monopolistic 47
    perfect 47
    world market 121
competition law 26
competition policy xii
competitive advantage 101,
    111, 257, 273
competitiveness 22, 117, 132,
    133, 149, 151, 153–5,
    156(n10), 222, 269
    international 266–7
components 195, 271
Comprehensive Scheme for Studying
    Cost of Cultivation of Principal
    Crops (COC, India) 104–8, 122,
    127(n7–8), 128(n10)
    C2 (farmer's own labour and
        resources included as costs at
        market prices) 104–5, 106,
        116, 123t, 126t
    CL2 (farmer's family labour
        cost not included) 105,
        116, 123t, 126t
    CP2 (cost of family labour and
        rent on farmer's own land
        not included) 105, 116,
        123t, 126t
    CR2 (rent on farmer's own land not
        included) 105, 116, 123t, 126t
    estimated regression equation for
        fertilizer use, for yield
        adjustment 126t
    fertilizer nutrient consumption and
        prices 124t
    gains in returns at external
        prices from paddy cultivation
        districts of Andhra
        Pradesh 127t
    gains in returns at external prices
        from paddy cultivation
        estimated with alternative cost
        concepts 126t

parameters underlying calculation
    of returns 125t
    rice per hectare (1996) 123t
computable general equilibrium (CGE)
    models 8, 74, 227, 228
Congo, Democratic Republic
    (ex-Zaire) 194, 197t, 220, 240f,
    241, 244f, 246t, 249, 255t
Congo Republic (Brazzaville) 197t,
    205t
Consolidated Tariff Schedules (CTS)
    database 188(n10)
consumer demand 76
consumers 16, 46, 47, 52, 64, 95,
    236, 245
    EU 49
    two-stage budgeting 206–7
consumption, domestic 152
contingent protection 16, 19
copper 194, 203t, 204
corporatization 101
corruption 58, 198, 283(n21)
cost structures 149
Costa Rica 196t, 202t,
    238, 240f, 243, 244f, 250t,
    251t, 255t
costs 58
    negotiation and adjustment 37
    processing, handling,
        transport 112
Côte d'Ivoire 197t, 243, 244f, 246t,
    250t, 254t, 255t
Cotonou Agreement, 49, 140, 154,
    192t, 198, 199, 225
    'EU–ACP Partnership
        Agreement' 246
    see also Everything But Arms
        Initiative
cotton 17–18
countervailing duties (CVDs) 261,
    263, 264–5, 277, 281, 282,
    284(n28)
    benchmarks in calculating subsidy
        margins 267, 283(n12)
    against Brazil 272t, 278
    against India 273, 274t, 274,
        275, 278
    against Korea 277, 278t, 278,
        284(n30)
credit 15, 95, 276, 279
Croatia 251t, 255t
crops 229–30t, 233–4t
cross-conditionality 28
crustaceans 175, 176t, 183t

Cuba 247, 250t, 255t
currency
  depreciation 276–7
  devaluation 268, 270, 272, 275,
    283(n19)
  overvaluation 273
current account deficits 276
customs clearance times 31–2(n6)
customs duty 12, 100(box)
cut flowers 203t, 204
Cuttack 113t
Cyprus 252t
Czech Republic 251t, 255t

dairy products 43t, 44t, 67t, 81,
    82t, 85t, 85, 140, 142t, 143–5,
    146f, 146t, 148t, 150t, 223t,
    223, 224t, 229–30t, 231, 232,
    233–4t, 241, 242f
Das, S. 129
data 76, 139
  bilateral trade 207
  bound tariffs 187
  cost of cultivation (India) 122–7
  sectoral 231
  trade liberalization and
    returns from land 104–9,
    127–8(n7–9)
data constraints/limitations 93–4,
    104, 106–9, 116, 127(n6–7), 164,
    188(n11, n13), 207, 228, 277(n27)
Datta, S. K. 96, 96t
debt-to-equity swaps 271
debt forgiveness 271
delays 283(n21)
Delhi 96t
demand 117, 128(n14), 135, 276
  excess 134f, 134
  external 262
  price and income elasticities 76
depreciation 277(n27), 282(n9)
Derbez, E. 182
destination principle 282(n9)
developed countries 23, 27, 30,
    31(n5), 46, 131, 143t, 144t,
    146t, 148t, 150t, 150, 151,
    162, 170, 185, 269
  agricultural policy distortions 55, 57
  agricultural support policies 25
  applied tariffs on crustaceans 176t
  capital goods imports 265–6
  duty-free market access for
    developing countries and
    LDCs 181t

economic results of freeing
  trade 190–218
export subsidies prohibited 263,
  265, 282(n4)
preference margin 145
developed countries, rest of 229t
  exports (percentage changes,
    EBA) 233t
  welfare changes (EBA) 231t, 232
developed-country trade barriers and
  LDCs
  benefits of tariff elimination 214
  economic results of freeing
    trade 190–218
  estimating equation 207–8
  key questions 191–2
  methodology 206–9, 216(n26–9)
  trade implications of existing
    preferences 209–11, 216(n30)
  trade implications of removal of
    existing preferences 211–14
  unilateral trade liberalization 190
developed-developing country
  divide xii, 3
developing countries 4, 5, 48, 66–7t,
    74, 78n, 178, 188(n14), 266
  agricultural liberalization (political
    feasibility) 6, 92–129
  agricultural policy reform 40
  agricultural price distortions 45
  applied tariff rates 184
  bilateral trade with OECD 70–1
  diversity 66
  food policy liberalization 42
  food-importing 52–3
  impact of agricultural trade reform
    (OECD study) 73
  impact of EU sugar
    regime 259(n20)
  impact of fifty percent liberalization
    in EU of border measures
    relating to wheat
    (simulation) 76, 76t, 77–81
  impact of OECD agricultural
    reforms 81–7
  large 6
  market access 10–33
  maximization of gains from WTO
    negotiations on agriculture 19
  net exporters (tropical
    products) 70, 89(n3)
  net food-importing 37
  net importers (temperate
    products) 70

net trade position (programme crops) 70
OECD domestic support and 63–91
oppose further agricultural trade liberalization 18
products of export interest 161, 162, 185, 187(n1), 191
'stand to gain from OECD measures that decouple domestic support from production decisions' 71
structural weaknesses 279, 281
tariff-preference erosion in OECD markets 59(n4)
trade liberalization, 42, 59(n5)
trade liberalization (between each other) 'stunted' 193
trade patterns 66–72, 89(n2–3)
trade shares of products affected by agricultural subsidies (1995–8) 17t
trading status 74, 83
TRQ gains in EU market 138–50, 155–6(n3–11)
use of EU TRQs 143t, 143–4
value of agricultural TRQs 130–57
welfare impact of re-instrumentation 86, 86t, 89
WTO Doha Round 10–33
see also least-developed countries; low-income countries
development 3–9, 30, 154, 193, 256
balanced 277
links between trade and 258
rural 152
tariff preferences as policy instrument 219–20
unbalanced 276
development
agenda 15
assistance 4, 16, 30
issues 214
priorities (national identification) 29
'relevance' 29
strategy (import-substitution) 268–75, 283(n13–21)
Dewbre, J. 77
diamonds 220, 221t
Diao, X. 55–6
Diaz-Bonilla, E. 55
'differentiation' (WTO rules) 27
Dimaranan, B. xvii, 60, 74, 83, 87, 89, 89(n5), 90

distance 101, 207
distribution/distributors 12, 24
diversification 25, 193, 256, 257, 279
Djibouti 194, 197t, 215(n16)
Doha: Special Session on Agriculture 130
Doha Development Agenda (DDA, November 2001–) xii, 4, 10, 38
industrial tariffs, LDCs, and 161–89
market-access barriers 39, 39t
potential gains 39–46, 59(n3–6)
sectoral output 43t
sectoral trade balance 44t
welfare gains 41t
Doha Ministerial Declaration (WTO, 2001) 8, 26, 37, 161, 180, 261, 282(n2)
duty-free, quota-free market access for LDCs 181, 188(n16), 189, 214
modalities 187(n1)
paragraph 14 26
paragraph 16 164, 182, 187(n1)
paragraph 42 59(n8), 188(n16), 215(n1)
paragraph 44 26
paragraph 50 182
product coverage 161, 182, 187(n1)
Doha Ministerial Declaration: Work Programme (WTO, 2001) 188(n16), 248
Doha Ministerial Meeting (WTO, 2001) 37, 50, 282(n6)
Doha Round/Doha negotiations 7, 66, 211, 261, 281
agriculture 60(n13)
developing countries 10–33
'Draft Elements of Modalities for Negotiations on Non-Agricultural Products' 185
Harbison draft 132, 151–3, 156(n12)
importance of extending TRQs 154
importance of SSA/developing country participation 45–6, 48
market access 15–13
Mauritius proposal to Special Session on Agriculture 154
policy implications 57–9
reciprocal MFN liberalization and unilateral trade preferences 23–5, 29–30, 31

Doha Round/Doha negotiations (*continued*)
  trade agenda at national level 12–15
  WTO rules and SDT 25–9, 30, 31–2 (n6–8)
Dollar, D. 38
domestic agricultural support (OECD) model 63–91
  comprehensive reform 81–7, 89(n6)
  'decoupling' 64, 65, 71, 73, 89(n1)
  effect of reductions 71
  experimental design 76–7, 76t
  fifty percent cut in domestic support in all OECD countries (simulation) 77, 81–4, 87–8, 89(n6)
  fifty percent cut in market price support in all OECD countries (simulation) 77, 84–7, 88
  fifty percent liberalization of border measures relating to wheat in EU15 (simulation) 76, 76t, 77–81
  four classifications 76
  impact on developing countries 64, 73–4, 78–87, 89(n6)
  impact on OECD agriculture 64
  literature review 72–3, 89(n4)
  methodology 73–7
  model design 73–6
  policy re-instrumentation 77–8, 84–7, 89
  policy implications 87–9, 89(n7–8)
  reduction (impact on developing countries) 81–4
  results and discussion 77–87, 89(n5–6)
domestic distortions, theory of 279
domestic reform/own reform 5, 18–19, 20, 22, 24, 29, 30
domestic support xii, 6, 9n, 17t, 19
  OECD countries 24
Dominican Republic 196t, 200, 202t, 244f
double taxation 282(n9)
drawback regimes 14
drugs (narcotics) 194, 196, 215(n20)
DSB (WTO: Dispute Settlement Body) 263, 282(n4)
  Brazil-Canada aircraft financing case 271, 282–3(n11)

durum 140
Duty Entitlement Pass Book (DEPB, India) 274
dyes and paints 203t, 204
dynamic gains 46

East Africa 198
East Asia 14t, 220
EBA *see* Everything But Arms (EBA) Initiative
EBA Council Regulation (2001–) 192t
EBA sugar 247, 249
econometrics 74, 89(n8), 191
  trade-reduction v. trade diversion 8, 206–8
economic
  cooperation 58–9
  development 11, 27, 196
  efficiency gains 45
  gain 45
  growth xii, 10, 37, 38–9, 59(n1–2), 261, 267, 275, 278, 283(n16, n18)
  liberalization 269
  performance 23, 280
  performance (effect of export subsidies) 261, 262
  welfare 11, 18, 48, 64, 73, 77, 78, 88, 105, 231–5, 257, 279
Economic Partnership Agreements (EPAs) 199
economies of scale 46, 47, 94, 111
Ecuador 196, 203t, 204, 238, 240f, 243, 244f, 252t, 255t
education 29, 58
efficiency 16, 45, 55, 78, 232
  gain 87
  loss 86
eggs 140, 146f
Egypt 184, 250t
El Salvador 196t, 202t, 251t, 255t
elasticity of
  demand and supply 116
  domestic demand 72
  export demand 72
  exports 280
  import demand 236
  substitution 206, 207, 208
Elbehri, A., *et al.* (1999) 73, 90, 147, 157
  Hertel, T. 90, 157
  Ingco, M. D. 90, 157
  Pearson, K. 90, 157

electric machinery 168t, 169t, 171t, 173t
electrical machinery and equipment 202t
electronic goods 193
electronics and electrical goods 185
emerging economies 178
applied tariffs on crustaceans 176t
empiricism 48, 51, 53, 54, 55, 59(n2, n6), 82, 93, 138, 148, 152, 280, 281
employees 277
employment 23, 72, 105, 117, 119, 219
non-farm 53, 54
energy 21, 39, 39t, 44t, 282(n9)
entry barriers 21
environment 11, 24, 26
Equatorial Guinea 197t, 211, 244f
equity capital 262, 263, 271
Eritrea 197t, 251t
Essential Commodities Act (ECA, India) 95
Estonia 252t, 255t
Ethiopia 197t, 251t, 254t
Europe 6
Europe Agreements (CEE countries) 140
Europe and Central Asia 14t
European Centre for Development Policy Management 216(n23)
European Commission 225–6
author 253, 258(n16)
impact study of EBA 235
website 258(n7)
European Communities/ Community 155(n4), 192t, 220
European Community–India Agreement (sugar) 246, 248
European Council Regulations
No 3281/94 and No 1256/96 258(n6)
No 552/97 (24 March 1997) 259(n17)
No 602/98 (9 March 1998) 258(n6)
No 1260/2001 (19 June 2001) 247, 248, 259(n21)
European Economic Community (EEC) 194, 198
European Free Trade Area (EFTA) 66t, 68t, 70, 84, 86, 87, 232

European Union (EU15) 2, 5, 6, 20t, 60(n11), 66t, 86, 88, 131, 156(n11), 175, 180, 190, 191, 193, 206, 207, 274t
agricultural imports 7, 141, 143, 150–1
agricultural reform, proposed 64, 89(n1)
applied tariffs on crustaceans 176t
applied tariffs on industrial products 173t, 174t
applied tariff rates 189(n18)
author 216(n23)
barriers to agriculture-based trade 214
barriers against imports from Bangladesh 59–60(n10)
bound tariffs on industrial products 165t, 167, 168t, 169t, 171t
budgetary exposure 73
changes in imports from LDCs as result of eliminating all tariffs on LDC exports (2000) 212
Council Regulation No. 416/ 2001 222
CVDs against Korea 284(n30)
domestic price 49
duty-free access 9, 224
duty-free and quota-free access (developing-country exports) 49, 50, 51–2, 59(n8)
export subsidies (simulated reduction) 85t, 85
exports (percentage changes, EBA) 233t
farm incomes 77
farm incomes (simulation) 84
import tariffs (simulated reduction) 85t, 85
importance of TRQ trade in total agricultural imports 141, 142t, 155–6(n7)
imports from LDCs 209–10, 211, 214
LDC imports and preference programmes (2000) 209t
LDC share in total EU imports (2000) 221t
major imports from LDCs (2000) 221t
MFN and preferential tariffs facing LDC exports 183t

European Union (EU15) (*continued*)
  'most open market'   181
  non-ACP imports   49
  preference programmes   192t,
      198–9, 216(n23–5)
  preferential market-access
      arrangements for LDCs   220–7,
      258(n3–13)
  producer subsidy equivalent and
      components (1987, 2000)
      65t, 65
  protection rates on merchandise
      trade   229–30t
  removal of tariff barriers against
      LDCs   214
  'sensitive' and 'non-sensitive
      goods'   194, 222
  sugar market   8
  sugar regime   24
  tariff effects on trade
      (summary)   208t
  tariff escalation on textile
      products   179t
  tariffs on fish and fish
      products   172
  tariffs on leather   177t
  top sugar exporters (market share,
      2000)   250–2t
  trade   208
  trade specialization indices
      (1965–98)   68t, 70
  TRQ case study   132
  TRQ gains (for developing
      countries)   138–50,
      155–6(n3–11)
  welfare changes (EBA)   231t,
      232, 235
  wheat production   77, 78t
European Union: Common
      Agricultural Policy (CAP)
      235, 256
Everything But Arms (EBA) Initiative
      (EU, 2001–)   8, 23, 50, 181,
      190, 194
  aggregate worldwide distribution of
      gains and losses   227, 228–35
  background   222–6
  better labelled 'nothing but
      sugar'   238
  cane sugar export changes,
      254–5t
  distribution of liberalized products
      (by sectors)   224t
  duty-free, quota-free access   194

economics of non-reciprocal trading
      arrangements   226–7,
      258(n12–13)
  exports, percentage changes
      233–4t
  impact assessment   227–35
  implications for traditional sugar
      exporters   248–56, 259(n30–1)
  and LDCs   219–60
  methodologies   237
  preferences as development policy
      instrument   219–20
  sensitive products (model,
      data)   236–7, 258(n14–16)
  sensitive products (scenario 1: no
      LDC trade re-orientation)
      237–41, 243, 253,
      254t, 256
  sensitive products (scenario 2: LDC
      trade re-orientation)   237–8,
      241–3, 244f, 253–6
  sensitive products (scenarios)
      236–7
  sensitive products (sugar)   243–8,
      259(n19–29)
  simulation results   231–5, 237–43
  simulations   227, 258(n15)
  third countries   237
  welfare changes   231–5
  winners and losers   235–56,
      258–9(n14–31)
  see also Lomé Convention
exchange rates   94, 100(box), 110n,
      127(n2), 262, 273, 280
  crawling peg   268
  real   268, 280
Expenditure Reforms Commission
      (ERC, India)   121
export
  bias   269
  credit   266, 273, 279, 280, 284(n32)
  earnings   4
  expansion   227, 279
  financing schemes   269, 275
  financing system   270
  growth   275–6, 278, 280
  insurance   279
  markets   9, 66
  orientation   280
  performance   274, 284(n24)
  possibilities   116
  prices   6, 78t, 78, 79t, 79, 80, 81,
      83t, 83, 84, 86t, 87, 94, 150t
  production refunds   274

promotion 261, 269, 275–9, 280,
283–4(n21–31)
refunds 245, 248, 259(n22)
supply elasticities 236
surplus 132, 133
taxes 280
trade (merchandise) 282(n6)
export incentives 267–75, 276, 281,
280, 283(n13–21)
distinguished from 'export
subsidies' 265
fiscal measures 272
impact on export performance 280
import entitlement schemes 272
theory and evidence 279–81,
284(n32–5)
Export Promotion Programme
(Brazil) 270
export subsidies 9, 15, 19, 30, 72,
243, 245, 249, 261–86
agricultural 17t, 17–18
conferring a benefit to
recipient 262, 263,
284(n24, n31)
cut by fifty percent
(simulation) 84
de minimis 284(n30)
definition 262–3
level 264
multilateral discipline 262–4,
282(n3–7)
rationale 261, 279
volume of exports 264–5
wheat 78
see also subsidies
exporters 11, 12, 19, 110, 120, 132,
135, 139, 148–52, 154, 155(n6),
270, 281
developing-country 7, 73
LDC 247
successful 275
'unable to appropriate full value of
TRQ rent' 145
exports 17t, 18, 23, 45, 60(n11),
67–72, 87, 89(n5), 92, 96, 112,
156(n10), 207, 210, 212,
216(n20, n27), 232, 236, 241,
266, 272–3, 275, 276
agricultural 55, 56
developing countries 48–9, 52
diversification 195, 196
expansion 213
FOB value 273
LDC 17, 237, 253

manufactured 268, 273, 283(n15)
non-traditional 280
poor-country 39
'positive impact' for LDCs of
EBA 235
rice 93, 117
special and preferential
treatment 264
sugar 249, 259(n30)
wheat 77–8, 78t

facility investment loans 276
factor demand: nested-CES production
function 74
factor markets 74, 279
fair price shops (FPS) 111, 119
family labour 105, 117
FAOSTAT database 149, 156(n10)
farm harvest prices (FHP) 109, 112,
113t, 116, 128(n10)
farm households 55, 58
farm incomes 6, 72, 88–9, 89(n4)
OECD countries 64
real 64, 75
farm lobby 64, 99
farm product markets 5, 37–8
farmers 38, 46, 93, 95, 97, 104, 105,
112, 114, 117, 118, 121
near-subsistence 17–18
net transfers to 16–17
OECD 18
small-scale 17–18
fats and oils 43t, 44t, 224t
vegetable 43t, 44t, 67t, 82t, 85t,
214, 229–30t, 231, 233–4t
FCI *see* Food Corporation of India
Fertilizer Association of India
(FAI) 104, 108, 109
fertilizers 6, 74, 97–100, 104,
106, 107, 117, 118, 124–6t,
127(n4–5), 127–8(n8)
ammonium chloride
(AC) 100(box)
ammonium sulphate
(AS) 100(box)
calcium ammonium nitrate
(CAN) 100(box)
diammonium phosphate
(DAP) 99, 100t, 102f, 109,
110t
domestic industry 121,
128(n11)
dual pricing method 100(box), 121
estimate of protection 110t

fertilizers (*continued*)
  freeing of trade 114
  import price 109, 110t
  imports (India)
    101, 101t
  muriate of potash (MOP) 99,
    100t, 102f, 109, 110t
  nitrogenous (N) 121
  nutrient (N, P, K) data 109, 124t
  phosphatic (P) 99, 121,
    128(n14)
  potassic (K) 99, 128(n14)
  prices/pricing 94, 108, 114, 116,
    127(n2)
  price changes 108
  reforms 99–100, 127(n4–5)
  regional picture 110
  Retention Price and Subsidy (RPS)
    Scheme 97–9, 100t, 121,
    128(n11, 13–14)
  urea 99, 100(box), 100t, 102f,
    110t, 121, 128(n14)
Ffrench-Davis, R. 280
Fiji 9, 238, 246t, 249, 250t,
  253, 254t, 255t
finance 4, 12, 15, 21, 275
  storage of export merchandise
    (Brazil) 270
  financial assistance 25, 30
  'resource needs' 31
  financial sector 276, 278
Finger, M. 187(n2)
Fink, C. 31(n*)
Finland 247
fiscal constraints 31(n2), 281
fiscal neutrality 265
fish/fishing 43t, 44t, 155(n7),
  162, 167–70, 171t, 172–5,
  185, 221t, 229–30t, 233–4t
  intra-LDC protectionism 182
  MFN and preferential tariffs
    facing LDC exports 183t
  shrimps 258(n18)
  tuna 196
Fitzgerald, B. 279
FINEX 270
Floyd, J. E. 72
food 212, 231
  buffer stocks 95
  importing countries 38
  market prices 56, 57
  prepared 193, 213, 214
  price support 52
  processed 5, 40, 241

'other processed' 67t, 70, 82t, 85t,
  86–7, 142t, 143, 143t, 144t,
  146f, 146t, 148t, 150t
food
  aid 37, 58, 60(n14), 94
  distribution 119
  imports 40, 41t, 42, 43t, 44t
  insecurity 37, 54–7, 60(n12)
  prices 31, 42, 52–7
  production 58, 211
  products 51, 67, 229–30t, 231,
    233–4t, 241
  security 38, 58, 94–5, 118, 152
  self-sufficiency 52, 55, 56, 57
  stocks 58, 118
  supplies 66
  trade 210
Food Corporation Act (India,
  1964) 119
Food Corporation of India (FCI,
  1965–) 94, 97, 104, 111, 112,
  117, 118
  future role 119
  phases of rice-marketing 119–20
  price policy (conflicting
    objectives) 95
footwear 162, 167–72, 173t, 175–6,
  185, 193, 195, 196, 210, 212, 213
forced labour 258(n17)
foreign direct investment (FDI) 20,
  26, 262
foreign exchange 95, 280,
  283(n24)
Foreign Investment Promotion Act
  (FIPA), Korea 277
forestry 43t, 44t, 229–30t,
  233–4t
Former Soviet Union (FSU) 67t, 68t,
  69n, 71t, 72, 78n
France 89(n1), 247, 279
Francois, J. 47, 60, 89
Frandsen, S. 73
free market 117
free trade 93, 112, 116,
  188(n13), 279
  differential impacts 3
  economic results 190–218
  sources of conflict 3–4
  unequal gain 117
free-trade agreements (FTAs)
  15, 199
free-trade areas/zones 48, 101t
French Overseas Departments
  (FODs) 248

fruits 43t, 44t, 67t, 82t, 85t,
141–8, 148t, 150t, 151, 154,
202t, 223t, 223, 224t, 229–30t,
231, 233–4t, 241
furskins 175, 221t

Gabon 197t, 204, 205t, 205
Gambia 197t, 210
gas/natural gas 98, 127(n4), 229–30t,
233–4t
liquefied natural gas (LNG) 121
GATT *see* General Agreement on
Tariffs and Trade
General Agreement on Trade in
Services (GATS), 46–7
mode one 22, 23
mode two 22
mode three 22–3
mode four 22, 23
General Agreement on Tariffs and
Trade (GATT) xii, 4, 16, 19, 23,
25, 50, 161, 177, 192, 198–9, 214,
216(n24), 247
Article XXIV 226
Article XXVIIIbis (of GATT 1994)
182, 187(n1)
'enabling clause' (1971–) 192, 194,
214, 215(n5), 225, 226
waivers 215(n5)
Generalized System of Preferences
(GSP, 1971–) 8, 49, 51, 190–5,
197–204, 204t, 210, 211, 214,
220–3, 225, 256, 257,
258(n3, n5–6, n17)
criticism 192–3
'differential treatment' 226–7
duty-free treatment 195
elimination of import ceilings 195
first non-reciprocal preference
programme 192–3
'limited range of products'
192–3
quantitative restrictions
193, 194
schemes 188(n16)
single preferential tariff rate (zero)
proposed 24–5
status 24
'in Triad' 193–5
George Washington University:
Institute of Brazilian
Issues 283(n13)
Germany 89(n1), 245, 269
Ghana 197t

Ghosh, N. xvii
Giambiagi, F. 269
glass 193
Global Trade Analysis Project
(GTAP) model 5–6, 8, 39, 42, 51,
53, 88, 227
editions:
GTAP1–4 73
GTAP Pre-Release 3: 228
GTAP4 59(n3), 228
GTAP5 69n, 71n, 73, 76, 86,
228, 235
GTAP5.0.1 228
general:
applied general equilibrium
model (Purdue
University) 40
database 59(n3), 73, 74, 69n,
71n, 73, 76, 86, 89(n2), 228
first-cut disaggregation 73
qualifications to global modelling
results 46–8
standard 75–6
standard multi-region
model 59(n3)
globalization 46
goats 140
'good practice' 11
goods 17
goods and services 15, 29
goods trade/merchandise trade 40,
43t, 44t
global protection (costs) 16
import market-access barriers 39,
39t
liberalisation 48
manufactures and agricultural 21
reform 42
removal of barriers/tariffs 40, 47
government 3, 277
government
intervention 267, 275, 276
loans 263
policy 280
procurement (transparency) 26
programmes 281
governments 10–11, 18, 45, 46
communist 193
Denmark, Finland, Norway, Sweden,
UK xiii
developing countries (three-fold
challenge) 11
developing-country 19
national 49

grains   5, 9n, 64, 65, 66, 87, 95
  coarse and cereals ('crsgrns')   67t,
    82t, 84, 85t, 85, 87, 89(n2)
  'green channel' treatment   12[–]14
'Green Revolution'   116
Grenada   196t
Gross Domestic Product (GDP)   207,
  215(n20), 216(n28), 264, 276,
  282(n7)
Gross National Product (GNP)   275,
  280, 282(n5)
GSP   *see* Generalized System of
  Preferences
GTAP Consortium   59(n3)
Guatemala   196t, 202t, 250t, 252t
Guha-Khasnobis, B.   xvii, 215(n*)
Guinea   197t
Guinea-Bissau   197t
Gulati, A.   97
Gulati, A., *et al.* (1994)   96, 96t, 129
  Chhabra, V.   129
  Das, S.   129
  Sharma, A.   129
  Sharma, K.   129
Guyana   9, 196t, 238, 246t, 250t,
  254t, 255t

Haiti   196, 196t, 209n
Haldia   101, 102t, 102,
  103t, 104
Halevi, N.   280, 284(n35)
Harmonized System (HS) of tariff
    classification   155(n5), 202t,
    203t, 205t, 247
  chapters 1 to 24   155(n7)
  chapter 25   156(n7)
  2-digit   210, 223t, 224t
  4-digit   152, 156(n10), 177t,
    177–8, 183t, 187
  6-digit   152, 181, 187(n4–5),
    188(n14), 207, 208,
    221n, 223t
  8-digit   41, 142t,
    155(n5–6), 222
Harris, J. R.   60(n14)
Haryana ('HRY')   107, 112, 113t,
  114, 119, 123t, 124t, 125t, 126t,
  127–8(n8), 128(n10)
Haveman, J. D.   xvii, 206, 208n,
  216(n30), 217
headage-based payments   65
headgear   210, 213
health   29
health and safety   14

heavy manufacturing and chemical
  industries (HCI)   276
Hertel, T.   xvii, 60, 72, 73, 74, 78, 83,
  87, 89, 89(n4–5), 90, 157, 228
Hertel, T., *et al.* (1996)   73, 90
  Dimaranan, B.   90
  Martin, W.   90
  Yanagishima, K.   90
hides and skins   213, 221t
High Power Fertilizer Pricing
    (Marathe) Committee
    (India)   121
high-income countries
  agricultural liberalization   42
  potential welfare gains from full
    trade liberalization   41t
highways/roads   111, 275
hinterland   109, 110
'History of UNCTAD 1964–84'
  (1985)   258(n1)
Hoda, A.   282(n*, n3)
Hoekman, B.   xvii, 18, 32(n7), 51, 52,
  60, 88, 89, 89(n8)
Honduras   196t, 200, 202t, 244f
Hong Kong   163, 164, 188(n11, n13),
    251t, 279
  bound tariffs on industrial
    products   166t, 167, 168t,
    169t, 171t
household income   54
households   54
  poorer   56
  poorest   57
  urban   56, 57
HS   *see* Harmonized System
Huang, J.   53–4
Huff, K. M.   78
hukou system   54
Hummels, D.   75
Hungary   66t, 241, 250t, 251t, 255t

Ianchovichina, E.   51, 53–4,
  228, 235
Iceland   251t
implementation costs   11, 27–8
  'opt-out' provision (suggested)   27
  resource-intensive rules   28–9
import
  agents   7, 151
  liberalization   273, 276
  licences   147t, 272
  prices   78, 79t, 79, 80, 83t,
    83, 86t, 87, 206
  quotas   40

regimes (simple and
     transparent) 164
restrictions 56
surges 18–19
import-substitution 9, 220, 261, 264,
     267, 275, 278, 284(n26)
     Brazil 268–72, 283(n13–19)
     India 272–5, 283(n20–1)
importers 24, 110, 112
importing countries
     high-income 39t
     low-income 39t
imports 8, 11, 16, 17t, 18, 67, 68–9t,
     70–2, 82, 86–7, 96, 121, 128(n14),
     141, 142t, 150, 151, 195, 206–11,
     216(n27), 236, 245, 270, 276
     agricultural 55
     anti-dumping initiations (1995–9) 20
     domestic demand 236
     duty-free 162–3, 205
     fertilizers (India) 97, 99
     LDC 17
     massive increases 226
     MFN bound duty-free 163
     non-dutiable 203t
     non-TRQ 155(n6)
     notified 156(n8)
     preferential 243
     TRQ 155(n6)
     world 164, 187(n5)
incentives 95
     financial 275
income level 207, 216(n28)
income redistribution 3
India 9, 18, 20t, 25, 30, 43t,
     44t, 67t, 164, 220, 246, 246t,
     250–1t, 253, 254t, 261, 262,
     265–7, 278–80, 282(n10),
     283(n18), 284(n33)
     agricultural development 'high
          priority' 117
     applied tariff rates 184
     applied tariffs on crustaceans 176t
     applied tariffs on industrial
          products 173t, 174t
     bilateral trade with OECD 71t, 71
     bound tariffs on industrial
          products 166t, 167–70, 171t
     comprehensive OECD domestic
          support reform
          (simulation) 82
     economic reforms (1991-) 273
     exemption of tax on export
          profits, 274

'export promotion capital goods'
     scheme 274
exports of agricultural goods 96–7
fertilizer pricing 97–100,
     127(n4–5)
GDP 282(n7)
government minimum support
     price 104
impact of EU15 wheat MPS reform
     (simulation) 79t
impact of OECD domestic support
     reform 82, 83t
impact of trade liberalization on rice
     exporters 6, 92–129
import-substitution development
     strategy 272–5, 283(n20–1)
internal distances 96
market channels and
     institutions 97
MFN and preferential tariffs facing
     LDC exports 183t
     regional dimension 108, 112
     regional imbalance in
          agriculture 116
rice export 97
rice market at a cross-roads 94–7,
     127(n3)
subsidy burden 99
tariff escalation on textile
     products 179t
tariffs on leather 177t
tariffs on textiles and clothing 177
trade liberalization and returns from
     land 92–129
trade specialization indices
     (1965–98) 68t, 70
welfare impact of
     re-instrumentation 86t
India: Agricultural and Processed Food
     Export Development Authority
     (APEDA) 104
India: Department of Economics and
     Statistics (DES) 104, 116
India: Directorate-General of
     Commercial Intelligence and
     Statistics (DGCIS) 104, 109, 111
India: Ministry of Agriculture
     (MOA) 109, 122, 128(n10)
India: Ministry of Agriculture: *Bulletin
     on Food Statistics* (BFS) 104
Indian Government (Government of
     India/GOI) 93, 104, 117, 118
     agricultural price policy 122
     author 282(n8)

Indian Government (Government of
India/GOI) (*continued*)
export promotion
schemes 283(n21)
foodgrain policy 94
Indian Railways 111
Indonesia 5, 20t, 59(n6), 66t, 68t,
70–1, 71t, 72, 79t, 83t, 86t, 251t
industrial
economies 14t
policies 277
products 51, 164, 165t, 194
industrial tariffs
bound 164, 165t
current situation 164–80,
187–8(n8–15)
four-digit level 172
general landscape 164–72,
187–8(n8–12)
LDCs, and DDA 161–89
market access (unfinished
business) 162–4,
187(n3–7)
modalities for negotiations 182,
184–6, 189(n18)
sector-specific landscape 172–80,
188(n13–15)
industrialization 53, 271
industries
import-competing 19, 20
OECD countries 11
policy instruments 187
relocation 277
subsidized 78
infant-industry argument 279
inflation 268, 269, 283(n16, n18)
informal fees 32(n6)
informal sector 55
Information Technology Agreement
(Ministerial Declaration on
Trade in Information Technology
Products, ITA, 1996) 163,
187(n7)
infrastructure 29, 59(n2),
93, 214, 262, 271,
275, 279
input
costs 93
markets 93, 94,
115–16, 118
prices 108
subsidies 64, 65t, 65, 72,
89(n4–5)
input-based payments 72

inputs 15, 77, 104, 107, 108,
127(n7), 265–6, 270, 272, 273,
274, 282(n10)
farm-owned 74, 75
fertilizers 114
free trade 116
intermediate 268
non-traded 105, 106, 107,
108–9, 128(n9)
purchased 74, 75
tradable 117
traded 105–6, 109
value-added aggregate 75
variable 88
Institute of Development Studies
(IDS), University of
Sussex 259(n30)
institutional capacity 27,
32(n6)
institutions 13t, 59(n2), 235
insurance 15
interest rates 266, 275, 276
'official' v. 'market' 283(n23)
subsidies 276
interests (differential) 27–9
international financial institutions
(IFIs) 28
International Monetary Fund
(IMF) 277
internet 22
investment 12, 46, 47, 76, 276,
277, 284(n26)
public 15
trade-related 30
investment climate 25, 29
investors 48, 263
Iran 250t
iron 205t, 272t, 274t
Israel 20t, 250t, 280, 284(n33)
Ingco, M. D. 90, 157, 187(n2)

Jamaica 244f, 246t, 250–1t,
254t, 255t
Japan 5, 8, 50, 66t, 175, 176, 180,
182, 190, 193, 206–8, 211–14,
229t, 250t, 269, 276
applied tariff rates 189(n18)
applied tariffs on
crustaceans 176t
applied tariffs on industrial
products 173t, 174t
bound tariffs on industrial
products 166t, 167, 168t,
169t, 171t

export subsidies (simulated reduction) 85t
exports (percentage changes, EBA) 233t
farm incomes (simulation) 84
GSP 220
import tariffs (simulated reduction) 85t, 85
imports 213
imports from LDCs 210
LDC imports and preference programmes (2000) 209t
market access 51
MFN and preferential tariffs facing LDC exports 183t
producer subsidy equivalent and components (1987, 2000) 65t, 65
tariff effects on trade (summary) 208t
tariff escalation on textile products 179t
tariff-elimination 212–13
tariffs on fish and fish products 172, 175
tariffs on leather 177t
trade specialization indices (1965–98) 68t, 70
welfare changes (EBA) 231t, 232
Japan: Ministry of Economics, Trade and Industry 195
Jensen, H. G. 73
just-in-time (JIT) supply chain management 12
jute 111, 178, 179t

Kahkonen, S. 97
Kakinada 102t, 102, 103t
Kandla 96t, 101, 101t, 102–3, 113t
free trade zone 101t, 103t
sea 101t, 102t, 103t
Karnal (Haryana) 96t, 113t
Keeney, R. xvii, 74, 83, 87, 89(n5)
Kenana sugar refinery (Sudan) 259(n31)
Kenya 197t, 246t, 251t, 255t
Kim, K. S. 280
Korea, Republic of (South Korea) 9, 20t, 66t, 163, 164, 180, 251t, 261, 262, 265, 267, 280, 281, 283(n15), 284(n33)
applied tariffs on crustaceans 176t
applied tariffs on industrial products 173t, 174t

bound tariffs on industrial products 166t, 168t, 169t, 171t
CVDs against 277, 278t, 278, 284(n30)
export promotion development strategy 275–9, 283–4(n22–31)
farm incomes (simulation) 84
GDP 264, 282(n7)
MFN and preferential tariffs facing LDC exports 183t
producer subsidy equivalent and components (1987, 2000) 65t, 65
tariff escalation on textile products 179t
tariffs on leather 177t
trade and industrial policies 283(n22)
trade specialization indices (1965–98) 68t, 70
Korean government 276, 277–8
Kraay, A. 38
Krueger, A. O. 59(n2)

labour 50–1, 54, 59(n9), 74, 77, 78t, 81
agricultural 56, 57
demand 55, 56, 57
farmer's own 104
foreign 22
global gains from allowing temporary entry 31(n3)
landless farm 105
non-farm 56
skilled 31(n3)
unskilled 31(n3), 55
labour law 279
labour market 22, 54, 105
labour rights 24, 194
labour standards xii, 11
Laird, S. xvii, 51, 187(n2), 258(n14–15), 259
laissez-faire 58
Lamy, P. 219
land 53, 54, 65, 72, 75, 81, 89(n5)
contribution to world price change 82t
impact of trade liberalization on returns (India) 92–129
land borders 207
land payments 88
land rents 78t, 105

land rights   58
land-based payments/subsidies   6,
    65t, 65, 76, 77, 81, 84, 89(n6)
    'win–win' scenario   72, 88
land-lease market   105
landlessness   105
language   207
Laos/Lao PDR   194, 210, 238
Laroche Dupraz, C.   xvii
Latin America   5, 14t, 141, 143t,
    144t, 145–51, 153, 154, 163,
    229t, 238, 243
  distribution of binding
    coverage   172t
  exports (percentage changes,
    EBA)   233t
  trade specialization indices
    (1965–98)   68t
  TRQ trade with EU   143
  welfare changes (EBA)   231t
Latin America, Rest of ('RlatAm')   67t
  bilateral trade with OECD   71t
  impact of EU15 wheat MPS reform
    (simulation)   79t
  price of wheat imports
    (simulation)   81
  impact of OECD domestic support
    reform (simulation)   83t, 84
  trade specialization indices
    (1965–98)   68t
  welfare impact of
    re-instrumentation   86t
Latvia   250–1t
least-developed countries (LDCs,
    1971–)   8–9, 15–16, 17, 25,
    31(n1, n5), 59(n8), 51, 52, 143t,
    144t, 146t, 148t, 150t, 151, 153,
    282(n5)
  Asian   241
  customs clearance times, 31–2(n6)
  duty-free access (97 percent of EU
    imports, 1999)   181
  duty-free, quota-free access to EU
    markets   49
  EBA   219–60
  exemption from tariff reductions,
    186
  export-enhancement (US
    programmes)   199–205
  exports   5, 191–2, 193, 214, 215
  failure to offer each other
    preferential schemes   182
  impact of EU15 wheat MPS reform
    (simulation)   79t

  industrial tariffs and DDA   161–89
  market-access issues   180–2, 183t,
    188(n16–17)
  non-ACP   220, 222, 258(n4)
  pre-EBA market access
    (to EU)   222
  preferential market-access
    arrangements (EU)   220–7,
    258(n3–13)
  products of export interest   191
  re-orientation of exports
    to EU   238
  share in EU market (2000)   224t
  share of world exports   232
  special needs and interests   182
  special treatment   225
  tariff barriers   214–15
  trade shares of products affected by
    agricultural subsidies
    (1995–8)   17t
UN-classification   49, 50
UN-defined group   27
  see also developing countries;
    low-income countries
leather/leather goods   162, 167–72,
    173t, 175–6, 180, 185, 195,
    229–30t, 231, 233–4t
Lebanon   251t
Lesotho   197t, 205t, 210
less than full reciprocity (LFR)   182,
    185–6, 187(n1)
  level of binding coverage   184–5
  NAMA context   184
liberalization   11, 12
Liberia   197t
linen   178, 180
literature
  agricultural subsidies   72–3, 89(n4)
  barriers to trade in services   31(n4)
  CGE simulations   228
  export subsidies   279
  post-Uruguay Round non-industrial
    tariff landscape   161,
    187(n2)
  preferential export credit and
    export insurance   279
  trade liberalization   73
  trade preferences   23–4
  value of improved TRQ
    access   131
Lithuania   250t
live animals   141–7, 148t, 150n,
    224t, 241, 242f
livelihood security   152

livestock   43t, 44t, 67t, 67, 81,
   83, 229–30t, 233–4t
   developing country trade with
      OECD (1997)   71t, 72
   trade specialization indices   68–9t, 70
loan guarantees   262, 263, 274, 275
loans   262, 271, 275, 284(n31)
   buyer's credit   271
   interest-free   284(n24)
   supplier's credit   271
local content   264, 271
location/geography   6, 66, 104,
   107, 108
Lomé Conventions (I–IV,
   effective 1976–2000)   49,
   50, 140, 143, 145, 148, 192t,
   198–9, 205–6, 246
   Article   174(2)(b)   225
   see also Yaoundé
low-income countries   12, 14, 25,
   31, 31(n2), 153
   international food prices   52–7
   policy implications   57–9
   potential welfare gains from
      full trade liberalization   41t
   poverty and food insecurity   54–7,
      60(n12)
   trade liberalization, agriculture
      and poverty   37–62
   trade policies (national
      priorities)   13t
   see also developing countries;
      least-developed countries
Lucknow   113t

Macao/Macau   163, 251t
macroeconomic
   environment   275
   policy   262
   problems   269
   stability   59(n2)
Madagascar   9, 197t, 205t, 210,
   211, 238, 241, 243, 246t, 247,
   249, 250t, 254t
Madhya Pradesh (MP)   107, 112–15,
   115f, 117, 123t, 124t, 125t, 126t
Maghreb   143t, 144t, 146t, 148t,
   150t, 151
maize   238, 239f
Malawi   9, 197t, 228, 229t, 241, 243,
   246t, 247, 249, 250t, 254t
   exports (percentage changes,
      EBA)   233t
   welfare changes (EBA)   231t, 238

Malaysia   20t, 164, 166t, 168t,
   169t, 171t, 173t, 174t, 176t,
   177t, 178, 180, 251t, 280
   see also ASEAN4
Maldives   210, 213
Mali   197t
Malta   251t
manufacturers   93
manufactures ('mnfc')   39t, 41t,
   43t, 44t, 67t, 223, 256
   light   39
   'not elsewhere specified'   168t,
      169t, 171t, 172, 173t
   OECD tariffs   21
   'other'   229–30t, 233–4t
   trade barriers   42
   unskilled-labour-intensive   53
   world price change (simulated   50
      percent reduction in OECD
      domestic support)   82t, 84
   world price change (simulated   50
      percent reduction in OECD
      market price support)   85t
manufacturing   5, 219,
   231, 266
   developed-country trade
      barriers   190–218
   Everything But Arms (EBA)
      Initiative   219–60
   export subsidies   261–86
   industrial tariffs, LDCs, and
      DDA   161–89
   light   275, 276
   labour-intensive   15, 42, 275
   market access   7–9, 159–286
   protectionism   57
Marahnao, C. A.   283(n13)
market
   channels (Indian rice)   97, 97,
      111, 113t, 113n, 119–20
   distortions   5
   disturbances   226
   economy/forces   99, 198
   failure   21, 279
   imperfections   279
   liberalization   276
   prices   104
market access   xii, 4, 11, 30, 39, 45,
   46, 88, 130, 131, 132, 134, 136–8,
   149–52, 241, 245, 257–8, 269
   ACP countries   225
   agriculture   6, 8, 16–19
   anti-dumping initiations
      (1995–9)   20t

market access (*continued*)
Cairns Group 60(n13)
current situation 164–80
duty-free 9, 181t, 195,
196, 198, 199, 222,
224, 231, 256
duty-free, quota-free 49, 50, 51–2,
59(n8), 181, 188(n16), 189, 214,
219, 223, 225, 227, 236–7,
258(n12)
'effective' 184
focal points and negotiating
modalities 21–3, 31(n5)
formula approach 24
general landscape 164–72
improving 15–23, 31(n1–5)
industrial products 162–4,
187(n3–7)
LDCs 180–2, 183t,
188(n16–17)
manufacturing 7, 159–286
MFN 9
non-reciprocity 162
preferential 151, 188(n16), 249
raw cane sugar exports 248
reciprocal MFN liberalization 25
services 20–1, 31(n3–4)
textiles and clothing 19–20
uncertainty 223
Market Effects of Crop Support Measures
(OECD, 2001) 72
market price support (MPS) 6, 64,
65t, 65, 76, 77, 81
impact of cuts 73
reduction by 50 per cent 77, 78t,
84–7, 88
market-sharing agreements 19
marketing 55, 111, 145
dual system (India) 93
marketing charges 96, 96t
markets 273, 279
developed-country 39
developing-country 39, 187
domestic and overseas 46
domestic product and factor 38
expansion 117–18
fertilizers 99
foreign 117
home 16
input 112
international 14, 59(n2), 78–9, 270
liberal domestic 59(n2)
middle-income countries 30
opening up 46

output 93, 94, 112, 116, 118
retail 119
third-country 279
uncompetitive 111
wholesale 119
world/global 84, 96, 99, 117,
237, 156(n11)
market share 133, 149, 226, 238,
243, 249, 253, 256
Martin, W. 31(n*), 59(n5–6), 60, 73,
89, 90
Matthews, A. xvii
Mattoo, A. 31(n*), 51, 228, 235
Mauritania 197t, 210, 213, 220
Mauritius 9, 51, 59(n7), 60(n11),
131, 154, 197t, 238, 246t, 249,
254t, 255t
cane sugar exporter to EU 250t,
253
maximum supply needs (MSN)
247–8, 259(n29)
McCulloch, N. 59(n2)
McDougall, R. A. 79
McKay, A. 59(n2)
meat/meat products 43t, 44t,
64, 65, 67t, 67, 73, 81–3,
85t, 85, 141, 143–9, 150t,
150n, 223t, 223, 224t, 229–30t,
231, 232, 233–4t, 241
MENA *see* Middle
East/North Africa
merchandise liberalization 31(n3)
Mercosur 269
metals 168t, 169t, 171t, 173t, 204
Mexico 5, 20t, 66t, 68t, 70, 75,
164, 165t, 168t, 169t, 171t,
173t, 174t, 176t, 177t, 177–8,
179t, 195, 250t, 284(n33)
MFN *see* most-favoured nation
MFN barriers (agriculture/textiles) 48
MFN liberalization 23–5, 50
avoids 'wasteful trade diversion' 49
MFN principle 131
MFN protection 231
MFN rate 194
MFN sugar 247, 248
preferential tariff quota 247
MFN tariffs 11, 130, 134, 138, 139n,
150, 152–4, 162, 183t, 209, 211,
212, 221t, 222, 226
applied 170, 236
bound duty-free 7
reduction 131
Michaely, M. 284(n35)

Michalopoulos, C. 31(n*), 32(n7)
Middle East 12, 143t, 144t, 146t, 148t,
 150t, 151, 230t, 231t, 232, 234t
Middle East/North Africa
 (MENA) 14t, 67t
 bilateral trade with OECD 71t,
  71, 72
 impact of OECD domestic support
  reform (simulation) 83t, 84
 impact of EU15 wheat MPS reform
  (simulation) 79t
 price of wheat imports
  (simulation) 81
 terms of trade 79t, 80
 trade specialization indices
  (1965–98) 69t, 70
 welfare impact of
  re-instrumentation 86, 86t, 87
middle-income countries 13t, 30
migration 54, 60(n14)
Milanovic, B. 280
milk 64, 65
Millennium Development Goals
 (MDGs, 2015) 21, 181
millers 97
Miloslavsky, E. 215(n*)
mineral products 168t, 169t, 171t,
 172, 173t, 210, 211, 213
minerals 39, 39t, 43t, 44t, 199,
 229–30t, 233–4t
mining 204
models
 dynamic v. static 48
 'path-dependent logic' 237
molasses 238, 242f
 top exporters to EU (market share,
  2000) 250–2t
molluscs 175
Monge-Roffarello, L. xvii, 259
monitoring 28, 64
monoculture 257
monopoly power 94
Monson, T. 279
Monteiro, S. S. M. 283(n13)
Monterrey (2002) 4, 31
Montserrat 196t
Moreira, M. M. 268, 269, 283
 (n13, n15)
Morocco 250t, 252t
most-favoured nation (MFN)
 definition 192
 GATT clause 192
 non-preferential market access 256
 progressive liberalization 257

motor vehicles
 automobiles/cars 180, 271
 parts/accessories/components 185,
  188(n14)
 trucks 180
 vehicles 205t
movement of 'natural persons' xii,
 50–1, 59(n9)
 temporary entry of foreign
  workers 22
Mozambique 197t, 210, 228,
 230t, 238, 241, 249, 251t,
 253, 254t, 255–6
 exports (percentage changes,
  EBA) 234t
 welfare changes (EBA) 231t,
  232, 235
Multifibre Agreement (MFA) 177
multilateral trade negotiations
 (MTNs) 37
 categories 167, 168t, 169t, 170,
  171t, 172, 173t
 reform process 38
Mumbai/Bombay 101, 101t,
 102t, 102, 103t, 113t
Myanmar 9, 194, 238, 241, 243, 249,
 251t, 254t, 258–9(n17)

NAFTA see North American Free
 Trade Agreement
Nair-Reichert, U. 206, (208n), 217
NAMA (non-agricultural market
 access) 161, 182, 184
Namibia 197t
narcotic crops 156(n12)
natural fibres 229–30t, 233–4t
Nayyar, D. 283(n21)
negotiating modalities 21–3
 request-offer approach 21
 Swiss-type formula 21, 31(n5)
Nepal 210, 241, 254t
Netherlands Antilles 196t, 251t,
 253, 254t, 255t
New Zealand 20t, 64–5, 65t, 66t,
 68t, 70, 189(n18), 179t, 250t
newly-industrializing
 countries 53
Ng, F. 18, 31(n*), 51, 52, 88,
 89(n8)
Nhava Shiva 102t
Nicaragua 196t, 252t
Niger 197t, 241, 243, 254t
Nigeria 131, 197t, 204, 205t, 205

Ninety-Nine Percent Initiative
(Japan, 2001–)   8, 190,
215(n16), 257
duty-free, quota-free market
access   195
nominal protection coefficient
(NPC)   96, 96t, 127(n3)
non-agricultural market access
(NAMA)   161, 182, 184
non-agricultural products   261
non-basmati rice   92–3
calculation of farmgate free-trade
price   109–12
characteristics   93, 96
distribution   118
dual channel market (India)
98f, 104
export price   94, 127(n2)
export routes   101–2
farmers 'unlikely to gain from
export'   117
fertilizer pricing   97–100
gains at external prices   112–16,
128(n10–11)
gains from free trade in
output   115f
gains from free trade in output and
input with yield
adjustments   115f
Indian market   94–7, 98f,
127(n3)
'open market'   97
policy transition (1991–2002)   95t
non-electric machinery   168t, 169t,
171t, 173t
non-reciprocity   30, 187
non-tariff barriers (NTBs)   8,
12, 140, 182, 185, 187(n1),
188(n16), 207, 228,
257, 269
frequency (developing countries,
1989–98)   14t
non-trade conditionality   24
non-transparent specific duties   18
North Africa   220
North America   6, 75, 88
North American Free Trade Agreement
(NAFTA)   195, 229t, 231t,
232, 233t
Norway   179t, 184, 189(n18), 250–1t,
255t
nuts   43t, 44t, 142t, 143t, 144t,
145, 146f, 146t, 148t, 150t,
202t, 229–30t, 233–4t

Oceania   232
OECD   *see* Organisation for Economic
Co-operation and Development
Organisation for Economic
Co-operation and Development
(OECD)   276
agricultural reforms (impact on
developing countries)   81–7,
87–9
AgLink model   73
agricultural policy reform   40
author   72, 73, 74, 75, 88, 187(n2)
countries   9n, 10, 16, 17, 24, 25,
31(n3), 59(n4), 66t
data   89(n2)
domestic support and developing
countries   63–91
export credit arrangement   266,
282–3(n11)
farm income   77, 88–9, 89(n5)
farm income   81, 84
industry   11
net trade position (programme
crops)   70
PSE data   76
subsidized economies   5–6
subsidy reform necessary   18–19
trade shares of products affected by
agricultural subsidies
(1995–8)   17t
see also domestic agricultural
support model
Office of US Trade
Representative   188(n17),
215(n17), 216(n21)
oil/petroleum   31(n1), 98, 128(n14),
196, 202t, 204, 205t, 205,
216(n20), 221t, 229–30t, 233–4t
oil companies   127(n4)
oil shocks   97, 268
oils and oilseeds   5, 9n, 43t, 44t,
67t, 82, 82t, 84, 85t, 87, 89(n2),
142t, 143, 221t, 224t, 229–30t,
233–4t
Olarreaga, M.   18, 31(n*), 51, 52, 88,
89(n8), 228, 235
openness   48, 59(n2)
opportunity cost   105
origin principle   282(n9)
Orissa (ORS)   107, 112–15, 115f,
117, 128(n12), 123–6t
output   72, 88, 104, 114
free trade   115, 116
wheat   77, 78t

output subsidies 65t, 65, 72, 73, 76, 89(n5)
contribution to world price change 82t
over-rebate of state value-added tax (Brazil) 270
Oxfam 259(n20), 259(n30)

Pakistan 250–1t
Panagariya, A. 227
Panama 196t, 238, 240f, 243, 244f
Panchamukhi, V. R. 280
Papua New Guinea 251t
Paraguay 251t, 254t, 255t, 269
partial equilibrium 51–2, 253
  see also SMART model
peace 55
Pearson, K. 90, 157
performance monitoring 32(n6)
Peru 20t, 196, 203t, 204
Petrapol 127(n6)
Philippines 251t, 255t
  see also ASEAN4
phosphates 220
Pinera, J. 280
Pinheiro, A. C. 268, 269
plant fibre 43t, 44t
Poland 66t, 164, 178, 241, 250t, 251t, 255t
  applied tariffs on crustaceans 176t
  applied tariffs on industrial products 173t, 174t
  bound tariffs on industrial products 165t, 168t, 169t, 170, 171t
  exports of live animals 9
  tariff escalation on textile products 179t
  tariffs on leather 177t
  tariffs on textiles and clothing, 177–8
political economy 18, 20, 84, 88, 283(n11)
political influence 130
polyester textured filament yarn (PTY) 274t
polyethylene terephthalate (PET) 274t
Port Trusts (India) 101
ports 94, 96t, 107, 108, 109, 111, 112, 275
  coefficient of variation (CV) 102, 103t
  distances from 110

facilities 110
fertilizer imports (1998–9) 101t
hinterland 101
India's external trade 101–4, 127(n6)
land 127(n6)
non-basmati rice exports 102t, 102f, 103t
sea 101t
Portugal 247
POSCO 278
'Positive Agenda for Reform' for agriculture (OECD, 2002) 6, 88
poultry 140
poverty 4, 30, 95, 119
  absolute 38
  landless rural 55, 56, 57
  links with economic growth and trade 38–9, 59(n1–2)
  policy implications 57–9
  rural 93, 117
  trade liberalization and agriculture in low-income countries 37–62
poverty-alleviation 117, 155
poverty-reduction xii, 10, 198
poverty-reduction strategy papers (PRSPs) 28
power plants 275
Prebisch–Singer thesis 219, 223
precious metals 168t, 169t, 171t, 172, 173t, 203t, 204
predictability 29
preference imports 199
preference margin 135, 145, 147, 148, 150, 151
  unit preference margin 133
preference programmes 188(n17), 191, 195–9, 216(n24, n30)
  by EU 198–9, 216(n23–5)
  by USA 195–8, 215–16(n17–22)
  for Africa 197–8
  for Andean Nations 196–7
  for Caribbean 195–6
  eligible countries 196–7t
  unilateral 8, 214
preferences 15, 162, 208, 209, 209t, 210, 211, 212t
  development policy instrument 219–20
  disadvantages 257
  non-reciprocal 220
  pre-EBA 235
  see also tariff preferences; trade preferences

preferential
  agreements 132
  financing for trading companies
    (Brazil) 270
  medium- and long-term financing
    for manufactured exports
    (Brazil) 270
  tariffs 183t
  trading arrangements 226–7,
    258(n12–13)
  working capital financing for export
    (Brazil) 269–70
Preferential Trading Agreements
  (PTAs) 5, 7–8
price
  channel 281
  differentials 237, 256
  distortions 6
  elasticity of export supply 236
  gaps (domestic-world) 75
  index (regional household's) 75
price-fixing agreements 19
prices 15, 95, 126t
  agricultural 56
  border 17
  calculations 109–12
  CIF 6, 107, 109
  consumer 54–5
  domestic 77, 96t, 108, 109, 124t,
    134, 135, 137
  domestic aligned with
    international 104
  domestic market 133
  domestic support 18
  estimate of protection 113t
  EU 49, 156(n11), 245
  export 107, 111, 117, 156(n11),
    232, 284(n32)
  external 92, 109
  external product 109
  farm harvest 112
  farmgate 107, 109, 112, 113t, 121,
    124t
  fertilizer domestic/imported 125t
  FOB 6, 94, 96t, 107, 109, 110, 111,
    112, 113t
  food 52–3, 57
  free-trade 114
  global 94
  import 6, 96t, 109, 124t, 128(n11),
    135, 232, 236
  input 106, 108, 128(n9)
  international 49, 93, 110, 111
  output 107

paddy domestic 125t
paddy export 125t
port 109
post-harvest 128(n10)
producer 17, 55, 89(n5), 106
producer (domestic
  market) 128(n11)
product 106, 108
R1 (prevailing) 112, 113t, 114t,
  115f, 127t
R2 (external output and prevailing
  input) 112, 114t, 115f, 127t
R3 (external output and tradable
  input price yield
  unadjusted) 114t, 114
R4 (external output and tradable
  external input price yield
  adjusted) 114t, 115f, 127t
regional dimension 109
relative 39, 106, 108, 114
statutory sale 121
sugar 243, 245, 259(n21)
supply 133
unit export 149
wheat 89(n5)
wholesale 128(n10)
  see also world prices
primary products 41t, 45, 53, 268
private sector 93, 95, 97, 270
private traders 94, 111, 119
privatization 101, 269
processing 112
producer groups 235
producer nominal protection
  coefficient 17
Producer Support Estimates (PSE)
  64–6, 65t, 72, 75, 89(n5)
  data 76
  definition 64
  impact on developing-country
    welfare 64
producer-support (agriculture) 72
  re-instrumentation 72
producers 47, 59(n2)
  agricultural 64
  direct payments (impact of
    cuts) 73
  import-competing 46
'producing centres' 111,
  112, 113t
product categories
  definitions 187(n8)
product coverage 186, 214
product markets 115, 279

product standards 15
production 57, 58, 94, 107
  additional 49
  agricultural 55, 211
  domestic 128(n14)
  for domestic market 269
production costs 138, 149
production subsidies 15, 271,
    277–8, 281
  discretionary and
      non-discretionary 278–9
productivity 48, 270
products 156(n10), 187, 202t,
    269, 273
  agricultural 57, 60(n13)
  milled 140, 223, 224t
  perfect substitutes
      (assumption) 89(n8)
  temperate 70
PROEX Programme: Preferential
    Export Financing (1991–) 270
PROEX-Equalization 270, 271
PROEX-Financing 270–1
profits 50, 104, 105, 279
programme commodities/crops 9n,
    67t, 67, 81, 83, 86, 87, 89(n2)
  developing country trade with
      OECD (1997) 71t, 71
  domestic support 70
  trade specialization indices
      5–6, 68–9t
protection/protectionism 16, 21,
    31(n5), 46, 86, 93, 113t, 114, 117,
    128(n10–11), 155, 175, 182
  agricultural 16, 52, 55, 56, 63
  EU (merchandise trade) 229–30t
  by EU/OECD countries, 'supported
      by subset of developing
      countries' 50, 52, 154
  manufacturing 57
  measure 109
  pre-EBA 232
  residual 162, 187
  service sector 57
Prowse, S. 32(n7)
Prusa, T. 19
PSE *see* Producer Support Estimates
psychology 275
public
  administration 12
  procurement 128(n12)
  sector 93, 127(n4), 270,
      274, 278
'public interest clauses' 20

Punjab (PJB) 107, 112–15, 115f, 117,
    119, 123–6t
purchasing power (of poor) 55
Purdue University (USA) xvii, 40
Pursell, G. 273, 283(n20)

Quad countries (Canada, EU, Japan,
    USA) 51–2, 163, 164, 167, 172,
    175, 176, 178, 181, 182
quality 14
quantitative restrictions
    (QRs) 273
quota rent 132, 135, 136, 137, 138,
    139n, 152, 153–4
  unit quota rent 133
quota tariffs 154
quotas 25, 60(n11)
  global 153
  non-tariffed product 140

Rae, A. N. 73, 88, 89(n6–7)
railway freight rates 111
railways 94, 95, 119, 180
Rajpur 113t
ratios
  domestic price to border
      price 127(n3)
  import price to domestic
      price 109
  input–output (input ratio) 106,
      107
Ravallion, M. 54
raw materials 39, 128(n14),
    178, 273
raw milk 67t, 82t, 85t
re-instrumentation 77–8, 78t,
    84–7, 89
  welfare impacts 86, 86t
Reagan, R. W. 193
real world 54
recession 276, 283(n16)
reciprocity xii, 45, 50
red tape 16
reform
  market-oriented 277
  political economy 4
  pro-competitive 15
refund schemes 274
regional agreements 226
regional studies
  trade liberalization and returns
      from land (India) 92–129
regional trade agreements
    (RTAs) 11, 162

regulation 21
Reincke, U. 187(n2)
remittances 54, 55
rent transfers 150, 151, 156(n11)
rent-seeking behaviour 19
rents (economic) 7, 24, 130, 132,
    133, 139, 144, 145, 149, 150–1,
    154, 155(n6)
  division 147, 147t
  exports from developed
    countries 147
repayment time 266, 271
reserves
  for export losses 276, 283–4(n24)
  for overseas market
    development 276, 284(n25)
resource-allocation 52, 227, 263
resource-reallocation 47
retailers 24, 111
Retention Price and Subsidy (RPS)
    Scheme 97–9, 121, 128(n11)
returns from land
  data and theoretical
    framework 104–9,
    127–8(n7–9)
  impact of trade liberalization
    (India) 92–129
rice 43t, 44t, 51, 85, 89(n2), 93, 117,
    181, 194, 223–5, 226, 231–6, 238,
    239f, 241–3
  broken 241
  milled 140
  paddy ('pdrice') 67t, 82t, 85t,
    89(n2), 229–30t, 232, 233–4t
  processed ('pcrice') 67t, 82t, 85t,
    89(n2), 229–30t, 232, 233–4t
  see also non-basmati rice
Robinson, S. 55
Roe, T. 55–6
Romania 9, 241
rubber 162, 167–72, 173t, 175–6
Ruggiero, R. 219
rules of origin 24, 59(n10),
    193, 194, 195, 198, 214,
    235, 257
rum 155(n3), 241
rural areas 53, 93, 117
Russia/Russian Federation 188(n13),
    251t, 283(n19)
Rwanda 197t, 238, 240f, 243, 244f

safeguard measures 16, 19, 40, 51,
    222, 225–6
safety belts 188(n14)

Saint Kitts and Nevis 196t, 246t,
    250t, 255t
Saint Lucia 196t, 244f
Saint Vincent and Grenadines 196t
Sala-i-Martin, X. 38
Samoa 244f
sanitary and phyto-sanitary (SPS)
    barriers 59(n10), 241
São Tomé and Príncipe 197t, 213
Saudi Arabia 251t
savings 76
scarce resources 128(n14)
  administrative and financial 27
SCM Agreement see WTO Agreement
    on Subsidies and Countervailing
    Measures
Seattle: WTO Ministerial Meeting
    (1999) xii, 37
sectoral
  intervention 219
  output 43t
  trade balance 44t
sectors 210, 228, 235, 257
  capital-intensive 269
  specific 278
self-employment 105
Senegal 32(n6), 197t, 210, 213,
    249, 250t
'sensitive' products/sectors 23, 24,
    51, 211, 225, 236–41, 242f, 256
  protectionism 57
  special case of sugar 243–8,
    259(n19–29)
services 11, 14, 22, 43t, 44t, 67t,
    232, 233–4t
  barriers to trade 46–7
  global protection (costs) 16
  market access 20–1, 31(n3–4)
  trade in 50
  world price change (simulated 50
    percent reduction in OECD
    domestic support) 82t, 84
  world price change (simulated
    50 per cent reduction in
    OECD market price
    support) 85t
Seychelles 197t
Sharma, A. 129, 273, 283(n20)
Sharma, K. 129
Sharma, P. 97
Shatz, H. J. xviii, 216(n30)
sheep 140, 238
shipbuilding 271
shippers 110

shipping rates 101
shocks 97, 268, 279
Shorrocks, A. i, xii, xiii
Sidhu, D. S. 97
Sierra Leone 197t, 249, 251t
Singapore 163, 164, 188(n11),
  251t, 284(n33)
  bound tariffs on industrial
    products 166t, 167, 168t,
    169t, 171t
  see also ASEAN4
Singapore Issues 186
Singapore Ministerial Meeting
  (WTO, 1996) 190, 214, 219
Single Undertaking approach
  (Uruguay Round) 10, 26
skills 50
Slovak Republic 250t, 252t
Slovenia 251t
Small Island Developing States
  (SIDS) 131
SMART model 227, 236, 237,
  238, 253, 258(n14)
SMEs 266, 270, 277
  foundation fund 276
Sohn, C-H. 283(n22–3)
Solomon Islands 210, 211
Somalia 197t, 254t
Somwaru, A. 55–6, 228, 235
sorghum 238, 241
South Africa 20t, 43t, 44t, 51,
  197t, 205t, 220, 250t, 251t,
  254t, 274t
South African Customs Union
  (SACU) 45
South America 75
South Asia 14t, 17, 37, 38, 42,
  43t, 44t, 53
  anti-export bias 12
  net food imports 45
  net importer of agricultural
    products 53
South Asia, 'Rest of' (RsoAsia) 67t
  bilateral trade with OECD 71t,
    71, 72
  impact of EU15 wheat MPS reform
    (simulation) 79t
  impact of OECD domestic support
    reform 83t
  trade specialization indices
    (1965–98) 68t
  welfare impact of
    re-instrumentation 86, 86t
South Korea *see* Korea, Republic of

special and differential treatment
  (SDT) 23, 25–9, 30,
  31–2 (n6–8), 152
  'rule-related' 27
  two forms 152
  WTO rules 25–9, 31–2 (n6–8)
special preferential sugar (SPS)
  247–8, 249, 253, 255, 259(n26–9)
special products (SP) 152
Special Tax Treatment Control Law
  (STTCL), Korea 277
specialization 270
  inappropriate 257
Spencer, B. J. 279
Sri Lanka 251t, 252t, 279, 280
Srinivasan, T. N. 272
STABEX (commodity export earnings
  stabilization scheme) 198
stability 219
standard deviations 165t, 166t
Standard Industrial Classification
  (SIC) 207, 208
State Bank of India 275
state governments (India) 95
state intervention (EU sugar
  market) 243, 259(n20)
state value-added tax (ICMS),
  Brazil 268
steel 193, 205t, 271, 272t, 272, 274t,
  275, 277, 278t, 278, 279
Steel Authority of India Limited
  (SAIL) 275
Stern, R. 31(n4)
Stevens, C. 32(n7)
stones, gems and precious
  metals 185
strategic trade theory 279
Strutt, A. 59(n6), 73, 88,
  89(n6–7)
Sub-Saharan Africa (SSA)/ 'Rest of
  SSA' 5, 8, 12, 14t, 37, 38, 42, 43t,
  44t, 47, 52, 55, 67t, 198, 228,
  230t, 232, 257
  bilateral trade with OECD 71t, 72
  economic welfare gain
    (potential) 45
  export prices 79t, 80
  exports 51
  exports (percentage changes,
    EBA) 234t
  impact of EU15 wheat MPS reform
    (simulation) 79t
  impact of OECD domestic support
    reform (simulation) 83t

Sub-Saharan Africa (SSA)/
  'Rest of SSA' (*continued*)
  net food imports 42
  price of wheat imports
    (simulation) 81
  trade liberalization 45
  trade specialization indices
    (1965–98) 69t
  welfare changes (EBA) 231t, 232
  welfare impact of
    re-instrumentation 86t
subsidies 17, 18, 121, 248
  agricultural 24, 25
  consumer 58
  direct and indirect 283(n20)
  domestic 63
  intermediate input 76, 81, 82t
  production and export
    (agricultural) 10
  region-specific (Korea), 277
  variable input 64, 65
  see also export subsidies
subsidy reform 18–19
Sucupira, R. 283(n13)
Sudan 9, 194, 197t, 238, 241, 244f,
    249, 250t, 254t, 259(n31)
sugar 8, 9, 24, 51, 59(n7), 60(n11),
    81, 140–9, 150t, 151, 154, 181,
    194, 223, 224t, 225, 226, 229–30t,
    231, 233–4t, 235, 236, 238, 239f,
    241, 242f, 257
  domestic quota 248
  'EBA' 247, 259(n25)
  EBA (implications for traditional
    exporters) 248–56
  EBA implications (transitional
    period) 248–9
  EBA implications (longer
    period) 249–56
  EU producers 247, 253
  four trade arrangements 246–8,
    259(n24–9)
  'MFN' 247, 248, 249
  non-preferential 246
  policy distortions 17
  'preferential' (ACP countries and
    India) 246, 238, 253, 259(n24)
  price support (EU) 245, 248,
    259(n21, n24)
  quota A 243, 245, 259(n21)
  quota B 243, 245, 259(n21)
  quota C 243, 245
  quota allocations 246t
  raw 67t, 82t, 85t, 85, 89(n2)

refined ('refsgr') 67t, 82t, 85t,
    89(n2)
  'special preferential' (SPS) 247–8,
    249, 259(n26–9)
sugar beet/beet sugar 67t, 82t, 85t,
    85, 89(n2), 229–30t, 232, 233–4t,
    249, 250–2t
sugar cane/cane sugar 67t, 82t, 85t,
    85, 89(n2), 229–30t, 232, 233–4t,
    246, 249, 253, 255–6
  export changes 254–5t
  top exporters to EU (market share,
    2000) 250–2t
sugar producers 243, 245
sugar refineries 243, 248,
    259(n29)
Sugar Traders Association
  (UK) 259(n19)
sulphanilic acid (AS) 274t
'sunset rules' 277
Supper, E. 187(n2)
suppliers 133–8, 155
  developing-country 132
  foreign 236
  in quota 134
supply/supply side 74, 135–6, 262, 276
supply and demand 93, 116
Suriname 196t
surveys, firm-specific 93
Swallow, A. xiii
Swaziland 197t, 246t, 250t,
    254t, 255t
Switzerland 164, 188(n11, n13),
    250–1t, 255t
  bound tariffs on industrial
    products 165t, 168t, 169t,
    171t
  producer subsidy equivalent
    and components (1987,
    2000) 65t, 65
synthetic fibres 178, 179t
Syrian Arab Republic 250t
SYSMIN (ACP mineral exports) 199

tafia 155(n3), 241
Taiwan 40, 164, 170, 172, 173t, 174t,
    176t, 177t, 179t, 284(n33)
Tandon, R. 283(n21)
Tangermann, S. 140
Tanzania 9, 67t, 197t, 228, 230t, 238,
    241, 243, 246t, 247, 249, 250t, 254t
  bilateral trade with OECD 70–1, 71t
  exports (percentage changes,
    EBA) 234t

impact of EU15 wheat MPS reform
(simulation) 79t
impact of OECD domestic support
reform (simulation) 83t
trade specialization indices
(1965–98) 69t, 69n
welfare changes (EBA) 231t
welfare impact of
re-instrumentation 86t
tariff
barriers xii, 16, 19, 188(n16), 223t,
228
bindings 19
data 216(n29)
elimination 185, 191, 209, 212,
212, 215, 219, 221t
escalation 161, 162, 175, 176t,
177–8, 179t, 180, 182, 187,
187(n1)
peaks 10, 15, 19, 21, 23, 52, 131,
161, 162, 169t, 170, 174t, 177,
182, 187, 187(n1)
quotas 225, 235, 246
rates 14t, 21, 22, 47
reduction 18, 185, 186, 236, 269
structures 172, 177, 188(n10)
tariff lines
bound 165t, 166t
bound duty-free 165t, 166t
non-*ad valorem* 164, 165t, 166t,
167, 172, 188(n12)
tariff preferences 37, 209, 216(n29)
erosion 38, 59(n4)
erosion by global trade reform
48–52, 59–60(n7–11)
MFN 52
partial equilibrium approach 51–2
see also preferences; trade
preferences
tariff rate quotas (TRQs) 6–7, 16, 18
assessed rent v. preference margin
by commodity sector
(1997–99) 146f
bilateral 132, 149, 154
bilateral TRQ, less competitive
supplier with underfill 133,
137f, 137–8
bilateral TRQ, more competitive
supplier with underfill 133,
135f, 135–6
binding 133, 135, 136,
137, 138, 144, 145, 147,
150, 152
non-binding 133, 138

binding characteristics, 130, 132,
155(n2)
characteristics 130
'current access' (EU) 140, 141, 153
developed-country share to TRQ
trade 143
division of rents (by TRQ import
arrangement) 147t, 148
drawback of approach 132
export prices (1997–9) 150t
export surplus 134–8, 139t, 139n,
149, 150, 152, 153
exporters 'unable to appropriate full
value of rents' 151
extension 154–5
fill rates 141, 142t, 145, 152,
156(n8, n12)
global 132
global TRQ with underfill and no
MFN supply 133–5
import value (actual) 151
importance in total EU agricultural
imports (1997–9) 141, 142t,
143, 155–6(n7)
in-quota tariff 130, 131, 136, 138,
140, 145, 152, 153, 154,
156(n12)
LDCs 'obtain almost no benefit'
from 144
'little new market access'
created 132
mandatory filling, 131
measurement problems 156(n10)
'minimum access' (EU) 140, 153
motivation 130
no MFN supply 133, 137
out-of-quota tariff 140
over-quota imports 133, 135–8
over-quota (MFN) tariff 130, 131,
135, 136, 138, 140, 145, 149,
153, 155
policy implications 153–5
preference margin on EU TRQ
trade (1997–9) 144–8,
156(n8)
preference margin (global) 145
quota volume 130
regime-switching 132, 155(n2)
rent accruing to developing
countries (EU TRQ trade,
1997–99) 145, 148, 148t
rent (actual) in EU TRQs 146f, 149
rent created in EU TRQs
(1997–99) 146t

tariff rate quotas (TRQs) (*continued*)
  sustainability of trade
    positions 148–50
  three typical cases 133
  underfill 130, 131, 133
  usage of EU TRQs by country
    grouping (1997–9) 143t
  use of EU TRQs by developing
    countries 143t, 143–4
  value to developing countries 7,
    130–57
  welfare effects (EU TRQs) 144–50,
    156(n-8–11)
  welfare gains 132, 138, 139
tariff-line level 132, 237–8, 241
tariffication 130, 140, 150
tariffs/import duties 8, 12, 39, 49, 50,
    82, 84–5, 87, 187(n1), 194, 208,
    235, 243, 271, 272, 280
  ad valorem 221n
  applied 162–3, 170, 177, 179t, 184,
    211, 236
  applied average 176t
  applied MFN 170, 236
  average applied 161
  average bound rate 165–6t, 167
  binding (developing
    countries) 162
  binding (number of tariff
    lines) 162
  bindings 188(n10)
  bound 21–2, 31(n5), 31(n5),
    162–7, 170, 171t, 177, 184–6,
    187(n5), 236, 245
  bound (disaggregated level) 167,
    168t
  bound (non-agricultural) 161–2
  bound duty-free 163,
    167, 187(n4)
  distribution of binding
    coverage 172t
  elimination 182, 212–13
  exemption 282(n6)
  high 48, 161, 162, 167, 177,
    180, 182, 187(n1), 188(n9),
    206, 237, 269
  highest 24, 172, 175
  in-quota 133
  multilateral negotiations 7, 163
  non-agricultural 7, 161–89
  non-preferential 162
  over-quota (T) 133
  post-Uruguay Round
    non-industrial 161, 187(n2)

preferential 162, 236
  reduction 7, 21, 31(n5), 245,
    259(n23)
  remission (aggregate and
    generalized rates) 266
  revenue-collection
    purposes 31(n2)
  scope of bindings 171t
  simple average of bindings at MTN
    category level 167, 168t
  sugar imports 246
  unbound 170
  uniform 31(n2)
tax
  base 279
  credits 276, 284(n26)
  exemptions/rebates/refund 262,
    265, 269, 271, 274, 280
  incentives 268, 275, 277
  measures 277
Tax Exemption and Reduction
    Control Law (TERCL),
    Korea 277, 284(n28)
tax on industrial production (IPI),
    Brazil 268
taxation 12, 55, 78, 272
  for balanced development 277
  consumption 58
  corporate 284(n24)
taxpayers 16, 64
technical assistance/cooperation 23,
    25, 28, 30, 45, 58–9
technology 21, 94, 98, 104, 106, 107
technology transfer 47
telecommunications 15, 21, 22
'temporary admission' 12
terms of trade (TOT) 11, 42, 45, 78,
    79t, 79, 81–3, 86–8, 219, 232
terrorism 193, 198
textiles 39–42, 43t, 44t, 46, 48, 51,
    53, 57, 162, 167–72, 173t, 176–80,
    185, 188(n13–15), 193, 195–8,
    210–13, 221t, 229–30t, 231, 232,
    233–4t
  market access 19–20
  multilateral trade rules 176
  plastic-coated 178, 179t
  quantitative restrictions 176–7
  quotas 19, 25
  rubberized 178, 179t
  synthetic 178
  tariff escalation 177–8, 179t
  tariffs on leather 177t
  see also apparel

Thailand 164, 173t, 174t, 178, 180, 238, 250–2t, 276, 280
  bound tariffs on industrial products 166t, 168t, 170, 171t
  MFN and preferential tariffs facing LDC exports 183t
  non *ad valorem* tariffs 188(n12)
  tariff escalation on textile products 179t
  see also ASEAN4
Thomas, M. 55
Thompson, W. 77
Thursby, J. 206, (208n), 217
time 12, 19, 106, 109, 185, 225
time-series analysis 280
tobacco products 229–30t, 233–4t
TOBIT regression framework 207
Todaro, M. P. 60(n14)
Togo 197t, 211, 241, 243
Tokyo Round (1973–9) 26, 31(n5)
town and village enterprises (TVEs) 53
trade 3–9, 72, 107, 116
  bilateral 75, 207
  'can be worse than direct aid' 52
  cross-border 20, 22
  impact on returns 108
  internal (India) 104
  international 92
  links with poverty and economic growth 38–9, 59(n1–2)
  private and public service institutions 15
  URAA 'boxes' 63
  see also goods/merchandise trade; world trade
trade
  balance 42
  creation 9, 227, 236, 238, 239f, 242f, 253, 258(n15)
  deficits 276
  distortions 42, 64, 84, 88, 130
  diversion 8, 9, 24, 30, 49, 52, 206–7, 208, 208t, 232, 235, 236, 238, 239f, 241, 242f, 257, 258(n15)
  elasticities 75
  facilitation 26
  gains 88
  orientation 267, 268–75, 283(n13–21)
  patterns 191
  policies 13t
  reduction 8, 206, 207, 208, 208t

re-orientation 241, 253
restructuring 277
shocks 279
specialization indices 67
theory 281
Trade Act (USA, 1974) 193
trade agenda: national level 12–15
  'behind the border' 14–15
  border barriers 12–14
  core NTBs (developing countries, 1989–98) 14t
  national priorities 13t
  tariff rates by region (1978–99) 14t
trade barriers 53, 253
  economic results of freeing trade 190–218
  reciprocal reduction 15
  reduction 29
  removal 45
Trade and Development Act (USA, 2000) 193, 195, 197–8, 216(n20)
trade liberalization 149, 191, 211, 261
  agriculture and poverty in low-income countries 37–62
  definition 104
  erosion of tariff preferences 48–52, 59–60(n7–11)
  full 40, 41t
  literature 73
  merchandise 22
  multilateral 151, 154
  non-discriminatory 30, 31
  policy implications 57–9
  qualifications to global modelling results 46–8
  returns from land (India) 92–129
  unilateral 190
trade preferences 29–30, 31, 131, 155
  historical 66
  margins 24
  unilateral 23–5
  see also preferences; tariff preferences
trade reform 47, 269–70, 273
  agreement-specific approach 27–8
  agricultural 37–8
  country-based approach 28
  domestic 11, 45, 46
  qualifications to global modelling results 46–8
Trade and Tariff Act (USA, 1984) 193

trading system
  openness and predictability
    (tariffs) 165–6t, 167
  political economy 4–5, 10–33
  transaction costs 12, 283(n21)
  transition economies 143t, 144t,
    146t, 148t, 150t, 170, 229t
  exports (percentage changes,
    EBA) 233t
  trade policies (national
    priorities) 13t
  welfare changes (EBA)
    231t, 232
transparency 26, 29, 46, 118,
  131, 257
transport 12, 15, 21, 76, 107, 127(n3)
transport charges/costs 94, 96, 101,
  116
transport equipment 167, 168t, 169t,
  170, 171t, 173t, 178, 212
transport services 46
travel goods 162, 167–72,
  173t, 175–6
Triad countries (EU, Japan, USA) 8,
  190–1, 191–2, 215
  changes in imports from LDCs as
    result of eliminating all tariffs
    on LDC exports (2000) 212
  GSP in 193–5
  implications of preferences
    205–14, 216(n27–30)
  LDC imports and preference
    programmes (2000), 209t
  non-reciprocal preference
    programmes 195–9
Trinidad and Tobago 196t, 202t,
  246t, 250t, 252t, 255t
TRIPS (Trade-Related Intellectual
  Property Rights) 10, 25, 27
tropical forests 194
tropical products 70, 142t, 143,
  156(n12)
TRQ gains for developing countries in
  EU market 138–50
  background 139–44, 155–6(n3–7)
  welfare effects of EU TRQs 144–50,
    156(n-8–11)
TRQs see tariff rate quotas
Trueblood, M. 228, 235
Turkey 20t, 66t, 164, 178, 250–1t,
  255t, 279, 280–1
  applied tariffs on crustaceans 176t
  applied tariffs on industrial
    products 173t, 174t

bound tariffs on industrial
    products 165t, 167, 168t,
    169t, 170, 171t
  tariff escalation on textile
    products 179t
  tariffs on leather 177t
  tariffs on textiles and clothing,
    177–8
  trade specialization indices
    (1965–98) 68t, 70
Turks and Caicos Islands 196t
Turrini, A. xviii, 51, 187(n2), 259

Uganda 193, 197t, 228, 230t,
  240f, 244f, 246t, 247
  exports (percentage changes,
    EBA) 234t
  welfare changes (EBA)
    231t, 232
Ukraine 252t
uncertainty 19, 22, 24, 47, 223
'UNCTAD Handbook on EU GSP
  Scheme' 258(n5)
UNCTAD-TRAINS project/
  database 216(n29), 228, 236,
    258(n15)
underemployment 55
unit export price 156(n11)
unit preference margin 138, 145,
  155(n6)
unit price 144
unit quota rent 136, 137, 138,
  155(n6)
  definition 133
United Arab Emirates 251t, 255t
United Kingdom 198, 247, 279
United Nations: Third Conference
  on LDCs 181
United Nations Conference on
  Trade and Development
  (UNCTAD) xvii, xviii,
    192, 214
  author 51, 60(n10–11), 228, 235,
    258(n3–4, n18)
  GSP database 236, 258(n15)
United Nations Economic and Social
  Council 190
United Nations General
  Assembly 190
United Nations University: World
  Institute for Development
  Economics Research
  (UNU-WIDER, Helsinki) i, xii,
    xiii, xvii, 215(n*)

United States of America 5, 8, 15–16,
    17, 20t, 24, 51, 60(n11), 66, 66t,
    82, 94, 131, 155(n3), 178, 180,
    190, 193, 207, 216(n20), 238,
    250t, 251t, 254t, 255t, 269, 271,
    272t, 274t, 277, 278, 279
  applied tariff rates 189(n18)
  applied tariffs on
    crustaceans 176t
  applied tariffs on industrial
    products 173t, 174t
  barriers to imports from LDCs 211
  bound tariffs on industrial
    products 165t, 167, 168t,
    169t, 171t
  cereal exports 9
  changes in imports from LDCs as
    result of eliminating all tariffs
    on LDC exports (2000) 212
  consumers 206
  developing-country
    export-enhancement 199–205
  dutiable, non-dutiable,
    educed-dutiable imports 200
  duty-free access (92 percent of
    imports from AGOA-eligible
    countries) 188(n17)
  export subsidies (simulated
    reduction) 85t
  growth rate of US total imports and
    US preference imports 201f
  GSP 220
  import tariffs (simulated
    reduction) 85t, 85
  imports 8, 204, 208
  imports from LDCs 210, 214
  LDC imports and preference
    programmes (2000) 209t
  MFN and preferential tariffs facing
    LDC exports 183t
  preference imports relative to total
    imports 200f, 200
  preference programmes 191t
  preferential schemes 258(n12)
  producer subsidy equivalent and
    components (1987, 2000)
    65t, 65
  proposed complete elimination of
    duties on non-agricultural
    products 184
  tariff adjustment effects 209
  tariff effects on trade
    (summary) 208t
  tariff elimination 212–13

  tariff escalation on textile
    products 179t
  tariffs on leather 177t
  trade contracts 208
  trade diversion 238
  trade performance under Caribbean
    programmes 201–2t
  trade specialization indices
    (1965–98) 68t, 70
unskilled labour 50–1, 59(n9)
URAA *see* Uruguay Round Agreement
    on Agriculture
Uruguay 269
Uruguay Round 5, 18, 26, 28, 30,
    37, 39, 40, 42, 43t, 44t, 46, 59(n6),
    199, 261, 262
  agriculture 16–17
  'hangover' 10–11, 130, 155(n1), 161
  request-offer approach 21
Uruguay Round: Agreement on
    Agriculture (AoA/URAA) 6, 63,
    95, 130, 153, 245
  Annex One 156(n7)
  Annex Two 58
  Article Five 246
  'box, amber' (trade-distorting
    payments) 63
  'box, blue' (production-limiting
    payments) 63, 89(n6)
  'box, green' (non-trade-distorting
    payments) 63
  TRQs (EU) 139–40, 145, 150–1,
    155(n3)
Uruguay Round: Agreement on
    Textiles and Clothing (ATC)
    19, 40, 177
US Congress
  author 215(n17), 216(n21)
  House of Representatives 193
  Senate 193
US Customs Service
    (author) 216(n21)
US Farm Act (May 2002) 65
USSR: preference
    programmes 215(n5)
Uttar Pradesh (UP), 107,
    112–17, 123t, 124t, 125t,
    126t, 127(n8)

value-added tax 268, 271
vegetables 43t, 44t, 67t, 82t,
    85t, 141–8, 148t, 150t, 151,
    154, 203t, 211, 223, 224t,
    229–30t, 231, 233–4t, 241

Vehmaan-Kreula, J.   xiii
Venezuela   20t, 196, 215(n20),
     251t, 279
vested interests: opposed to
     multilateral trade
     liberalization   257
Vietnam   67t, 68t, 69n, 70–2, 79t,
     83t, 86t
Vijayawada   113t
Viner, J.   227
Vishakhapattanam   101, 101t, 102t,
     102, 103t, 113t

Walmsley, T.   31(n3),
     59(n9)
Wang, Z. K.   32(n7)
watches   193, 196
water   118
websites   258(n11)
     European Commission   258(n7)
     George Washington
          University   283(n13)
     WTO   155(n1), 282(n3)
West Africa   17
West Bengal (WB)   107, 112, 113t,
     114, 123–6t, 127(n6), 128(n12)
Westphal, L. E.   280
wheat   43t, 44t, 67t, 78t, 84, 87,
     89(n2, n5), 140
     prices   78, 80
     world price change (simulated   50
          per cent reduction in OECD
          domestic support)   82t
     world price change (simulated   50
          per cent reduction in OECD
          market price support)   85t, 85
wheat bran   241
wheat flour   241
Wijnbergen, S.   280
Winters, L. A.   16, 31(n*), 31(n3),
     32(n7), 59(n2, n6, n9)
wood/wood products   168t, 169t,
     171t, 172, 173t, 210, 213
wool   178, 179t
worker rights   198
world
     economy   48, 269
     production   40
World Bank   31(n*), 48, 51, 53,
     216(n28)
world prices   12, 18, 31, 75, 78t, 79t,
     79, 80, 83t, 83, 86t, 87
     agricultural   64, 73, 89(n1)
     changes   82t, 84, 85t, 85

distortions   88
     sugar   17, 245, 259(n22)
world trade   25, 40
     distortions   38, 81–2
     duty-free items   163
     industrial products   7
     LDC share   256
World Trade Organization
     (WTO)   xvii, 40, 49, 50, 141,
          155(n4), 199, 248, 276
     agreements   225
     agriculture   35–157
     author   39, 187(n2, n8), 188(n9)
     bananas case   154
     bound reform commitments   46
     'core business'   161
     country proposals   282(n8)
     'development credibility' deficit   xii,
          4, 10
     disciplines   73
     dispute-settlement   49
     disputes   249
     'domestic ownership'   4
     jurisprudence   281, 284(n29)
     market access committee   21
     members   7, 37, 42, 52, 163, 184,
          187(n5), 188(n16), 249
     ministerial declaration on
          'coherence'   28, 32(n8)
     modalities for negotiations   182,
          184–6, 189(n18)
     multilateral negotiations   256
     official documents   155(n1)
     overview   1–33
     rule-based, reciprocity-driven
          organization   xii
     Russia not a member   188(n13)
     schedules   47
     trade and development   3–9
     website   155(n1), 282(n3)
     see also Doha Round
WTO: Agreement on Customs
     Valuation   32(n6)
WTO: Agreement on Subsidies and
     Countervailing Measures (SCM
     Agreement, 1995–)   261–86
     Annex VII   263, 264,
          282(n5, n7)
     countervailing measures   264–5
     duty remission (aggregate and
          generalized rates)   266
     export credit   266
     export incentives   267–75,
          283(n13–21)

export incentives (theory and
    evidence) 279–81, 284(n32–5)
export-promotion development
    strategy (South Korea) 275–9,
    283–4(n22–31)
import-substitution development
    strategy 268–75, 283(n13–21)
improvements and clarifications
    (sought by developing
    countries) 265–7,
    282–3(n8–12)
inclusion of capital
    goods in definition of
    inputs consumed 265–6,
    282(n10)
'injury to domestic industry'
    provision 263, 264, 282(n1)
international
    competitiveness 266–7,
    283(n12)
multilateral discipline on
    subsidies 262–4, 282(n3–7)
'other' developing countries 263–4
specificity test 263, 277, 281,
    284(n29)
WTO: Cancún Ministerial Conference
    (2003) xii, 182, 186
WTO: Committee on
    Agriculture 147, 156(n9)
WTO: Committee on Subsidies and
    Countervailing Measures
    (SCM) 282(n6)
WTO: Committee on Trade and
    Development 188(n16)
WTO: Dispute Settlement Body
    (DSB) 263
WTO: Fourth Ministerial Meeting see
    Doha Ministerial Meeting
WTO: General Council 29,
    182, 186
WTO: Negotiating Group on Market
    Access 182, 185, 186
WTO: rules
differential interests and
    capacities 27–9, 31(n6–8)
eligibility for exemptions 27–8
exemptions or deferrals 23, 29

'getting the rules right' 25, 26,
    27, 29
'ownership' in developing
    countries 29, 30
'one size may not fit all' 29
rejection of reciprocity 29
SDT 25–9, 30, 31–2 (n6–8)
waivers 220
WTO: Secretariat 188(n16)
WTO: Singapore Ministerial Meeting
    (1996) 190, 214, 219
WTO: Sub-Committee on LDCs 181,
    188(n16)
WTO: Trade Policy Review 277

Yanagishima, K. 90
Yang, J. 283(n22–3)
Yao, S. 42, 45
Yaoundé Conventions (1964–)
    192t, 198
see also ACP (Africa, Caribbean,
    Pacific) countries
Yeats, A. 258(n14–15)
Yemen 243, 244f
yields 106, 108, 114, 116, 125t, 123t,
    127t, 127(n7)
Yim, H.-S. 283(n22–3)
Yu, W. 73
Yugoslavia 284(n33)

Zambia 9, 67t, 78, 194, 197t, 228,
    230t, 238, 243, 249, 250t, 254t
bilateral trade with OECD 70–1,
    71t, 72
export prices 79t, 80
exports (percentage changes,
    EBA) 234t
impact of EU15 wheat MPS reform
    (simulation) 79t
impact of OECD domestic support
    reform (simulation) 83t
trade specialization indices
    (1965–98) 69t
welfare changes (EBA) 231t, 232
welfare impact of
    re-instrumentation 86t
Zimbabwe 197t, 246t, 250t, 255t